Communications in Computer and Information Science 1729

More information about this series at https://link.springer.com/bookseries/7899

Sanjaya Kumar Panda · Rashmi Ranjan Rout ·
Ravi Chandra Sadam ·
Bala Venkata Subramaanyam Rayanoothala ·
Kuan-Ching Li · Rajkumar Buyya (Eds.)

Computing, Communication and Learning

First International Conference, CoCoLe 2022
Warangal, India, October 27–29, 2022
Proceedings

Editors
Sanjaya Kumar Panda
National Institute of Technology
Warangal, India

Rashmi Ranjan Rout
National Institute of Technology
Warangal, India

Ravi Chandra Sadam
National Institute of Technology
Warangal, India

Bala Venkata Subramaanyam Rayanoothala
National Institute of Technology
Warangal, India

Kuan-Ching Li
Providence University
Taichung, Taiwan

Rajkumar Buyya
University of Melbourne
Melbourne, VIC, Australia

ISSN 1865-0929 ISSN 1865-0937 (electronic)
Communications in Computer and Information Science
ISBN 978-3-031-21749-4 ISBN 978-3-031-21750-0 (eBook)
https://doi.org/10.1007/978-3-031-21750-0

This Springer imprint is published by the registered company Springer Nature Switzerland AG
The registered company address is: Gewerbestrasse 11, 6330 Cham, Switzerland

Preface

The First International Conference on Computing, Communication, and Learning (CoCoLe 2022) took place during October 27–29, 2022, and was hosted and sponsored by the National Institute of Technology (NIT) Warangal, Telangana, India.

The CoCoLe conference focuses on three broad areas of computer science and other allied branches, namely computing, communication, and learning. It provides a unique platform for academicians, researchers, scientists, engineers, practitioners, industry personnel, developers, and students to exchange state-of-the-art methods, present and publish their research findings, and deliberate on contemporary topics in the areas of computing, communication, and learning. The main aim of CoCoLe is to provide quality publications to the research community and to provide directions for further research.

For CoCoLe 2022, we received 117 full paper submissions. Each submission was reviewed by three to four Technical Program Committee members and reviewers of national and international repute in a single-blind process. Based on the reviews, the conference chairs decided to accept 25 full papers and one short paper for presentation at the conference, with an acceptance rate of 22%. We would like to express our sincere gratitude to all the authors and co-authors who submitted their work to this conference. Our special thanks go to all Technical Program Committee members and reviewers, who generously offered their expertise and time, which helped the conference chairs to select the papers and prepare the conference program.

We were fortunate to have eight esteemed academicians as our advisory committee members. Their constant support and guidance helped us to plan this conference successfully. We were also fortunate to have five invited keynote speakers: Mohammad S. Obaidat from the University of Texas Permian Basin, USA, and the University of Jordan, Jordan, Vincenzo Piuri, from the University of Milan, Italy, Sudip Misra, from IIT Kharagpur, India, Sung-Bae Cho from Yonsei University, South Korea, and Marcin Paprzycki from the Systems Research Institute, Polish Academy of Sciences, Poland. Their talks gave us the unique opportunity to listen to leaders in their fields.

A number of people worked very hard to make this conference a huge success. First, we wish to express our thanks to the steering committee members for planning the first edition of the conference at NIT Warangal, India. Further, we wish to extend our thanks to the registration chairs, session management chairs, publicity chairs, publication chairs, website management chairs, and student volunteers for their valuable suggestions and coordination. Lastly, we thank the faculty members of the Department of Computer Science and Engineering (CSE), NIT Warangal, Telangana, India, for their timely support.

The Department of CSE, NIT Warangal, the host of the conference, provided various support and facilities for organizing the conference. Particularly, we express our sincere gratitude to N. V. Ramana Rao, the Chief Patron of this conference and the Director of NIT Warangal, and S. Ravi Chandra, the Patron of this conference and the Head of the Department of CSE, for their continuous support.

The conference program was prepared with the help of EasyChair for efficient and smooth handling of all activities from paper submissions to preparation of the proceedings. We thank Communications in Computer and Information Science (CCIS), Springer, for publishing the conference proceedings, and the International Journal of Computational Science and Engineering (IJCSE), Inderscience, the International Journal of Embedded Systems (IJES), Inderscience, and Connection Science, Taylor & Francis, for publishing extended versions of selected papers.

We hope you will find the papers in this collection helpful and inspiring for further research.

October 2022

Sanjaya Kumar Panda
Rashmi Ranjan Rout
Ravi Chandra Sadam
Bala Venkata Subramaanyam Rayanoothala
Kuan-Ching Li
Rajkumar Buyya

Organization

Steering Committee

Sanjaya Kumar Panda	NIT Warangal, India
Rashmi Ranjan Rout	NIT Warangal, India
Ravi Chandra Sadam	NIT Warangal, India
Bala Venkata Subramaanyam Rayanoothala	NIT Warangal, India

Advisory Committee

Rajkumar Buyya	University of Melbourne and Manjrasoft, Australia
Mohammad S. Obaidat	University of Texas Permian Basin, USA, and University of Jordan, Jordan
Sajal K. Das	Missouri University of Science and Technology, USA
D. V. L. N. Somayajulu	IIITDM Kurnool and IIITDM Kancheepuram, India
Manoj Singh Gaur	IIT Jammu, India
Narasimha Sarma N. V. S.	IIIT Trichy, India
Shyam Sundar Pattnaik	NITTTR Chandigarh, India
C. R. Tripathy	BPUT Rourkela, India

General Chairs

Kuan-Ching Li	Providence University, Taiwan
Rajkumar Buyya	University of Melbourne and Manjrasoft, Australia
Bala Venkata Subramaanyam Rayanoothala	NIT Warangal, India

Program Chairs

K. Ramesh	NIT Warangal, India
Ch. Sudhakar	NIT Warangal, India

Technical Program Committee

Aakanksha Sharaff	NIT Raipur, India
Abhimanyu Kumar	NIT Uttarakhand, India
Abhinav Tomar	NSUT Delhi, India
Achyuth Sarkar	NIT Arunachal Pradesh, India
Alekha Kumar Mishra	NIT Jamshedpur, India
Amit Garg	IIIT Kota, India
Amit Joshi	MNIT Jaipur, India
Amiya Kumar Rath	NAAC, India
Anand Bihari	VIT Vellore, India
Anil Jadhav	SCIT Pune, India
Anshul Agarwal	VNIT Nagpur, India
Anshul Verma	BHU Varanasi, India
Ansuman Mahapatra	NIT Puducherry, India
Anurag Singh	NIT Delhi, India
Arabinda Dash	SUIIT Burla, India
Arka Prokash Mazumdar	MNIT Jaipur, India
Arti Jain	JIIT Noida, India
Arun Agarwal	SOA University, India
Arun Kishor Johar	Chandigarh University, India
Asish Dalai	VIT Andhra Pradesh, India
Ashok Kumar Das	IIIT Hyderabad, India
Ashok Kumar Turuk	NIT Rourkela, India
Ashok Patel	VIT Bhopal, India
Asis Tripathy	VIT Vellore, India
B. Acharya	NIT Raipur, India
B. B. Gupta	NIT Kurukshetra, India
B. Satya Sekhar	IIT Jammu, India
Bala Prakasa Rao Killi	NIT Warangal, India
Balu L. Parne	SVNIT Surat, India
Benazir Neha	KIIT University, India
Bhabendu Kumar Mohanta	GITAM University, India
Bharat Gupta	NIT Patna, India
Bibhu Mohanty	SOA University, India
Binayak Kar	National Taiwan University of Science and Technology, Taiwan
Biswajit R. Bhowmik	NITK Surathkal, India
Bunil Kumar Balabantaray	NIT Meghalaya, India
Chandrakanta Mahanty	GIET University, India
Chintan Bhatt	PDEU Gandhinagar, India
Chouhan Kumar Rath	NIT Durgapur, India
D Chandrasekhar Rao	VSSUT Burla, India

Damodar Reddy Edla	NIT Goa, India
Debashreet Das	VIT Vellore, India
Debasis Gountia	OUTR Bhubaneswar, India
Debasis Mohapatra	PMEC Berhampur, India
Deepak Ranjan Nayak	MNIT Jaipur, India
Deepak Singh Tomar	MANIT Bhopal, India
Deepsubhra Guha Roy	VIT Vellore, India
Devashree Tripathy	Harvard University, USA
Devendra Yadav	NIT Rourkela, India
Devesh C. Jinwala	SVNIT Surat, India
Diptendu Sinha Roy	NIT Meghalaya, India
Durga Prasad Mohapatra	NIT Rourkela, India
Gargi Bhattacharjee	IIT Jodhpur, India
Gauri Shankar Dewangan	Chandigarh University, India
Greeshma Lingam	NIT Warangal, India
Hemraj Lamkuche	SIT Pune, India
Ila Sharma	MNIT Jaipur, India
Indrajeet Gupta	Bennett University, India
Jagadeesh Kakarla	IIITDM Kancheepuram, India
Jai Prakash Verma	Nirma University, India
Jitendra Kumar Rout	NIT Raipur, India
Jyoti Prakash Sahoo	SOA University, India
Jyoti Prakash Singh	NIT Patna, India
K. V. Kadambari	NIT Warangal, India
Kalyan Kumar Jena	PMEC Berhampur, India
Khumanthem Manglem Singh	NIT Manipur, India
Kshira Sagar Sahoo	SRM University, Andhra Pradesh, India
Kshiramani Naik	VSSUT Burla, India
Kumar Abhishek	NIT Patna, India
Lalatendu Behera	NIT Jalandhar, India
Lalatendu Muduli	Utkal University, India
Lov Kumar	BITS Hyderabad, India
M. Madhubala	IARE College, India
M. S. Patel	Amruta Institute of Engineering and Management Sciences, India
Mahasweta Sarkar	San Diego State University, USA
Manas Ranjan Prusty	VIT Vellore, India
Manjubala Bisi	NIT Warangal, India
Masilamani V	IIITDM Kancheepuram, India
Mohammad Shameem	IIT Dhanbad, India
Monalisa Jena	Fakir Mohan University, India
Mohd Zuhair	Nirma University, India

Mrutyunjaya Panda	Utkal University, India
Mukesh Kumar	NIT Patna, India
Munesh Singh	IIITDM Jabalpur, India
Nabajyoti Mazumdar	IIIT Allahabad, India
Nagesh Salimath	PDA College of Engineering, Kalaburagi, India
Neelamadhab Padhy	GIET University, India
Niladri Bihari Puhan	IIT Bhubaneswar, India
Niranjan Panigrahi	PMEC Berhampur, India
Nitin Singh Singha	NIT Delhi, India
P. Rangababu	NIT Meghalaya, India
P. Santhi Thilagam	NITK Surathkal, India
Pabitra Mohan Khilar	NIT Rourkela, India
Padmalochan Bera	IIT Bhubaneswar, India
Pawan Kumar	NIT Rourkela, India
Pawan Kumar Patidar	Poornima Group of Colleges, India
Prabhat Dansena	University of Hyderabad, India
Pradeep Kumar Roy	IIIT Surat, India
Pranesh Das	NIT Calicut, India
Prasant Kumar Sahu	IIT Bhubaneswar, India
Pratyay Kuila	NIT Sikkim, India
Pravati Swain	NIT Goa, India
Praveen Kumar K V	Sapthagiri College of Engineering, India
Preeti Chandrakar	NIT Raipur, India
Preeti Ranjan Sahu	NIST Brahmapur, India
Preeti Soni	IIT (ISM) Dhanbad, India
Priya Ranjan Muduli	IIT (BHU) Varanasi, India
Priyambada Subudhi	IIIT Sri City, India
Priyanka Parimi	NIT Warangal, India
Priyanka Singh	SRM University, Andhra Pradesh, India
R. Padmavathy	NIT Warangal, India
Radhashyam Patra	VSSUT Burla, India
Rahul Hiremath	Symbiosis Centre for Management and Human Resources Development, India
Rahul Kumar Vijay	Banasthali Vidyapith, India
Rajendra Prasad Nayak	GCE Bhawanipatna, India
Rakesh Ranjan Kumar	CVRGU, India
Rakesh Ranjan Swain	IIT Kanpur, India
Ramalingaswamy Cheruku	NIT Warangal, India
Ranjan Kumar Behera	BIT Mesra, India
Ranjita Das	NIT Mizoram, India
Rashmi Panda	IIIT Ranchi, India
Ravi Maddila	MNIT Jaipur, India

Ravi Verma	VIT Bhopal, India
Roshni Pradhan	KIIT University, India
S. Gopal Krishna Patro	K L University, India
S. Karthick	NIT Andhra Pradesh, India
Sachi Nandan Mohanty	ICFAI University, India
Sai Krishna Mothku	NIT Tiruchirappalli, India
Sampa Sahoo	C V Raman Global University, India
Sandeep Kumar Dash	NIT Mizoram, India
Sangharatna Godboley	NIT Warangal, India
Sangram Ray	NIT Sikkim, India
Sanjeet Kumar Nayak	IIITDM Kancheepuram, India
Sanjib Kumar Nayak	VSSUT Burla, India
Sanjib Kumar Raul	NIT Warangal, India
Santi Kumari Behera	VSSUT Burla, India
Santosh Kumar Das	Sarala Birla University, India
Santosh Kumar Sahu	ONGC Dehradun, India
Sarat Nayak	Yonsei University, South Korea
Satish Vemireddy	KLA Corporation, India
Satya Prakash Sahu	NIT Raipur, India
Satyajit Nayak	IIT Kharagpur, India
Satyasai Nanda	MNIT Jaipur, India
Satyendra Singh Yadav	NIT Meghalaya, India
Sharmila Subudhi	SOA University, India
Shelly Sachdeva	NIT Delhi, India
Shraban Apat	Geetanjali College of Engineering and Technology, India
Siba Mishra	Zoho Corporation, India
Sibarama Panigrahi	SUIIT Burla, India
Sibun Parida	SOA University, India
Sitanshu Sekhar Sahu	BIT Mesra, India
Situ Rani Patre	NIT Rourkela, India
Slokashree Padhi	NIT Warangal, India
Sohan Kumar Pande	SIT Sambalpur, India
Sourav Kanti Addya	NITK Surathkal, India
Sourav Kumar Bhoi	PMEC Berhampur, India
Srinivas Naik N	IIIT Naya Raipur, India
Srinivas Sethi	IGIT Sarang, India
Sriram Kailasam	IIT Mandi, India
Subasish Mohapatra	OUTR Bhubaneswar, India
Subhransu Padhee	SUIIT Burla, India
Suchismita Chinara	NIT Rourkela, India
Sudhansu Bala Das	NIT Rourkela, India

Sugyan Mishra	NIT Durgapur, India
Sujata Pal	IIT Ropar, India
Sujit Das	NIT Warangal, India
Suneet Gupta	Bennett University, India
Sunil Gautam	Nirma University, India
Suraj Sharma	IIIT Bhubaneswar, India
Surendra Singh	NIT Uttarakhand, India
Suryakant Panda	IIT Patna, India
Sushil Kumar	NIT Warangal, India
Sushree B. Priyadarshini	SOA University, India
T. M. Asif	NIT Warangal, India
Tapan Kumar Sahu	IIIT Bhubaneswar, India
Tapas Kumar Mishra	SRM University, Andhra Pradesh, India
Tribikram Pradhan	Tezpur University, India
Umakanta Majhi	NIT Silchar, India
Uma Shankar Ghugar	GITAM University, India
Urvashi Prakash Shukla	Banasthali Vidyapith, India
Valentina Emilia Balas	Aurel Vlaicu University of Arad, Romania
Vasundhara	NIT Warangal, India
Venkateswara Rao Kagita	NIT Warangal, India
Yogendra Gupta	SKITMG Jaipur, India

Contents

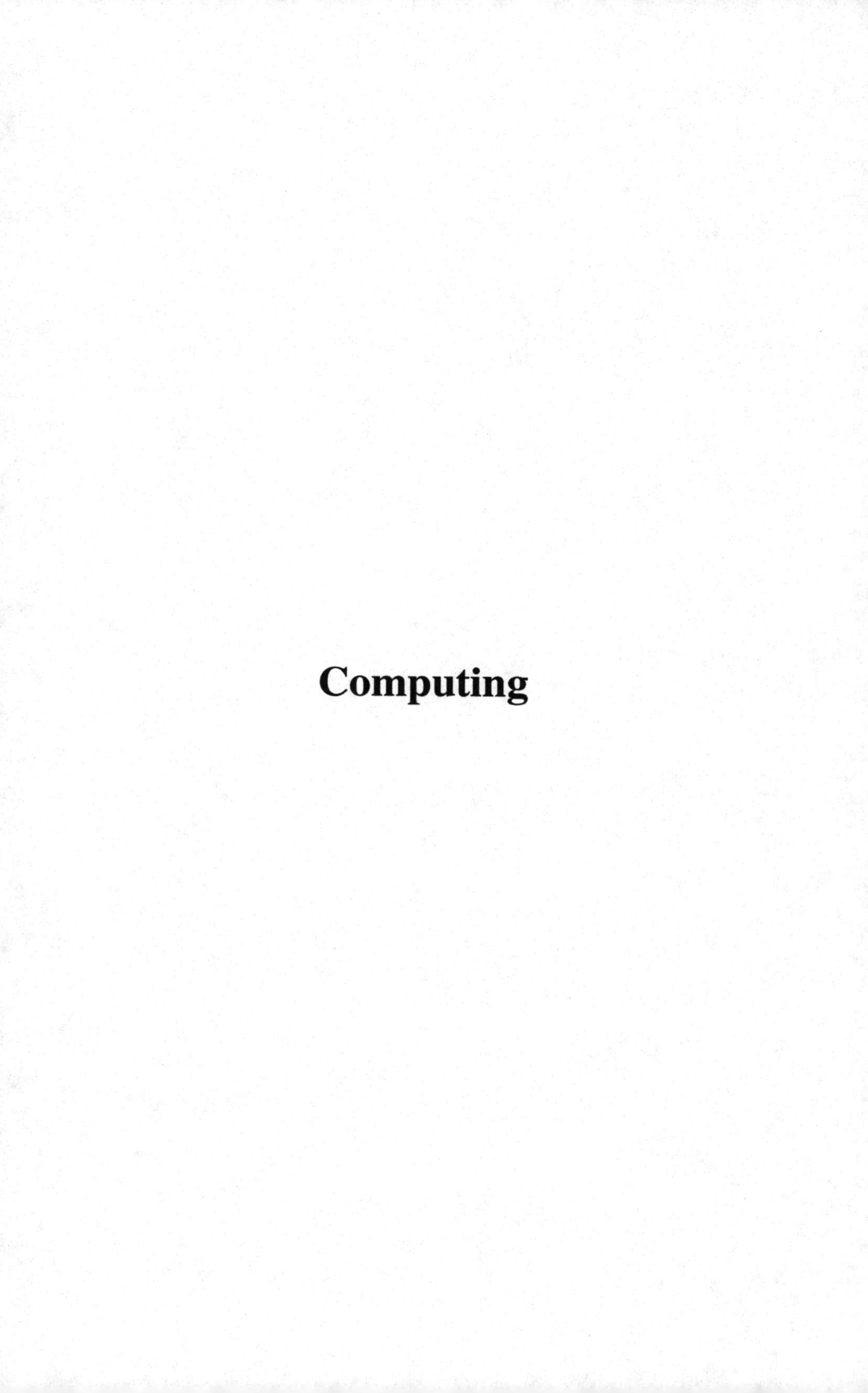

Computing

A Lightweight Block Cipher for Cloud-Based Healthcare Systems

Hemraj Shobharam Lamkuche[1(✉)], Krishnakumar Singh[2], and Kaustubh Shirkhedkar[2]

[1] Symbiosis University of Applied Sciences, Indore, India
hemraj.lamkuche@gmail.com
[2] Symbiosis Centre for Information Technology, Pune, India
krishnakumar@scit.edu, Kaustubh.Shirkhedkar@gmail.com

Abstract. The expansion of remote-based digital healthcare-based IoT systems has accelerated the transfer of medical data through the IoT platform. This study proposes a unique model based on intelligent encryption algorithms in light of lightweight block ciphers, which will secure healthcare data transmitted via IoT devices to cloud systems; overall system is integrated with fog and edge computing to capture and process the data close to fog and edge devices. Compared to conventional encryption techniques, the suggested approach requires the least amount of time to generate cipher text information. The time complexity is decreased to 4.2 ms, and the power consumption is reduced to 7.97 mW, which also improves performance.

Keywords: IoT · Block cipher · Cryptanalysis · Security · Fog computing · Edge computing

1 Introduction

Some data, like healthcare, are crucial and need high security during transmission. We will integrate edge computing with fog computing for data pre-processing at the sensor level, which will help us improve response time and conserve bandwidth. Edge computing aids in integrating applications with data sources such as edge servers or IoT devices. Distributed computing framework helps improve the response time, enhance bandwidth availability, and faster insights. Fog computing is a decentralized computing framework connecting IoT data sources and the cloud, and it helps the cloud to handle the data produced by IoT devices.

Edge computing or Fog computing can be used for: Analyzing the time-sensitive data at the network edge instead of moving entire IoT data to the cloud, Acting on IoT data within milliseconds, and. Sending only selected data to the cloud for longer-term use, in case required for Analysis. This paper discusses how cryptography can be performed over the signal data embedded in an image or direct image data using lightweight encryption in an IoT environment [1–10]. The work is limited to low-powered devices like IoT sensor networks, per- invasive devices, etc. To evaluate the cryptographic images, data analysis

S. K. Panda et al. (Eds.): CoCoLe 2022, CCIS 1729, pp. 3–14, 2022.
https://doi.org/10.1007/978-3-031-21750-0_1

is done based on parameters like several pixel change rate (NPCR), unified average changed intensity (UACI), mean absolute error (MAE), mean squared error (MSE), peak signal-to-noise ratio (PSNR), etc. Data Analysis means systematically applying logical and statistical methods or techniques so that it is possible to describe and evaluate data to generate results. As this data analysis is done on cryptographic images in this paper, it is referred to as cryptanalysis. This paper aims to enhance the algorithm's performance by reducing time and space complexity. Justification A comparative analysis between various algorithms is done based on time complexity and power consumption to analyze if the goal is achieved. Section 2 of this paper begins with various related works. This is followed by Sect. 3, which explains the Proposed Model. Section 4 covers all the information about the implementation of the model. In Sect. 5, there is Analysis of our model is done based on various parameters. Finally, the paper is concluded in Sect. 6.

2 Related Work

Elhoseny et al. [1] developed a model for hybrid encryption over diagnostic textual data embedded in the medical images, and the encryption was done using a combination of AES and RSA. The system's performance was evaluated on six parameters: mean square error, peak signal-to-noise ratio, bit error rate, correlation, structural content, and structural similarity. Darwish et al. [2] presented a new and different concept of integrating Cloud Computing and the Internet of Things for various healthcare applications. This paper presents the state-of-the-art and gap Analysis to analyze the multiple proposals available for Cloud IoT-Health systems. Shehab et al. [3] researched security concerns in IoT networks. The paper discussed essential security requirements like confidentiality, integrity, and authentication. This paper did a comparative study on different attack types and their behaviors. The threat of attack is characterized by high-level, medium-level, and low-level attacks. Also, it suggests the solutions which are possible when attacks are encountered. Anwar et al. [4] developed a technique by which it is possible to secure all image types, and it mainly focuses on medical images. The paper aims to ensure that the integrity of medical information is maintained, the availability of medical images is there, and proper authentication is done so that only authorized people can access that information. Xunjun Chen et al. [5] developed a lightweight cryptographic algorithm for the resource-constrained environment. This paper shows that cryptanalysis of lightweight block cipher Hummingbird-1 might lead to an efficient differential attack with non-negligible probability, which shows ideal security cannot be achieved on a block cipher. Chunguang et al. [6, 7] proposed that stream ciphers are also effective ways of image encryption, and there can be a different permutations. Some block ciphers used to encrypt images in this paper are DES, AES, and SMS4. Showkat et al. [8] developed a model for image security using a hybrid algorithm. It does a secure force algorithm for fast power calculation in LTE and Arnold function to improve reinforcement systems so that the transmission is fast and effective. Truong et al. [9] surveyed and proposed a scheme dedicated to lightweight encryption, which would be significant for TIMS in an insecure channel. The proposed method has 5 phases: registration phase, pre-computing phase, authentication phase, biometrics update phase, and lost card revocation phase. Results show elliptic curve is better in terms of security and efficiency. Bashir et al. [10]

proposed a technique for encryption of images based on shifted image blocks and AES. As per the algorithm developed for a moved image block, first, it divided the image into multiple blocks where every block had a large number of pixels. It then shuffled the blocks using the shift technique on the original image, in which rows and columns were moved to generate a new image. This unique image was then considered as input for the AES algorithm, which was used to encrypt the pixels of the shifted image. It's considered that chaotic cryptanalysis aims to share the details about secret keys used for encryption under various security models.

3 Proposed System for Secure Healthcare System

The framework proposed is the security model. Figure 1 shows a flow chart of the process. This process begins with data collection in the form of a signal from the sensors. The data is then embedded into an image by the method of steganography. FFT is applied to compress the frequency data. Information is further optimized based on four parameters: size, power consumption, memory utilization, and computation. It is then encrypted and transmitted in the IoT environment through IoT devices.

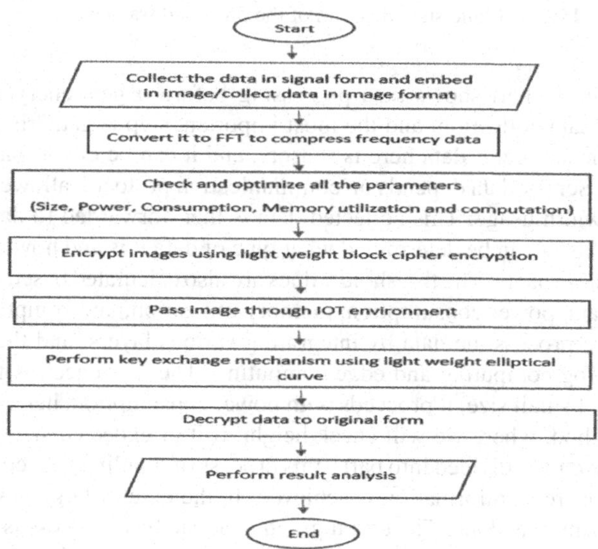

Fig. 1. Flow chart – proposed model

The data is then decrypted to its original form using a key. Results are generated, and Analysis is performed on the results [1–10]. The state diagram depicts a dynamic perspective of the system's event-ordered behavior. Figure 2 shows the proposed framework's system execution. When the input is complete, the block size implementation process begins. The data is read from the system's memory. The stack is then saved as a Serial In Parallel Out (SIPO). The encryption process begins with this stored data and continues until all of the data is encrypted. This encrypted data is transferred into the system memory as a Parallel In Serial Out (PISO) stack. The system memory rereads all pixel data before implementing the block size solution.

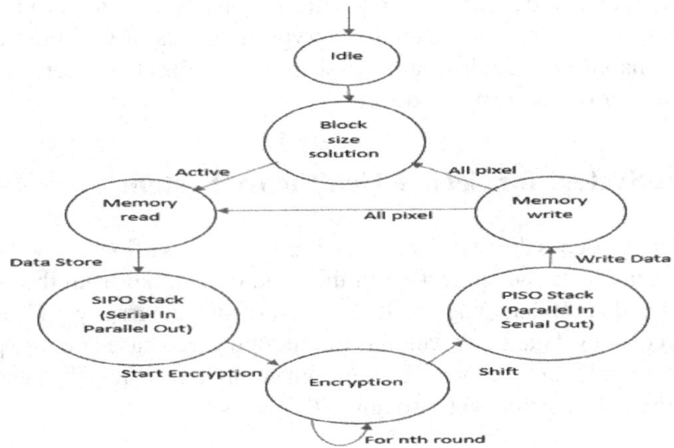

Fig. 2. Finite state diagram of the proposed framework

In Fig. 2, a flow chart shows data processing before it gets encrypted. The process begins with data collection, and the most important step is gathering relevant and accurate data. The source of data here is sensors, and it can be either wired sensors or wireless sensors. Sensor data depends on communication protocol, allowed latency, and acceptable bandwidth usage. This collected data is then forwarded to data acquisition and control. By this, it can be determined what type of data it is and how much power it consumes from the sensors. The threshold values are also calculated based on parameters like the size of data, power consumption, memory utilization, and computation. At this point, we will pre-process the data by integrating various layers, and the primary two layers would be fog computing and edge computing. The first check is for the size of the data. In case of small size, it proceeds with power consumption, here we will follow conventional method, where we will check height, if it of expected size but in case its large size then the data is divided into parts, this process of dividing data continues till the considerable measure of information is achieved. In the case of large power consumption, data optimization is done. The cryptography and analysis process is demonstrated in Fig. 3. The method shows that the key exchange mechanism is done once the image is encrypted. By using this key, image decryption is done. Once the process of cryptography is completed, cryptanalysis begins. There are three types of Analysis performed here. PSNR, NPCR, UACI, correlation coefficient, etc., are calculated as a part of the statistical data analysis. Comparative Analysis is conducted for various algorithms to analyze time complexity and energy consumption. The algorithm's security is verified by critical Analysis, which uses brute force attack, related key attack, and an avalanche effect.

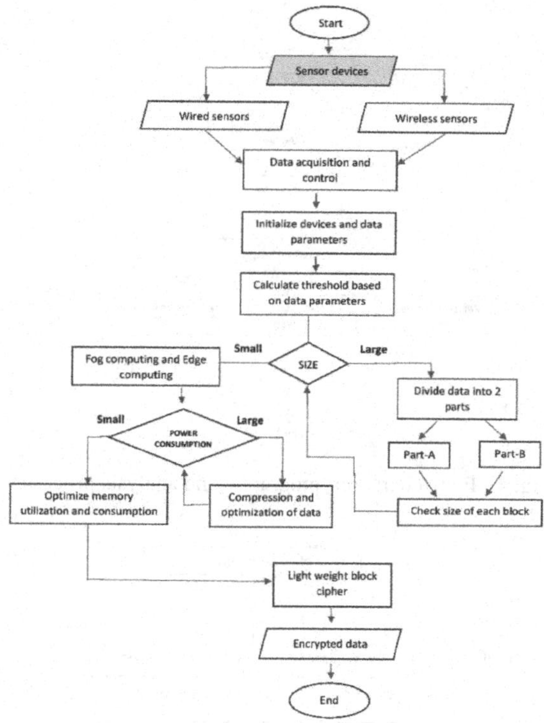

Fig. 3. Flow chart – data collection and encryption process

The key exchange mechanism is performed using the lightweight elliptical curve technique. In this network plaintext block of 64-bit along with the key, P will be input, and a series of permutation operations will start where transformation will be done on the position of pixels. The re-ordering will form a key (P-boxes); it continues for all m positions. At the end of the mth round, the substitution operation takes place where Key S is input along with the permutation value, and transformation is done on the pixel value to attain keys (S-boxes). Diffusion is the process that scatters the statistical structure, and confusion is a process that makes the relation between key and ciphertext very complex. Decryption can be done by inverting the S-boxes and P-boxes and using the keys in reverse order, as shown in Fig. 4 and Fig. 5, respectively.

Figure 5 shows that the input image from the healthcare system is forwarded using IoT sensors. Then a sequence of operations is performed on the input image to generate a cipher image, as shown below.

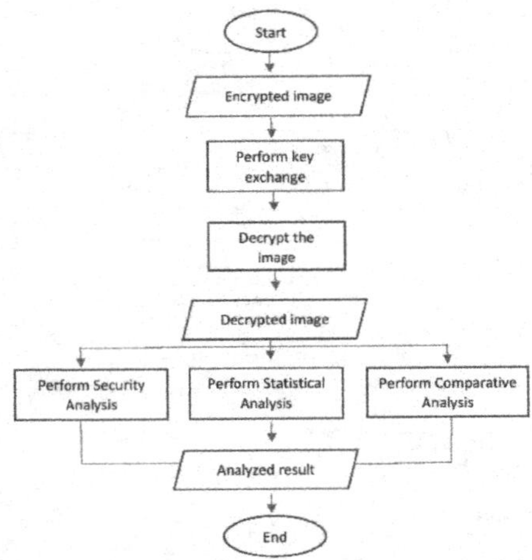

Fig. 4. Flow chart – cryptography and analysis process

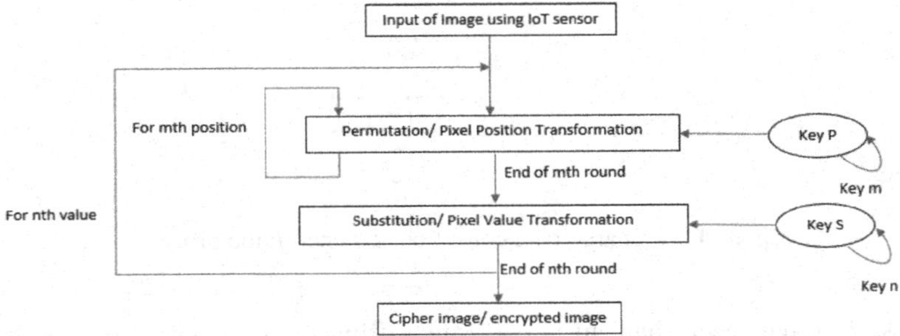

Fig. 5. Proposed permutation-substitution based architecture

4 Software Implementation

The implementation is done in 2 steps. MATLAB and Python scripts are used to implement the algorithms. Step 1 has the entire process done for information security, and step 2 has the security analysis on the image and performance analysis of the algorithm. In step 1, the data is collected from sensor devices in the form of Full Color Anatomical Images and converted to grayscale. These grayscale images are taken as input. For further process, calculation of threshold for parameters like the size of data, power consumption, memory utilization, and computation are done on data. So that, based on these four parameters, data optimization can be performed. This data is then encrypted by lightweight, innovative encryption using Algorithm 1 below. It is then transmitted through the IoT environment; key exchange is done using a light.

Algorithm-1: Proposed Encryption Scheme

A: Input Plaintext of 8-byte Divide A into two 4-byte splits: AL, AR
For i = 1 to 14: AL =AL XOR P (i)
AR = AR XOR (P (i) XOR F (AL))
AL = AL XOR H (AR)
Switch AL and AR
End for Loop
Shift AL and AR (Undo the last switch) AL = AL XOR P15
AR = AR XOR P16
Switch AL and AR AL = AL XOR P17 AR = AR XOR P18
Re-combine AL and AR
Lastly, 8-byte Ciphertext (B) is produced
Encryption: Input: 64-bit(8-byte) Plaintext Output: 64-bit(8byte) Ciphertext Generated.

Elliptical curve for decryption and the data is again decrypted to the original form using Algorithm 2 below. In step 2, security analysis and performance analysis are conducted. Security analysis is done on parameters like: (i) Brute force attack, (ii) Related key attack, (iii) Avalanche effect, (iv) Absolute error between sequences of images, (v) Histogram analysis, (vi) Image Entropy, (vii) Profile Plots, (viii) Correlation Coefficient, (ix) NPCR & UACI randomness test, (x) PSNR & MSE. Performance evaluation is done by comparative Analysis based on time complexity and power consumption with various algorithms.

Algorithm-2: Proposed Decryption Scheme

The input of 8-byte (B) Ciphertext Divide B into two 4-byte splits:
BL, BR BL = BL XOR P18
BR = BR XOR P17
Switch BL and BR BL = BL
XOR P16 BR = BR XOR P15
For i = 14 to 1: BR = BR XOR H (BL)
BL = BL XOR (P (i) XOR F (BR)) BR = BR XOR P (i)
Shift BL and BR (undo the last switch). End For Loop
Re-combine BL and BR
Lastly, 8-byte original Plaintext (A) is produced
Decryption: Input: 64-bit(8-byte) Ciphertext Output: 64-bit plaintext

5 Results and Findings

Full-color anatomical medical images are used for the data set, as shown in Table 1. These images are generated by an X-Ray machine, ultrasound scanner, mammography, MRI scan, computed tomography scan, etc., and used for detecting and treating various diseases by revealing the structural anatomical variances concerning the normal bio-logical process. These images are then converted to a grayscale image to increase the level of complexity and performance of the encrypted image. The images used are from the Kaggle repository and the National library of medicine, which are open-source, and non-copyrighted images used for education and research. The dataset used for the proposed model all images used in a research paper are copyrighted free images, as shown in Table 1, demonstrating the actual image on which encryption was accomplished, the image encoded, and the image decoded obtained by enabling the decryption methodology. Such initial images, encoded images, and decoded images were analyzed. (Source-kaggle-https://www.nlm.nih.gov/research/visible/full_color_png.html).

5.1 Statistical Analysis

For the performance assessment, the statistical analysis is done on parameters like NPCR, UACI, MSE, MAE, PSNR, Image Entropy Histogram, correlation coefficient, and profile plots. These parameters will determine the quality of our proposed model. The NPCR/UACI are calculated using the below formula:

$$\begin{aligned} \mathrm{D(i,j)} = \{0,\ & if\ Q^1(i,j) = Q^2(i,j) \\ 1,\ & if\ Q^1(i,j) \neq Q^2(i,j)\} \end{aligned} \tag{1}$$

$$NPCR : N(Q1,\ Q2) = \sum\ (D(i,j) \times 100\% \tag{2}$$

$$UACI : U(Q1,\ Q2) = \sum\ |(Q1(i,j) - (Q2(i,j)| \times 100\% \tag{3}$$

Q1 and $Q2$ are the pixels of encrypted and decrypted images, respectively. F is the most significant pixel value, and n is a total number of pixels. Net pixel change rate (NPCR) and unified average changing intensity (UACI) examine the influence of one-pixel change on the complete cipher image. NPCR and UACI test the strength of picture encryption algorithms/ciphers against differential assaults. High NPCR/UACI scores indicate differential attack resistance. Table 2 shows the calculated values of NPCR and UACI. The computed average NPCR value is 99.6081, which shows the image has high resistance against attacks.

5.2 Accuracy

PSNR. Peak Signal-to-Noise Ratio is calculated to determine the quality measure between the original and reconstructed/compressed image. MSE is the mean square of differences in the pixel values between corresponding pixels of two images. MAE to check absolute error between sequences of images. It is calculated by the mean of the

Table 1. Dataset used for the proposed model all images used in a research paper are copyrighted free images

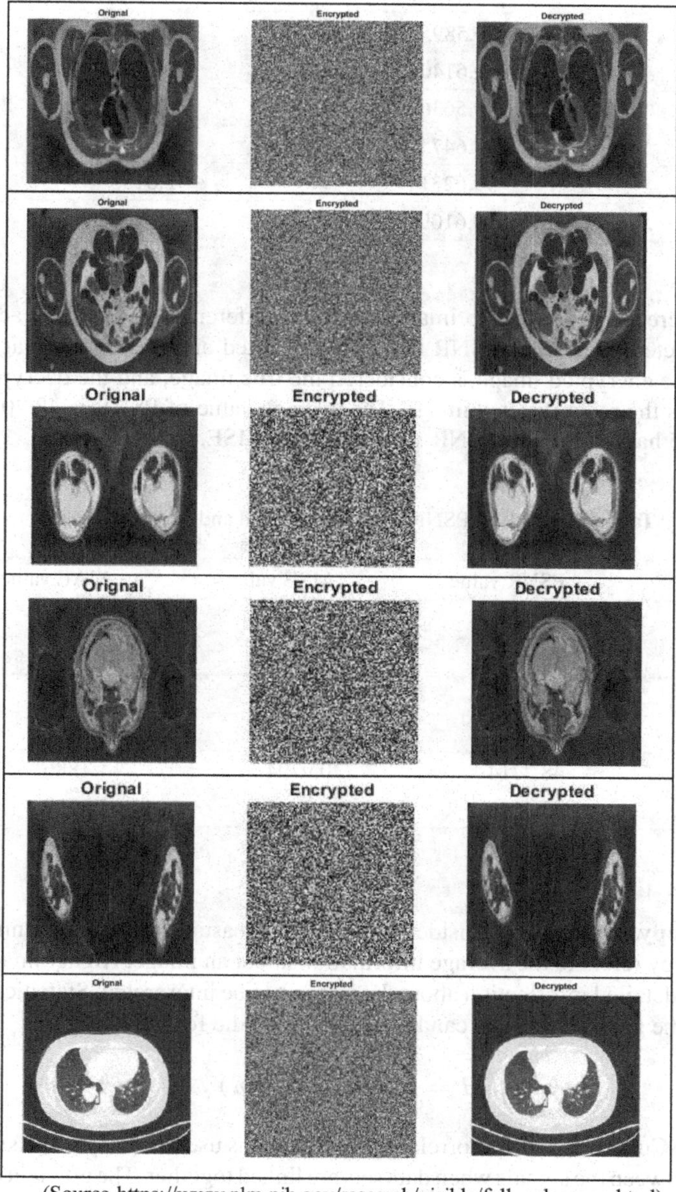

(Source-https://www.nlm.nih.gov/research/visible/full_color_png.html)

Table 2. Result of NPCR and UACI on healthcare images

Images used	NPCR value	UACI value
Image-1.png	99.5895	26.2511
Image-2.png	99.6140	24.3790
Image-3.png	99.5636	26.9870
Image-4.png	99.6475	29.4142
Image-5.png	99.6231	32.6158
Image-6.png	99.6109	19.3716

absolute difference between two images. It is the difference between the actual value and the expected value. The PSNR between encrypted and decrypted image is given in Table 3, the encrypted image is considered the true image, and the decrypted image is regarded as the reconstructed image. The average value of PSNR is 48.2085. In this case, Image 5 has the highest PSNR value and least MSE.

Table 3. Result of PSNR between encoded and decoded image

Images used	PSNR value	MSE value	MAE value
Image-1.png	48.2022	0.9837	1.1888
Image-2.png	48.2127	0.9813	1.1849
Image-3.png	48.2079	0.9924	1.1813
Image-4.png	48.2069	0.9926	1.1851
Image-5.png	48.2214	0.9794	1.1886
Image-6.png	48.1999	0.9842	1.1929

Image Entropy. Entropy is considered a perfect measure of the randomness of the cipher. Entropy refers to the average information about an image. Higher image entropy means more detailed information about the image can be interpreted. Statistically, image entropy for the grayscale image can be calculated by the formula:

$$H = -\sum k\, p_k\, log_2(p_k)$$

Correlation Coefficient. The correlation coefficient is used to analyze the similarity or difference between the signals when data sets are linked together. The efficient encryption method eliminates the correlation. The formula used is:

$$r = \frac{p\sum xy - (\sum x)(\sum y)}{\sqrt{p(\sum x^2) - (\sum x)^2}\sqrt{p(\sum x^2) - (\sum y)^2}}$$

Decryption Time. The more time takes for decryption, the more secure the algorithm is. If the algorithm takes a long time to execute, there is less probability of occurrence of an attack. As shown in Table 4, the average decryption time taken by the proposed algorithm is 4.183 ms.

Table 4. Result of time taken for decryption

Images	Total decryption time
Image-1.png	03.6 ms
Image-2.png	03.7 ms
Image-3.png	04.8 ms
Image-4.png	04.1 ms
Image-5.png	04.3 ms

As per the Analysis, for different sizes of images, when time is calculated for various algorithms, the proposed model takes minimum time, showing it has the best performance among all algorithms shown in Table 5 below.

Table 5. Comparative analysis based on the time complexity

Images	Size (kb)	Proposed model	AES	BLOWFISH
Image-1.png	84.5	4.20	11.17	5.25
Image-2.png	83.8	4.11	10.91	5.13
Image-3.png	73.4	3.30	8.77	4.13
Image-4.png	79.2	3.75	9.83	4.63
Image-5.png	65.1	2.90	7.71	3.63

5.3 Key Analysis

To ensure security, brute force attacks, related acute attacks, and an avalanche effect were performed on the encrypted image. Brute Force Attack: All the possible vital combinations were tried for brute force to get the original image. The maximum number of attempts was 2key-size. The more the key's size or the number of bits in the key, the more time it takes to break the cipher. Related Key Attack: For related key attacks, several keys were generated which had mathematical relation with the original key, and these keys were applied to the ciphertext to get the decrypted image. However, all these attacks cannot break security which shows the algorithm is quite secure. Avalanche Effect: For the avalanche effect, the bits of image pixels were changed, and a slight change generated more than 50% change in output. The proposed system also satisfies avalanche effect criterion in generating complex cipher at the end of each round, a small change in input produces high degree of cipher data using proposed scheme.

6 Conclusion

The proposed framework uses lightweight cryptography and builds a permutation substitution network based on the algorithm. Based on the analysis results, it can be concluded that the main objective of time optimization, space optimization, and performance enhancement is achieved. The use of fog computing and cloud computing helps in enhancing the optimization at the data pre-processing layer. Various attacks like brute-force and related key attack could not break the security to decrypt the ciphertext. Hence, it can be said that by using a lightweight block cipher encryption scheme, it is possible to perform secure data transmission.

References

1. Pramod, D., Lamkuche, H.S.: CSL: FPGA implementation of lightweight block cipher for power-constrained devices. Int. J. Inf. Comput. Secur. **12**(2/3), 349–377 (2020). https://doi.org/10.1504/ijics.2020.10023595
2. Lamkuche, H.S., Pramod, D., Onker, V., Katiya, S., Lamkuche, G., Hiremath, G.R.: SAL–a lightweight symmetric cipher for Internet of Things. Int. J. Innov. Technol. Explor. Eng. **8**(11), 521–528 (2019)
3. Kumar, S., Kumar, D., Lamkuche, H.S.: TPA auditing to enhance the privacy and security in cloud systems. J. Cyber Secur. Mobil. **10**, 537–568 (2021)
4. Elhoseny, M., Ramírez-González, G., Abu-Elnasr, O.M., Shawkat, S.A., Arunkumar, N., Farouk, A.: Secure medical data transmission model for IoT-based healthcare systems. IEEE Access **6**, 20596–20608 (2018). https://doi.org/10.1109/ACCESS.2018.2817615
5. Darwish, A., Hassanien, A.E., Elhoseny, M., Sangaiah, A.K., Muhammad, K.: The impact of the hybrid platform of internet of things and cloud computing on healthcare systems: opportunities, challenges, and open problems. J. Ambient. Intell. Humaniz. Comput. **10**(10), 4151–4166 (2017). https://doi.org/10.1007/s12652-017-0659-1
6. Shehab, A., et al.: Secure and robust fragile watermarking scheme for medical images. IEEE Access **6**, 10269–10278 (2018). https://doi.org/10.1109/ACCESS.2018.2799240
7. Anwar, A.S., Ghany, K.K.A., El Mahdy, H.: Improving the security of image transmission. Int. J. Bio-Med. Inform. E-Health **3**(4), 7–13 (2015)
8. Chen, X., Zhu, Y., Gong, Z., Luo, Y.: Cryptanalysis of the lightweight block cipher hummingbird-1. In: 2013 Fourth International Conference on Emerging Intelligent Data and Web Technologies, Xi'an, pp. 515–518 (2013). https://doi.org/10.1109/EIDWT.2013.92
9. Bashir, A., Hasan, A.S.B., Almangush, H.: A new image encryption approach using the integration of a shifting technique and the AES algorithm. Int. J. Comput. Appl. **42**(9), 38–45 (2012)
10. Li, C., Lin, D., Feng, B., Lü, J., Hao, F.: Cryptanalysis of a chaotic image encryption algorithm based on information entropy. IEEE Access **6**, 75834–75842 (2018)

Developing a Cloud Intrusion Detection System with Filter-Based Features Selection Techniques and SVM Classifier

Mhamad Bakro[1(✉)], Rakesh Ranjan Kumar[1], Sukant K. Bisoy[1], Mohammad Osama Addas[2], and Dania Khamis[2]

[1] Department of Computer Science and Engineering, C. V. Raman Global University, Bhubaneswar 752054, India
mhwb14794@gmail.com

[2] Department of Computer Science and Engineering, Siksha 'O' Anusandhan, Bhubaneswar 751030, India

Abstract. The rising usage of the cloud nowadays and its usage in various domains have made it more essential for all, which has led to an expansion in the size of data kept in the cloud. Data is the gold of our era; thus, it is important to protect it against any attacks. The intrusion detection system IDS is considered among of the most important solutions that address security issues and threats in the different models of cloud service delivery. IDS-based on machine learning (ML) has been developed to monitor and analyse data packets to detect abnormal behaviours and new attacks. The datasets utilized for these objectives are generally vast and include a lot of features, making computing very time-consuming. It is crucial to pick relevant features to include in the model, which produce better results and require less computation time than using all of the features. In this paper, we developed a system that combines filter-based feature selection with the support-vector-machine (SVM) model as a classifier. The NSL-KDD, Kyoto, and the CSE-CIC-IDS-2018 datasets are used to validate our system. We have compared with many existing methodologies and found that our proposed system outperformed the others in terms of accuracy, recall, precision, F-measure, and false-alarm rate.

Keywords: Filter-based feature selection · SVM · NSL-KDD · Kyoto · CSE-CIC-IDS 2018

1 Introduction

Cloud computing has become important in different aspects recently due to its simplicity of usage and correlation between payment and demand [1,2]. Different service kinds are delivered through the Internet as part of cloud computing (CC) such as IaaS, PaaS , and SaaS [3,4]. Security fears are growing daily along with an increase in its use. The hackers are making every effort to get unauthorised access to the cloud's data. Securing data and information on the

S. K. Panda et al. (Eds.): CoCoLe 2022, CCIS 1729, pp. 15–26, 2022.
https://doi.org/10.1007/978-3-031-21750-0_2

cloud has grown to be exceedingly difficult. An effective IDS is needed to protect such data [5]. Today, machine learning plays a critical part in many security-related fields. To construct a robust IDS model in this circumstance, we also used machine learning [6]. A dataset containing the attack recordings is required for the implementation of an effective IDS. The volume of the datasets that are accessible is enormous, and many of its features are unnecessary. When features don't make much of an impact on a prediction model's accuracy, they are deemed irrelevant. The dataset's irrelevant features must be eliminated, and only the relevant features must be chosen in order to increase predictive performance and minimize computing costs. To exclude such features and choose a subset of features that provides greater accuracy while requiring less computing time, we offered filter techniques that include information gain, gain ratio, and chi-square. Also, we have used SVM as a classifier to determine the normal and malicious packets, this would result in an effective IDS. The suggested approach is verified on the NSL-KDD, Kyoto, and CSE-CIC-IDS 2018 datasets and comparison with other approaches.

Our study is arranged as follows: Sect. 2 represents some previous work, Sect. 3 offers the proposed approach, Sect. 4 is concerned with the experimental outcomes, and Sect. 5 is the conclusion.

2 Related Work

Here, we review some earlier research on AI-based intrusion detection systems. In an effort to decrease the input dimension while enhancing the classifier's performance, Kasongo and Sun presented a DL-based intrusion detection system IDS utilising FeedForward-DNN along with a feature selection approach employing IG as a filter method. The NSL-KDD was used to test their system [7]. The authors proposed an IDS consisting of an improved conditional variational AutoEncoder (ICVAE) and DNN. The data dimension is reduced, and the DNN hidden layers' weight is initialised employing the learned-ICVAE encoder. The ICVAE decoder can provide a variety of unknown attack instances and balance the training data set, which increases the detection rate of minorities. DNN played a dual role as a feature extraction model and a classifier [8]. Peng et al. developed an approach for building and optimising the structure of the DBN-IDS model in a few hidden layers' range. The initial optimization solution is designed using the PSO technique, which is based on fish swarms. The initial particle swarm of the GA optimization PSO algorithm is made up of the initial optimization solution. Their approach then optimises the DBN-IDS model and has achieved high classification accuracy with the speed of detection [9]. The authors suggested a fuzzy aggregation method that employs the MDPCA and DBNs. MDPCA is used to split the imbalance of the training set into many subsets with related sets of attributes to minimize the intricacy of the training subsets and enable the model to get the best detection accuracy. An individual sub-DBNs classifier is trained for each subset. These sub-DBNs can act as classifiers and minimise data dimensionality. Based on the weights of fuzzy membership, the output of sub-DBN classifiers is combined [10]. Multiple convolutional layers are used by T. Su et al. to extract the local features of traffic data in their BAT-MC model, which has a two-phase learning of the BLSTM and awareness on the time series features for intrusion detection. Each packet's traffic bytes are utilised by the BLSTM layer to extract features. A packet vector may be created from each data packet. To create a network flow vector, these packet vectors are combined and feature learning is applied through the attention layer [11]. Ieracitano et al. introduced an IDS based on an autoencoder (AE) driven intelligent and statistical analysis. To extract the optimal and more correlated features, they applied data analytics, statistical approaches, and the latest developments in ML theory. The AE architecture, which had a single hidden layer with 50 units, provided these correlated features [12]. Samriya and Kumar designed the FCM-SMO model that merges between spider-monkey optimization algorithm for reducing the dimensionality of the dataset and select the features which are fed into fuzzy clustering for classification. The suggested system produces improved accuracy and decreased computation time [13]. The authors suggested a hybrid IDS that integrates the advantages of signature intrusion detection systems - developed using the C5 decision tree classifier - and anomaly intrusion detection systems - developed using the one-class SVM. This approach detected both well-known attacks and zero-day threats, with a low FAR and a high detection rate [14]. Zhang et al. presented a MFFSEM. The four benchmark datasets are broken down into multiple basic feature datasets based on the correlation of the traffic data, and then by permutation and combination, a number of comprehensive feature datasets are produced. Permutation and combination boost the variety of fundamental classifiers, increase the robustness of MFFSEM, and provide mutual support among many features [15]. As a pre-processing stage for CNN that serves as a classifier, Shams et al. proposed a novel technique called CAFE. They used feature selection approaches like ERT and SKB to minimize the dimensionality of the input data and decrease the time of classification, since the feature extraction approach maximizes the dimension of the input data and raises the detection time. A fine-tuning method was also applied to enhance the effectiveness. Validating of the system was performed using four datasets that included host and network-based data instances [16].

The aforementioned studies show the significant importance of IDSs in securing the existing systems against threats, but we have observed that the detection rate (DR) and accuracy of threat detection were lower than expected, also most of them haven't concentrated to provide an extensive feature set. As is common knowledge, the efficacy of an IDS is determined by its DR, Acc, and FAR values. To guarantee higher detection outcomes, a suitable feature collection has to be chosen. As a consequence, we were motivated to create an efficient IDS employing filter-based feature selection.

3 Methodology

The proposed IDS includes pre-processing phase. The collection of filter techniques together constitutes the final feature set. The final classification results are derived from the SVM model after it has been trained on the feature set. Figure 1 illustrates the suggested system.

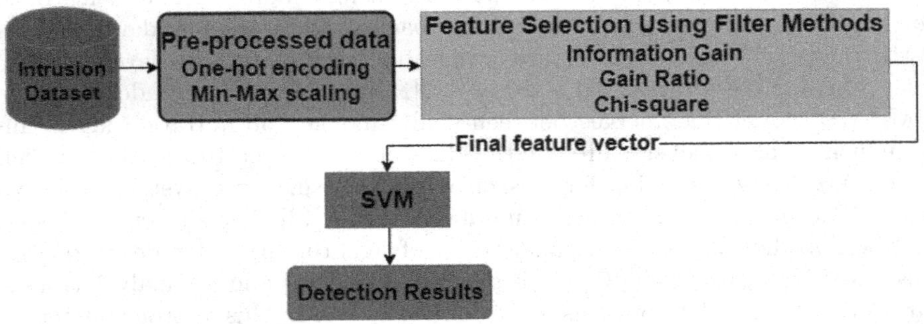

Fig. 1. Block diagram of the suggested design

3.1 Pre-processing

The dataset is initially pre-processed by removing noisy, incomplete, and duplicate values. Then, we are using one-hot encoding to get the numeric form of variables, and min-max scaling for reducing the scope of values to a specific range. Thus, we keep one valid numeric value. Finally, we divide the preprocessed data into the training and testing parts.

3.2 Feature Selection

To determine the most related features and form the feature vector, we used filter techniques such as IG, GR, and CS:

Information Gain IG: It is a reduction in class entropy from an initial state to the known state of an attribute value, in which the entropy is considered the probability distribution of the dataset and is computed as follows [17]:

$$H(S) = -\sum P(s)\log_2 \ P(s) \tag{1}$$

where $P(s)$ is the probability distribution of the observations s, variable s is a member of class S, and $H(s)$ is the entropy prior to the observation of a variable in class S. By comparing the entropy of the dataset before and after a change, information gain is computed as follows:

$$Information\ Gain(A, S) = H\left(S\right) - H\left(S, A\right) \tag{2}$$

where $H(S)$ is entropy before the observation of attribute A and $H(S, A)$ is entropy following the observation of attribute A, and $IG(A, S)$ is information gain of attribute A given class S.

Gain Ratio GR: It determines the ratio of entropy to attribute information gain. GR is a method to enhance the IG score. GR is given as follows [18]:

$$Gain\ ratio(S, A) = \left(H\left(S\right) - H\left(S, A\right)\right)/H\left(A\right) \tag{3}$$

Chi-Square CS: Is a statistical test that is used to ascertain if 2 variables are correlated or not [18]. CS is calculated as follows:

$$X^2 = \sum_{ij} \left(O_{ij} - E_{ij}\right)^2/E_{ij} \tag{4}$$

where O and E refer to observed and expected values, respectively, X^2 denotes the value of CS, and i and j are two variables.

3.3 Classification Approach

The real objective of IDS is to identify whether flowing data are normal or malicious and to achieve that we used the SVM model.

SVM: It is a supervised ML technique, that is used for classifying various data types and is considered the most efficient compared to all ML models and that is our reason for choosing it [19]. SVM separates data by creating one or more hyperplanes or lines in a high-dimensional space, and the best ones are chosen based on how well they break the data up into classes. By using kernels, SVM is able to find these hyperplanes and address the linear and non-linear issues [20]. The hyperplane is indicated as follows [21]:

$$Hyperplane\left(x\right) = w^T\left(x\right) + b \tag{5}$$

where the w, x, and b represent the weight vector, the input, and the bias value, respectively.

4 Implementation and Result Analysis

This section has demonstrated the datasets and the performance measures that we used and analysed the results of our system. The experiment was run on the Google Colab platform using python with the Scikit-learn library on an Intel processor Core i5.

4.1 Dataset

These Benchmark datasets are used to verify our proposed:

NSL-KDD: It is the most dataset used by researchers, which is an advanced form of the KDD Cup-99 dataset. It includes normal and abnormal instances with 42 features. Attacks can be classified as DOS, R2L, U2R, and Probe [22]. The NSL-KDD is illustrated in Table 1.

Table 1. The NSL-KDD dataset

	Normal	DOS	Probe	R2L	U2R	Total
KDDTrain+	67,343	45,927	11,656	995	52	**125,973**
KDDTest+	9,711	7,460	2,421	2,885	67	**22,544**

Kyoto: It was gathered from the honeypot and other servers installed at the University of Kyoto between 2006 and 2015. The dataset has 24 features from both KDD-99 and honeypot. The instances can be categorized as known and unknown attacks and normal packets [23]. The Kyoto is shown in Table 2.

Table 2. The Kyoto dataset

	Normal	Known attack	Unknown attack	Total
Train	43,190	157,429	9,184	**209,803**
Test	10,827	39,360	2,264	**52,451**

CSE-CIC-IDS-2018: It is an enhanced version of CSE-CIC-IDS-2017. This dataset includes 84 features and 7 traffic patterns, including benign, DoS attacks, DDoS attacks, web attacks, brute force attacks, botnet attacks, and infiltration attacks. These patterns are categorised into 14 classes [24]. The CSE-CIC-IDS-2018 is demonstrated in Table 3.

4.2 Evaluation Criteria

These performance criteria demonstrate the efficiency of our intrusion detection system in recognising the packets. They are computed mathematically using the confusion matrix CM, which consists of the prediction and actual results of our system. Four categories of CM exist as follows: False Negative (FN), a positive sample that has been incorrectly determined to be a negative sample. False Positives (FP) occur when negative samples are mistakenly interpreted as positive ones. True Negative (TN), which are really negative samples, are accurately identified as such. Positive samples are considered to be True Positives (TP), which are truly positive samples. Equations 6, 7, 8, 9, and 10 are used to measure the performance of the model.

Table 3. The CSE-CIC-IDS 2018 dataset

Pattern	Attack Type	Train	Test
Benign	–	15,469	3,939
DoS Attack	DoS attacks-Hulk	6,093	1,466
	DoS attacks-Slowloris	973	246
	DoS attacks-GoldenEye	2,923	717
	DoS attacks-SlowHTTPTest	2,575	640
DDoS Attack	DDoS attacks-LOIC-HTTP	7,521	1,885
	DDOS attack-LOIC-UDP	573	150
	DDOS attack-HOIC	9,146	2,328
Web Attack	Brute Force-XSS	189	51
	Brute Force-Web	249	63
	SQL Injection	52	11
Brute-force	SSH-Bruteforce	3,491	851
	FTP-BruteForce	3,511	865
Botnet	Bot	4,062	976
Infiltration	Infiltration	2,997	768
Total	–	**59,824**	**14,956**

- **Accuracy:** It is the proportion of successfully identified instances to all instances.

$$Accuracy\ Acc = \frac{TP + TN}{TP + TN + FP + FN} \tag{6}$$

- **Precision:** It measures the proportion of attacks that were successfully predicted to all the instances that were attacked.

$$Precision\ P = \frac{TP}{TP + FP} \tag{7}$$

- **Recall:** It is the proportion of all instances that were successfully detected as attacks to all instances that are really attacked. Also, known as the detection rate.

$$Detection\ Rate\ DR = Recall\ R = \frac{TP}{TP + FN} \tag{8}$$

- **False Alarm Rate:** It is the proportion of incorrectly predicted Attack instances to all Normal instances.

$$False\ Alarm\ Rate\ FAR = \frac{FP}{FP + TN} \tag{9}$$

- **F-measure:** It is a method for evaluating a system's performance by looking at its recall and precision.

$$F - measure\ F = \frac{2\,(P * R)}{(P + R)} \tag{10}$$

4.3 Result Analysis

By the implementation, the confusion matrix for datasets are calculated as shown in Fig. 2, which will be used to compute the evaluation criteria of multi-class classification.

Table 4 illustrates the outperforming of the results of our proposal compared to other recent other works in terms of Acc, and the macro average of Precision P, Recall R, and F-measure based on the NSL-KDD dataset.

Table 4. Comparing the results of our proposal and the recent other works based on NSL-KDD.

No.	*Year*	*ReferenceNo.*	*Methodology*	*ACC*	*P*	*R*	*F*
1	2019	[7]	FFDNN	86.62	–	–	–
2	2019	[8]	ICVAE-DNN	85.97	97.39	77.43	86.27
3	2019	[9]	AFSA-GA-PSO-DBN	82.36	–	–	–
4	2019	[10]	MDPCA-DBN	82.08	97.27	70.51	81.75
5	2020	[11]	BAT-MC	84.25	–	–	–
6	2020	[12]	AE	87.00	87.85	82.04	81.21
7	2020	[13]	FCM-SMO	86.00	84.70	88.40	86.50
8	2020	[14]	C5+OC-SVM	83.24	–	–	–
9	2021	[15]	MFFSEM	84.33	74.61	96.43	84.13
10	2021	[16]	CAFE-CNN	83.43	–	–	–
IG+GR+CS - SVM				98.09	96.24	88.53	91.87

While Table 5 represents the results of the proposed model according to the Kyoto and the CSE-CIC-IDS 2018 datasets.

Table 5. The simulation outcomes of the proposed model according to the Kyoto and the CSE-CIC-IDS 2018 datasets.

Methodology: IG+GR+CS - SVM	*ACC*	*P*	*R*	*F*
The Kyoto dataset	96.42	90.53	96.23	92.96
The CSE-CIC-IDS 2018 dataset	99.89	93.02	92.93	92.97

Figure 3 shows the superior performance of our proposal's findings in terms of FAR and DR for each class in the NSL-KDD when compared to two prior works.

Our study reduced the consumption of resources and the outcomes were excellent compared to earlier studies, but we will endeavour to improve performance by choosing other strategies to determine appropriate features and handling the issue of unbalanced data.

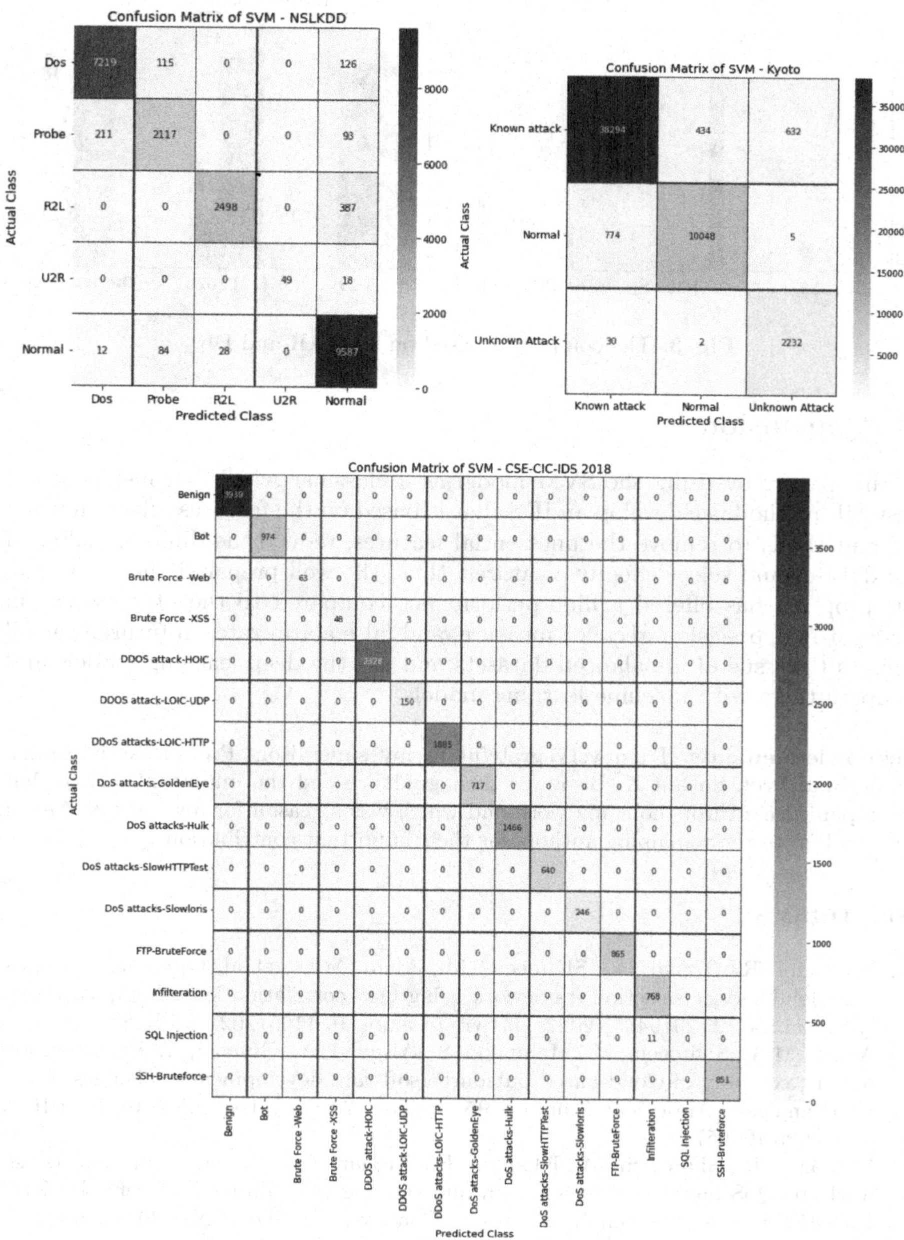

Fig. 2. Confusion Matrix of the NSL-KDD, the Kyoto, and the CSE-CIC-IDS 2018 datasets.

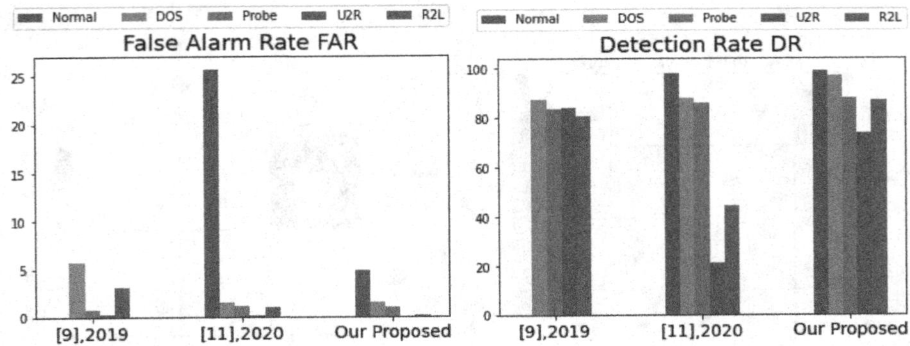

Fig. 3. The comparing based on the FAR and DR

5 Conclusion

In this paper, by using the SVM model as a classifier which is considered the best ML method, we develop an IDS that is based on the features selection using filter methods to remove the unessential features, reduce the dimensionality of the dataset and select effective features, thus, the well prepared the dataset in our proposal has offered a high-performance compared to the other works in terms of Acc, precision, recall, f-measure, and false alarm rate. In future, we will address the issue of imbalanced datasets and use the deep learning models and compare them with machine learning models.

Acknowledgements. I am very grateful to my supervisors Prof. Rakesh Ranjan Kumar and Prof. Sukant K. Bisoy for their guidance and the important advice that accompanied me throughout my work and which was a reason for my success. Also, I am thankful to the remaining authors for their important contributions.

References

1. Kumar, R.R., Tomar, A., Shameem, M., Alam, M.D., et al. Optcloud: an optimal cloud service selection framework using QoS correlation lens. Comput. Intell. Neurosci. **2022**, 2019485 (2022). https://doi.org/10.1155/2022/2019485
2. Akbar, M.A., Shameem, M., Mahmood, S., Alsanad, A., Gumaei, A.: Prioritization based taxonomy of cloud-based outsource software development challenges: fuzzy AHP analysis. Appl. Soft Comput. **95**, 106557 (2020). https://doi.org/10.1016/j.asoc.2020.106557
3. Kumar, R.R., Shameem, M., Khanam, R., Kumar, C: A hybrid evaluation framework for QoS based service selection and ranking in cloud environment. In: 2018 15th IEEE India Council International Conference (INDICON) (2018). https://doi.org/10.1109/INDICON45594.2018.8987192
4. Bakro, M., Bisoy, S.K., Patel, A.K., Naal, M.A.: Performance analysis of cloud computing encryption algorithms. In: Das, S., Mohanty, M.N. (eds.) Advances in Intelligent Computing and Communication. LNNS, vol. 202, pp. 357–367. Springer, Singapore (2021). https://doi.org/10.1007/978-981-16-0695-3_35

5. Bakro, M., Bisoy, S.K., Patel, A.K., Naal, M.A.: Hybrid blockchain-enabled security in cloud storage infrastructure using ECC and AES algorithms. In: De, D., Bhattacharyya, S., Rodrigues, J.J.P.C. (eds.) Blockchain based Internet of Things. LNDECT, vol. 112, pp. 139–170. Springer, Singapore (2022). https://doi.org/10.1007/978-981-16-9260-4_6
6. Kilincer, I.F., Ertam, F., Sengur, A.: Machine learning methods for cyber security intrusion detection: datasets and comparative study. Comput. Netw. **188**, 107840 (2021). https://doi.org/10.1016/j.comnet.2021.107840
7. Kasongo, S.M., Sun, Y.: A deep learning method with filter based feature engineering for wireless intrusion detection system. IEEE Access **7**, 38597–38607 (2019). https://doi.org/10.1109/ACCESS.2019.2905633
8. Yang, Y., Zheng, K., Chunhua, W., Yang, Y.: Improving the classification effectiveness of intrusion detection by using improved conditional variational autoencoder and deep neural network. Sensors **19**(11), 2528 (2019). https://doi.org/10.3390/s19112528
9. Wei, P., Li, Y., Zhang, Z., Tao, H., Li, Z., Liu, D.: An optimization method for intrusion detection classification model based on deep belief network. IEEE Access **7**, 87593–87605 (2019). https://doi.org/10.1109/ACCESS.2019.2925828
10. Yang, Y., Zheng, K., Chunhua, W., Niu, X., Yang, Y.: Building an effective intrusion detection system using the modified density peak clustering algorithm and deep belief networks. Appl. Sci. **9**(2), 238 (2019). https://doi.org/10.3390/app9020238
11. Tongtong, S., Sun, H., Zhu, J., Wang, S., Li, Y.: BAT: deep learning methods on network intrusion detection using NSL-KDD dataset. IEEE Access **8**, 29575–29585 (2020). https://doi.org/10.1109/ACCESS.2020.2972627
12. Ieracitano, C., Adeel, A., Morabito, F.C., Hussain, A.: A novel statistical analysis and autoencoder driven intelligent intrusion detection approach. Neurocomputing **387**, 51–62 (2020). https://doi.org/10.1016/j.neucom.2019.11.016
13. Samriya, J.K., Kumar, N.: A novel intrusion detection system using hybrid clustering-optimization approach in cloud computing. In: Materials Today Proceedings (2020). https://doi.org/10.1016/j.matpr.2020.09.614
14. Khraisat, A., Gondal, I., Vamplew, P., Kamruzzaman, J., Alazab, A.: Hybrid intrusion detection system based on the stacking ensemble of c5 decision tree classifier and one class support vector machine. Electronics **9**(1), 173 (2020). https://doi.org/10.3390/electronics9010173
15. Zhang, H., Li, J.-L., Liu, X.-M., Dong, C.: Multi-dimensional feature fusion and stacking ensemble mechanism for network intrusion detection. Futur. Gener. Comput. Syst. **122**, 130–143 (2021). https://doi.org/10.1016/j.future.2021.03.024
16. Shams, E.A., Rizaner, A., Ulusoy, A.H.: A novel context-aware feature extraction method for convolutional neural network-based intrusion detection systems. Neural Comput. Appl. **33**(20), 13647–13665 (2021). https://doi.org/10.1007/s00521-021-05994-9
17. Omuya, E.O., Okeyo, G.O., Kimwele, M.W.: Feature selection for classification using principal component analysis and information gain. Expert Syst. Appl. **174**, 114765 (2021). https://doi.org/10.1016/j.eswa.2021.114765
18. Nisha Arora and Pankaj Deep Kaur: A Bolasso based consistent feature selection enabled random forest classification algorithm: an application to credit risk assessment. Appl. Soft Comput. **86**, 105936 (2020). https://doi.org/10.1016/j.asoc.2019.105936

19. Liu, L., Wang, P., Lin, J., Liu, L.: Intrusion detection of imbalanced network traffic based on machine learning and deep learning. IEEE Access **9**, 7550–7563 (2020).https://doi.org/10.1109/ACCESS.2020.3048198
20. Wang, D., Zhang, Z., Bai, R., Mao, Y.: A hybrid system with filter approach and multiple population genetic algorithm for feature selection in credit scoring. J. Comput. Appl. Math. **329**, 307–321 (2018). https://doi.org/10.1016/j.cam.2017.04.036
21. Soumaya, Z., Taoufiq, B.D., Benayad, N., Yunus, K., Abdelkrim, A.: The detection of parkinson disease using the genetic algorithm and SVM classifier. Appl. Acoust. **171**, 107528 (2021). https://doi.org/10.1016/j.apacoust.2020.107528
22. Canadian institute for cybersecurity and university of new brunswick, NSL-KDD | datasets | research | canadian institute for cybersecurity | UNB. 2009. https://www.unb.ca/cic/datasets/nsl.html. Accessed 03 Mar 2022
23. Kyoto university. Traffic data from Kyoto university's honeypots (2006). https://www.takakura.com/Kyoto_data/new_data201704/. Accessed 03 Mar 2022
24. C.I. for Cybersecurity. IDS 2018 Datasets Canadian Institute for Cybersecurity (2018). https://www.unb.ca/cic/datasets/ids-2018.html. Accessed 03 Mar 2022

A Study on Effect of Learning Rates Using Adam Optimizer in LSTM Deep Intelligent Model for Detection of DDoS Attack to Support Fog Based IoT Systems

Surya Pavan Kumar Gudla[1](✉) and Sourav Kumar Bhoi[2]

[1] Department of Computer Science and Engineering, NCR- PMEC Berhampur, Faculty of Engineering, BPUT, Rourkela 769015, Odisha, India
pavan1980.mca@gmail.com

[2] Department of Computer Science and Engineering, PMEC (Govt.), Berhampur 761003, India
sourav.cse@pmec.ac.in

Abstract. The conceptual underpinnings of machine learning and artificial intelligence have been significantly impacted by deep learning, which has experienced substantial practical success. A deep learning model's (DL) performance is influenced by a number of hyperparameters during model formation. The learning rate is one of them (LR). The examination of the widely used Adam optimizer's LR impact on performance metrics and the choice of the best LR with no ambiguity for future research are the main objectives of this work. The DDoS SDN dataset and Long Short Term Memory (LSTM) DL model are used in the research to support the work for attack detection in fog-based IoT systems for security purposes. It was discovered that Adam Optimizers' default LR 0.001 is the best; however, when huge batch sizes are taken into account, LR 0.01 proved to be better in the numbers of performance metrics but the noise is too high. As a result, it is decided that the LR 0.001 is the most appropriate value while building a DL model using the Adam optimizer.

Keywords: Adam optimizer · Deep learning · Learning rate · LSTM

1 Introduction

Deep Learning, a neural network architecture the most in-demand word in the present technical era stands atop machine learning. It is highly used to train the model on large volumes of data obtaining efficient results in means of performance metrics. Due to its popularity, it's widely used in disparate domains like medical image processing, natural language processing, object detection, and cyber security attack detection. In the domain of security, IoT-based cloud computing implementation it is needed to have a fog plane in the middle where we can provide the security measures using deep learning concepts as IoT is having its constrained nature. Many studies are going on in the field of security of fog computing for the usage of deep learning algorithms and motivated us to study the

S. K. Panda et al. (Eds.): CoCoLe 2022, CCIS 1729, pp. 27–38, 2022.
https://doi.org/10.1007/978-3-031-21750-0_3

effect of learning rate in the implementation. Deep learning learns to create a statistical model as a result of the non-linear transformation of its input. Emphases go on until the result has arrived at an adequate degree of exactness. It is capable of learning the traits at different abstraction levels of the data formed by the blend of low-level traits without relying totally upon human-made traits. To create a robust deep learning model various methods can be considered such as learning rate decay, activation function, optimizer, batch size, weight initialization, transfer learning, and dropout [1–5]. Although deep learning has flexible nature, deep care is needed in which learning rate is considered a choice to make more effective. Learning rate (LR), a hyperparameter makes the model either converge or diverge concerning loss/cost function based on adjusting the weights of the network using the optimizer [6–10]. There are different optimizers like Gradient Descent [17], Stochastic Gradient Descent (SGD) [10, 11, 17], Mini Batch Stochastic Gradient Descent, SGD+Momentum [12, 17], AdaGrad [14, 17], Ada Delta [15, 17], RMS Prop [17], Adam [16, 17], and AdaBelief [18] used to optimize a cost function. In gradient descent-like algorithms, the baseline for updating weights of a DNN is constructed as

$$Wt_{t+1} = Wt_t - \eta \nabla C \tag{1}$$

From Eq. (1) C is the cost function, ∇C is the gradients, t + 1 is the new iteration, and the learning rate is η, which controls the degree of the update to the parameter Wt at cycle t + 1. The cost function may either converge or diverge or sometimes may stall out and can be optimized based on the choice of the best learning rate. In getting off a better learning rate policy on training models, deep learning needs adjusting of learning rates at various stages using annealing methods. As for cost function as the baseline, annealing methods [19] use three reduction rules the Linear reduction (LR) rule, the Geometric reduction (GR) rule, and the slow-decrease (SD) rule.

$$LR\ Rule : Wt = Wt - \emptyset(Wt) \tag{2}$$

$$GR\ Rule : Wt = Wt \times \emptyset(Wt) \tag{3}$$

$$SD\ Rule : Wt = \frac{Wt}{1 + a.Wt} \tag{4}$$

where Wt is the weight, $\emptyset(Wt)$ is the weight reduction function, and the arbitrary constant is denoted as a. These annealing methods are used for weight updating in the backpropagation of neural networks and achieved by optimizers. In a deep learning environment, we use various optimizers for noise removal by smoothening effect and use momentum to converge at global minima without getting stuck at local minima. In this paper, we focus on the deep learning model Long Short Term Memory (LSTM) evaluated against different learning rates and batch sizes using the Adam optimizer. It is an adaptive method for learning rate adjustment strategy and also includes better momentum than other optimizers.

The contributions are:

1. We study Adam optimizer on different learning rates considering DDOS-SDN Dataset.

2. We study Adam optimizer with the best learning rate considering different batch sizes on DDOS-SDN Dataset.
3. Experimental results proved to converge on a learning rate of 0.001 with the Adam optimizer effectively for small batch sizes.

The rest of the work follows Sect. 2 presents the related work, Sect. 3 discusses various existing optimizers, Sect. 4 presents the dataset's overview, Sect. 5 describes the results and discussion, and the conclusion is presented in Sect. 6.

2 Related Work

In this section research papers are discussed [1–5] related to different optimizers used in Deep Learning and come up with a confined conclusion regarding Adam optimizer usage with different learning rates against different batch sizes. Ling Liu et al. [1] worked on selecting the best learning rates for learning deep neural networks. Things are carried out by doing three individual functionalities (i) considering 13 available learning rate functions and related policies by checking different parameters, (ii) proffered metrics for assessing and differentiating LR policies using cost and validity (iii) developed an LR benchmarking mechanism. All the above three functionalities can select the best LR for obtaining high accuracy. Chang Young Yu et al. [2] proposed a meta-learning method for dynamic adjustment of learning rates for faster convergence. They implemented the method on three different datasets on four different frameworks and obtained better results than other optimizers and concluded that it performs worse on combined with adaptive optimizations methods. Zhao, Huizhen, et al. [3] proposed a novel energy index-based optimization method (EIOM) for dynamic adjustment of LR in backpropagation. This model is built on different Machine Learning (ML) algorithms such as Logistic Regression, Multilayer Perceptron, and Convolutional Neural Network (CNN). From the results, EIOM showed better performance, however, applying on CNN needs extra exertion. Hertel, Lars, et al. [4] discussed a hyperparameter optimization library for ML called Sherpa. It is used for problems with high computations with more iterative functions while doing hyperparameter investigation and optimization for the improvement of metrics in ML. Zhang, Hongwei, et al. [5] proposed the Adal optimizer that speeds up convergence by enhancing the gradient in the beginning phase, and later the gradient shrinks in balancing the optimization and smoothens the noise. Adal optimizer stood for both theoretical and experimental proof. Similar studies can be found in [6–20].

The research gap that is identified in the above study is that no one has discussed in clear regarding the selection of a particular learning rate for the Adam optimizer to achieve better performance metrics considering a security dataset. Researchers working on attack detection systems, security in the Fog layer, and related areas using deep learning concepts have ambiguity in choosing the specific LR. In this work, we worked on the Adam optimizer against different learning rates and batch sizes. For this, we considered the DDoS SDN dataset [21].

3 Optimizers

Different learning rates have different effects on training neural networks. The choice of learning rate will decide whether the network converges or diverge. In conventional optimizers learning rates are given with an initial value and gradually increase or decrease during training based on strategy. Later on, compared to conventional optimizers, the dynamic adjustment strategy for learning rates is being used in the training process which has a positive effect. A selection of appropriate learning rates will increase the performance metrics. Here we are going to discuss different types of optimizers and their impact on the cost function [1, 17].

3.1 Gradient Descent (GD)

Gradient Descent (GD): An optimization strategy that can be used in every algorithm when training models. It is easier to comprehend and execute deep learning models with better performance by reducing loss function through updating weights in backpropagation. The weight updating is done by using Eq. 1. The gradient can also be considered as a slope where weight changes can be computed concerning changes in the loss. The model can learn quickly as the slope steeps about the higher gradient. Yet, assuming the slope is zero, the model quits learning. This optimizer takes the whole dataset as input and does forward propagation and backward propagation for weight updating by minimizing the loss function. Due to consideration of the whole dataset, it requires more resources and is computationally expensive. To mitigate this problem a new optimizer called SGD came into existence.

3.2 Stochastic Gradient Descent (SGD)

In SGD, each record is taken at one time random rather than the whole dataset for each iteration, and hence this process is named stochastic. Although it requires fewer resources and is less computationally expensive than GD, leads to slow convergence concerning noise and therefore Mini Batch SGD came into existence. In Mini-Batch SGD, the records are taken batch-wise.

3.3 SGD+Momentum

An optimizer SGD+Momentum is used to smoothen the noise that is high in SGD and Mini-Batch SGD and also allows for faster convergence which is not obtained in GD using momentum. To remove the noise from the data we need some moving average in means of exponentially weighted average [17]. Exponential weighted average looks like the below Eq. 5

$$Ve_t = \beta \times Ve_{t-1} + (1 - \beta)Se_t \tag{5}$$

where Ve_t is the new sequence and Se_t is the original sequence, β is the smoothening constant where the value lies between [0, 1]. The SGD+Momentum equation can be written as

$$Ve_t = \beta \times Ve_{t-1} + (1 - \beta) \times \nabla C \tag{6}$$

The weight updation can be written as

$$Wt_{t+1} = Wt_t - \eta Ve_t \tag{7}$$

When the β value is 0.0 it means gradient descent without momentum and η is the learning rate.

3.4 Adagrad

In the above-said optimizers, the learning rates are fixed but the learning rates can be made adaptive using the Adagrad optimizer on the iteration for each parameter. It doesn't require any momentum for weight updating as compared to SGD+Momentum and is less complex [17]. The weight updating can be done as

$$Wt_{t+1} = Wt_t - \eta'.\nabla C \tag{8}$$

To compute the dynamic learning rate η' in the Adagrad we have

$$\eta' = \frac{\eta}{\sqrt{\alpha_t + \theta}} \tag{9}$$

where $\alpha_t = \sum_{i=1}^{t} (\nabla C)^2$, θ is a small positive integer called fuzz factor and its default value is 10^{-7}. By α_t value, it is evident that at some time step it will become very near to 0, thus the model will not converge and the default of η is 0.01.

3.5 RMSProp

Root Mean Square Prop, an improvement of Adagrad with adaptive learning rate. An exponentially weighted average of gradients is considered rather than a sum of squared gradients as in Adagrad. In Adagrad the denominator value reaches a maximum high after a good many iterations and thus the learning rate diminishes to the least value [17]. The weight updating in RMSProp is carried out as

$$Wt_{t+1} = Wt_t - \eta''.\nabla C \tag{10}$$

where η'' is given as
$\eta'' = \frac{\eta}{\sqrt{\alpha'_t + \theta}}$ and α'_t are given as

$$\alpha'_t = \beta.\alpha'_{t-1} + (1 - \beta).(\nabla C)^2 \tag{11}$$

The default value of η is 0.001, θ is 10^{-6} and β is 0.9.

3.6 Addelta

RMsProp and Adadelta are developed in the same year and both are enhancements of Adagrad only. Adagrad highly concentrates on the learning rate parameter but in Adadelta the learning rate parameter is totally replaced with exponentially weighted averages squared gradients denoted by the X [15, 17, 20]. The Weight updating equation is given as

$$Wt_{t+1} = Wt_t - \frac{\sqrt{X_t + \theta}}{\sqrt{\alpha'_t + \theta}}.\nabla C \quad (12)$$

where X_t can be calculated as

$$X_t = \beta.X_{t-1} + (1 - \beta)(\nabla C)^2 \quad (13)$$

The default value of β is 0.95 and the fuzz factor θ is 10^{-6}.

3.7 Adam

An adaptive moment estimation (Adam), the composition of momentum and RMSProp. It considers the exponentially weighted average of gradients denoted as ‘m’ and the square root of the exponentially weighted average of squared gradients (RMSProp) as α' which divides the learning rate η. It uses the accumulative history of gradients and converges faster compared to other optimizers [16, 17, 20]. The weight updating equation is given as

$$Wt_{t+1} = Wt_t - \frac{\eta}{\sqrt{\hat{\alpha}_t + \theta}}.\hat{m}_t \quad (14)$$

where $\hat{m}_t$ and $\hat{\alpha}_t$ are bias corrections given as

$$\hat{m}_t = \frac{m_t}{(1 - \beta_1^t)} \quad (15)$$

$$\hat{\alpha}_t = \frac{\alpha'_t}{(1 - \beta_2^t)} \quad (16)$$

m_t *and* α'_t is calculated by

$$m_t = \beta_1.m_{t-1} + (1 - \beta_1)(\nabla C) \quad (17)$$

$$\alpha'_t = \beta_2.\alpha'_{t-1} + (1 - \beta_2)(\nabla C)^2 \quad (18)$$

The default values of η, β_1, β_2, and θ are 0.001, 0.9, 0.999, and 10^{-8} respectively. There are several variants of Adam optimizer like Adamax (extension by the same authors of Adam), Nadam (Nesterov and Adam optimizer) AMSGrad. A novel optimizer called AdaBelief came into existence which shows better speed in convergence and generalization. In the present work, we focus on the popular widely used Adam optimizer against different learning rates and the best learning rate with different batch sizes.

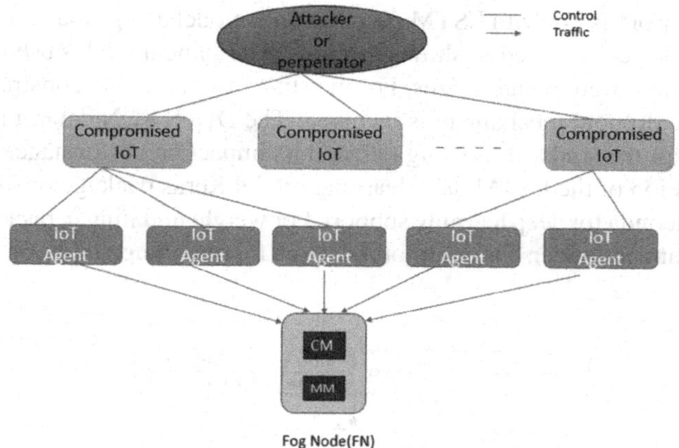

Fig. 1. DDoS attack model [23].

4 DDoS Attack Model

The way DDoS attacks occur in any fog environment can be depicted as shown in Fig. 1. Usually, they are carried out in the below stepwise manner [23, 24]:

1. An attacker who employs IoT devices to carry out attacks.
2. IoT agents are controlled by IoT devices that are compromised.
3. IoT agents, who are compromised by Master Compromised IoT devices, flood packets to Fog nodes.

5 Overview of Dataset

The considered DDoS SDN is browsed Mendeley Data [21] with 104345 rows and 23 features. Dataset used to recognize traffic type as harmless or vindictive in light of TCP Syn assault, UDP flood assault, and ICMP assault. Complete 23 features are accessible including Switch id, Packet count, byte count, and numerous so with all out of 1,04,345 rows of information. The traffic characterization is marked as 0 for harmless and 1 for the malignant client. The dataset is redone to 15 features of which 14 are highlights out of which one is a categorical feature named protocol and 01 is the target variable. The target variable is binary classified with 0 (benign user) and 1 (assailant).

6 Results and Discussion

The functioning of the Adam optimizer against different learning rates and the best learning rate with different batch sizes is gauged using the python anaconda Jupyter Notebook platform. The machine used for this gauging incorporates Windows 11 OS, core i7 processor, 3.30 GHz processor speed, and 16 GB RAM. The LSTM deep learning model is used in this work as mentioned for different learning rates using the Adam optimizer. The functioning is gauged for accuracy, F1-score, Precision, and Recall.

The present work is run with LSTM deep learning model using Adam as an optimizer where the model is constructed as shown in Fig. 2. The same model is used for different learning rates and different batch sizes. For the study, we have also constructed another model where no dropout mechanism is involved. The DDoS SDN dataset mentioned in Sect. 4 is used for the study of learning rate and its impact on performance metrics. For the implementation of the LSTM deep learning model Keras package on TensorFlow is installed in Anaconda for deep learning support. For weight updating in backpropagation, we used the Adam optimizer. The matplotlib is used for obtaining graphs on performance metrics.

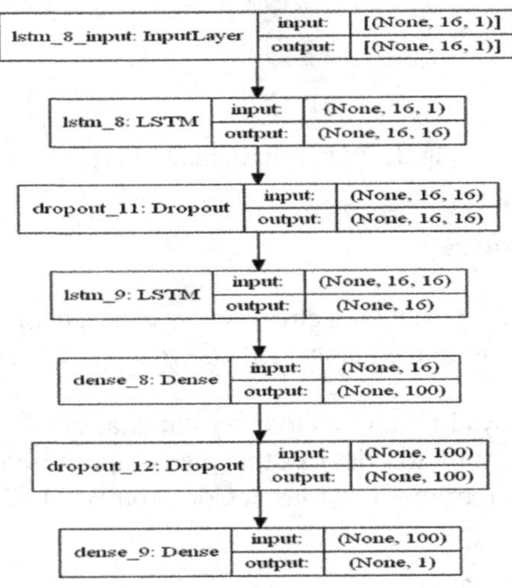

Fig. 2. Constructed model of LSTM for the study of Adam optimizer.

Table 1. Performance metrics of LSTM DL model against different learning rates

DL model-BS	LR used for Adam optimizer	Accuracy (%)	Precision (%)	Recall (%)	F1-score (%)
LSTM-10	0.01	96.17	96.22	94.03	95.11
	0.001	**99.79**	**99.54**	**99.95**	**99.74**
	0.0001	98.38	97.71	98.21	97.96
	0.001-no dropout	99.73	99.55	99.77	99.66
LSTM-32	0.01	98.57	97.33	99.11	98.21
	0.001	**99.52**	**99.3**	**99.5**	**99.4**
	0.0001	96.74	95.55	96.26	95.9
	0.001-no dropout	99.75	99.54	99.83	99.68

(*continued*)

Table 1. *(continued)*

DL model-BS	LR used for Adam optimizer	Accuracy (%)	Precision (%)	Recall (%)	F1-score (%)
LSTM-64	0.01	99.32	99.39	98.91	99.15
	0.001	**99.43**	**99.19**	**99.39**	**99.29**
	0.0001	95.22	92.12	96.18	94.11
	0.001-no dropout	99.54	99.64	99.19	99.41
LSTM-128	0.01	98.99	98.69	98.77	98.73
	0.001	**98.91**	**98.05**	**99.22**	**98.63**
	0.0001	95.03	92.64	95.01	93.81
	0.001-no dropout	99.21	98.71	99.31	99.01

Table 1 shows the performance metrics of the LSTM DL model against different learning rates and different batch sizes. The metrics tabled here are the average values given at the end of 100 epochs. For some learning rates and batch sizes, it is found that the convergence happened better and showed better metrics after certain epochs which are not reflected the same in the average after 100 epochs. In these cases, we understand the constructed model robustness by the ROC-AUC curve. By Table 1 it is evident that the Adam optimizer showed better results at a 0.001 learning rate with small batch sizes.

In any deep learning model implementation, the aim is to have less validation loss and maximum accuracy. In Fig. 3 the training loss and validation loss are depicted against epochs considering the different batch sizes with the same 0.001 LR as it is proven the best. Figure 3 says the training loss is best for batch size 10 and for validation loss it's nearly the same for batch sizes 10 and 32 but the time taken for convergence is more.

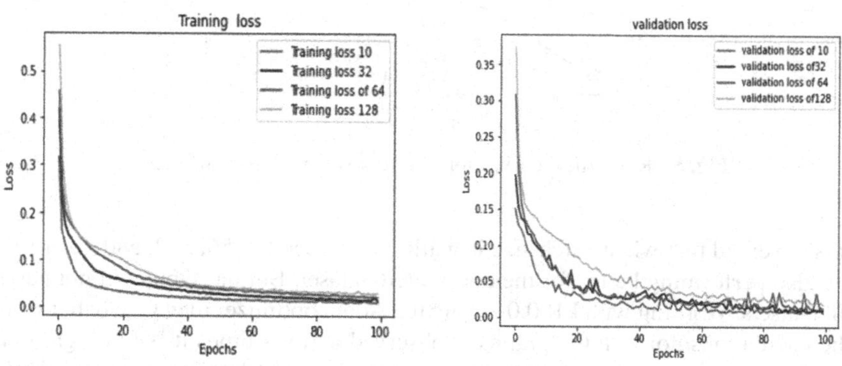

Fig. 3. Training loss and validation loss of LSTM DL model for different batch sizes.

We found how the training loss and validation loss vary by different learning rates with the same batch size-32 in Fig. 4. It is clear from Fig. 4 that validation loss for 0.0001

LR is very high and a learning rate of 0.001 is shown as a better training and validation loss. It is evident that training and validation loss is better for the model without dropout with LR 0.001.

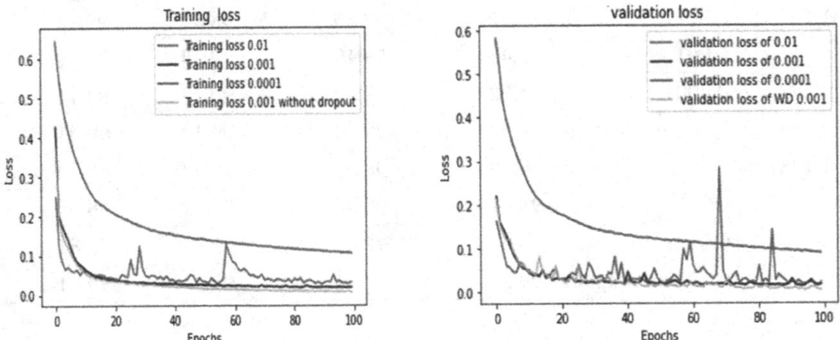

Fig. 4. Training loss and validation loss of LSTM DL model for different LRs.

When a dataset is imbalanced, accuracy is not treated as an appropriate measure and we investigated the model performance for f1-score and ROC curves and AUC scores. It is evident from Table 1 and Fig. 5 that both prevailed respectively for the learning rate of 0.001.

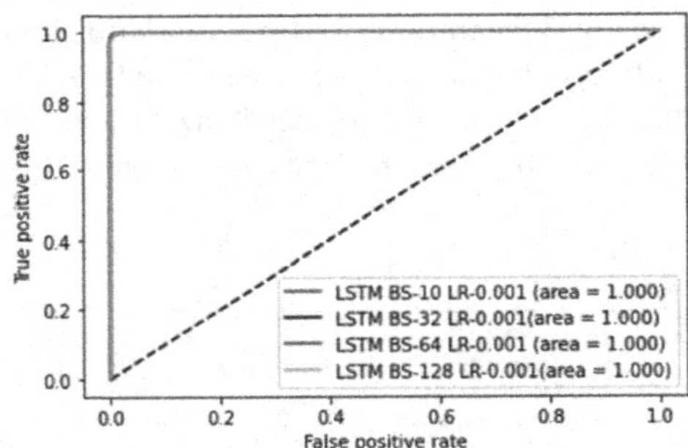

Fig. 5. ROC-AUC curves for different BSs with the same LR

It is observed that when batch size is getting increased to 256, 512, and 1024 LR of 0.01 is also performing better for the considered dataset. But the same will not happen for all datasets. Working with LR 0.01 using the Adam optimizer may give better results but the oscillations/noise in the graphs is observed and yet times it is too high. Large datasets having more number of attributes, more sparsity, and datasets having categorical attributes gone through one-hot encoding during the preprocessing need to be run with large batch sizes rather than small ones. Here model needs to be constructed accordingly i.e. based on the selected dataset model needs to be constructed well by taking the appropriate number of hidden layers in terms of neurons or cells. The Adam optimizer doesn't need much support from the dropout mechanism or L2 regularization scheme. It is evident from the present work in Table 1 and Fig. 4. Even the Adam optimizer needs those help in constructing the specific DL model and the data we dealt with.

7 Conclusion

In this work, we investigated the functioning of the LSTM DL model using the most widely accepted Adam optimizer against different LRs and BSs for obtaining the best performance metrics. The results show the LR 0.001 performed better than others (0.1, 0.01, and 0.0001) on BSs 10, 32, 64, and 128. For the same BSs, the LR 0.1 do not work. The increase in batch sizes allows us to work with LR 0.1 (512, 1024, etc.) with low performance. When BS is large for the considered DDOS SDN dataset 0.01 performed well compared to the LR 0.001. This issue is checked by considering a novel large dataset like IoTID20 [22] with more attributes, and more complex in nature and found that LR 0.001 is only the better as the LR 0.01 is providing more noise in convergence. The Adam optimizer is proven the best in our case still it is questioned for the performance related to generalization for the proved best LR.

Conflict of Interest. There is no conflict of interest.

References

1. Wu, Y., et al.: Demystifying learning rate policies for high accuracy training of deep neural networks. In: 2019 IEEE International Conference on Big Data (Big Data). IEEE (2019)
2. Yu, C., et al.: LLR: learning rates by LSTM for training neural networks. Neurocomputing **394**, 41–50 (2020)
3. Zhao, H., et al.: Research on a learning rate with energy index in deep learning. Neural Netw. **110**, 225–231 (2019)
4. Hertel, L., et al.: Sherpa: robust hyperparameter optimization for machine learning. SoftwareX **12**, 100591 (2020)
5. Zhang, H., et al.: AdaL: adaptive gradient transformation contributes to convergences and generalizations. arXiv preprint arXiv:2107.01525 (2021)
6. LeCun, Y., et al.: Gradient-based learning applied to document recognition. Proc. IEEE **86**(11), 2278–2324 (1998)
7. Krizhevsky, A., Ilya, S., Hinton, G.E.: Imagenet classification with deep convolutional neural networks. In: Advances in Neural Information Processing Systems, vol. 25 (2012)
8. Schaul, T., Zhang, S., LeCun, Y.: No more pesky learning rates. In: International Conference on Machine Learning. PMLR (2013)
9. Ruder, S.: An overview of gradient descent optimization algorithms. arXiv preprint arXiv: 1609.04747 (2016)
10. He, K., et al.: Deep residual learning for image recognition. In: Proceedings of the IEEE Conference on Computer Vision and Pattern Recognition (2016)
11. Bottou, L.: Stochastic gradient descent tricks. In: Montavon, G., Orr, G.B., Müller, K.-R. (eds.) Neural Networks: Tricks of the Trade. LNCS, vol. 7700, pp. 421–436. Springer, Heidelberg (2012). https://doi.org/10.1007/978-3-642-35289-8_25
12. Qian, N.: On the momentum term in gradient descent learning algorithms. Neural Netw. **12**(1), 145–151 (1999)

13. Sutskever, I., et al.: On the importance of initialization and momentum in deep learning. In: International Conference on Machine Learning. PMLR (2013)
14. Duchi, J., Hazan, E., Singer, Y.: Adaptive subgradient methods for online learning and stochastic optimization. J. Mach. Learn. Res. **12**(7), 2121–2159 (2011)
15. Zeiler, M.D.: Adadelta: an adaptive learning rate method. arXiv preprint arXiv:1212.5701 (2012)
16. Kingma, D.P., Ba, J.: Adam: a method for stochastic optimization. arXiv preprint arXiv:1412. 6980 (2014)
17. Soydaner, D.: A comparison of optimization algorithms for deep learning. Int. J. Pattern Recognit. Artif. Intell. **34**(13), 2052013 (2020)
18. Guide to latest AdaBelief optimizer for deep learning (analyticsindiamag.com). Accessed Jan 2022
19. https://towardsdatascience.com/optimization-techniques-simulated-annealing-d6a4785a1de70. Accessed Jan 2022
20. https://towardsdatascience.com/deep-learning-optimizers-436171c9e23f. Accessed Jan 2022
21. Ahuja, N., Singal, G., Mukhopadhyay, D.: DDOS attack SDN dataset. Mendeley Data **V1** (2020). https://doi.org/10.17632/jxpfjc64kr.1
22. Ullah, I., Mahmoud, Q.H.: A scheme for generating a dataset for anomalous activity detection in IoT networks. In: Goutte, C., Zhu, X. (eds.) Canadian AI 2020. LNCS (LNAI), vol. 12109, pp. 508–520. Springer, Cham (2020). https://doi.org/10.1007/978-3-030-47358-7_52
23. Douligeris, C., Mitrokotsa, A.: DDoS attacks and defense mechanisms: a classification. In: Proceedings of the 3rd IEEE International Symposium on Signal Processing and Information Technology (IEEE Cat. No. 03EX795). IEEE (2003)
24. Gudla, S.P.K., et al.: DI-ADS: a deep intelligent distributed denial of service attack detection scheme for fog-based IoT applications. Math. Probl. Eng. **2022**, 1–17 (2022)

Comparative Study of Workflow Modeling Services Based on Activity Complexity

Anisha Kumari[(✉)], Manoj Kumar Patra, and Bibhudatta Sahoo

Department of Computer Science and Engineering, National Institute of Technology, Rourkela, Odisha, India
anishamishracs@gmail.com

Abstract. Serverless computing has been widely used in several applications, where tasks are represented through an independent stateless functions. These stateless functions can be orchestrated in the form of workflow and can be deployed and executed in serverless frameworks. A number of serverless frameworks have emerged recently to provide orchestration services for serverless workflow. It is necessary to explore the potential of serverless frameworks which can be helpful for developers in taking business decisions. The performance of a serverless framework depends on several complexities associated with the serverless workflow. In this paper, we have focused on the effect of activity complexity associated with the workflow. The activity complexity of a workflow refers to the number of functions in the serverless application. A comparative analysis of various serverless workflow services based on change in performance parameters based on activity complexity is presented. The performance parameters such as overall function time, overhead time, and total response time are considered as the evaluation parameters. The extensive comparison has been done by considering both sequential and parallel workflow, which have been generated by various workflow services. Some of the findings are also presented for comparative analysis. This could be a potential resource for the application developers who have focused on serverless computing.

Keywords: Serverless computing · Workflow · Activity complexity · Function-as-a-service · AWS Lambda

1 Introduction

Serverless computing is a new paradigm in cloud computing that enables developers to build and deploy applications on cloud platforms without having to manage any of the underlying infrastructure, such as load-balancing, auto-scaling, and operational monitoring. Serverless computing was developed by Amazon Web Services (AWS) [1], which was acquired by Microsoft in 2014. The enormous benefits that serverless computing offers have made it an increasingly popular subject in both academic circles and the business world. It is anticipated that the market for serverless computing will increase to more than 8 billion dollars annually by the year 2021. Developers create a prototype of an event-driven application using serverless computing. The application is made up of a

S. K. Panda et al. (Eds.): CoCoLe 2022, CCIS 1729, pp. 39–51, 2022.
https://doi.org/10.1007/978-3-031-21750-0_4

group of interdependent functions, which are referred to as serverless functions. Each function is responsible for a single logical job. In current history, cloud vendors had also started rolling out serverless workflow services (for example, AWS Step Functions [2]), the goal of which is to reliably orchestrate serverless functions to facilitate easier coordination among these functions. Particularly, a serverless workflow provides developers with the ability to only specify the operational logic among functions, as opposed to requiring to execute this logic using complex function calls that are nested inside one another. Because of this, a considerable amount of time and effort may be saved.

Complex application scenarios, such as machine learning pipelines and data processing pipelines, may be completed in a more time and effort efficient manner with the assistance of serverless workflow. As interest in serverless computing grows and present serverless computing becomes more reliant on serverless workflow, it is critical to characterize existing serverless workflow services. On the one hand, it may assist developers in better appreciating the benefits and drawbacks of various cloud services so that they can make more informed decisions about which ones to use. The flip side of this is that cloud providers may use the information in this study to better target their services. Serverless workflow services have not yet been well studied as far as we can tell.

The complexity of serverless workflow is highly affect the performance of application which deployed and executed in serverless platform. In this paper, we have defined the complexity of a workflow in term of number of activity orchestrated in an application. We have investigated the rate of change of performance parameters over different activity complexity on four major serverless workflow services such as Microsoft Azure [3], AWS Step Functions [4], Openwhisk [5] , and Google Cloud Composer [6]. The performance of the four workflow services is compared with various parameters which includes function execution time, orchestration overhead time, workflow execution time, etc. under different activity complexity exist in the application. The effect of activity complexity is compared in both parallel and sequential workflow. This study could be a potential source for selecting the appropriate workflow service tool for investigating various activities in the serverless application.

The paper is structured as follows: in Sect. 2 we have presented the motivation toward the comparative analysis of workflow service frameworks. In Sect. 3, we have presented a short overview of the recent developments in serverless platforms for scientific workflows. In Sect. 4, we have discussed in detail about the serverless workflow modeling concepts. Section 5 describes features comparison of several serverless workflow services. Section 5 presents study about workflow execution in various serverless platforms. The experiment and result is presented in Sect. 6. The conclusion and the possible future work is presented in Sect. 7.

2 Motivation

The motivation towards the research work may be described as these folds:

- The motivation for this study is that a serverless environment has more to offer developers, architects, and service providers of software applications than

traditional server-based environments, even though the fact its acceptance is inadequate or at the very least, is not highly utilized due to certain aspects. Because of this, moving to a serverless framework requires a thoughtful shift, similar to what architects and developers may do when microservices are well-suited to a certain architectural style. Serverless computing adoption relies on several criteria, as well as several non-arbitrary concerns which needs to be explored in an effective way.
- The goal of current research work is to develop a uniform serverless workflow modeling concept and implementation prototype. For this purpose, the existing function orchestration technologies of a selection of cloud platforms are analyzed and commonly supported control flow capabilities as well limitations are researched.
- Detail comparative analysis is necessary as this could be a potential source for the researchers and developers in order to make prior decision for lunching their applications in serverless frameworks.

3 Related Work

The serverless paradigm has previously been employed in a wide range of contexts, such as the Internet of Things, data processing, edge computing, system security, scientific workflow, system security, and so on [13,14]. Serverless architectures are more cost-effective than monolithic or microservices, according to most au- thors. Extensive research by Wang et al. [7] employed more than 50,000 function instances to assess the architectural frameworks and resource management practices of Google Cloud Functions, AWS Lambda, and Azure Functions. McGrath et al. [15] conducted preliminary tests on Azure Functions, AWS Lambda, IBM OpenWhisk and , Google Cloud Functions, and discovered that AWS lambda's scalability, cold-start latency [8], and throughput are superior to those of alternative platforms. Serverless workflow services are something that prominent cloud providers have created in order to facilitate the coordination of operations inside serverless applications [12]. In 2018, Lopez and his colleagues analyzed a variety of serverless workflow services, paying particular attention to the designs and programming of these services [9]. On the other hand, the information that can be seen on the official website has been brought up to date. Python and JavaScript are two examples of supported languages by Azure Durable Functions at the current count. Serverless workflow services were used by Akkus et al. [10] to run an image processing pipeline. They found that workflows take substantially longer to execute in total than the time required to perform a single function in a single process. A portion of the time overhead will be utilized to orchestrate the scheduling of serverless processes, as their research has shown. An orchestration architecture called Triggerflow was recently described by Kijak et al. [11]. They discussed that Directed Acyclic Graphs and State machines are just two examples of the many process models that may be integrated into this flexible, trigger-based orchestration system. It is also becoming more common to use serverless workflow services. However, their results give a picture of orchestration techniques, performance baselines, and suggestions for developers to build de- pendable and gratifying applications and to assist cloud providers in enhancing service efficiency.

4 Serverless Workflow Modeling Concepts

4.1 Serverless Computing

One of the most talked-about technologies today is the serverless computing framework, which enables users to create and run their applications in a low-overhead, high-throughput [14] setting that is monitored by automation. Just because we call it "serverless" doesn't imply there are no servers involved. In the background, the server is still active. The user's experience is unaffected by the location of the application's server. The shift of administration and configuration obligations from the customer to the provider is a crucial factor in the service's rising popularity [16, 19]. Clients need just submit their application for execution on the cloud, with no attention to the environment in which it will run or the resources it will need. Auto-scaling, pay-as-you-go charging, rapid deployment, little user intervention, support for many runtimes, etc. are just a few of the advantages of serverless computing. Cloud service providers must also do ongoing checks, keep logs, and provide security measures. The program is not tied to a single server, thus it may be executed on the server that is geographically closest to the client, as a result, it significantly reduces response time compared to other technologies.

4.2 Function as a Service

FaaS, or Function as a Service, is a cloud computing service that allows developers or clients to run their piece of code in response to an event without the complicated infrastructure that is typically required when developing and deploying microservices applications [6, 18]. Each individual process in a serverless architecture is represented by a stateless function. The functions may each run in their own container, which provides a completely separate environment for their execution. Typically, the provider does not consider the environment while allocating and provisioning resources. As such, a serverless application may be seen as the coordination of stateless, decoupled services. By initiating certain web API events, the user may get the service. The execution environment and resource setup are taken care of transparently for the user. Like an object in an Object-Oriented Language or a function in the Functional Programming paradigm, a function on a serverless platform is the building block upon which applications are built.

4.3 Serverless Application as Workflow Model

According to the Workflow Modeling Coalition, "workflow" refers to "the automation of a business process, in whole or in part, during which task, documents, or information are conveyed from one participant to another for the response, according to a set of procedural rules" [19,20]. A business process can be defined as a set of one or more linked procedures or activities which collectively realize a business objective or strategic goal, normally within the context of an organizational structure defining functional roles and relationships [21]. In other words, a business process is a set of one or more linked procedures or activities which collectively realize a business objective or policy goal [22]. Workflows may be modeled using workflow modeling languages with a workflow modeling tool [23]. One example of a modeling tool is Bizagi Modeler [26], which can be used to create workflows in the BPMN workflow modeling language [25]. The execution of modeled workflows is managed with the help of a workflow management systems. The workflow management system builds an executable process definition from the initial workflow model. For the example of Bizagi Modeler, Bizagi Studio and Bizagi Automation fulfill this role.

The serverless application decouples its business logic into a series of serverless functions hosted on FaaS platforms. It uses required cloud resources such as message queue, bucket storage, and pub/sub messaging service to develop a stateless as well as an event-driven software system [24]. To complete the business logic of the application, interactions among disconnected services are essential. Many times, a coordinator is necessary to connect the various parts of an application, deal with events that occur across different functions, and to set off the appropriate processes based on business logic. Such a coordinator is usually provided by a message queue or a pub/sub messaging service or an event bus such as AWS Step Functions Express Workflow.

5 Feature Comparison of Serverless Workflow Services

A number of serverless workflow services have been emerged to provide functional orchestration services [17]. However, we have considered four most popular workflow services for comparison, which includes Amazon Step Function, Google cloud Composer, Microsoft Azure Function and Openwhisk. In comparison with that private cloud platforms, the application processes used by these services are far more standardized and more developed. We have compared the characteristics of various serverless workflow systems based on the following dimensions, which we determine by going through the official documentation. The overall comparison based on these features are presented in Table 1.

- *Time deadline for execution*: It is defined as maximum allowable time limit for execution, which can be configured in the frameworks.
- *Orchestration policy*: It is defined as the rule and standards specified for orchestration in serverless frameworks.
- *Transmission payload size:* It is defined as the maximum allowable size of payload that can be transmitted from one function to another in the workflow.
- *Degree of parallelism*: It is defined as the extent to which parallelism is supported by the frameworks.

Table 1. Comparative analysis of various serverless workflow model services

Serverless Workflow Services	Time deadline	Orchestration policy					Payload size	Degree of parallelism	Inheritance support	Runtime
		SDL	State machine	DAG	Function Orchestration	FDL				
AWS Step Function	Dual mode support 5 min(standard) 1 year (express)	✓	✓	×	×	×	256 KB	✓	✓	Java, C#, F#, python, Go, Ruby, C++
Google Cloud Composer	No limitation	×	×	✓	✓	×	×	✓	×	python, C#, Javascript
Microsoft Azure Function	No limitation	×	×	×	✓	✓	×	✓	✓	C#, Javascript, F#, Powershell, Python
Openwhisk	1 year	×	×	✓	✓	×	32 KB	✓	✓	C++, Javascript, pyhton, Go

Note: SDL-State Definition Language; DAG-Directed Acyclic Graph; FDL: Flow Definition Language

- *Support for inheritance*: It is defined as the extend to which a part or a full workflow can be reused in other application.
- *Runtime*: It is defined as the languages that can be supported by the frameworks.

Table 1 shows the results of the feature comparison of various serverless workflow model services.

The workflow service tools differs in the way functions are orchestrated in the workflow. In AWS State Function and Openwhisk, workflow is orchestrated by using State Machine and Flow definition language respectively. but Microsoft Azure Function employs a novel kind of function (named Orchestrator Functions) whereas Google Cloud Composer creates workflows by generating a Directed Acyclic Graph (DAG). Some of the tools are having constraints on data payload limits where as some others does not have any payload limit. It entirely depends on the user requirement can be explicitly specified by the developers. In Microsoft Azure Function and Google Cloud Composer, developers are allowed to specify their data payload limit where as in case of Amazon Step Function, the maximum transmission payload size is estimated to be 256KB and in Openwhisk it is 32 KB. In some of the literature work, it has been observed that the payload limit of Microsoft Azure Function is having larger data transmission payload capacity as compared to Amazon Step Function and Google Cloud Composer has less payload limit as compared to Openwhisk i.e., 32 KB. Each of the mention tools in Table 1. supports parallelism in developing serverless workflow.

Two different versions of subscription are available for Amazon Step Function and Openwhisk such as Standard and express. In standard the workflow can run for one year duration but for express mode, it can execute for five minute which usually suitable for event processing. Inheritance feature is supported in Amazon Step Function, Microsoft Azure Function and Openwhisk. But it is not supported by Google cloud composer tool.

6 Experiments and Results

The performance of the workflow heavily depends on the activity complexity of a serverless application. It also depends on the structure of the serverless workflow i.e, whether the request for invocation to the functions are in sequential or parallel. The effectiveness of four serverless workflow frameworks such as AWS Stepfunction, Google Cloud Composer, Microsoft Azure Function and Openwhisk in term of activity complexity is verified by generating two serverless workflow of both sequential and parallel types. The detail of the experimental setup and the dataset are presented in subsequent sections.

6.1 Experimental Setup and Dataset Preparation

The effect of workflow activity complexity on execution of application is verified in term of rate of response time, overhead time and function execution time. For the sake of simplicity, the cold-start delay in between the consecutive function call are not considered. The cold-start delay is considered only for the first function call in the workflow. It is to be noted that the overall function time for sequential and parallel workflow has been measured in different manner. In case of sequential workflow, the overall function time is the sum of execution time required for each functions where as In parallel workflow, it is the different between the completion time of last function to the starting time of the first function.

The activity complexity in sequential and parallel workflow has different effect on the performance of serverless execution. In our work, we have generated two different variety of workflow in four different workflow service frameworks. These workflows are then deployed and executed in their respective platforms. Each of the workflow has different combination of functions. As most of the serverless applications demand for more CPU intensive function and less number of IO intensive function, we have kept the ratio for IO, CPU and network intensive function as 2:3:4. However, this ratio is not always fixed, It can be configured differently for different types serverless applications. It can be noted that some of the CPU intensive and I/O intensive functions can be parallelized but network intensive function are executed in sequential manner only.

6.2 Evaluation Parameters

To compare the performance of serverless platforms in term of activity complexity, the following parameters are considered:

- *Overall function execution time*: It represents the total time required to execute all the functions in the serverless workflow. It is measured differently for sequential and parallel workflow. In sequential workflow, it is the sum of execution time for all the individual function where as for parallel workflow, It the time difference between the finishing time for the last function and the starting time of the first function that exist in the workflow.
- *Overhead time*: It is the time required for the orchestration process in the workflow. It includes function scheduling, simplifying the complex structure like merging parallel branches, handling loop, cycle etc., information flow between the function, container setup time etc. More is the overhead time,

less will be overall response time. The overhead time of a workflow usually more than the function execution time.

- *Total response time:* The total response time of a serverless workflow execution is the time difference between time when the first request from the client-side is initiated to the response received from the cloud provider side. It also includes the overall execution time along with the network latency between the server-side to client-side.

6.3 Results and Discussion

The activity complexity of a serverless application is represented through the number of functions available in the workflow. The effect of activity complexity on the performance of serverless workflow is analyzed in different platforms. The rate of change in function execution time, overhead time and the overall response time is recorded by increasing the activity complexity (No. of functions) from 5 to 100.

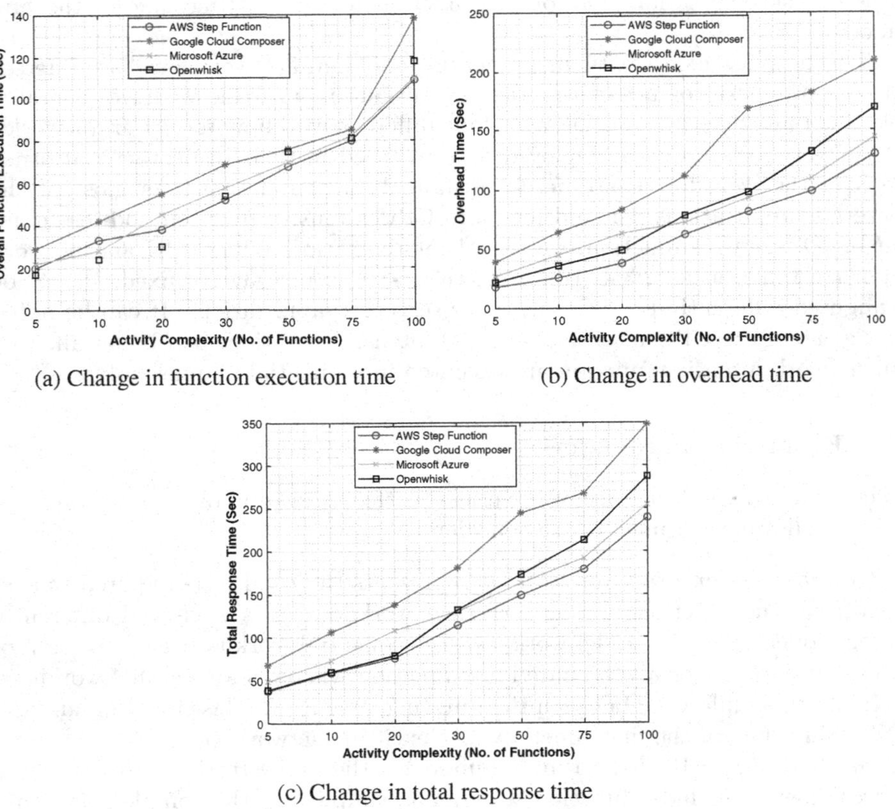

(a) Change in function execution time

(b) Change in overhead time

(c) Change in total response time

Fig. 1. Comparative analysis of serverless frameworks in term of effect of activity complexity of sequential workflow

Comparative Analysis in Sequential Workflow: The comparative analysis of various frameworks in term of change in execution time with respect to activity complexity for a sequential workflow is shown in Fig. 1. It can be observed that the overall time increases when the number of functions increases in the workflow. Figure 1a shows comparative analysis of various workflow services in term of change in overall function execution time with respect to activity complexity in the sequential workflow. It can be observed that in Google Cloud Composer, the function execution time increases more rapidly as compared to other frameworks, when the number of functions increases. The openwhisk framework has least overall function time when the activity complexity increases upto 30 number of function and beyond that the Google Cloud Composer outperforms other frameworks in term of overall function time. The overall function response time is found to be same for all the workflow services when the number of function is 75 in sequential workflow. The rate of change of function time is more in case of Openwhisk framework from the activity complexity changes from 20 to 50.

Figure 1b shows the change of overhead time with respect to the activity complexity in sequential workflow. It can also be observed that the overhead time increases with increase in activity complexity in all the frameworks. Google cloud composer is found to have highest overhead time as compared to all other workflow services for all activity complexity. AWS Step Function is found to have less overhead time as compared to all the workflow services. The overhead time in parallel workflow is less as compared to Microsoft azure when the activity complexity is upto 30. However, when the activity complexity exceed 30 Microsoft Azure has better overhead time as compared to Openwhisk. Comparative analysis of serverless workflow services in term of total response time is presented in Fig. 1c. It can be observed from Fig. 1c, that Google cloud composer has peak total response time as compared to all the workflow service providers. In Google cloud composer, the total response time increases linearly upto the activity complexity 30. However, when the activity complexity exceed 30, the rate of change of response time increases in non-linear fashion. It can also be observed that the total response time is same for both openwhisk and AWS Step function when the activity complexity increases from 5 to 20. When the activity complexity exceed 20, AWS Step function service outperforms Openwhisk framework in term of Total response time.

Comparative Analysis in Parallel Workflow: The comparative analysis of serverless workflow services for parallel workflow in term of overall function time, overhead time and total response time is shown in Figs. 2a, b and c respectively. It can be observed that the overall function time, overhead time and total response time is found to be less in parallel workflow as compared to sequential workflow in all the workflow services as some of the function can be executed concurrently. Google cloud composer framework has found to be more function response time, overhead time and total response time as compared to other workflow services which is clearly observed from Fig. 2a, b and c respectively. The overhead time and total response time in AWS Step Function is better as compared to Google

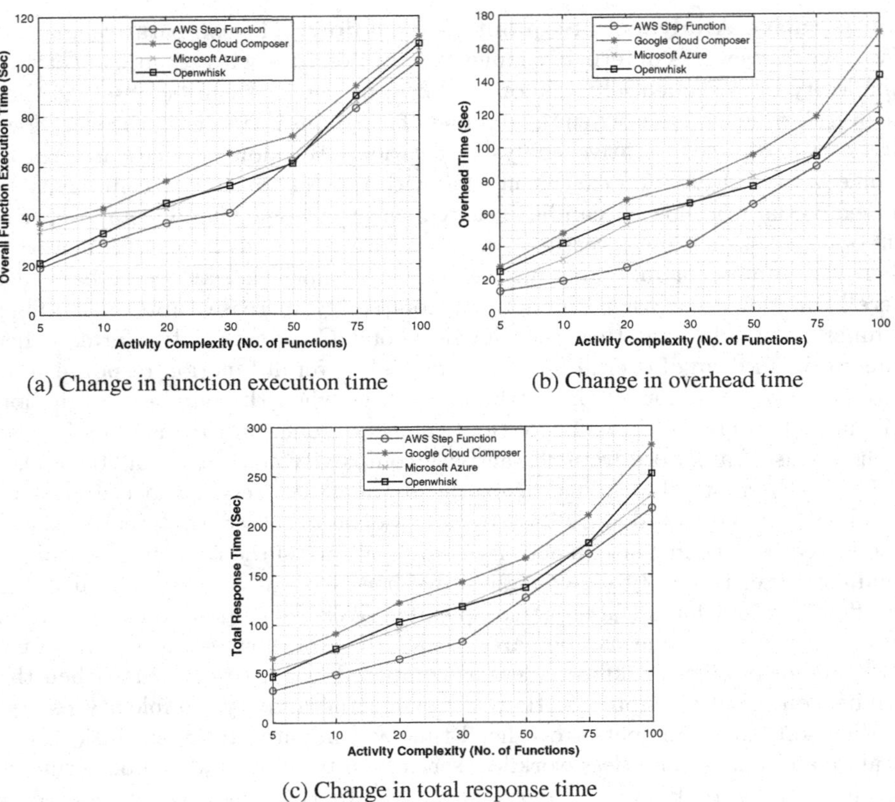

(a) Change in function execution time

(b) Change in overhead time

(c) Change in total response time

Fig. 2. Comparative analysis of serverless frameworks in term of effect of activity complexity of parallel workflow

cloud composer, Openwhisk and Microsoft Azure in all the activity complexity. It can also be observed that the rate of change in function execution time, overhead time and total response time is more when the activity complexity exceed beyond 50 in all the workflow services.

The box plot analysis of total response time for various serverless workflow services is presented in Fig. 3. The average response time is measure for various activity complexity and the same is presented in the form of boxplot.The comparative analysis of serverless framework in sequential workflow and parallel workflow is shown in Fig. 3a and b respectively. It can be observed that the mean response time in Amazon Step Function is better as compared to other workflow services in both sequential and parallel workflow. The average response time in GCC is highest as compared to all other framework. The highest response time has reached upto 350 and 290 s in case of GCC in sequential and parallel workflow respectively. It can also be observed that the response time in parallel workflow is less as compared to sequential workflow in all the serverless frameworks.

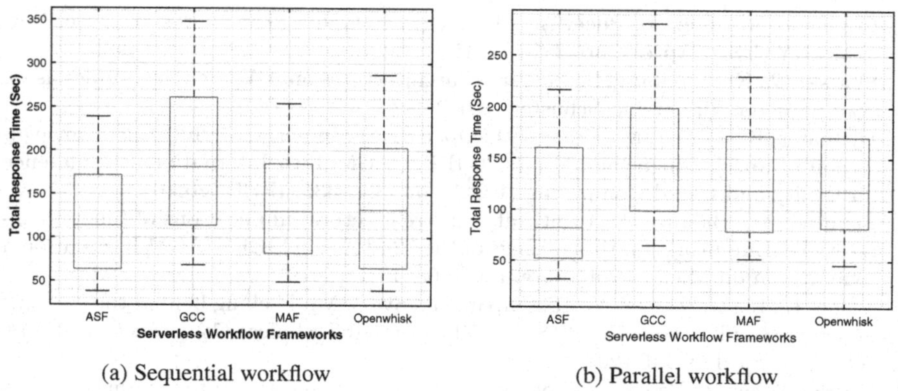

(a) Sequential workflow (b) Parallel workflow

Fig. 3. Boxplot analysis of serverless frameworks in term of overall response time Note: ASF-AWS Step Function; GCC-Google Cloud Composer; MAF-Microsoft Azure Function

7 Conclusion

In this paper, an empirical study on comparison of various serverless workflow services, such as Microsoft Azure, AWS Step Functions, Google Cloud Composer, and Openshisk in term of activity complexity is presented. The comparative analysis is performed based several features such as the data payload limit, the orchestration way, and the parallelism support available, language etc. In this paper, we have focused on activity complexity which represents the number of serverless function orchestrated in the serverless workflow. The serverless workflow services are compared based on the rate of change of performance due to activity complexity. The performance of the serverless framework is considered in term of overall function execution time, overhead time and total response time. It has been concluded from the experiments that AWS Step Function service has better performance as compared to Microsoft Azure, Google cloud composer, and Openwhisk. The rate of change of total response time is very high for Openwhisk framework as compared to other workflow services. It can be concluded that the performance of execution of serverless heavily depends on the activity complexity existing in the workflow.

In future, this work can be extended by considering the cold-start delay in measuring the performance. Other complexity like data-flow complexity, function-complexity can also be considered for comparative analysis of workflow services in future.

References

1. A. E. C. Cloud, Amazon web services. Accessed 9 Nov 2011
2. Buddha, J.P., Beesetty, R.: The Definitive Guide to AWS Application Integration. Apress, Berkeley, CA (2019). https://doi.org/10.1007/978-1-4842-5401-1

3. Copeland, M., Soh, J., Puca, A., Manning, M., Gollob, D.: Microsoft azure. New York, NY, USA: Apress, pp. 3–26 (2015)
4. Sbarski, P., Kroonenburg, S.: Serverless architectures on AWS: with examples using Aws Lambda. Simon and Schuster (2017)
5. Djemame, K., Parker, M., Datsev, D.: Open-source serverless architectures: an evaluation of apache openwhisk. In: 2020 IEEE/ACM 13th International Conference on Utility and Cloud Computing (UCC), pp. 329–335. IEEE (2020)
6. Shahrad, M., Balkind, J., Wentzlaff, D.: Architectural implications of function-as-a-service computing. In: Proceedings of the 52nd Annual IEEE/ACM International Symposium on Microarchitecture, pp. 1063–1075 (2019)
7. Wang, L., Li, M., Zhang, Y., Ristenpart, T., Swift, M.: Peeking behind the curtains of serverless platforms. In: 2018 USENIX Annual Technical Conference (USENIX ATC 18), pp. 133–146 (2018)
8. Lee, S., Yoon, D., Yeo, S., Sangyoon, O.: Mitigating cold start problem in serverless computing with function fusion. Sensors **21**(24), 8416 (2021)
9. García López, P., Arjona, A., Sampé, J., Slominski, A., Villard, L.: Triggerflow: trigger-based orchestration of serverless workflows. In: Proceedings of the 14th ACM International Conference on Distributed and Event-Based Systems, pp. 3–14 (2020)
10. Akkus, I.E., et al.: {SAND}: Towards {High-Performance} serverless computing. In: 2018 Usenix Annual Technical Conference (USENIX ATC 18), pp. 923–935 (2018)
11. Kijak, J., Martyna, P., Pawlik, M., Balis, B., Malawski, M.: Challenges for scheduling scientific workflows on cloud functions. In: 2018 IEEE 11th International Conference on Cloud Computing (CLOUD), pp. 460–467. IEEE (2018)
12. Baldini, I., et al.: Serverless computing: current trends and open problems. In: Chaudhary, S., Somani, G., Buyya, R. (eds.) Research Advances in Cloud Computing, pp. 1–20. Springer, Singapore (2017). https://doi.org/10.1007/978-981-10-5026-8_1
13. Kaewkasi, C.: Docker for serverless applications: containerize and orchestrate functions using OpenFaas, OpenWhisk, and Fn. Packt Publishing Ltd (2018)
14. Kumari, A., Behera, R.K., Sahoo, K.S., Nayyar, A., Kumar Luhach, A., Prakash Sahoo, S.: Supervised Link Prediction using Structured-Based Feature Extraction in Social Network, p. e5839. Practice and Experience, Concurrency and Computation (2020)
15. McGrath, G., Brenner, P.R.: Serverless computing: design, implementation, and performance. In: 2017 IEEE 37th International Conference on Distributed Computing Systems Workshops (ICDCSW), pp. 405–410. IEEE (2017)
16. Quevedo, S., Merchán, F., Rivadeneira, R., Dominguez, F. X.: Evaluating apache openwhisk-FaaS. In: 2019 IEEE Fourth Ecuador Technical Chapters Meeting (ETCM), pp. 1–5. IEEE (2019)
17. Kumari, A., Sahoo, B., Behera, R.K., Misra, S., Sharma, M.M.: Evaluation of integrated frameworks for optimizing QoS in serverless computing. In: Gervasi, O., et al. (eds.) ICCSA 2021. LNCS, vol. 12955, pp. 277–288. Springer, Cham (2021). https://doi.org/10.1007/978-3-030-87007-2_20
18. Copik, M., Calotoiu, A., Taranov, K., Hoefler, T.: FaasKeeper: a blueprint for serverless services. arXiv preprint arXiv:2203.14859 (2022)
19. Behera, R.K., Rath, SK., Jena, M.: Spanning tree based community detection using min-max modularity. Procedia Comput. Sci. **93**, 1070–1076 (2016)

20. Sreekanti, V., Subbaraj, H., Wu, C., Gonzalez, J.E., and Hellerstein, J.M.: Optimizing prediction serving on low-latency serverless dataflow. arXiv preprint arXiv:2007.05832 (2020)
21. Kumari, A., Patra, M.K., Sahoo, B., Behera, R.K.: Resource optimization in performance modeling for serverless application. Int. J. Inf. Technol. **14**, 2867–2875 (2022). https://doi.org/10.1007/s41870-022-01073-x
22. Wen, J., Liu, Y.: An empirical study on serverless workflow service. arXiv preprint arXiv:2101.03513 (2021)
23. Ivan, C., Vasile, R., Dadarlat, V.: Serverless computing: an investigation of deployment environments for web APIs. Computers **8**(2), 50 (2019)
24. Behera, R.K., Das, S., Jena, M., Rath, S.K., Sahoo, B.: A comparative study of distributed tools for analyzing streaming data. In: 2017 International Conference on Information Technology (ICIT), pp. 79–84. IEEE (2017)
25. Chinosi, M., Trombetta, A.: BPMN: an introduction to the standard. Comput. Stan. Interfaces **34**(1), 124–134 (2012)
26. Studer, R.: Modeling workflow patterns through a control-flow perspective using BPMN and the BPM modeler Bizagi (2009)

Granular Access Control of Smart Contract Using Hyperledger Framework

Ashis Kumar Samanta(✉) and Nabendu Chaki

Department of Computer Science and Engineering, University of Calcutta, Kolkata, India
aksdba@caluniv.ac.in, nabendu@ieee.org

Abstract. The blockchain is an emerging technology and is used in various applications for data security and trustworthiness. One fundamental technique of blockchain is that any changes incorporated by the authorized user in the system have been inserted into the transaction and would be traceable. The smart contract access control mechanisms have gained considerable attention since its applications. However, there are no systematic efforts to analyze existing empirical evidence. To this end, we aim to synthesize literature to understand the state-of-the-art of smart contract-driven access control mechanisms concerning underlying platforms, utilized blockchain properties, nature of the models, and associated test beds and tools. The attribute-based access control access rights are granted to users by evaluating suitable attributes. An essential aspect of access control is to preserve the user's identity accessing a service. This paper's objective is to propose an access control mechanism of smart contracts to ensure that only authorized users can access the authorized component of the object in the Hyperledger framework.

Keywords: Smart contract · Blockchain · Access control · Hyperledger · Network security · Distributed network · Granular access · Ethereum

1 Introduction

Blockchain technology is one of the demanding technologies in the security domain of sharing data. The immutable property of the blockchain helps to make the transnational data transparent and trustworthy. The blockchain is a continuously growing database chain of permanent records, "blocks," linked and secured using a cryptography-based hash function (Fig. 1).

A smart contract is one of the techniques of communication of blockchain applications, where different security issues have been considered. Subsequently, the probable solutions to those security concerns are proposed by various researchers. Therefore, the smart contract property of the blockchain provides an extra mileage to this technology. The smart contract is a self-driven and self-executing contract written in digital code between two or more people without

S. K. Panda et al. (Eds.): CoCoLe 2022, CCIS 1729, pp. 52–64, 2022.
https://doi.org/10.1007/978-3-031-21750-0_5

involving any third person [2]. The transactions of smart contracts can be executed, and the data can be stored on a pear- to- pear distributed network. This digital data is updated in real-time and intended to be maintained on geographically uncoordinated nodes that may not know each other. The smart contract is deployed to all authorized nodes on a network through decentralization, which effectively prevents modifications from maintaining transparency [2].

The blockchain is designed as a public, private, consortium network depending on a specific application area. Permission is required to access the database, and also for making any transaction in case of private blockchain. In case of a public blockchain, the networks allow any one to participate in the network. The database is open to access, and no permission is required to join the network. In case of consortium blockchain, must have some common objective with some mutual agreements. The consensus algorithm like proof of work (PoW), proof of stake (PoS), delegated proof of stake (DPoS), proof of capacity (PoC), proof of authority (PoA), proof of elapsed time (PoET), and proof of importance (PoI) are used to maintain the security and privacy of blockchain. Hyperledger Fabric, Bitcoin, Ethereum, EOSIO, Codra are the important popular frameworks used to develop the blockchain network [1].

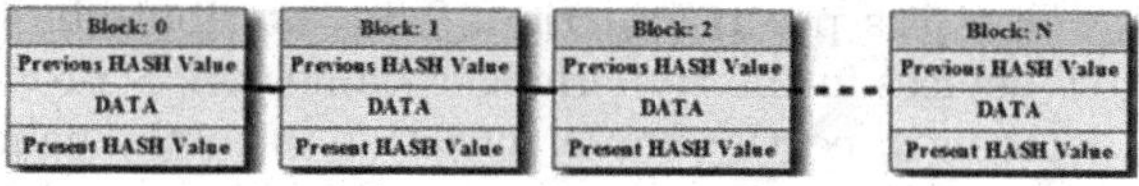

Fig. 1. Blocks in blockchain technology

The smart contract is required a granular level of access control of different access policies. The Hyperledger Fabric, the blockchain development framework and platform is implemented by "The Linux Foundation" [3]. The Hyperledger allows to development of the private blockchain and the object level access control policy of transnational assets that can be assigned to the object of participants.

The access control rules are needed to be defined for a particular smart contract in the Hyperledger framework (Fig. 2). The objective of this article is to proposed a granular level access control of the object of the asset defined in the Hyper Ledger rather than the access control of the object of the asset itself as a whole.

2 Literature Review

The searching of initial keywords evident that there are an appreciably substantial amount of research works related to the access control mechanism of a smart contract. Some of the papers are discussed below;

The access control issues of the Internet of Things (IoT) on the Ethereum environment are addressed in the proposed work of the authors of the paper

```
rule Default {
    description: "Allow all participants access to all resources"
    participant: "org.example.Participant_1"
    operation: READ, CREATE, UPDATE
    resource(v): "org.example.mynetwork.*"
    transaction(tx): "org.example.SampleTransaction"
    condition: (v.owner.getIdentifier() == m.getIdentifier())
    action: ALLOW
}
```

Fig. 2. Definition of access rule in Hyperledger

[2]. In the proposed smart contract consisting of multiple access control contracts(ACCs) providing static access right of subject object pair and dynamic access right of validation of subjects,one judge contract (JC) dynamically identify and analysis them is behavior of the device and one register contract (RC) to combine the function of previous two, to achieve the access control of IoT in distributed systems. The work proposed by the authors [1] an auditing system on blockchain "distributed Attribute-Based Access Control (ABAC)". The system provides a transparency mechanism to both, the access requester and owners of the resources based on Hyperledger Fabric. The authors demand the higher efficiency and low computational overheads of the proposed system. The authors also stated the evaluation results 270 transactions per second, with an average latency of 0.54 s per transaction. The "attribute-based access control(ABAC)" of IoT devices in the Hyperledger framework is proposed in a work [4]. The authors demonstrated the implementation with the help of Raspberry Pi 4B. Data security and data privacy are maintained through the application of blockchain implementation using Hyperledger in foreign trade management. The secure authentication of the blockchain transactions makes the data more secure without any third-party involvement which also reduces the external threats [3]. In the paper, the authors proposed a blockchain-based access control model to provide the benefit of the data owner. The access privileges of the data are intensively defined by the data owner so that along with the access control auditable support can also be provided for smart contracts [5]. A smart contract implementation of the examination system of a large university in India is done using the Hyperledger framework. The data access data and the information would be secured by maintaining the privacy of the data and the data is acceptable to society and all with transparency and trustworthy with reducing cost [11]. An enhanced "Bell-Lapadula" access controlled policy (Read, remark, update, and delete) model is proposed by the author in paper [6] for the healthcare network system in Hyperledger fabric environment. Each pear in this blockchain has a clearance level to access the transaction without keeping the history but only the important part of the transaction is maintained. In another work, the authors in paper [7] analyze the attack of different components of blockchain in the Hyperleger framework. The components are components, namely, consensus, chaincode, network, and privacy-preserving mechanisms.The authors also suggested the corresponding solutions to address the said risks. In paper [8,12], the authors proposed a solution model of access control of big data using the smart contract. The authors also included the access paradigm of "Identity- Based Access Con-

trol (IBAC)", and "Role-Based Access Control (RBAC)" of smart contracts in a platform of Hyperledger Composer. In both cases, the access parameters request access, grant access, revoke access, verify access and view asset is taken into consideration. The "role-based access control (RBAC)" of a smart contract is defined in the paper [9].The data of electronic health record(EHR) systems is preserved through the implementation of blockchain for the quality of healthcare services. The security and privacy threat on the data are also important as healthcare data is accessible by different users. The access control model is developed with the help of encryption technology to maintain the security and privacy of EHR [10].

The proposed research works on access control of smart contracts strengthening the security issues from various aspects. Most of the work proposed the model to address the issues of access control the data of IoT devices through its interfaces. However,the research works are also directed towards the scope of future research domains.

2.1 Findings

The intensive study of the above research works intends to focus on a broader context of security access of smart contracts in Hyperledger frameworks. The main extracts that have been extracted from the above study are below.

1. The function [2] of RC is the combination of ACC and JC. What are the extra advantages of incorporation of ACC and JC over RC.
2. The solutions proposed in [8], how the owner of the data would be benefited through smart contract is silent about.

2.2 Gap Analysis

It is important to emphasize that the above-discussed research work covers a wider domain relevant to smart contract security and privacy. However,there are still some areas of application that are yet to be addressed for access control issues of smart contract technology.

1. There is a scope of development of access control in the Hyperledger framework that needs to be incorporated to benefit both parties involved in the smart contract [8].
2. The previous work [11], highlighted the fact that the access control permission of any object of the asset can be assigned to any user as a hole. The fact is much interesting that there may be a security issue as some of the attributes are sensitive to give access to the other user. Therefore the designing of attribute level security of te asset in smart contract is under its scope.

2.3 Problem Definition

The advantage of using the Hyperledger framework is that it supports private blockchain. The code of assets and participants are written in the model file

(.cto). The security for the permission level is written in the access control file (.acl) file.The security rules need to define. The programming interface support assigning the access operations are READ, UPDATE, CREATE and DELETE permission on an individual object (specified by object code) of the user or participants. The action policy of the per- missions is either allow or deny. The complicacy of the system the permission of the object of the asset is assigned to the participants along with all attributes of the objects. The other problem arises when the policy of the same business is changed as the same customized permission can not be assigned to a different user in a single rule. The smart contract in Hyperledger cannot assign the attribute level permission to the users. Such limitations could lead to security breaches for private blockchain.

In this article, an effort is given to address the issues that the access permission of attribute level of asset may be assigned or withdrawn to the single or number of participants.

3 Methodology

The accessibility issue raises further complications at the time of assigning permission for a private blockchain (in .acl file). The access control rules of Hyperledger need to be defined as shown in Fig. 2. The definition of rules contains the descriptions of the rule, the participant code, The operation that needs to be performed. The operations are confined to the reading, create, update and delete operations. The resource code needs to mention the object code of the asset and the transaction code is also needs to be furnished.There is an option to incorporate the condition within the rule that needs to be defined and finally, the action is required to define either allow or deny.

The problem is that the read/update/delete permission assigned to a particular object of the asset is retained for the specific participant's code in the smart contract. This work aims to handle this double-folded problem and enhance the usage of the smart contract in the Hyperledger framework system. Eventually, we have proposed the counter measures to enhance the technical efficiency and accessibility of the smart contract in the Hyperledger framework and also to balance the flexibility issues.

3.1 Proposed Solutions

In Hyperledger Composer, a separate model file that only contains the prime conditions of a smart contract for both the participants. The file generally contains three object classes that are assets, participants, and transactions. In that case, if there is any malicious edition in the logic of the smart contract, the contract can execute only after the mutual consent of both the participant.

The Operations in the Hyperledger composer tool are controlled by the Access Control file (.acl). Different access control permissions are given to different users or participants. This may lead to certain vulnerabilities if the access

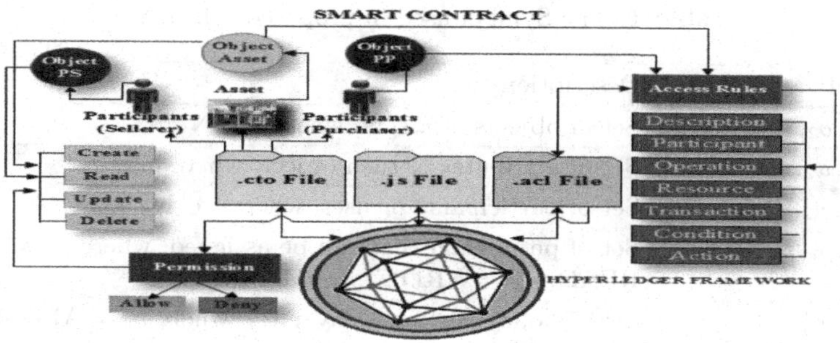

Fig. 3. Definition of access rule in Hyperledger

control is not properly administered. The basic symbols are used in proposed solutions are refereed in Table 1.

The proposed solution of Access Control Mechanism tries to address the anonymity of the access control policies of all attributes of the asset is restricted to the user other than admin. The defined access policy that is supported by the Hyperledger is Read, Write or Create, Update and Delete.

1. The assignment of access policy of a single attribute of the asset object can be assigned to a single user.
2. The assignment of access policy more than one attribute (but not all the attributes of the class) can be assigned to a single user.
3. The assignment of access policy single attribute can be assigned to multiple users.
4. The assignment of access policy more than one attribute can be assigned to multiple users.

Case-1: Permission of Single Attribute to Single Participant. The access control of a single attribute is assigned to a single participant shown in equation (1) and Fig. 4. The set of permission and set of actions have defined in Table 1 and shown in Fig. 3. The implementation of the proposed rule over the existing rule is defined in Fig. 5. The proposed changes are marked in blue color.

$$
\begin{gathered}
o_j.a_k = u_i.\sum_{m=1}^{m} p_m.s_n \\
o_j \subseteq O, u_i \subseteq U, a_k \subseteq A \\
p_m \subseteq P \text{ and } \sum_{m=1}^{m} p_m = p_1 \bigcup p_2, s_n \subset S, \text{i.e. either } s_n = s_1 \text{ or } s_n = s_2 \\
\text{where } j, k, i \in N \text{ and } m, n \in \{1, 2\}
\end{gathered} \tag{1}
$$

The k_{th} attribute of the j_{th} object of the asset is assigned the permission p_m along with the action s_n to the user u_i. The proposed system in comparison of the existing system is shown in Fig. 5. The corresponding algorithm (Algorithm-1) is also expressed with a function singleAttributeSingleParticipant().

Table 1. The Symbol used in proposed solution

Symbol	Descriptions
O $\{o_1, o_2, o_3 \ldots, o_n\}$	Set of objects of assets, where n ∈ N
A $\{a_1, a_2, a_3 \ldots, a_m\}$	Set of attributes of each object, where m ∈ N
U $\{u_1, u_2, u_3 \ldots, u_t\}$	Set of participants or user, where t ∈ N
P $\{p_1, p_2, p_3 \ldots, u_t\}$	Set of permission that can be assigned ,where p_1 = READ, p_2 = WRITE, p_3 = UPDATE
S $\{s_1, s_2\}$	Set of policy (Allow, Deny, etc.), where s_1 = ALLOW, s_2 = DENY
$=$	Assign the permission and policy
$\bigcup$	Used to concatenate the permission and policy
$\neq$	Withdraw the permission and policy

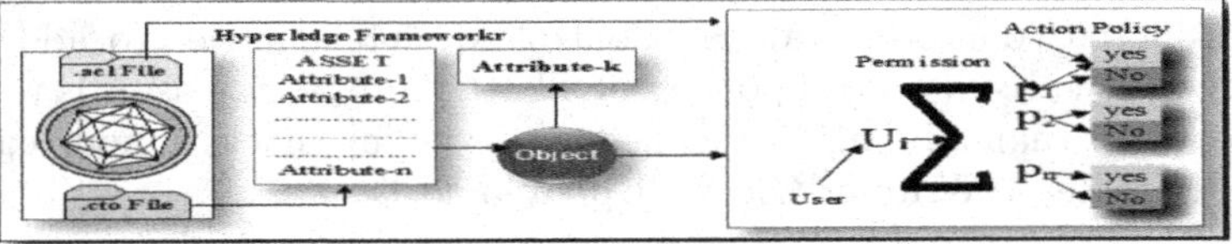

Fig. 4. Permission of single attribute to single participant

```
Existing System
rule SampleConditionalRule {
   description: "Description of the ACL rule"
   participant(m): "org.example.SampleParticipant"
   operation: READ, UPDATE
   resource(v): "org.example.SampleAsset"
   condition: (v.owner.getIdentifier() == m.getIdentifier())
   action: ALLOW
}
```

```
Proposed System
rule SampleConditionalRule {
   description: "Description of the ACL rule"
   participant(m): "org.example.Participant#p1"
   operation: READ, UPDATE
   resource(v): "org.example.#OBJ.A1"
   condition: (v.owner.getIdentifier() == m.getIdentifier())
   action: ALLOW
}
```

Fig. 5. The proposed rule definition of case-1 (Color figure online)

Case-2: Permission of Multiple Attribute to Single Participant. The access control of multiple attributes (but may not all the attributes) is assigned to a single participant shown in Eq. 2 and Fig. 6. The set of permission and set of actions have defined in Table 1 and shown in Fig. 3. The implementation of the proposed rule over the existing rule is defined in Fig. 7. The proposed changes are marked in blue color.

$$\begin{gathered} o_j . \sum_{k=1}^{k} a_k = u_i . \sum_{m=1}^{m} p_m . s_n \\ o_j \subseteq O, u_i \subseteq U \\ a_k \subseteq A \text{ and } \sum_{k=1}^{k} a_k = a_1 \bigcup a_2 \bigcup a_3 \cdots \bigcup a_k \\ p_m \subseteq P \text{ and } \sum_{m=1}^{m} p_m = p_1 \bigcup p_2, s_n \subset S, \text{i.e. either } s_n = s_1 \text{ or } s_n = s_2 \\ \text{where } j, k, i \in N \text{ and } m, n \in \{1, 2\} \end{gathered} \tag{2}$$

The number of attributes of the j_{th} object of the asset is assigned the permission p_m, along with the action s_n to the user u_i. The proposed system in comparison to the existing system is shown in Fig. 7. The corresponding algorithm

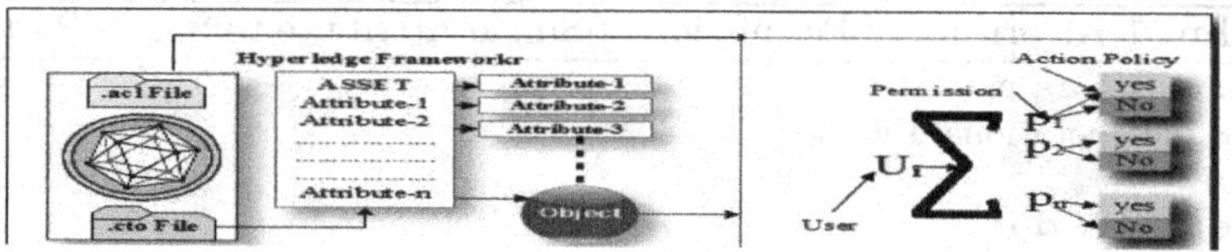

Fig. 6. Permission of multiple attributes to single participant

Existing System
```
rule SMRule {
   description: "Description of the ACL rule"
   participant(m): "org.example.SampleParticipant"
   operation: READ, UPDATE
   resource(v): "org.example.SampleAsset"
   condition: (v.owner.getIdentifier() == m.getIdentifier())
   action: ALLOW
}
```

Proposed System
```
rule SMRule {
   description: "Description of the ACL rule"
   participant(m): "org.example.Participant#p1"
   operation: READ, UPDATE
   resource(v): "org.example.#OBJ.A1 U #OBJ.A2 U ..."
   condition: (v.owner.getIdentifier() == m.getIdentifier())
   action: ALLOW
}
```

Fig. 7. The proposed rule definition of case-2 (Color figure online)

(Algorithm-2) is also expressed with a function MultipleAttributeSingleParticipant().

Case-3: Permission of Single Attribute to Multiple Participant. The access control of a single attribute is assigned to a single participant shown in Eq. 3 and Fig. 8. The set of permission and set of actions have defined in Table 1 and shown in Fig. 3. The implementation of the proposed rule over the existing rule is defined in Fig. 9. The proposed changes are marked in blue color.

$$\begin{gathered} o_j.a_k = \sum_{i=1}^{i} u_i.\sum_{m=1}^{m} p_m.s_n \\ o_j \subseteq O, a_k \subseteq A \\ u_i \subseteq U \text{and} \sum_{i=1}^{i} u_i = u_1 \bigcup u_2 \bigcup u_3 \cdots \bigcup u_i \\ p_m \subseteq P \text{ and } \sum_{m=1}^{m} p_m = p_1 \bigcup p_2, s_n \subset S, \text{ i.e. either } s_n = s_1 \text{ or } s_n = s_2 \\ \text{where } j,k,i \in N \text{ and } m,n \in \{1,2\} \end{gathered} \tag{3}$$

The k_{th} attribute of the j_{th} object of the asset is assigned the permission p_m along with the action s_n to the user u_i. The proposed system in comparison to the

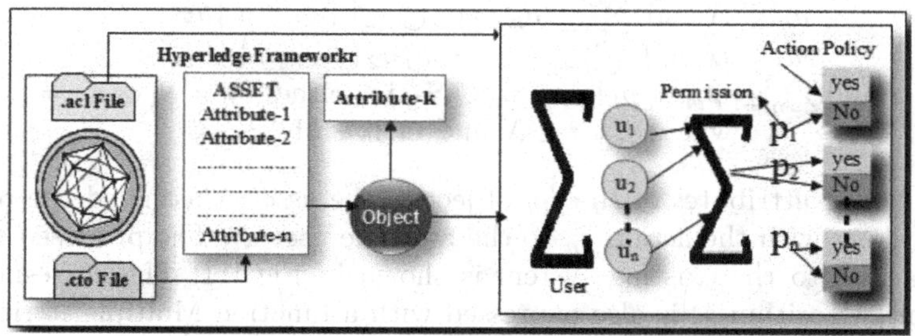

Fig. 8. Permission of single attribute to multiple participant

Algorithm 1 Algorithm of Permission of Single Attribute to Single Participant

Require: o_j, a_k, u_i, N ▷ inputs

create the operational set p_m
$m \leftarrow 1$
while $m < N$ **do**
  Provide the value for s_m
  if s_m = ALLOW **then**
    $u_i.o_j.a_k = p_{m_1} \bigcup p_{m_2} \bigcup \cdots$
  else
    $u_i.o_j.a_k \neq p_{m_1} \bigcup p_{m_2} \bigcup \cdots$
  end if
  m=m+1
end while

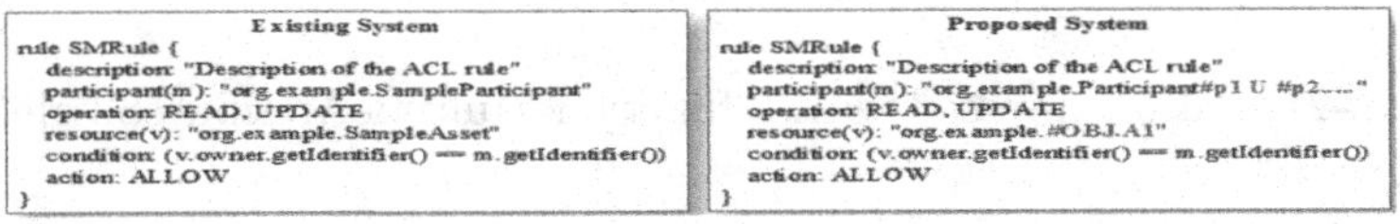

Existing System

```
rule SMRule {
   description: "Description of the ACL rule"
   participant(m): "org.example.SampleParticipant"
   operation: READ, UPDATE
   resource(v): "org.example.SampleAsset"
   condition: (v.owner.getIdentifier() == m.getIdentifier())
   action: ALLOW
}
```

Proposed System

```
rule SMRule {
   description: "Description of the ACL rule"
   participant(m): "org.example.Participant#p1 U #p2...."
   operation: READ, UPDATE
   resource(v): "org.example.#OBJ.A1"
   condition: (v.owner.getIdentifier() == m.getIdentifier())
   action: ALLOW
}
```

Fig. 9. The proposed rule definition of case-3 (Color figure online)

existing system is shown in the Fig. 9. The corresponding algorithm (Algorithm-3) is also expressed with a function SingleAttributeMultipleParticipant().

Case-4: Permission of Multiple Attribute to Multiple Participant. The access control of multiple attributes (but may not all the attributes) is assigned to multiple participants shown in Eq. 4 and Fig. 10. The set of permission and set of actions have defined in Table 1 and shown in Fig. 3. The implementation of the proposed rule over the existing rule is defined in Fig. 11. The proposed changes are marked in blue color.

$$
\begin{gathered}
o_j.\sum_{k=1}^{k} a_k = \sum_{i=1}^{i} u_i.\sum_{m=1}^{m} p_m.s_n \\
o_j \subseteq O \\
a_k \subseteq A \text{ and } \sum_{k=1}^{k} a_k = a_1 \bigcup a_2 \bigcup a_3 \cdots \bigcup a_k \\
u_i \subseteq U \text{ and } \sum_{i=1}^{i} u_i = u_1 \bigcup u_2 \bigcup u_3 \cdots \bigcup u_i \\
p_m \subseteq P \text{and} \sum_{m=1}^{m} p_m = p_1 \bigcup p_2, s_n \subset S \text{ , i.e. either } s_n = s_1 \text{ or } s_n = s_2 \\
\text{where } j, k, i \in N \text{ and } m, n \in \{1, 2\}
\end{gathered}
\tag{4}
$$

The number of attributes of the j_{th} object of the asset is assigned the permission p_m, along with the action s_n to the multiple user u_i. The proposed system in comparison to the existing system is shown in Fig. 11. The corresponding algorithm (Algorithm-4) is also expressed with a function MultipleAttributeMmultipleParticipant().

Algorithm 2 Algorithm of Permission of Multiple Attribute to Single Participant

Require: o_j, u_i, N, N_1 ▷ inputs

create the operational set p_m
$k \leftarrow 1, m \leftarrow 1$
while $k < N_1$ **do**
    Provide the asset object a_k
    while $m < N$ **do**
        provide the value of s_m
        if s_m = ALLOW **then**
            $u_i.o_j.(\ a_1 \bigcup a_2 \bigcup a_3 \ldots\ ) = p_{m_1} \bigcup p_{m_2} \bigcup \ldots$
        else
            $u_i.o_j.(\ a_1 \bigcup a_2 \bigcup a_3 \ldots) \neq p_{m_1} \bigcup p_{m_2} \bigcup \ldots$
        end if
        m=m+1
    end while
    k=k+1
end while

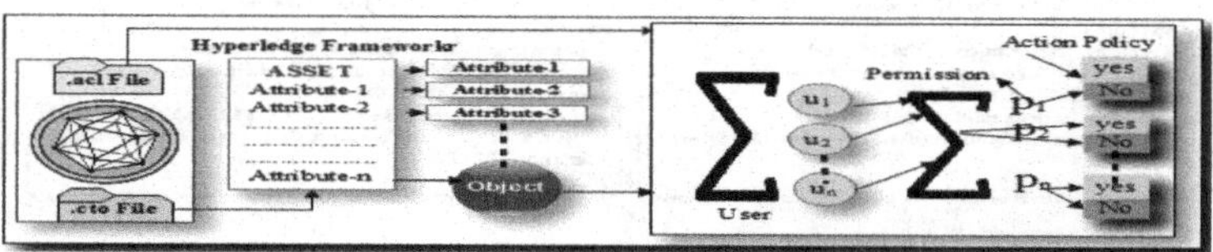

Fig. 10. Permission of multiple attribute to multiple participant

3.2 Discussion and Analysis

The security of data is one of the primary and basic needs from the users point of view. The object level access control is already available in hyperledger framework. The advantages of this proposed attribute level access control solution directly or indirectly benefit the participants of the smart contract and the smart contract itself and reduce the security threat of the smart contract. The granularity level, efficiency, complexity, business exposure and security of the proposed system is discussed in Table 2 below.

Algorithm 3 Permission of Single Attribute to multiple Participant

Require: o_j, a_k, u_i, s_t, N_2, N ▷ inputs

Create the operational set p_m
$i \leftarrow 1$, $m \leftarrow 1$,
while $i < N_2$ **do**
    Provide the user object u_i
    while $m < N$ **do**
        provide the value of s_m
        if s_i = ALLOW **then**
            $(u_1 \bigcup u_2 \bigcup u_3 \ldots) .o_j.a_k = p_{m_1} \bigcup p_{m_2} \bigcup \cdots$
        else
            $(u_1 \bigcup u_2 \bigcup u_3 \ldots) .o_j.a_k \neq p_{m_1} \bigcup p_{m_2} \bigcup \cdots$
        end if
        m=m+1
    end while
    i=i+1
end while

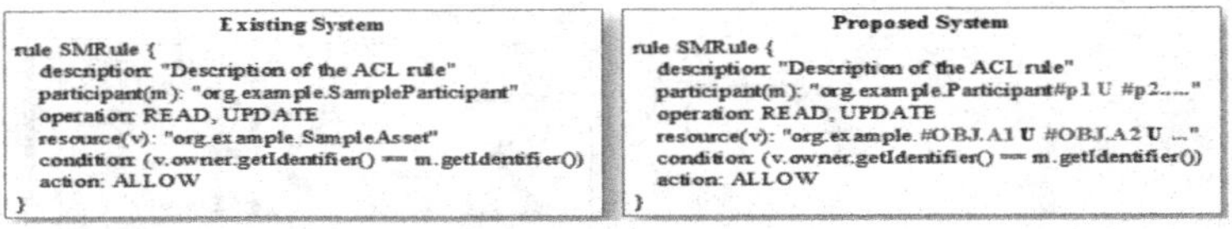

Existing System

```
rule SMRule {
   description: "Description of the ACL rule"
   participant(m): "org.example.SampleParticipant"
   operation: READ, UPDATE
   resource(v): "org.example.SampleAsset"
   condition: (v.owner.getIdentifier() == m.getIdentifier())
   action: ALLOW
}
```

Proposed System

```
rule SMRule {
   description: "Description of the ACL rule"
   participant(m): "org.example.Participant#p1 U #p2....."
   operation: READ, UPDATE
   resource(v): "org.example.#OBJ.A1 U #OBJ.A2 U ..."
   condition: (v.owner.getIdentifier() == m.getIdentifier())
   action: ALLOW
}
```

Fig. 11. The proposed rule definition of case-4

Table 2. Analysis of Proposed Method of Granularity Access in Hyperledger

Sl.No.	Descriptions	Existing System of Hyper ledger Composer	Impact of the Proposed System
1	Granularity level	The access permission exists at the object level	The access permission is fixed at the attributes level of the object
2	Efficiency	Efficiency is lower than that of the proposed system as the access permission is assigned at the object level	Efficiency will be increased as finer granularity increases the possibility of more users accessing the system simultaneously
3	Complexity	Complexity is lower as the access permission is assigned at the object level	Complexity will be increased due to finer granularity
4	Business Exposure	The lack of efficiency in terms of accessibility at the object level is discouraging for the user	Due to the enhancing security status, the adaptability of technology would attract the user
5	Security	The existing security level is under threat due to the object level access control and the access of the unwanted attributes need to be compromised	The attribute level access control would enhance the security and privacy by reducing the challenges of attribute level access control

Algorithm 4 Permission of Multiple Attribute to multiple Participant

```
Require: o_j, N_1, N_2, N                                          ▷ inputs
Require o_j, N_1, N_2, N                                           ▷ inputs
Create the operational set p_m
i ← 1, k ← 1, m ← 1
while i < N_2 do
    Provide the user object u_i
    while k < N_1 do
        Provide the asset object a_k
        while m < N do
            provide the value of s_m
            if s_i = ALLOW then
                ( u_1 ⋃ u_2 ⋃ u_3 ...) .o_j.( a_1 ⋃ a_2 ⋃ a_3 ...) = p_{m_1} ⋃ p_{m_2} ⋃ ...
            else
                ( u_1 ⋃ u_2 ⋃ u_3 ...) .o_j.( a_1 ⋃ a_2 ⋃ a_3 ...) ≠ p_{m_1} ⋃ p_{m_2} ⋃ ...
            end if
            m=m+1
        end while
        k=k+1
    end while
    i=i+1
end while
```

4 Conclusion

This paper proposed a granular access control system using smart contracts in the Hyperledger framework. The security access control of the smart contract is enhanced by assigning the permission attribute-based instead of permission of the hole object. The hole object access permission of the smart contract is within the scope of the Hypeerledger framework. In this proposed system the access control method of the single attribute to a single user, multiple attributes to a single user, single attribute to multiple users, and multiple attributes to multiple users are recommended. The proposed solution combines the accountability and anonymity requirements with blockchain technology for the access control of service delivery.

The extension of this work, security access control of the smart contract, is a plan using game theory in the future as it is within the scope.

References

1. Rouhani, S., Belchior, R., Cruz, R.S., Deters, R.: Distributed attribute-based access control system using permissioned blockchain. World Wide Web **24**(5), 1617–1644 (2021). https://doi.org/10.1007/s11280-021-00874-7
2. Zhang, Y., Kasahara, S., Shen, Y., Jiang, X., Wan, J.: Smart contract-based access control for the internet of things. IEEE Internet Things J. **6**(2), 1594–1605 (2019)

3. Toapanta, S.M.T., Gallegos, L.E., Villalta, M.G., Saltos, N.S.M.: A hyperledger technology approach to mitigate the risks of the database in foreign trade management. In: 2020 3rd International Conference on Information and Computer Technologies (ICICT), pp. 313–319 (2020)
4. Iftekhar, A., Cui, X., Tao, Q., Zheng, C.: Hyperledger fabric access control system for internet of things layer in blockchain-based applications. Entropy **23**(8), 1054–1054 (2021)
5. Laurent, M.: A Blockchain based Access Control Scheme. In: 15th International Conference on Security and Cryptography, pp. 168–176 (2018)
6. Kumar, R., Tripathi, R.: Scalable and secure access control policy for healthcare system using blockchain and enhanced Bell-LaPadula model. J. Ambient Intell. Hum. Comput. **12**, 2321–2338 (2021)
7. Brotsis, S., Kolokotronis, N., Limniotis, K., Bendiab, G., Shiaeles, S.: On the security and privacy of hyperledger fabric: challenges and open issues. In: 2020 IEEE World Congress on Services, pp. 197–204 (2020)
8. Uchibeke, U., Schneider, K.A., Kassani, S., Deters, R.: Blockchain access control ecosystem for big data security. In: 2018 IEEE International Conference on IoT (iThings) GreenCom and IEEE Cyber, Physical and Social Computing (CPSCom), pp. 1373–1378 (2018)
9. Ultra, S.J.D.: Pancho-Festin: a simple model of separation of duty for access control models. Comput. Secur. **68**, 69–80 (2017)
10. Rezaeibagha, F., Mu, Y.: Distributed clinical data sharing via dynamic access-control policy transformation. Int. J. Med. Inform. **89**, 25–31 (2016)
11. Samanta, A.K., Sarkar, B.B., Chaki, N.: A blockchain-based smart contract towards developing secured university examination system. J. Data Inf. Manage. **3**, 237–249 (2021)
12. Working, H.A., (WG), G.: Hyperledger Architecture 1 (2017)

Cyclomatic Complexity Analysis for Smart Contract Using Control Flow Graph

Shantanu Agarwal, Sangharatna Godboley(✉), and P. Radha Krishna

National Institute of Technology, Warangal, India
agarwa_mc19127@student.nitw.ac.in, {sanghu,prkrishna}@nitw.ac.in

Abstract. Smart Contracts, which are embedded in block-chains, allow for the automatic fulfillment of contractual obligations without the need for a reliable third party. Due to this, companies can save administration and service costs, and improve their processes which in turn improve efficiency and reduce risks. EthIR framework is one of the most precise instruments available, with a high success rate. Smart-Contracts need to ensure that they have a minimal number of flaws and vulnerabilities is critical. In this work, we present a Control Flow Graph to apply Cyclomatic Complexity for analyzing smart contracts. Our approach uses EtiIR framework, for creating a CFG from an Etherium Virtual Machine smart contract.

Keywords: Control flow graph · Blockchain · Cyclomatic complexity · Ethereum · Ethereum virtual machine · Smart contracts

1 Introduction

The Blockchain is a distributed database that records all peer-to-peer network transactions. Nodes in a Blockchain system cooperate in a distributed system to secure and maintain a set of shared transaction records [22].

Nakamoto[1] released the first cryptocurrency namely "Bitcoin" in 2008 that uses the Blockchain as a decentralized infrastructure platform. It enabled users to send cryptocurrencies with no need on relying on a centralized authority in a secure manner. Ethereum, NXT, and Hyperledger Fabric also support "bitcoins". Ethereum facilitates smart contracts as building blocks for Blockchain applications. Smart contracts are programs that allow users to translate traditional contracts into their digital form as shown in Fig. 1. Blockchain stores the information in blocks. Each block has a specific hash number as well as a link to

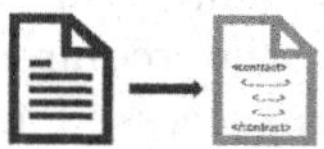

Fig. 1. Conversion to digital Contract

[1] https://bitcoin.org/bitcoin.pdf.

S. K. Panda et al. (Eds.): CoCoLe 2022, CCIS 1729, pp. 65–78, 2022.
https://doi.org/10.1007/978-3-031-21750-0_6

the preceding block. Blockchain is a distributed, immutable ledger that makes it easier to record transactions and track assets in a Blockchain network. The sharing and validation of digital contract in Blockchain are shown in Figs. 2 and 3. The consensus protocol used by the Blockchain network is used to record and validate new transactions produced by blocks. In terms of value, a Blockchain network can track transactions and reduces risk and expenses for all parties involved.

As a result, the Blockchain system is less susceptible to failures or attacks. The contracting parties must agree on the contract's terms, and the contractual terms are converted into a programming code. Essentially, the code is a collection of conditional statements that explain several outcomes for a future transaction. When the code is generated, it is saved in the Blockchain system and reproduced among the Blockchain members. Every machine on the network then executes and implements the code. If a contract term is met and confirmed by all Blockchain network participants, the appropriate transaction is carried out [11].

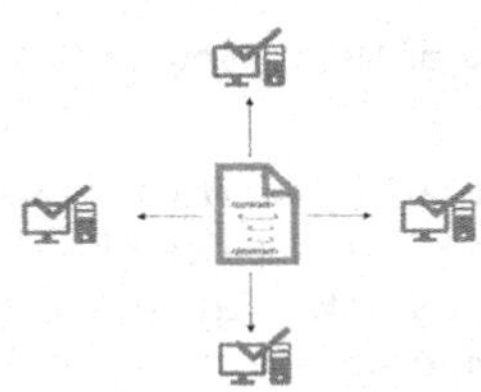

Fig. 2. Sharing of digital contract in Blockchain

The conditions of a smart contract, unlike those of a regular contract, are executed as code based on a Blockchain. Smart contracts as shown in Fig. 4 allow developers to construct Apps that take benefit of Blockchain's reliability, security, and accessibility Traditional Contract contains three main stages: (i) Contract preparation, (ii) Contract negotiation, and (iii) Contract fulfilment [25]. The First level lays out the requirements for an agreement's success. The contract negotiation level enables a common method of payment, deliverables, milestones, and other issues to be reached. Finally, the contract success level deals with the contract's actual implementation as well as specific responsibilities within the agreement. Smart contracts are computer programs that contain functionalities that cannot be corrupted and are implemented in a Blockchain and can store values. Ethereum is the most widely used platform for deploying smart contracts. Ethereum's smart contracts are executed using EVM where each node in the network has a sole object of EVM, allowing anyone to create and deploy smart contracts. programs typically use

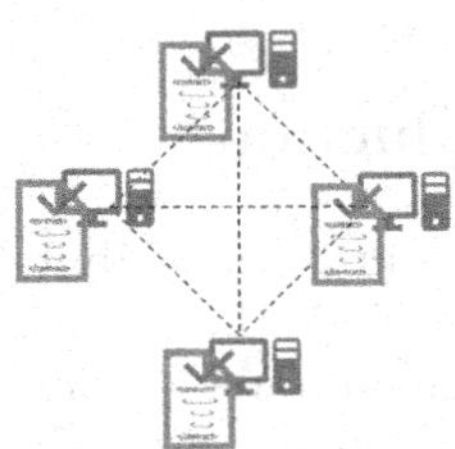

Fig. 3. Validation of digital contract in Blockchain

high-level programming languages like Solidity to create their code. The high-level code is converted into EVM bytecode for the EV to execute. EVM operates with 256-bit words is a large endian virtual computer and is built on stacks. It allows users to form contracts or send transactions to existing contracts with payloads that indicate the contract's interaction or extra information. Function calls, for example, are defined using the first four bytes of the SHA3 encoding of the function signature supplied with a transaction. A function Object() function will be called when a contract is created. This function will only be called once, and no other transactions will be able to call it. However, the initial bytecode will always be the smart contract's entry point, therefore there is no difference between creating a contract and running a transaction. There are four alternative ways to handle data, which makes it quite difficult. The first one has previously been mentioned: while performing a transaction, it may be associated with a data load, which may be retrieved using the CALLDATALOAD, CALLDATASIZE, and CALLDATACOPY instructions.

Compilers utilize data-flow analysis as one of the major technologies for generating programs and performing static analysis. It requires determining the various memory values that may exist at different points in the program. Control Flow Graph (CFG) can be obtained from a program and used to generate this data flow. On the other hand, Software Testing and Debugging is an important and expensive phase in Software Development (in our context software is considered as a contract) [6,12–19]. During the coding phase, the Cyclomatic Complexity (CC) can be computed and accordingly the developers can ensure the complexity of the software.

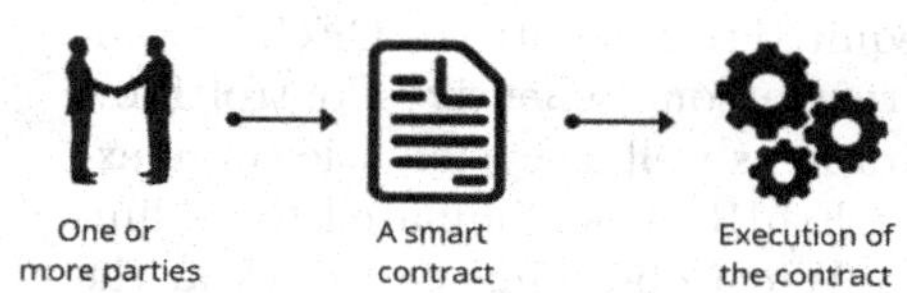

Fig. 4. Smart contracts in Blockchain in comparison to the traditional contracts

It is a directed graph that depicts the flow of a program as it runs; edges in a CFG correspond to different possible flows. Nodes, which are groupings of instructions that are always implemented in a sequential manner and do not contain any jump instructions, constitute the basic blocks of a program. The edges represent the possible leaps between the various fundamental blocks. As an output, nodes and edges may be easily distinguished in a variety of these languages. The programs follow initial instruction, the target of a non-conditional jump instruction or conditional jump instruction, or the block's first instruction is the instruction after the branch instruction. The Jump, an exception, or the program the last command can all be used as the block's final instruction. Edges are created by using a jump instruction to connect each node to a block that starts at the jump's target address. The pathways which are linearly independent in a code's cyclomatic complexity are a set of indicators of its complexity. cyclomatic complexity is used to measure a program's complexity. CFG can be used for calculating software's complexity. A directed edge joins two nodes in the graph which represent the smallest group of instructions in a program. e.g. a source code without a control flow diagram, cyclomatic complexity will be 1 and there will be only one path. In the same way, any source code with one "if-statement" will have two routes so CC will be 2. i.e. for true and false. The two basic blocks of the program are connected by the edge which is called a digraph of control flow as it may be unidirectional i.e. from first to second. Therefore, Cyclomatic Complexity would be defined as, **CC = E - N + 2** where, N = Total number of nodes in the CFG, E = Total number of edges in the CFG. EthIR is a tool that converts low-level EVM bytecode into a control flow graph (CFG) [10].

EthIR is a tool that builds a CFG and analyses smart contracts to identify possible errors [2]. However, because the information from the contract is generated over a set number of rounds, this analysis is neither sound nor full. In other circumstances, it also bypasses some of the information required to generate the CFG. To construct a comprehensive Control Flow Graph as well as cyclomatic complexity, EthIR* has eliminated these limits. When obtaining pathways in the Control Flow Graph, we can see how non-existing paths might be detected in the following example. A specific flow in a CFG can be seen in Fig. 5. We assume there is the first step between blocks 345 and 658, but we make the example more simple. Within the graph, we can detect four alternative paths: P1: 345 → 481 → 123 → 341, P2: 658 → 481 → 123 → 341, P3: 345 → 481 → 123 → 768, P4: 658 → 481 → 123 → 768. Figure 6 depicts the situation when all stack values are added at the beginning of nodes by us. Two of the paths found above are possible, while the other two are not really possible. We are dealing with this as nodes that are common to multiple paths are cloned but can result in unclear flows. Cloning is the process of duplicating common nodes, one for each conceivable path. We can avoid ambiguous pathways by ensuring that distinct paths cannot share nodes. These nodes have the same instructions, but they are completely independent of the graph's perspective. In the example above, nodes 481 and 123 are shared by two pathways. The graph presented in Fig. 7 is obtained by cloning them. There are only two paths to choose from, which match the ones that are possible.

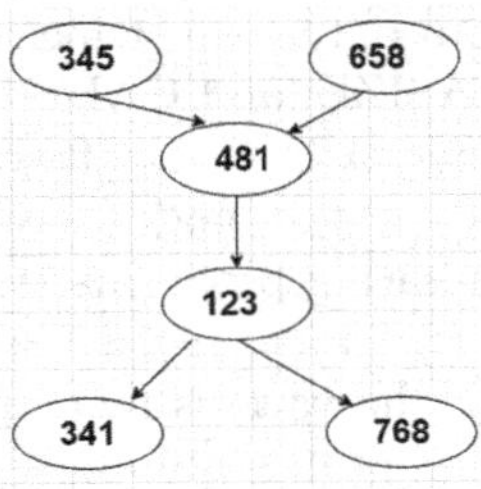

Fig. 5. Initial CFG

2 Related Work

The term "smart contract" refers to a legal contract that can be automated [2]. They have created a simple semantic architecture for legally enforceable smart contracts based on legal documentation, as well as a smart contract template. Parameters are collected from legalized papers and used to link legal agreements to standardized data modules. Other tools, like Gastap, rely on this representation to infer properties about the EVM code [3].

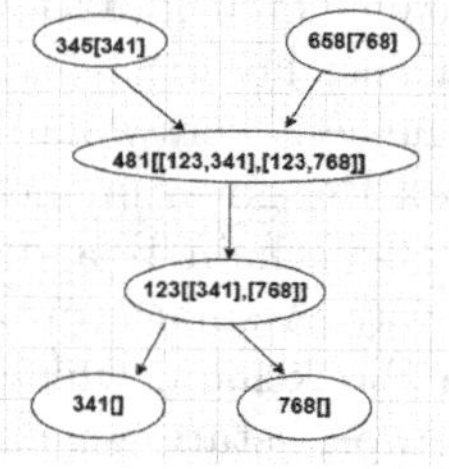

Fig. 6. Initial CFG with annotated stacks

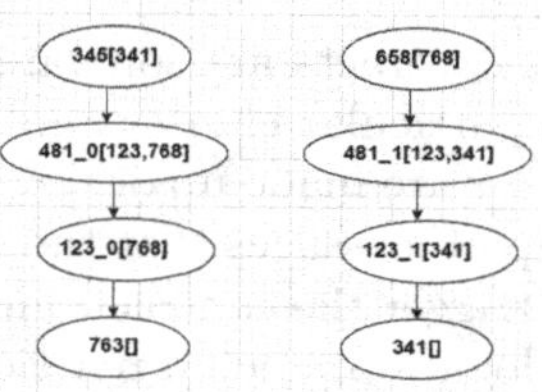

Fig. 7. Cloned CFG

The most well-known Blockchain platform for smart contracts is Ethereum. Smart contracts are deployed by sending the smart contract's bytecode to the Blockchain. It is not possible to change already deployed smart contracts with code alteration because the data in the Blockchain cannot be changed, even if these contracts have errors. Furthermore, there is currently no explained classification framework for Ethereum smart contract bugs, as well as no documented criteria for detecting errors in smart contracts, making it difficult for developers to fully comprehend the negative effects of bugs and design new approaches to detect bugs. To close the gap, we gathered as many smart contract defects SmartInspect, an innovative software developed by the authors, enables contract developers to better visualise and understand the contract's stored state without having to re-deploy or write ad-hoc code, as possible from various sources and divided them into nine categories in [24].

Debugging smart contracts is a time-consuming and difficult operation once they have been deployed. The code can not be re-executed. Analysis of a single attribute is impossible because the data is encrypted and encoded [23].

Bragagnolo, S. et al. [7], Smart contracts are used in prediction markets, financial services and the Internet of Things (IoT), to name a few. However, there are still several difficulties to be addressed in the future, like data exposure.

Clack, C. D. et al. [9]. The authors give a thorough review of Blockchain-based smart contracts. First, a comprehensive overview of smart contracts is provided, encompassing the fundamental structure, operational processes, platforms, and programming languages. Second, application scenarios are examined, as well as current problems. Finally, recent smart contract developments and potential development tendencies, such as parallel Blockchain, are examined. It is intended to serve as a guide and resource for future research initiatives.

Amani, S. et al. [5] shows that, even third-party beneficiaries are mentioned in some contracts. These contracts are intended to affect a non-contracting party. The majority of civil litigation focuses on resolving and battling over contractual obligations. For both individuals and organisations, a better approach to managing the contracts would be a boon. Not to mention the enormous amount of paperwork the government would save in the form of verification and attestations. A Blockchain is a distributed ledger that records transactions in an immutable way. A smart contract accesses two elements of the ledger programmatically a Blockchain, which axiomatically records the history of all transactions, and a world state, which maintains an archive of the current value of these states, as it is generally the present value of an object that is required [4]. Smart contracts are bits of software that were created to automate transactions by utilising the trusty computational features of a Blockchain network. They are terms that two parties can agree on while signing a contract in an untrustworthy environment.

Smart contracts are software that implements a logical sequence of steps in line with particular clauses and norms, and they are still used in the computing world. They are made up of three parts: the contract logic's computational code. The group of messages that the smart contract can receive and reflect the events that will trigger the contract; and the collection of functions that will trigger the contract logic's predicted reactions [8]. Physical agreements can be transformed into executable programs, which are referred to as smart contracts in the business [10]. To open up a slew of fresh options when a smart contract is performed, governance rules for any type of business object are automatically enforced.

3 Problem Approach

When compared to ordinary distributed applications, smart contracts have unique characteristics. On the one side, some smart contract systems, such as Ethereum, are built on open networks that anyone may join. Contracts, on the other hand, cannot be amended once they have been deployed owing to the unchangeable nature of Blockchain, therefore hackers can take advantage of this weakness. Furthermore, because smart contracts are commonly used for security, the transfer of digital assets and privacy is critical. Complexity [20] is a software statistic that provides a quantitative measure of a program's logical complexity. The number of unique routes in a program's basis set that provide an upper bound on the number of tests required to ensure that all statements are executed at least once is referred to as the Cyclomatic Complexity of the program. In Smart Contracts, Cyclomatic Complexity is critical. So, in this work, we will use a control flow graph to calculate the Cyclomatic complexity of a smart contract. Figure 8 shows the framework of Cycl-Sol to compute the cyclomatic complexity report for a smart contract.

EthIR* has been updated to include the suggested method. In Sect. 3.1, we will go over the basics of how to make a Control Flow Graph with the EthIR* tool, and then in Sect. 3.2, we will we explain how to compute Cyclomatic Complexity with the Control Flow Graph. Additionally, now we will discuss how

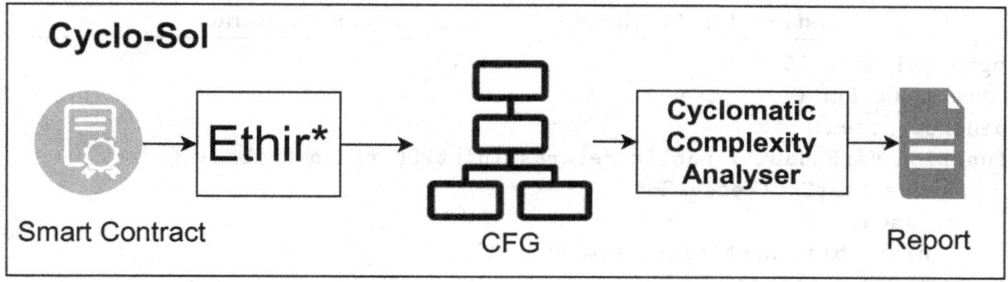

Fig. 8. Framework of Cyclo-Sol

the EthilR* works, we will analyse the findings received from the code in the conclusion section utilising the above architecture.

3.1 Creation of CFG

We will explain how the CFG is cloned and generated. We shall grow the abstract states following these equations rather than solving the equation system, as initially indicated in [1]. Initially, only the block at address 0 and the initially empty stack are taken into account. We get a final stack by symbolically executing all of the bytecodes in each block. Once we are at the end block, we will find the following cases-

- Case (1): If we have not come to the end of the bytecode yet. This indicates that the following bytecode will start a new block. As an output, before cloning the following block, we will get all blocks which are associated with this address (i.e. its duplicates and initial block) and differentiate their corresponding first stacks to the recent execution's last stack. Simply the CFG's information is updated by adding another edge from the current node to the previously created node if another block shares the initial stack. Otherwise, we create a new node in the CFG to represent the new forked block, as well as another edge from the previous block that points to it, and then again and again the process is repeated with an entirely new created block. The next block address can be found in a variety of methods, depending on the final bytecode. The final bytecode is JUMP, before executing JUMP, the next block location is at the stack's top. JUMPI is the last bytecode, here we must determine whether or not the routes should be explored that are related to an already used branch. As a result, we investigate each of the two possibilities in turn, we use the jump target address and the current program counter plus one as the next block address. JUMP and JUMPI aren't the last bytecodes. As a result of the lack of a branch instruction, the next address is equal to the program counter plus one.
- Case (2): We are at the last node. Due to the examination of the present path is complete, no additional changes are done.

Listing 1.1. Solidity Code of Lottery Smart Contract

```
pragma solidity ^0.4.18;
contract Random {
  uint256 _seed;
  function maxRandom() public returns (uint256 randomNumber) {
    _seed = uint256(keccak256(
        _seed,
        block.blockhash(block.number - 1),
        block.coinbase,
        block.difficulty
    ));
    return _seed;
  }
  // return a pseudo random number between lower and upper bounds
  // given the number of previous blocks it should hash.
  function random(uint256 upper) public returns (uint256 randomNumber) {
    return maxRandom() % upper;
  }
}
contract Lottery is Random {
   struct Stage {
      uint32 maxNum;
      bytes32 participantsHash;
      uint winnerNum;
   }
   mapping (uint32 => Stage) public stages;
   address public owner;
   event Winner(uint32 _stageNum, uint _winnerNum);
   modifier onlyOwner() { require(msg.sender == owner); _;}
   constructor() public {
        owner = msg.sender;
    }
   function randomJackpot(uint32 _stageNum, bytes32 _participantsHash,
        uint32 _maxNum) external onlyOwner {
      require(_maxNum > 0);
      uint winnerNum = random(_maxNum);
      stages[_stageNum] = Stage(_maxNum, _participantsHash, winnerNum);
      emit Winner(_stageNum, winnerNum);
   }
}
```

3.2 Cyclomatic Complexity with the Help of Control Flow Graph

The term “Cyclomatic Complexity” can be defined as follows [21]:

- It’s a software metric that assesses a program’s code’s logical complexity, and it’s always greater than or equal to one.
- It counts how many linearly independent pathways there are in the program code.

– It counts how many decisions there are in the given computer code.

The control flow model of the computer code is used to calculate cyclomatic complexity.

– Nodes are code segments that do not have any branches.
– During the execution of a program, the edges represent potential control flow transfers.

Using the Control Flow Graph, we calculate the Cyclomatic Complexity, CC = E − N + 2, where, N = Total number of nodes in the CFG, E = Total number of edges in the CFG.

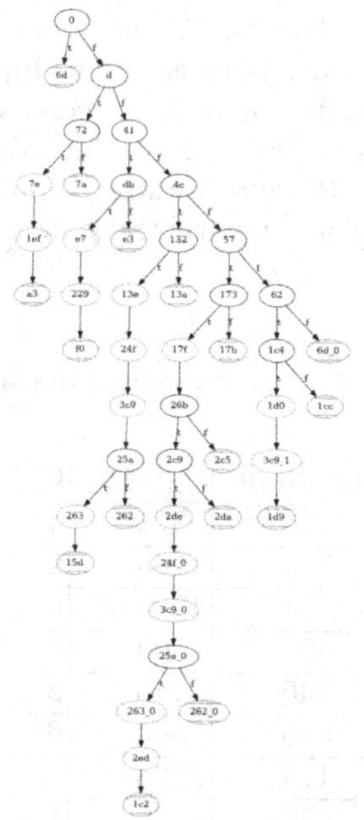

(a) CFG Of Lottery Contract

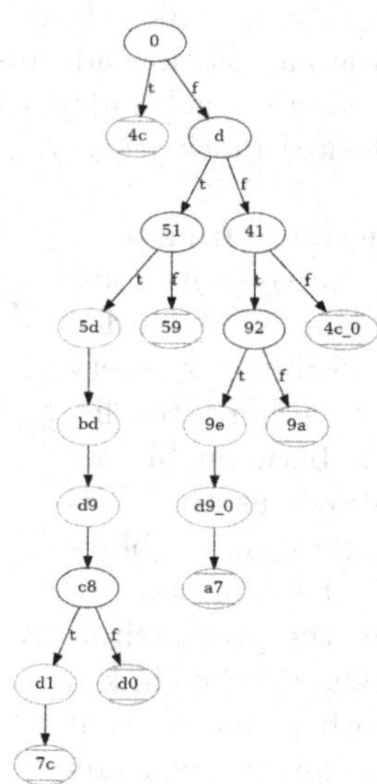

(b) CFG Of Random Contract

Fig. 9. Generated CFGs for Listing 1.1

4 Experimental Studies

The entire architecture is shown in Fig. 8 that depicts all of the process' intermediate representations. Ethir* has a CFG generated on top of it. It builds CFG and also focuses on [10] search security vulnerabilities and errors in smart contracts. As a result, we use EthIR's parser, which we enhanced to create EthIR*.

The EthIR* decompiler generates the whole Control Flow Graph for the contract under investigation. To accomplish this, every block is converted to a module that takes input storage, stack variables, Blockchain and memory data. Each block is converted to a module that takes stack variables as parameters, memory, Blockchain data and storage. We display the stack as independent stack variables that we passed to the functions since we are aware of the length of the stack at the beginning of the block. Each bytecode is converted into a high-level rule within each function, utilising the information obtained from the stack then, a call to the respective functions is included externally.

We generate the CFG implicitly with the help of EthIR* while conducting value propagation using the jump equations. We connect the bytecodes that refer to the same block in a structure before starting the execution so that we can directly run all of the instructions of a block. The first bytecode position is used to figure out these blocks. A sub-index is added to a block when it is copied to identify the copy. Because each duplicated block has its solitary identifier, we've provided a map that connects each original block's address to the index which is next available for copying to assign a sub-index when duplicating a block. If we're forking a previously forked block, we'll remove the old one and replace it with the new one.

Table 1. Cyclomatic Complexity of Smart Contracts using CFG

Smart Contract	# Nodes	# Edges	CC
advertisement.sol	375	377	4
auctusEther.sol	163	163	2
bitzCrypto.sol	1388	1392	6
blockSquareSereisA.sol	497	500	5
clockAuction.sol	245	246	3
coinchangex.sol	556	560	6
idice.sol	1124	1128	6
lotary.sol	47	46	1
pot.sol	262	263	3
validToken.sol	241	242	3

This differs from prior EthIR* implementations, which simply appended a new sub-index every time, it is hard to distinguish between blocks. This allows us to determine if a new block should be formed or whether the present iteration should be linked to another block that has previously been created during an investigation. If the block's associated stack has not been formed before, that is, if there isn't another previous block with a stack in the same equivalence class as the present stack which are using the same characteristics we picked for the evaluation, we will clone it.

Finally, we created a Control Flow Graph for Cyclomatic Complexity. With the help of this command,"**./ethir.py -s lottery.sol -cfg**", it builds a CFG in *dot* File[2]. After that we used *Graphviz tool*[3] with given command "**dot -Tpng**

[2] https://graphviz.org/doc/info/lang.html.
[3] https://graphviz.org/.

Contract-name.dot -o contract-name.png". We process the code shown in Listing 1.1. The generated CFGs for the functions *Lottery* and *Random* are shown in Figs. 9a and 9b. The final output report of our proposed approach for the Listing 1.1 is shown in Fig. 10. Graphviz is a graph visualisation software that is free and open source. Graph visualisation is a method of displaying structural data as abstract graph diagrams. Graphviz layout applications take simple written descriptions of graphs and convert them into useful diagrams in formats like pictures, and PDF for inclusion in other documents, or display in an interactive graph browser. Hyperlinks, tabular node layouts, fonts, colours, line styles, and custom shapes are just a few of the features available in Graphviz for concrete diagrams.

Here, nodes are coloured differently based on their type. Nodes which are yellow mentioning jump without condition with a JUMP instruction, while green nodes represent terminal nodes. Red nodes are those blocks which do not contain any jump instruction and are followed by the start of another block. The blue nodes are those nodes whose most recent bytecode is JUMPI. The edge which is evaluating its condition to True is represented by **t**, and the edge which evaluates its condition to False is represented by **f**. We looked at some smart contracts and discovered that Cyclomatic Complexity is good because it falls between 1 and 10, indicating that the smart contracts are well-coded and have less complexity.

```
shantanu@shantanu-HP-Notebook: ~/Downloads/EthIR-master/ethir
shantanu@shantanu-HP-Notebook:~/Downloads/EthIR-master/ethir$ ./ethir.py -s lotary.sol  -cfg
*************************************************************
Compilation time: 0.495028972626s
*************************************************************
File: Lottery
Build CFG: 0.186800003052s
OYENTE tool: 0.189233064651s
('Total Number of Nodes :', 47)
('Total Number of Edges :', 46)
('Cyclomatic Complexity :', 1)
Build RBR: 0.0115940570831s
*************************************************************
File: Random
Build CFG: 0.0646488666534s
OYENTE tool: 0.0656650066376s
('Total Number of Nodes :', 19)
('Total Number of Edges :', 18)
('Cyclomatic Complexity :', 1)
Build RBR: 0.00379204750061s
*************************************************************
The files generated by EthIR are stored in the following directory: /tmp/costabs/
```

Fig. 10. Output of our proposed approach

In out experimentation, we have executed a total number of 10 smart contracts. The results computed can observed in Table 1. Column 1 shows the name of the smart contracts executed. Column 2 shows the total number of Nodes. Column 3 shows the total number of edges. Column 4 shows the final results i.e. Cyclometic Complexity (CC). If the value of CC is lower than the contract is small and less complex. On the other hand, if the value of CC is higher than the contract is complex and big.

5 Conclusion and Future Work

Ethereum is the second most maximum valued cryptocurrency after Bitcoin which has been most popular in recent years. However, we may look for Ethereum to overtake Bitcoin in the coming time, since it has a lot of benefits and advantages above Bitcoin. It identifies users to build Apps and construct their smart contracts on the above of it. There are still lots of possibilities for smart contracts that have not been explored yet, and you'll have to wait and watch a few years to see all of their potential and their use in everyday life. One of the key reasons why decentralised technologies are becoming increasingly popular nowadays is the ability to communicate data without fear of centralised control. When people lose faith in a tool, the spirit of utilising it dies, and no one wants to participate. Finally, we have developed an algorithm that takes a contract as an input and gives the outputs as a Control Flow Graph and a Cyclomatic Complexity. This set of rules needs to take care of the cloning hassle with the aid of using making sure that doubtful paths inside the Control Flow Graph aren't detected.

In the future work, we will try to look at the application of smart contract. Subsequently, we try to find an efficient way o compute the complexity. Smart contracts are complex, and their applications go beyond basic asset exchanges. Legal processes, coverage premiums, crowdfunding agreements, and monetary derivatives are some of the fields wherein they can behaviour transactions. Smart contracts have the potential to dis-intermediate the legal and accounting professions by automating and simplifying mundane and repetitive tasks for which people currently pay huge fees to banks and lawyers. As smart contracts gain features like adjudication of traditional legal contracts and customised smart contract templates, lawyers' jobs may change in the future. Additionally, smart contracts' ability to govern behaviour and automate activities, and risk assessments and with the possibilities of real-time testing, can be useful for compliance Smart contracts also can automate IoT and edge computing tasks. A utility company, for example, may offer a service in which smart contracts react to changes in power pricing via devices embedded in power metres. When prices exceed a specific threshold, for example, a Smart Contract may utilise a special regulated IoT controller to turn off or reduce power-needed goods like air conditioners. Another potential application is the use of smart contracts in vending machines, which might release commodities in competition with bitcoin or traditional cash payments.

References

1. Albert, E., Correas, J., Gordillo, P., Román-Díez, A.H.-C.G., Rubio, A.: Analyzing smart contracts: from EVM to a sound control-flow graph. arXiv preprint arXiv:2004.14437 (2020)
2. Albert, E., Gordillo, P., Livshits, B., Rubio, A., Sergey, I.: EthIR: a framework for high-level analysis of Ethereum bytecode. In: Lahiri, S.K., Wang, C. (eds.) ATVA 2018. LNCS, vol. 11138, pp. 513–520. Springer, Cham (2018). https://doi.org/10.1007/978-3-030-01090-4_30

3. Albert, E., Gordillo, P., Rubio, A., Sergey, I.: Running on fumes-preventing out-of-gas vulnerabilities in Ethereum smart contracts using static resource analysis. arXiv preprint arXiv:1811.10403 (2018)
4. Alharby, M., Aldweesh, A., Moorsel, A.V.: Blockchain-based smart contracts: a systematic mapping study of academic research (2018). In: 2018 International Conference on Cloud Computing, Big Data and Blockchain (ICCBB), pp. 1–6 IEEE (2018)
5. Amani, S., Bégel, M., Bortin, M., Staples, M.: Towards verifying Ethereum smart contract bytecode in isabelle/hol. In: Proceedings of the 7th ACM SIGPLAN International Conference on Certified Programs and Proofs, pp. 66–77 (2018)
6. Barisal, S.K., Dutta, A., Godboley, S., Sahoo, B., Mohapatra, D.P.: Agility based coverage improvement. In: LASD 2022. LNBIP, vol. 438, pp. 170–186. Springer, Cham (2022). https://doi.org/10.1007/978-3-030-94238-0_10
7. Bragagnolo, S., Rocha, H., Denker, M., Ducasse, S.: Smartinspect: solidity smart contract inspector. In: 2018 International workshop on blockchain oriented software engineering (IWBOSE), pp. 9–18 IEEE (2018)
8. Canetti, R., Fischlin, M.: Universally composable commitments. In: Kilian, J. (ed.) CRYPTO 2001. LNCS, vol. 2139, pp. 19–40. Springer, Heidelberg (2001). https://doi.org/10.1007/3-540-44647-8_2
9. Clack, C.D., Bakshi, V.A., Braine, L.: Smart contract templates: foundations, design landscape and research directions. arXiv preprint arXiv:1608.00771 (2016)
10. Di Angelo, M., Salzer, G.: A survey of tools for analyzing Ethereum smart contracts. In: 2019 IEEE International Conference on Decentralized Applications and Infrastructures (DAPPCON), pp. 69–78 IEEE (2019)
11. Dziembowski, S., Eckey, L., Faust, S., Malinowski, D.: Perun: virtual payment hubs over cryptocurrencies. In: 2019 IEEE Symposium on Security and Privacy (SP), pp. 106–123. IEEE (2019)
12. Godboley, S., Dutta, A., Mohapatra, D.P., Das, A., Mall, R.: Making a concolic tester achieve increased mc/dc. Innovations Syst. Softw. Eng. **12**(4), 319–332 (2016)
13. Godboley, S., Dutta, A., Mohapatra, D.P., Mall, R.: J3 model: a novel framework for improved modified condition/decision coverage analysis. Comput. Stan. Interfaces **50**, 1–17 (2017)
14. Godboley, S., Dutta, A., Mohapatra, D.P., Mall, R.: Gecojap: a novel source-code preprocessing technique to improve code coverage. Comput. Stan. Interfaces **55**, 27–46 (2018)
15. Godboley, S., Dutta, A., Mohapatra, D.P., Mall, R.: Scaling modified condition/decision coverage using distributed concolic testing for java programs. Comput. Stan. Interfaces **59**, 61–86 (2018)
16. Godboley, S., Dutta, A., Pisipati, R.K., Mohapatra, D.P.: SSG-AFL: vulnerability detection for reactive systems using static seed generator based AFL. In: 2022 IEEE 46th Annual Computers, Software, and Applications Conference (COMPSAC), pp. 1728–1733. IEEE (2022)
17. Godboley, S., Gupta, K., Monika, R.G.: Av-AFL: a vulnerability detection fuzzing approach by proving non-reachable vulnerabilities using sound static analyser. In: ENASE, pp. 301–308 (2022)
18. Godboley, S., Mohapatra, D.P.: Towards agile mutation testing using branch coverage based prioritization technique. In: LASD 2022. LNBIP, vol. 438, pp. 150–169. Springer, Cham (2022). https://doi.org/10.1007/978-3-030-94238-0_9
19. Godboley, S., Mohapatra, D.P., Das, A., Mall, R.: An improved distributed concolic testing approach. Softw. Pract. Experience **47**(2), 311–342 (2017)

20. Hegedűs, P.: Towards analyzing the complexity landscape of solidity based Ethereum smart contracts. Technologies **7**(1), 6 (2019)
21. Mall, R.: Fundamentals of software engineering. PHI Learning Pvt. Ltd. (2018)
22. Mohanta, B.K., Panda, S.S., Jena, D.: An overview of smart contract and use cases in blockchain technology. In: 2018 9th International Conference on Computing, Communication and Networking Technologies (ICCCNT), pp. 1–4. IEEE (2018)
23. Vivar, A., Orozco, A.L.S., Villalba, L.J.G.: A security framework for Ethereum smart contracts. Comput. Commun. **172**, 119–129 (2021)
24. Zhang, P., Xiao, F., Luo, X.: A framework and dataset for bugs in Ethereum smart contracts. In: 2020 IEEE International Conference on Software Maintenance and Evolution (ICSME), pp. 139–150. IEEE (2020)
25. Zou, W., et al.: Smart contract development: challenges and opportunities. IEEE Trans. Softw. Eng. **47**(10), 2084–2106 (2019)

An Improved GWO Algorithm for Data Clustering

Gyanaranjan Shial[1,3], Chitaranjan Tripathy[2], Sibarama Panigrahi[1(✉)], and Sabita Sahoo[4]

[1] SUIIT, Sambalpur University, Burla, India
panigrahi.sibarama@gmail.com
[2] Biju Patnaik University of Technology, Rourkela, India
[3] VSSUT, Burla, India
[4] Sambalpur University, Burla, India

Abstract. Grey wolf optimization (GWO) is one among the most promising swarm intelligence based nature inspired meta-heuristic algorithm that improves its search process by mimicking the search for prey and attacking strategy of grey wolfs. To further improve its performance, here we have hybridized with Jaya algorithm that improves the exploration capability and hence maintains a trade between exploitation and exploration. An extensive simulation work is carried out to make a comparative analysis of our proposed method with respect to original GWO algorithm and three other meta-heuristic based clustering algorithms such as JAYA, PSO and ALO considering Accuracy, Sensitivity, Specificity and F-score performance measures. The proposed method is used to cluster each dataset taken from UCI machine learning repositories and the experiment is conducted for total 12 datasets separately. The statistical test of the proposed model is conducted by performing Friedman and Nemenyi hypothesis test and Duncan's multiple test. The obtained results from the statistical test show the superiority of our proposed method with respect to other meta-heuristic based clustering methods.

Keywords: Grey wolf optimization · Particle swarm optimization · JAYA algorithm · Ant lion optimizer

1 Introduction

Over the past few decades, meta-heuristic based optimization stands a reliable alternative in comparison to other optimization methods for solving mathematical problems. Among such for a variety of reasons, stochastic population based methods are most popular among researchers due to derivative free, have enough strength to overcome local convergence issue of non-convex problems and so on. Due to such advantages, several stochastic population based algorithm are predominately used, such as Particle Swarm Optimization algorithm (PSO) [1], Differential Evolution (DE) [2, 3], Genetic algorithm (GA) [4, 5] and Ant Colony Optimization (ACO) [6, 7] etc. In recent years some more nature inspired based stochastic optimization algorithms are developed such as

S. K. Panda et al. (Eds.): CoCoLe 2022, CCIS 1729, pp. 79–90, 2022.
https://doi.org/10.1007/978-3-031-21750-0_7

Grey Wolf Optimization (GWO) [8–10], Ant Lion Optimization (ALO) [11, 12], JAYA algorithm [12, 13], Whale Optimization Algorithm (WOA) [14] and Spider Monkey Optimization (SMO) [15] algorithms are developed.

The large variety of applications of nature inspired based stochastic algorithms proves its evidence of popularity among researchers in the field of engineering, science, medical and industrial applications. Due to stochastic nature, these algorithms gives different results in every run. Therefore obtaining optimal solution is a critical issue for these meta-heuristic based algorithms. Additionally, obtaining near optimal solutions is a challenging problem and can be overcome by improving the performance of existing algorithms. Therefore, for the improvement of performance researchers are giving their continuous effort by combining different operators or by hybridizing.

The GWO is a recently proposed nature inspired meta-heuristic based optimization algorithm that mimics the prey search and attacking procedure of grey wolfs. This algorithm was initially found by Canis lopus and proposed by Mirjalili et al. 2014 [10]. The algorithm is a very powerful optimization method that explores the search space with the use of three leader wolfs and improves the exploitation capability by their combine effort. However, this algorithm converges faster in comparison to other meta-heuristic algorithm and due to such behavior obtaining near optimal solution becomes infeasible. So, in this paper the mechanism of two different algorithms are combined to improve its performance. Therefore, the contributions of our research are as follows:

- Combining operators from two different algorithm such as JAYA and GWO.
- Jaya based perturbation is used to control the convergence speed of GWO search agents with the combine effort of leader wolf (alpha), mean leaders position ($leader_{avg}$) and one wolf selected randomly.
- Applying greedy selection while improving the search process.
- The superiority of our proposed method is established by comparing with the classical GWO algorithm and is also compared with the performance of other meta-heuristic based clustering methods such as PSO, JAYA, ALO based clustering methods considering 12 UCI machine learning benchmark datasets over 5 performance measures such as Accuracy, Sensitivity, Specificity and F-Score.
- The Friedman Nemenyi hypothesis test and Duncan's multiple range tests are applied to rank the methods separately for all five performance measures and by considering all datasets together respectively.

The rest of the paper is described in four remaining sections such as: Sect. 2 covers detail literature reviews including overview of partitional clustering method and meta-heuristic based optimization methods Sect. 3 describes about the methodologies, the problem formulations and proposed approach Sect. 4 presents Simulation works and result analysis. Finally, the conclusions are drawn in Sect. 5.

2 Literature Work

2.1 Partitional Clustering Algorithms

Basically, the problem of clustering can be solved using either of the two methods such as partitional and hierarchical clustering. Besides hierarchical clustering, partitional clustering method gives better solutions with less computational effort. The most famous K-means is one of the simple partitional clustering algorithm. However, the algorithm has major limitation that depends on initial assumption of cluster centers and converges to local optimal solutions. Therefore, most of the research focuses on proposing better clustering methods.

2.2 Grey Wolf Optimization

GWO is introduced by Mirjalili et al. [10, 16–18] that mimics the process of prey search and attacking procedure of the grey wolfs. This algorithm is comparatively simple, few parameters, convergences faster, better exploitation capability than other meta-heuristic algorithms. Moreover, the algorithm is most suitable for linear as well as complex optimization problems. Though GWO is a stochastic based meta-heuristic algorithm, the algorithm improves its search process by changing the movement directions of search agents from exploration to exploitation. However, due to fast convergence the algorithm still lacks the capability to balance between exploitation and exploration.

The algorithm improves its search process by considering the three best candidate solutions such as alpha (α), beta (β) and delta (δ). The remaining wolfs are assumed as omega that updates their positions with the leadership of three leader wolfs with hope to achieve near optimal solutions. The encircling behavior of each omega wolfs can be mathematically formulated as given in Eq. (1) and Eq. (2).

$$D = C \,.\, X_p(t) - X_i(t) \tag{1}$$

$$X_i(t+1) = X_p(t) - A \,.\, D \tag{2}$$

where t represents the current iteration, the value of A is are calculated as given in Eq. (3) and Eq. (4).

$$A = 2 * a * r2 - a \tag{3}$$

$$a = 2 - \frac{2 * t}{N} \tag{4}$$

where, N is the end criteria number of iteration and t is the current iteration.

Based on the above fact the GWO algorithm improves its exploration when $|A| > 1$ and similarly, the algorithm transit towards better exploitation when $|A| < 1$. Most generally, the algorithm has better exploration capability during the initial phase of iteration and later on converges towards near optimal solution with high degree of exploitation. Another parameter C helps to avoid local convergence by with its stochastic behavior as given in Eq. (5).

$$C = 2 \,.\, r1 \tag{5}$$

where, r_1 indicates a random number generated interval 0 to 1.

2.3 JAYA Algorithm

Jaya algorithm is proposed by Rao et al. in the year 2016 [13, 19–21]. It is also termed as parameter less algorithm which improves its search process using best and worst search agent. In each iteration, the algorithm achieves better solution by avoiding worst solution and by moving closer towards better solution. The algorithm has got great interest among researcher due to its motivational characteristics. This is also considered as most simple and flexible algorithm that does not need any control parameters to be tuned [20]. The most important aspect of JAYA algorithm is to avoid local convergence by running away from failures and simultaneously getting closer to success to obtain near optimal solutions.

3 Methodology

Clustering can be considered as a search problem that finds optimal cluster centers in order to form compact clusters. The exhaustive search towards clustering problem is an impractical solution and time consuming. A well-known approach to solve such problem is a heuristic approach that quickly finds near optimal solutions by sacrificing optimality and completeness. Additionally, meta-heuristic are the high-level heuristic algorithms that produces more accurate solution in an unknown search space. Therefore, with a hope to achieve near optimal solution for our clustering problem within feasible time domain, here in this paper we have used meta-heuristic based clustering approaches for obtaining near optimal cluster centers in order to form compact clusters. Most importantly, some amount of randomness and a few rules are the most important factors of all meta-heuristic algorithms for improving the search processes. These meta-heuristic algorithms simulates the idea of natural phenomena, such as evolutionary processes, animal behaviors, physics, birds or fish swarm behavior, bacteria foraging etc. However, obtaining higher efficiency is a challenging task for any meta-heuristic algorithms in order to apply it in any real problem domain. Moreover, this efficiency depends on two important factors such as explorative and exploitative search behaviors of an algorithm. Therefore, to control these two characteristics of an algorithm during the search process, most of the meta-heuristics uses some control parameters that allows periodic transition between exploration and exploitation. Therefore, considering the limitations of conventional clustering methods and the capabilities of recently proposed meta-heuristic algorithms, we have solved a set of clustering problems using our novel approach. The novelty of our proposed method uses the searching procedure of both GWO meta-heuristic algorithm and Jaya algorithm. In order to overcome the inappropriate explorative and faster convergence behavior of GWO, a hybrid explorative search behavior is incorporated into the search process of each search agents that improves the search process by escaping from local convergence with the combine effort of best wolf (alpha), mean leaders position ($leader_{avg}$) and a omega wolf (X_{rand}) selected randomly as given in Eq. (6).

$$X^1 = X_i + r_1(\alpha - X_i) - r_2\left(leader_{avg} - X_{rand}\right) \tag{6}$$

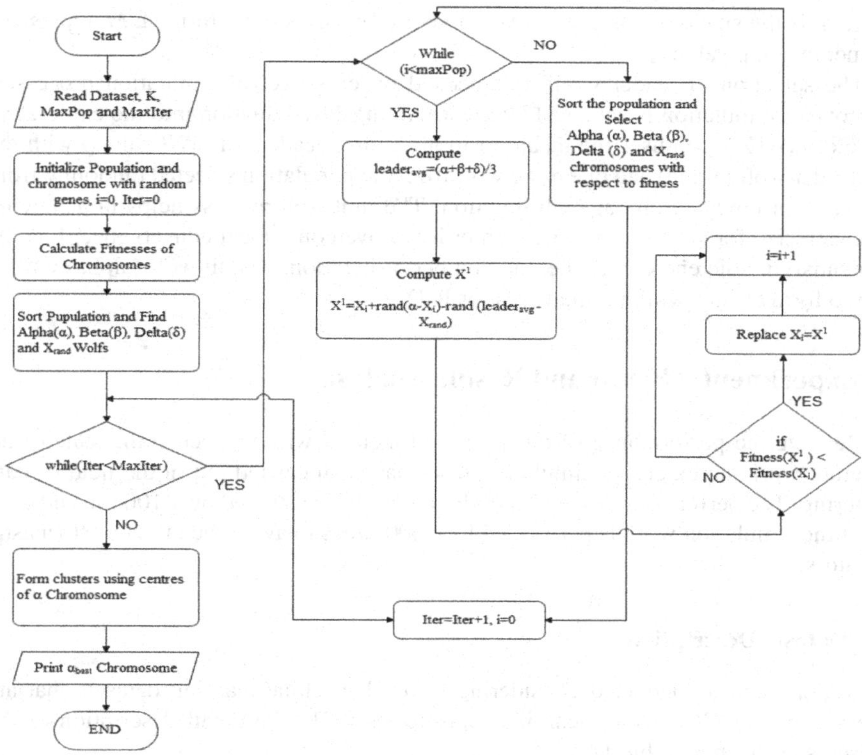

Fig. 1. Proposed enhanced GWO method for data clustering applications

Here, X_i is the ith omega wolf among the whole population and $r_1 and r_2$ are two random number provides stochastic behavior for the two terms that are attracted and propelled by best wolf (α) and mean position of leaders ($leader_{avg}$) respectively.

3.1 Proposed Clustering Methods Using Meta-heuristic Approaches

To address the problem of clustering and to form compact clusters a population based meta-heuristic approach is considered. Most importantly, in order to calculate the compactness value, here we have minimized the intra-cluster distance. The primary steps of our enhanced Grey wolf based clustering method is illustrated in Fig. 1.

The above figure shows major steps of our proposed methods such as population Initialization, fitness calculation and set of operations such as selection, crossover and mutation. In the initial step the solutions are formulated using a set of K number of randomly selected data points and termed as chromosome. Subsequently, the fitness of each chromosome are calculated using Intra-cluster distance (ICD) as given in Eq. (7).

$$ICD = \sum\nolimits_{j=1}^{k} \sum\nolimits_{i=1}^{k} M_i^j * \sqrt{\sum\nolimits_{q=1}^{d} \left(X_i^q - C_j^q\right)^2} \tag{7}$$

where, n is the size of dataset, K is the number of clusters to be formed, M represents the membership value

The selection of leader wolfs is preceded by crossover and mutation processes. Moreover the mutation is achieved by incorporating Jaya equation into the explorative phase of GWO which uses the mean position of three leaders of GWO along with the best leader wolf (alpha) and one more wolf from the population selected randomly from the group of omega wolfs at each iteration. The mutation process helps in achieving large step size for each search agents in order to overcome local convergence. Finally, after satisfying the end criteria i.e. the number of iteration, best fit wolf (alpha) will be used to form cluster with minimal error or ICD.

4 Experimental Setup and Result Analysis

To illustrate the performance of our proposed method with respect to the state of art literature work, an extensive simulation work has been carried out in the field of data clustering. The performance of each simulation work is measured over 100 run and each run of the simulation work is performed for 1000 times to avoid the effect of stochastic operators.

4.1 Dataset Description

The experiment is conducted considering 12 UCI machine learning datasets that are accessed from UCI machine learning repositories [22]. The detail description of the dataset is as given in Table 1.

Table 1. Dataset descriptions

Dataset name	Number of classes	Number of attributes	Attribute characteristics	No of instances
WBDC	02	09	Real	699
Bupa	02	06	Real, integer	345
Haberman's survival	02	03	Real	306
Hepatitis	02	19	Real, integer categorical	155
Indian liver patient	02	10	Real, integer,	583
Ionosphere	02	34	Real, integer	351

(continued)

Table 1. (*continued*)

Dataset name	Number of classes	Number of attributes	Attribute characteristics	No of instances
Iris	03	04	Real	150
Liver	02	06	Integer	345
Mammographic mass	02	06	Integer	961
Seeds	03	07	Real	210
WDBC	02	30	Real	569
Zoo	07	16	Integer	101

4.2 Result Analysis Using Individual Dataset

The 100 simulation results for each benchmark dataset are shown in Table 2. The standard deviation and the mean results for each clustering methods shows that our proposed method acquires highest occurrences of mean results i.e. 11 among 12 datasets in accuracy performance measures. Similarly, our proposed method also achieves highest mean results in 8, 7, 8 and 7 datasets in sensitivity, specificity and Precision and F-score performance measures respectively among same set of input datasets. Additionally, one can observe from the table that the proposed method and the most promising method are statistically equivalent in 1, 2 and 2 datasets respectively for Specificity, Precision and F-score performance measure. Therefore, the superior performance of our proposed method is confirmed for all five performance measure in Duncan's multiple range based statistical test.

Table 2. Performance of different meta-heuristic based clustering methods using Accuracy, Sensitivity, Specificity, Precision and F-score measures on 12 different benchmark Datasets

Dataset	Algorithms	Accuracy Mean ± Std. Dev.	Sensitivity Mean ± Std. Dev.	Specificity Mean ± Std. Dev.	Precision Mean ± Std. Dev.	F-score Mean ± Std. Dev.
Breast cancer wisconsin	Proposed	97.15 ± *0.48*^{b}	***0.97 ± 0.00***^{a}	*0.97 ± 0.02*^{c}	*0.98 ± 0.01*^{b}	*0.98 ± 0.00*^{a}
	GWO	***97.92 ± 0.10***^{a}	*0.96 ± 0.00*^{c}	***0.99 ± 0.00***^{a}	***0.99 ± 0.00***^{a}	***0.98 ± 0.00***^{a}
	JAYA	*97.09 ± 1.02*^{b}	*0.97 ± 0.01*^{b}	*0.97 ± 0.03*^{c}	*0.98 ± 0.02*^{c}	*0.97 ± 0.01*^{b}
	PSO	*97.14 ± 1.09*^{b}	*0.96 ± 0.01*^{d}	*0.98 ± 0.03*^{b}	*0.98 ± 0.02*^{b}	*0.97 ± .01*^{b}
	ALO	*95.71 ± .89*^{c}	*0.97 ± 0.01*^{bc}	*0.95 ± 0.03*^{d}	*0.95 ± 0.03*^{d}	*0.96 ± 0.01*^{c}
Bupa	Proposed	***68.20 ± 2.83***^{a}	*0.54 ± 0.12*^{a}	***0.79 ± 0.09***^{a}	*0.66 ± 0.07*^{b}	*0.58 ± 0.08*^{b}
	GWO	*66.96 ± 2.57*^{b}	*0.63 ± 0.08*^{bc}	*0.71 ± 0.10*^{b}	***0.69 ± 0.05***^{a}	***0.65 ± 0.04***^{a}
	JAYA	*63.87 ± 3.19*^{c}	*0.66 ± 0.09*^{ab}	*0.61 ± 0.13*^{c}	*0.64 ± 0.06*^{bc}	*0.65 ± 0.04*^{a}

(*continued*)

Table 2. (*continued*)

Dataset	Algorithms	Accuracy Mean ± Std. Dev.	Sensitivity Mean ± Std. Dev.	Specificity Mean ± Std. Dev.	Precision Mean ± Std. Dev.	F-score Mean ± Std. Dev.
	PSO	58.31 ± 4.26^{e}	0.59 ± 0.26^{c}	0.57 ± 0.26^{c}	0.63 ± 0.11^{c}	0.55 ± 0.17^{d}
	ALO	59.74 ± 2.88^{d}	$\mathbf{0.70 \pm 0.14^{a}}$	0.50 ± 0.16^{d}	0.59 ± 0.05^{d}	0.63 ± 0.06^{a}
Haberman's survival	Proposed	$\mathbf{77.07 \pm 1.06^{a}}$	$\mathbf{0.92 \pm 0.03^{a}}$	0.34 ± 0.07^{c}	$\mathbf{0.80 \pm 0.01^{a}}$	$\mathbf{0.86 \pm .01^{a}}$
	GWO	68.40 ± 2.49^{b}	0.75 ± 0.07^{b}	$\mathbf{0.62 \pm 0.09^{a}}$	0.67 ± 0.03^{b}	0.70 ± 0.03^{b}
	JAYA	67.77 ± 2.87^{b}	0.75 ± 0.10^{b}	0.61 ± 0.11^{a}	0.66 ± 0.04^{b}	0.70 ± 0.04^{b}
	PSO	58.25 ± 4.47^{d}	0.64 ± 0.29^{c}	0.52 ± 0.27^{b}	0.61 ± 0.20^{c}	0.57 ± 0.17^{d}
	ALO	60.31 ± 3.00^{c}	0.71 ± 0.19^{b}	0.50 ± 0.18^{b}	0.59 ± 0.04^{c}	0.63 ± 0.09^{c}
Hepatitis	Proposed	$\mathbf{80.39 \pm 1.10^{a}}$	0.13 ± 0.14^{d}	$\mathbf{0.98 \pm 0.03^{a}}$	$\mathbf{0.82 \pm 0.21^{a}}$	0.19 ± 0.16^{e}
	GWO	66.08 ± 4.12^{b}	$\mathbf{0.76 \pm 0.11^{a}}$	0.56 ± 0.11^{c}	0.64 ± 0.04^{b}	$\mathbf{0.69 \pm 0.05^{a}}$
	JAYA	64.63 ± 3.89^{c}	0.63 ± 0.17^{b}	0.66 ± 0.14^{b}	0.66 ± 0.06^{b}	0.63 ± 0.09^{b}
	PSO	59.01 ± 4.05^{d}	0.64 ± 0.25^{b}	0.54 ± 0.25^{c}	0.61 ± 0.07^{c}	0.58 ± 0.13^{c}
	ALO	58.05 ± 3.58^{d}	0.54 ± 0.19^{c}	0.62 ± 0.18^{b}	0.60 ± 0.05^{c}	0.54 ± 0.11^{d}
Indian liver patient	Proposed	$\mathbf{71.37 \pm 1.81^{a}}$	$\mathbf{0.88 \pm 0.10^{a}}$	0.30 ± 0.21^{b}	$\mathbf{0.77 \pm 0.04^{a}}$	$\mathbf{0.81 \pm 0.03^{a}}$
	GWO	$70.09 \pm .58^{b}$	0.63 ± 0.02^{b}	$\mathbf{0.77 \pm 0.02^{a}}$	0.74 ± 0.01^{b}	0.68 ± 0.01^{b}
	JAYA	68.85 ± 1.87^{c}	0.62 ± 0.07^{b}	0.76 ± 0.05^{a}	0.72 ± 0.02^{c}	0.66 ± 0.04^{b}
	PSO	65.67 ± 4.51^{d}	0.56 ± 0.15^{c}	0.76 ± 0.14^{a}	0.71 ± 0.07^{c}	0.61 ± 0.10^{c}
	ALO	66.24 ± 1.90^{d}	0.60 ± 0.11^{c}	0.77 ± 0.09^{a}	0.72 ± 0.05^{c}	0.62 ± 0.06^{c}
Ionosphere	Proposed	$\mathbf{82.57 \pm 3.47^{a}}$	0.60 ± 0.08^{b}	$\mathbf{0.95 \pm 0.05^{a}}$	$\mathbf{0.89 \pm 0.08^{a}}$	0.71 ± 0.06^{a}
	GWO	73.63 ± 5.74^{b}	$\mathbf{0.67 \pm 0.10^{a}}$	0.80 ± 0.13^{b}	0.78 ± 0.10^{b}	$\mathbf{0.72 \pm 0.07^{a}}$
	JAYA	70.53 ± 4.34^{c}	0.64 ± 0.12^{ab}	0.77 ± 0.13^{b}	0.75 ± 0.09^{c}	0.68 ± 0.07^{b}
	PSO	67.12 ± 5.76^{d}	0.63 ± 0.16^{b}	0.72 ± 0.17^{c}	0.72 ± 0.11^{d}	0.65 ± 0.10^{c}
	ALO	65.41 ± 4.93^{e}	0.63 ± 0.18^{b}	0.68 ± 0.15^{c}	0.69 ± 0.09^{e}	0.63 ± 0.12^{c}
Iris	Proposed	$\mathbf{97.66 \pm 1.41^{a}}$	$\mathbf{0.98 \pm 0.01^{a}}$	$\mathbf{0.99 \pm 0.01^{a}}$	$\mathbf{0.98 \pm 0.01^{a}}$	$\mathbf{0.98 \pm 0.01^{a}}$
	GWO	97.45 ± 1.13^{a}	0.97 ± 0.01^{a}	0.99 ± 0.01^{a}	0.98 ± 0.01^{a}	0.97 ± 0.01^{a}
	JAYA	97.25 ± 1.57^{a}	0.97 ± 0.02^{a}	0.99 ± 0.01^{a}	0.97 ± 0.02^{a}	0.97 ± 0.02^{a}
	PSO	81.61 ± 10.26^{c}	0.82 ± 0.10^{c}	0.91 ± 0.05^{c}	0.86 ± 0.09^{c}	0.79 ± 0.14^{c}
	ALO	94.61 ± 1.94^{b}	0.95 ± 0.02^{b}	0.97 ± 0.01^{b}	0.95 ± 0.02^{b}	0.95 ± 0.02^{b}
Liver	Proposed	$\mathbf{68.71 \pm 2.95^{a}}$	0.53 ± 0.10^{c}	$\mathbf{0.80 \pm 0.09^{a}}$	0.67 ± 0.07^{a}	0.58 ± 0.06^{b}
	GWO	65.83 ± 2.12^{b}	0.61 ± 0.10^{b}	0.71 ± 0.10^{b}	$\mathbf{0.68 \pm 0.05^{a}}$	$\mathbf{0.64 \pm 0.04^{a}}$
	JAYA	63.83 ± 3.45^{c}	0.63 ± 0.11^{b}	0.64 ± 0.14^{c}	0.65 ± 0.07^{b}	0.63 ± 0.04^{a}
	PSO	59.03 ± 3.63^{e}	0.61 ± 0.19^{b}	0.57 ± 0.21^{d}	0.61 ± 0.06^{c}	0.58 ± 0.10^{b}
	ALO	60.23 ± 3.12^{d}	$\mathbf{0.70 \pm 0.14^{a}}$	0.51 ± 0.16^{e}	0.60 ± 0.05^{c}	$0.63 \pm 0.05a$
Mammographic mass	Proposed	$\mathbf{80.14 \pm 2.59^{a}}$	$\mathbf{0.81 \pm 0.04^{a}}$	0.79 ± 0.06^{b}	0.82 ± 0.04^{a}	$\mathbf{0.81 \pm 0.02^{a}}$
	GWO	76.93 ± 3.63^{b}	0.73 ± 0.09^{b}	0.81 ± 0.08^{ab}	0.80 ± 0.06^{b}	0.76 ± 0.05^{c}
	JAYA	79.36 ± 3.26^{a}	0.75 ± 0.07^{b}	$\mathbf{0.84 \pm 0.05^{a}}$	$\mathbf{0.82 \pm 0.04^{a}}$	0.78 ± 0.04^{b}

(*continued*)

Table 2. (*continued*)

Dataset	Algorithms	Accuracy Mean ± Std. Dev.	Sensitivity Mean ± Std. Dev.	Specificity Mean ± Std. Dev.	Precision Mean ± Std. Dev.	F-score Mean ± Std. Dev.
	PSO	65.26 ± 6.48^{d}	0.56 ± 0.25^{d}	0.75 ± 0.22^{c}	0.75 ± 0.12^{c}	$0.58 \pm 0.18e$
	ALO	70.78 ± 3.86^{c}	0.68 ± 0.10^{c}	0.74 ± 0.10^{c}	0.73 ± 0.06^{c}	0.70 ± 0.05^{d}
Seeds	Proposed	$\mathbf{92.18 \pm 0.59^{a}}$	$\mathbf{0.92 \pm 0.01^{a}}$	$\mathbf{0.96 \pm 0.00^{a}}$	$\mathbf{0.92 \pm 0.01^{a}}$	$\mathbf{0.92 \pm 0.01^{a}}$
	GWO	91.78 ± 0.63^{a}	0.92 ± 0.01^{a}	0.96 ± 0.00^{a}	0.92 ± 0.01^{a}	0.92 ± 0.01^{ab}
	JAYA	91.67 ± 0.77^{a}	0.92 ± 0.01^{a}	0.96 ± 0.00^{a}	0.92 ± 0.01^{a}	0.92 ± 0.01^{ab}
	PSO	68.81 ± 15.09^{c}	0.69 ± 0.15^{c}	0.84 ± 0.08^{c}	0.72 ± 0.17^{b}	0.65 ± 0.19^{c}
	ALO	89.49 ± 1.12^{b}	0.90 ± 0.01^{b}	0.95 ± 0.01^{b}	0.90 ± 0.01^{a}	0.89 ± 0.01^{b}
WDBC	Proposed	$\mathbf{92.55 \pm .90^{a}}$	$\mathbf{0.97 \pm 0.01^{a}}$	0.85 ± 0.04^{d}	$\mathbf{0.92 \pm 0.02^{a}}$	$\mathbf{0.94 \pm 0.01^{a}}$
	GWO	91.03 ± 1.09^{b}	0.93 ± 0.03^{b}	0.90 ± 0.04^{b}	0.90 ± 0.03^{b}	0.91 ± 0.01^{b}
	JAYA	91.00 ± 1.36^{b}	0.90 ± 0.04^{c}	$\mathbf{0.92 \pm 0.03^{a}}$	0.92 ± 0.02^{a}	0.91 ± 0.02^{b}
	PSO	88.82 ± 3.64^{c}	0.90 ± 0.01^{c}	0.88 ± 0.07^{c}	0.89 ± 0.05^{c}	0.89 ± 0.05^{c}
	ALO	88.97 ± 1.14^{c}	0.90 ± 0.05^{c}	0.88 ± 0.06^{c}	0.89 ± 0.04^{c}	0.89 ± 0.01^{c}
Zoo	Proposed	$\mathbf{90.39 \pm .69^{a}}$	$\mathbf{0.86 \pm 0.01^{a}}$	$\mathbf{0.99 \pm 0.00^{a}}$	$\mathbf{0.85 \pm 0.03^{a}}$	$\mathbf{0.84 \pm 0.02^{a}}$
	GWO	73.30 ± 8.74^{b}	0.73 ± 0.09^{b}	0.96 ± 0.02^{b}	0.77 ± 0.12^{b}	0.72 ± 0.08^{b}
	JAYA	72.96 ± 8.49^{b}	0.73 ± 0.09^{b}	0.96 ± 0.01^{b}	0.77 ± 0.11^{b}	0.71 ± 0.08^{b}
	PSO	51.70 ± 11.13^{d}	0.52 ± 0.11^{d}	0.92 ± 0.02^{d}	0.51 ± 0.13^{d}	0.51 ± 0.11^{d}
	ALO	65.47 ± 8.56^{c}	0.66 ± 0.09^{c}	0.94 ± 0.01^{c}	0.65 ± 0.10^{c}	0.65 ± 0.09^{c}

Note: * means the same letters within a column for a single dataset are statistically equivalent to each other at confidence level = 95% considering Duncan's multiple range test

4.3 Analysis Using Non-parametric Test

To reject the Null hypothesis i.e. "there no significant mean performance difference of our proposed method with respect to all considered meta-heuristic based clustering methods" and to confirm the superiority of our proposed method, this time the Friedman and Nemenyi hypothesis based non-parametric test is performed on the obtained results separately for each performance measure. The Fig. 2, Fig. 3, Fig. 4, Fig. 5 and Fig. 6 presents the mean rank of GWO, JAYA, PSO, ALO and our proposed method across Accuracy, Sensitivity, Specificity and F-score performance measure. The result from this statistical test confirms highest mean rank by our proposed method in all performance measures considered for the performance evaluation.

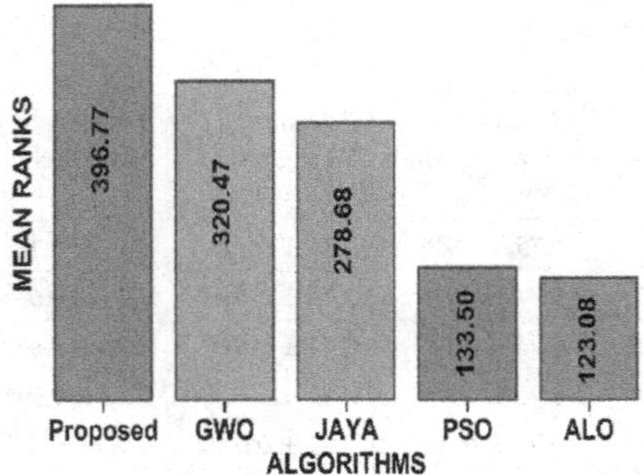

Fig. 2. Mean rank of GWO, JAYA, PSO, ALO and our proposed method based clustering on Accuracy performance measure using 12 benchmark datasets at P-value = .000 and critical distance = 1.8

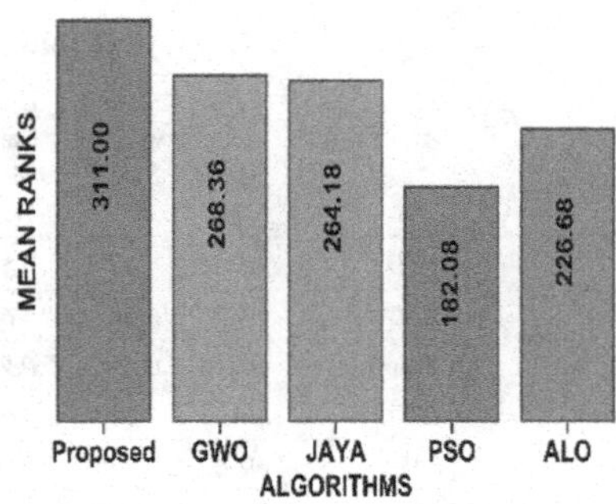

Fig. 3. Mean rank of GWO, JAYA, PSO, ALO and our proposed method based clustering on Sensitivity performance measure using 12 benchmark datasets at P-value = .000 and critical distance = 1.8

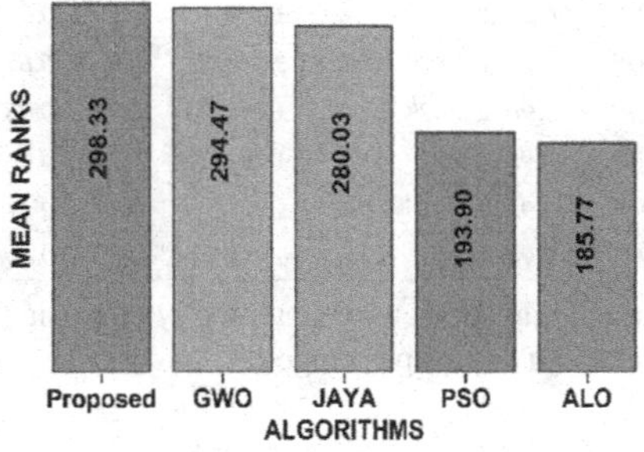

Fig. 4. Mean rank of GWO, JAYA, PSO, ALO and our proposed method based clustering on Specificity performance measure using 12 benchmark datasets at P-value = .000 and critical distance = 1.8

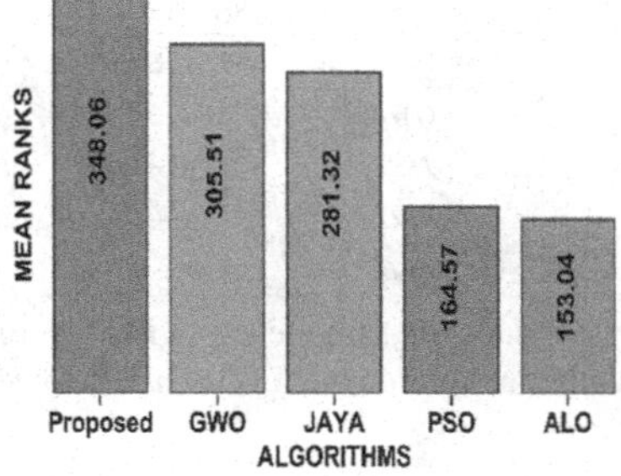

Fig. 5. Mean rank of GWO, JAYA, PSO, ALO and our proposed method based clustering on Precision performance measure using 12 benchmark datasets at P-value = .000 and critical distance = 1.8

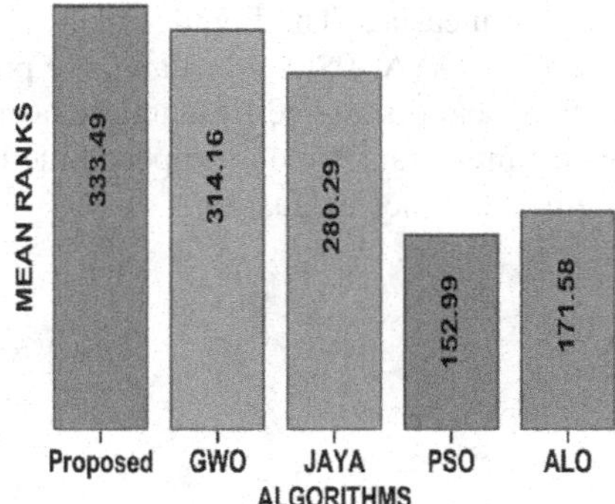

Fig. 6. Mean rank of GWO, JAYA, PSO, ALO and our proposed method based clustering on F-score performance measure using 12 benchmark datasets at P-value = .000 and critical distance = 1.8

5 Conclusion

The paper discusses about outstanding performance of our proposed meta-heuristic based clustering method. Therefore, our experimental work also includes additional four nature inspired swarm intelligence based meta-heuristic clustering methods such as GWO, JAYA, PSO and ALO based clustering for finding optimal cluster centers. Here, the proposed method is used to improve the performance over classical grey wolf optimization method. To test the performance of our proposed method, Duncan's multiple range test is conducted using the results obtained from all the clustering problems. The test suggests that our proposed method performs better in 11 different clustering problems among 12 considered problems except for Breast Cancer Dataset considering accuracy performance measure. Similarly, the proposed method also achieves superior performance in 8, 7, 8 and 7 datasets in sensitivity, specificity, precision and F-score performance measure respectively. The Friedman and Nemenyi hypothesis based non-parametric test is also conducted to test the significant rank difference among the meta-heuristic based clustering algorithms with our proposed method. The test performance rejects the Null hypothesis with a critical distance 1.8 and P-value .000. It also suggests that our proposed method obtains highest mean rank among the clustering algorithms. The overall statistical test confirms the superiority of our proposed method in comparison to the state-of-art meta-heuristic based clustering methods.

References

1. Kennedy, J., Eberhart, R.: Particle swarm optimization. In: Proceedings of ICNN 1995-International Conference on Neural Networks, vol. 4, pp. 1942–1948 (1995)
2. Draa, A., Bouzoubia, S., Boukhalfa, I.: A sinusoidal differential evolution algorithm for numerical optimisation. Appl. Soft Comput. **27**, 99–126 (2015)
3. Qin, A.K., Huang, V.L., Suganthan, P.N.: Differential evolution algorithm with strategy adaptation for global numerical optimization. IEEE Trans. Evol. Comput. **13**(2), 398–417 (2008)
4. Abualigah, L., Alkhrabsheh, M.: Amended hybrid multi-verse optimizer with genetic algorithm for solving task scheduling problem in cloud computing. J. Supercomput. **78**(1), 740–765 (2021). https://doi.org/10.1007/s11227-021-03915-0
5. Alba, E., Dorronsoro, B.: The exploration/exploitation tradeoff in dynamic cellular genetic algorithms. IEEE Trans. Evol. Comput. **9**(2), 126–142 (2005)
6. Shelokar, P.S., Jayaraman, V.K., Kulkarni, B.D.: An ant colony approach for clustering. Anal. Chim. Acta **509**(2), 187–195 (2004)
7. Dorigo, M., Di Caro, G.: Ant colony optimization: a new meta-heuristic. In: Proceedings of the 1999 Congress on Evolutionary Computation-CEC99 (Cat. No. 99TH8406), vol. 2, pp. 1470–1477 (1999)
8. Yu, X., Xu, W., Li, C.: Opposition-based learning grey wolf optimizer for global optimization. Knowl.-Based Syst. **226**, 107139 (2021)
9. Gao, Z.-M., Zhao, J.: An improved grey wolf optimization algorithm with variable weights. Comput. Intell. Neurosci. **2019**, (2019)
10. Mirjalili, S., Mirjalili, S.M., Lewis, A.: Grey wolf optimizer. Adv. Eng. Softw. **69**, 46–61 (2014). https://doi.org/10.1016/j.advengsoft.2013.12.007
11. Mirjalili, S.: The ant lion optimizer. Adv. Eng. Softw. **83**, 80–98 (2015)

12. Azizi, M., Mousavi Ghasemi, S.A., Ejlali, R.G., Talatahari, S.: Optimum design of fuzzy controller using hybrid ant lion optimizer and Jaya algorithm. Artif. Intell. Rev. **53**(3), 1553–1584 (2019). https://doi.org/10.1007/s10462-019-09713-8
13. Rao, R.: Jaya: a simple and new optimization algorithm for solving constrained and unconstrained optimization problems. Int. J. Ind. Eng. Comput. **7**(1), 19–34 (2016)
14. Mirjalili, S., Lewis, A.: The whale optimization algorithm. Adv. Eng. Softw. **95**, 51–67 (2016)
15. Bansal, J.C., Sharma, H., Jadon, S.S., Clerc, M.: Spider monkey optimization algorithm for numerical optimization. Memetic Comput. **6**(1), 31–47 (2014)
16. Akbari, E., Rahimnejad, A., Gadsden, S.A.: A greedy non-hierarchical grey wolf optimizer for real-world optimization. Electron. Lett. **57**, 499–501 (2021)
17. Karakoyun, M., Onur, I., İhtisam, A.: Grey Wolf Optimizer (GWO) algorithm to solve the partitional clustering problem. Int. J. Intell. Syst. Appl. Eng. **7**(4), 201–206 (2019)
18. Aljarah, I., Mafarja, M., Heidari, A.A., Faris, H., Mirjalili, S.: Clustering analysis using a novel locality-informed grey wolf-inspired clustering approach. Knowl. Inf. Syst. **62**(2), 507–539 (2019). https://doi.org/10.1007/s10115-019-01358-x
19. Dhiman, G., Kumar, V.: Spotted hyena optimizer: a novel bio-inspired based metaheuristic technique for engineering applications. Adv. Eng. Softw. **114**, 48–70 (2017)
20. El-Ashmawi, W.H., Ali, A.F., Slowik, A.: An improved Jaya algorithm with a modified swap operator for solving team formation problem. Soft Comput. **24**, 16627–16641 (2020)
21. Gunduz, M., Aslan, M.: DJAYA: a discrete Jaya algorithm for solving traveling salesman problem. Appl. Soft Comput. **105**, 107275 (2021)
22. Dua, D., Graff, C.: {UCI} Machine Learning Repository (2017). http://archive.ics.uci.edu/ml

Anticipation of Heart Disease Using Improved Optimization Techniques

Sibo Prasad Patro[1](✉), Neelamadhab Padhy[1], and Rahul Deo Sah[2]

[1] School of Engineering and Technology, Department of Computer Science and Engineering, GIET University, Gunupur, Odisha, India
{sibofromgiet,dr.neelamadhab}@giet.edu
[2] Department of CA and IT, DSPMU, Ranchi, India
rahuldeosah@gmail.com

Abstract. Heart disease is one of the major cause that leads to a reduce the life span of human beings. Hence it is important to find abnormal heart conditions at an early stage that helps to avoid sudden cardiac death. The optimization algorithms are adaptable and flexible enough to handle difficult non-linear problems. A heart disease prediction model is proposed using Bayesian Optimization of Support Vector Machine, Salp Swarm Optimized Neural Network Classifier, Particle Swarm Optimization, Ant colony, Gradient Descent and Gradient Descent + Particle Swarm Optimization to identify the presence of heart disease. The Proposed GD+PSO mixed optimization algorithms produced the highest accuracy with 99.92% on Cleveland dataset. The proposed algorithms' superiority is supported by numerous numerical, statistical, graphical, and comparative analyses involving numerous state-of-the-art algorithms. Finally, GD+PSO is suggested in this study for unconstrained optimization problems based on overall performance.

Keywords: Heart disease · Classification · Feature selection · Optimization · Performance measures

1 Introduction

Cardiovascular disease (CVD) is now on the emergence in the world today. According to WHO nearly 17 million people die each year due to heart diseases, specifically cardiovascular disease and peripheral arterial disease [1]. In the United States, cardiovascular disease is identified as the major cause of death. According to the American Heart Association, approximately 5,25,000 people have an early cardiac arrest and approximately 2,10,000 people repeatedly affected by heart attacks every year. According to the Centers for Disease Control, nearly half of these deaths in 1999 occurred before the patient received emergency services or hospital treatment [2]. Therefore, it is crucial to identify the key signs and lifestyle choices that lead to CVD. Before the diagnosis of CVD numerous tests are performed, such as BP, Cholesterol, Auscultation, ECG and blood sugar etc. When a patient's condition is critical, medicines must be started immediately, these tests can be lengthy and time-consuming, so it's critical to take priority of them [3]. Due to several lifestyle factors CVD occurs. It is very important to find out which dietary habits contribute to CVD.

S. K. Panda et al. (Eds.): CoCoLe 2022, CCIS 1729, pp. 91–102, 2022.
https://doi.org/10.1007/978-3-031-21750-0_8

Machine learning enables the acquisition of knowledge from huge amount of data. ML is the process of learning from past data and generalising it to create predictions about future data using an algorithm. Such problems can be identified as approximating function that maps input parameters to output parameters. By redefining the issue as function optimization, the problem of approximating can be resolved. Optimization function helps to minimize error, cost, or loss when fitting a ML algorithm. The goal of this paper is to classify the diagnostic tests and look at a few of the health behaviors that play a role in CVD. Due to versatility, intelligent optimization algorithms are widely used [4, 5]. PSO algorithm has been successfully implemented for cardiovascular disease due to simplicity and generality [6]. PSO, on the other hand, conveniently fell into the best local solution. With PSO, almost all issues in science and engineering have been resolved. PSO has been used to solve some of the most researched problems [7]. ACO algorithm developed for combinatorial optimization. ACO algorithms used for solving continuous optimization issues. These problems differ from discrete problems in that the choice variables have continuous domains [8]. Recently, the ACO technique was implemented in the data mining field to extract rule-based classifiers [9]. ACO is a metaheuristic for solving difficult complex optimization problems [10]. Data mining's main objective is to draw knowledge from data. The core of the multidisciplinary field of data mining combines machine learning, statistics, and databases [11, 12]. When newly discovered information will be used to support a choice made by a human user, comprehension is crucial. The user won't be able to interpret and validate the knowledge if it is not understandable to them. This can result in the user not having enough confidence in the knowledge to use it for decision-making, which could result in poor decisions [13]. ML algorithms has good performance, are simple to use, and require little computational work [14].

1.1 Problem Statement

Many studies have carried out previously to predict and categorize heart disease. However, the existing studies have concentrated on a particular machine learning techniques rather than on their optimization through the use of optimum methods. Few researchers also attempted to use hybrid optimization techniques for improved machine learning classification. Most studies in the literature that have been proposed exploit optimized methods with a focus on PSO, ACO, SS, and BO of Support Vector Machines. When all continuous attributes are down-sampled, the mining-relevant feature extraction attributes are chosen from among all the original attributes. The feature selection technique is more effective in reducing the dimensionality of the dataset, removing irrelevant data, and helping to increase learning accuracy and understanding of the results. This article's primary goal is to predict heart disease using various optimization algorithms. The following are the critical contribution towards this research:

Critical Contribution

- Data cleaning techniques applied on the dataset to enhance the accuracy of the model.
- Min-Max Scalar technique taken for normalizing the data.

- BO-SVM, SSA-NN, PSO, ACO, GD and Proposed (GD+PSO) optimization algorithms used for implementing the proposed model.
- We have applied several epochs on the dataset at various phases including the training, testing, and validating phase for calculating the results of MAE, RMSE, and MSE
- For enhancing the accuracy an implementation phase and validation phase were identified.

2 Literature Review

On various medical data sets, experiments are carried out using various classifiers and feature selection methods. Very few research works are carried out for heart disease classification. Many of them exhibit greater classification precision [15]. Using various machine learning and optimization techniques, researchers have recently made significant advancements in heart disease prediction.

Khourdifi, Y. et al. [15] proposed a Fast Correlated- Based Feature Selection technique to enhance the accuracy of heart disease classification by removing the redundant features. NB, K-NN, SVM, RF, and classification algorithms were used to perform the classification. PSO and ACO techniques were used to optimize an artificial neural network. The proposed hybrid technique applied on a HD dataset. The suggested optimized model using FCFB, ACO and PSO produced 99.65% accuracy for K-NN and 99.60% for RF. Gaddala, L. K. et al. [16] discussed various Swarm Optimization techniques such as Group Search Optimization, Swarm Intelligence, ACO, Artificial Bee Colony Optimization and PSO. In this research PSO performance was good compared to others. A Feed Forward of AI Network is used to classify diseased or non-diseased patients. Finally, the performance was compared to well-known other data sets in terms of accuracy, sensitivity, and specificity. Alkeshuosh, A. H. et al. [17] applied Particle Swarm Optimization technique for heart disease prediction. Intially, the Random Rules were encoded then optimized based on their accuracy by using the PSO Algorithm. The method was compared to the DT algorithm based on C4.5 on a ML Datasets. The test results demonstrated that the PSO outperformed C4.5 in terms of predictive accuracy and rule list size. The PSO method outperformed with 87% and C4.5 with 63% respectively. Satyananda, N. et al. [18] discussed Neural network models perform better compared to machine learning in the field of disease predictions but due to the presence of complex methods, neural networks take much computational time. A new technique is proposed using predictive optimization technique to improve the efficiency of the system in both time complexity and trade-off. OMLR algorithm was proposed in this study to improve the performance of the results, the algorithms produced an accuracy of 93.2% which is lesser time complexity comparable to existing studies. Bhardwaj, J. et al. [19] discussed algorithms for optimization can easily handle complicated nonlinear problems with exceptional resistance and versatility. In this research, various methods were examined and recorded, using different features to enhance the results for the categorization of heart diseases. Later, the PSO and ACO methods are used to optimize categorization based on various machine learning algorithms such as KNN, SVM, DT, and RF. This study compares various ml designs, analyzing the results on various domains such as exactness, recall, F1 score, and so on, and the highest accuracy is 87.0% using PSO and

ACO. Thilagamani, S. et al. [20] presented a survey highlighting DT, SVM, K-NN, NB, and genetic algorithms for heart disease prediction. As the study says, The multilayer perceptron classification rule algorithm can be used to improve the accuracy of heart disease diagnosis with a diagnosis alert system. Dulhare, U. N. et al. [21] discussed Classification is one of the data mining techniques, which helps to predict accurately the target class for each defined case in the given dataset. Linear classifiers, such as Naive Bayes (NB) models, are relatively stable in the face of minor differences or modifications in training data. PSO is an effective iterative optimization technique that chooses the most optimal features that contribute the most to the result, reducing computation time and increasing accuracy. The proposed technique helped to increase the classification performance and decrease the number of features.The combination of Naïve Bayes and PSO produced an accuracy of 87.91%. He, W. et al. [22, 23] proposed an evolutionary classification model using kernel extreme learning machine optimized with the help of an improved salp swarm algorithm. The STSSA-KELM KELM model designed for heart disease diagnosis based on optimized parameters and by taking the subset of features. The model outperformed for STSSA-KELM model with a classification accuracy of 84.40%, 69.02% for correlation coefficient, 87.30% for sensitivity and 81.70% for specificity.

Heart disease prediction becomes a challenging task using machine learning techniques. CVD is the leading cause of mortality all over the world. After various literature reviews from the existing research we found, that there are various statistical packages, diverse methods, and approaches used across identified studies. Most studies applied limited techniques in the data preprocessing phase. Different optimization algorithms were proposed by the previous studies which are outperformed with accuracy and performance metrics values that can be enhanced. BO-SVM, SSA, PSO, ACO, GD, and the combination of PSO+GD are introduced in this research to accurately identify the presence of heart disease.

3 Research Question

RQ1: Can it be possible to use optimization techniques to improve heart disease prediction accuracy?
RQ2: How the validation process helps to improve the performance of the model?

4 Proposed Model

A Heart disease prediction architecture is proposed using Optimization algorithms. The primary goal of the model is to enhance the accuracy using various optimization optimization techniques. In this section, the structure of the proposed model is presented. To develop an intelligent and highly reliable hyper-parameter optimization model for assessing early heart disease using imperative risk features. The model is divided in two phases: implementation phase and validation phase. In the first phase, we have taken BO-SVM, SSA, PSO, ACO, GD, and the combination of PSO+GD algorithms for evaluating the performance matrix and finding the learning accuracy. If the learning accuracy is achieved, then the second phase where the validation process is taken care of for CVD analysis. The detailed flow of the proposed model is shown in Fig. 1.

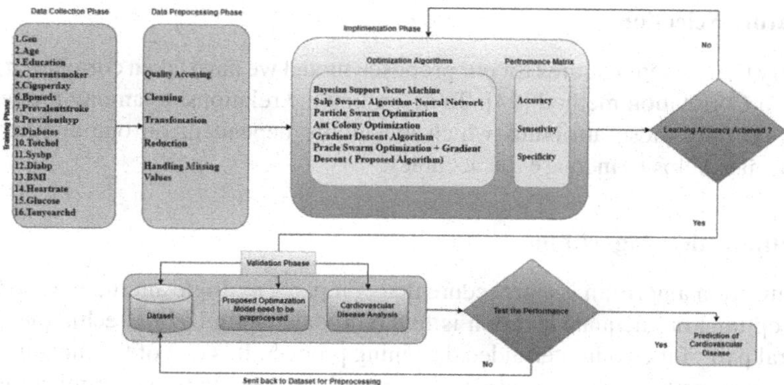

Fig. 1. The proposed Heart disease prediction architecture using optimization algorithms

4.1 Data Collection

For this research Framingham heart disease dataset from Kaggle ("https://www.kaggle.com/code/lauriandwu/machine-learning-heart-disease-framingham") and Cleveland heart disease dataset from the UCI repository (http://archive.ics.uci.edu/ml/datasets/Heart+Disease, accessed on 9 April 2020) taken for training and evaluating the proposed model. The Framingham dataset contains 16 features with 4238 records, out of 4238 samples, the numbers of healthy patients are 3594 and the number of sick patients is 644. The Cleveland dataset contains 14 features with 303 records, where 165 sick patients and 138 healthy patients are available. Risk factors from the patients' physical examinations, behavioral risk factors, and medical risk factors are available in both datasets.

4.2 Manual Exploration

Manual Exploration is one of the important techniques for developing machine learning algorithms. This phase helps for analyzing the given datasets, where we can label or rank the person is sick or not. After constucting the dataset various ML algorithms are applied to the training dataset.

4.3 Data Preprocessing

There are many missing and null values that exist in various attributes in the given dataset. This may lead to unbalanced observations and biased estimates. Hence, Data preprocessing helps us to make it easier to interpret the data. This procedure removes duplicates in data, otherwise, it may negatively affect a model's accuracy. The dataset is divided in to training and testing dataset with 70:30, 80:20 and 50:50 ratios. Imputation is a method for replacing missing data with a value based on other available details to preserve the majority of the information in the dataset. Because missing data can be problematic for many machine learning algorithms. Furthermore, we use MinMaxScaler to scale the features to the range [0, 1]. The removal process of noise improves the detection of heart disease.

4.4 Feature Selection

To identify the relevant features for our proposed model we have taken correlation matrix or Pearson Correlation method [24]. To determine the relationship among the features, we selected only those attributes which are highly dependent on one another. Such technique also helps to increase the accuracy.

4.5 Optimization Algorithms

An optimization algorithm is a procedure that compares multiple alternatives iteratively until an optimal or adequate solution is found. Today, Optimization technique became an integral part of the computer-aided designing process. It is one of the most important phenomena in getting better results in Machine Learning. Various optimization algorithms are used in this paper to find the performance metrics. Once the performance is evaluated then we applied a condition to identify whether the learning accuracy is achieved or not. If the learning accuracy is achieved then we move towards to validation phase, if the learning accuracy is not achieved then the optimization algorithms will repeat their process to improve the learning accuracy [25].

SSA: Is one of the optimization strategies. It replicates the behaviour of salps in nature. It consists of two groups, they are leaders and followers. The salp which is on the front side called a leader and others are called followers. The salps' point is defined in n-dimensions, which represent a problem's search area, and n represents the variables in the problem. These salps are looking for a food supply, which implies the swarm's aim. The position should be updated on a regular basis. The mathematical computation to find the salp leader is shown in the following Eq. (1)

$$x_j^i = \begin{cases} f_j + c_1\left(\left(ub_j - lb_j\right) \times c_2 + lb_j\right)c_3 \leq 0 \\ f_j - c_1\left(\left(ub_j - lb_j\right) \times c_2 + lb_j\right)c_3 < 0 \end{cases} \tag{1}$$

$$c_1 = 2e^{-\left(\frac{4l}{L}\right)^2} \tag{2}$$

$$x_j^i = \frac{1}{2}at^2 + v_0 t \tag{3}$$

$$x_j^i = \frac{1}{2}\left(x_j^i + x_j^{i-1}\right) \tag{4}$$

PSO: Swarm intelligence solves difficult issues by interacting with basic agents and their surroundings. This approach relies on the interaction of individuals: for each iteration the particle moves, the particle nearest to the optimal location informs the others of its location so they can adjust their trajectory. Every single member of the population is referred to as a particle in particle swarm optimization. Conventional PSO updates each particle's velocity and position after population initialization based on pbset and gbest as represented in the following Eq. (5 and 6). The effectiveness of every particle are assessed by cost functions after each iteration.

$$\mathrm{v^i[t+1] = w.v^i[t] + c_1 r_1\left(p^{i,best}[t] - p^i[t] + c_2 r_2\left(p^{i,best}[t] - p^i[t]\right)\right)} \tag{5}$$

$$p^i[t+1] = p^i[t] + v^i[t+1] \tag{6}$$

ACO: Utilizing some iterations, the ACO method investigates to identify the ideal feature subset. The main goal of the ACO method is to reduce redundancy. Each ant chooses the features with the lowest similarity to the features that were previously chosen. Consequently, if a feature is chosen by the majority of ants, it means that it is the least similar to the other features. The feature that receives the most pheromones will have a higher likelihood of being chosen in subsequent iterations by other ants. Finally, due to their similarity, the major traits that were chosen will have high pheromone values. As a result, the ACO method chooses the best features with the least amount of duplication. The following Eq. (7) shows the mathematical terms of ACO

$$T_{xy} \leftarrow (1-p)T_{xy+\sum_k \Delta T^k_{xy}} \tag{7}$$

$$\Delta T^k_{xy} = \left\{ \frac{Q/L_K \text{ ant k uses curve xy in its tour}}{0 \text{ otherwise}} \right. \tag{8}$$

GD (Gradient Descent): Finding the minimum value for a function is accomplished using the iterative optimization technique known as gradient descent. The general concept is to initialize the parameters with random values and then, at each iteration, move a little bit closer to the "slope". In supervised learning, gradient descent is frequently used to reduce the error function and identify the best parameter values. The mathematical process is shown in the following Eq. (9)

$$p_{n+1} = p_n - n\nabla f(p_n) \tag{9}$$

The important factor affecting the success of machine learning is training and testing the dataset. An effective training process enhances the performance of the model. After identifying the target column in the given dataset, the dataset spitted in to two smaller data sets to train the ML algorithm. The algorithm's test set serves as its training set. The dataset is divided into two parts, and then further divide the data for training and validation in the training set. We have Applied BO-SVM, SSA-NN, PSO, ACO, GD, and the combination of PSO+GD optimization algorithm to the dataset. The training and testing ratios of the proposed optimization techniques are depicted in Table 1.

Table 1. Training and testing ratios of the proposed optimization techniques

The ratio between training and testing	Accuracy	Sensitivity	Specificity
70:30	97.32	99.45	98.12
80:20	96.25	98.48	97.56
50:50	97.30	98.32	98.02

Table 2 shows the Accuracy is varying when the dataset is spitted into different ratios. We applied K-Fold cross-validation techniques with our proposed model. When the parameters of K are changed the average accuracy is changed which is shown in Table 2.

Table 2. K-Fold cross-validation techniques with our proposed model

Parameters of K	Average accuracy
When k = 3	It gives 97.36%
When k = 4	It gives 97.45
When k = 5	It gives 98.23
When k = 10	It gives 99.15

4.6 Performance Measure

Finally, the prediction model's accuracy, sensitivity and specificity performance is calculated. The model outperformed with good prediction accuracy. The accuracy metric defines the correctness of the machine learning classifier's prediction. The mathematical calculations for the performance parameters are computed are shown in Eqs. (14–17):

$$\text{Accuracy} = \frac{\text{TP} + \text{TN}}{\text{TP} + \text{TN} + \text{FN} + \text{FP}} \tag{10}$$

$$\text{Sensitivity} = \frac{\text{TP}}{\text{TP} + \text{FN}} \tag{11}$$

$$\text{Specificity} = \frac{\text{TN}}{\text{TN} + \text{FP}} \tag{12}$$

$$\text{MAE} = \frac{1}{\text{N}} \sum\nolimits_{\text{I}=1}^{\text{N}} |\text{Y}_\text{i} - \widehat{\text{Y}}| \tag{13}$$

$$\text{RMSE} = \sqrt{\text{MSE}} = \sqrt{\frac{1}{\text{N}} \sum\nolimits_{\text{i}=1}^{\text{N}} (\text{y}_\text{i} - \hat{\text{y}})^2} \tag{14}$$

$$\text{MSE} = \frac{1}{\text{N}} \sum\nolimits_{\text{i}=1}^{\text{N}} (\text{y}_\text{i} - \hat{\text{y}})^2 \tag{15}$$

In our proposed model to identify the error measurement we have applied several epochs on the dataset at various phases including the training, testing, and validating phase. At each epoch, the results for MAE, RMSE, and MSE outperformed with different ratios. The detailed results are shown in Table 3.

Table 3. Training, testing and validation phase

Training phase				Testing phase				Validation phase			
Errors	#0	#20	#40	Errors	#0	#20	#40	Errors	#0	#20	#40
MAE	1.7992	0.2951	0.1781	MAE	1.8452	0.3854	0.1782	MAE	1.9642	0.3954	0.1854
RMSE	1.2564	0.5723	0.4215	RMSE	1.3874	0.5854	0.5354	RMSE	1.3854	0.5960	0.5525
MSE	0.8954	0.3941	0.4247	MSE	0.9982	0.4785	0.5324	MSE	0.9972	0.4892	0.5435

5 Results and Discussion

In this section, the details of the experiments and evaluation scheme are presented. The experiment's goal was to evaluate the best algorithm for heart disease using various optimization techniques. The experiments for the proposed work are carried out under "Waikato Environment for Knowledge Analysis (Weka)" tool. Due to minimum selected attributes, tenfold cross-validation was applied. Each experiment was run ten times to avoid unstable operation results, and the MAE, RMSE, and MSE results were generated with different epoch times. We looked at each classifier's accuracy and efficiency in terms of model building time, correctly classified examples, incorrectly classified examples, and accuracy with optimization techniques. For dataset comparisons, performance measures after attribute selection, parameter tuning, and calibration are applied. The accuracy, sensitivity, and specificity values are calculated on both Cleveland and Framingham datasets. After successful validation, our proposed model produced a good accuracy for all the optimization algorithms on Cleveland dataset, the results are shown in Table 4.

Table 4. Performance evaluation of the Cleveland dataset

Name of the optimization technique	Accuracy	Sensitivity	Specificity
BO-SVM	93%	80%	82%
SSA-NN	80%	60%	79%
PSO	95%	87%	86%
ACO	96%	89%	88%
GD	99%	98%	99%
Proposed (GD+PSO)	99.92%	99%	99.26

The proposed model produced different results for BO-SVM, SSA-NN, PSO, ACO, GD and PSO+GD optimization algorithms, whereas the combination of GD+PCO produced the highest accuracy with 99.92% for the Cleveland dataset. The detailed accuracy of the Framingham dataset are shown in Table 5.

Table 5. Performance evaluation of the Framingham dataset

Name of the optimization algorithm	Accuracy obtained	Sensitivity	Specificity
BO-SVM	92%	79%	81%
SSA-NN	84%	69%	74%
PSO	93%	86%	85%
ACO	95%	88%	86%
GD	98%	97%	96%
Proposed (GD+PSO)	99.02%	99.01%	99.15%

The graphical representation for the performance evaluation of the Cleveland and Framingham dataset is shown in Figs. 2 and 3.

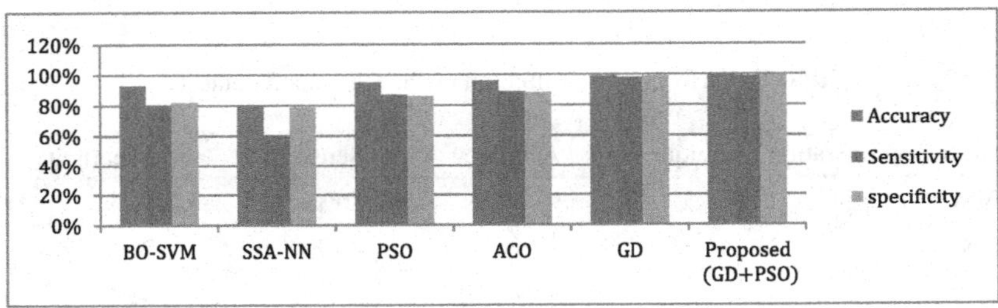

Fig. 2. Grpah representation for Cleveland dataset

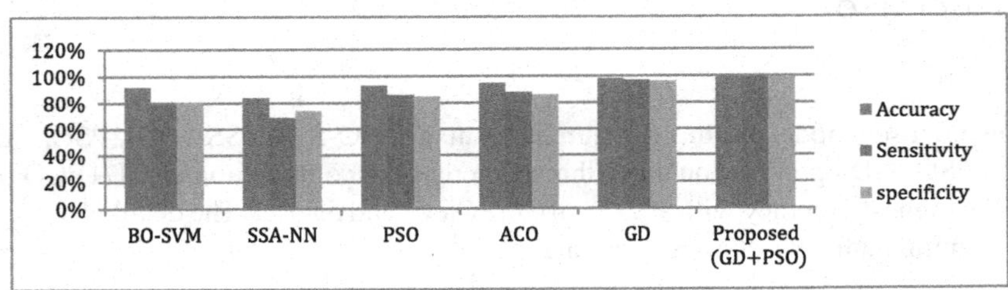

Fig. 3. Grpah representation for Framingham dataset

6 Conclusion

Heart disease become more frequent and one of the critical diseases over the globe. As a result, predicting the disease before becoming sick minimises the risk of death. This study proposed various optimization algorithms such as BO-SVM, SSA-NN, PSO, ACO, GD, and the combination of PSO+GD on the Cleveland and Framingham dataset.

In the initial phase, the dataset was trained to find the learning accuracy. If the learning accuracy is achieved then the testing datasets are validated for CVD analysis. Finally, we test the performance level. A hybrid optimization combination of Particle Swarm Optimization (PSO) and Gradient Descent (GD) produced an accuracy with 99.92% on the Cleveland dataset and 99.02% on the Framingham dataset. The results shows the Cleveland dataset accuracy is higher compared to the Framingham dataset. In this study, we conclude that PSO+GD will yield superior outcomes to the other available techniques for identifying heart disease.

References

1. Mackay, J., Mensah, G.A., Greenlund, K.: The atlas of heart disease and stroke. World Health Organization (2004)
2. Rumsfeld, J.S., Joynt, K.E., Maddox, T.M.: Big data analytics to improve cardiovascular care: promise and challenges. Nat. Rev. Cardiol. **13**(6), 350–359 (2016)
3. Centers for Disease Control and Prevention (CDC): State-specific mortality from sudden cardiac death--United States, 1999. MMWR. Morb. Mortal. Wkly. Rep. **51**(6), 123–126 (2002)
4. Kamkar, I., Akbarzadeh-T, M.R., Yaghoobi, M.: Intelligent water drops a new optimization algorithm for solving the vehicle routing problem. In: 2010 IEEE International Conference on Systems, Man and Cybernetics, pp. 4142–4146. IEEE (October 2010)
5. Gazzaz, N.M., Yusoff, M.K., Ramli, M.F., Juahir, H., Aris, A.Z.: Artificial neural network modeling of the water quality index using land use areas as predictors. Water Environ. Res. **87**(2), 99–112 (2015)
6. Zhang, Y., Wang, S., Ji, G.: A comprehensive survey on particle swarm optimization algorithm and its applications. Math. Probl. Eng. **2015**, 1–38 (2015)
7. Erdogmus, P.: Introductory chapter: swarm intelligence and particle swarm optimization. Part. Swarm Optim. Appl. **10**, 1–8 (2018)
8. Alshamlan, H.M., Badr, G.H., Alohali, Y.A.: Genetic Bee Colony (GBC) algorithm: a new gene selection method for microarray cancer classification. Comput. Biol. Chem. **56**, 49–60 (2015)
9. Ganji, M.F., Abadeh, M.S.: Using fuzzy ant colony optimization for diagnosis of diabetes disease. In: 2010 18th Iranian Conference on Electrical Engineering, pp. 501–505. IEEE (May 2010)
10. Xiong, W., Wang, C.: A novel hybrid clustering based on adaptive ACO and PSO. In: 2011 International Conference on Computer Science and Service System (CSSS), pp. 1960–1963. IEEE (June 2011)
11. Chen, Y., Miao, D., Wang, R.: A rough set approach to feature selection based on ant colony optimization. Pattern Recogn. Lett. **31**(3), 226–233 (2010)
12. Kabir, M.M., Shahjahan, M., Murase, K.: A new hybrid ant colony optimization algorithm for feature selection. Expert Syst. Appl. **39**(3), 3747–3763 (2012)
13. Jiang, Q., Shao, F., Gao, W., Chen, Z., Jiang, G., Ho, Y.S.: Unified no-reference quality assessment of singly and multiply distorted stereoscopic images. IEEE Trans. Image Process. **28**(4), 1866–1881 (2018)
14. Abdar, M., Książek, W., Acharya, U.R., Tan, R.S., Makarenkov, V., Pławiak, P.: A new machine learning technique for an accurate diagnosis of coronary artery disease. Comput. Methods Programs Biomed. **179**, 104992 (2019)
15. Khourdifi, Y., Bahaj, M.: Heart disease prediction and classification using machine learning algorithms optimized by particle swarm optimization and ant colony optimization. Int. J. Intell. Eng. Syst. **12**(1), 242–252 (2019)

16. Gaddala, L.K., Rao, D.N.N.M.: An analysis of heart disease prediction using swarm ıntelligence algorithms. Int. J. Innov. Eng. Technol. **6**(3), 081–087 (2018)
17. Alkeshuosh, A.H., Moghadam, M.Z., Al Mansoori, I., Abdar, M.: Using PSO algorithm for producing best rules in diagnosis of heart disease. In: 2017 International Conference on Computer and Applications (ICCA), pp. 306–311. IEEE (September 2017)
18. Satyanandam, N., Satyanarayana, C.: Heart disease detection using predictive optimization techniques. IJ Image Graph. Signal Process. **9**, 18–24 (2019)
19. Bhardwaj, J., Nagrath, P.: Anticipation of heart disease using machine learning algorithms optimised by feature optimisation. J. Multi Discipl. Eng. Technol. **13**(2), 103–106 (2020)
20. Thilagamani, S.: A survey on efficient heart disease prediction technique. Turk. J. Comput. Math. Educ. (TURCOMAT) **12**(9), 130–136 (2021)
21. Dulhare, U.N.: Prediction system for heart disease using Naive Bayes and particle swarm optimization. Biomed. Res. **29**(12), 2646–2649 (2018)
22. He, W., Xie, Y., Lu, H., Wang, M., Chen, H.: Predicting coronary atherosclerotic heart disease: an extreme learning machine with improved salp swarm algorithm. Symmetry **12**(10), 1651 (2020)
23. Patro, S.P., Padhy, N., Chiranjevi, D.: Ambient assisted living predictive model for cardiovascular disease prediction using supervised learning. Evol. Intel. **14**(2), 941–969 (2020). https://doi.org/10.1007/s12065-020-00484-8
24. Fang, X., Hodge, B.M., Du, E., Zhang, N., Li, F.: Modelling wind power spatial-temporal correlation in multi-interval optimal power flow: a sparse correlation matrix approach. Appl. Energy **230**, 531–539 (2018)
25. Patro, S.P., Nayak, G.S., Padhy, N.: Heart disease prediction by using novel optimization algorithm: a supervised learning prospective. Inform. Med. Unlocked **26**, 100696 (2021)

Decentralized Energy Management in Smart Cities Using Blockchain Technology

Preeti Chandrakar[1(✉)], Narendra K Dewangan[1], and Karan Chandrakar[2]

[1] National Institute of Technology Raipur, Raipur, CG 492010, India
pchandrakar.cs@nitrr.ac.in

[2] Indian Institute of Technology Delhi, New Delhi, India

Abstract. As electricity is a high demand technology in any society and city, the technology of distribution and billing must evolve within a certain time.There are lots of limitations present in current techniques, like we can't access live information of previous unit usage, users' privacy is also not maintained here, and one more important thing is that there is no transparency in the payment system. To solve such types of problems, we present a blockchain-based model for usage in smart cities. This will not only maintain transparency but will also maintain the anonymity of users. This paper determines how we can implement blockchain technology in smart cities to facilitate the development of smart cities and delivers a smart city ecosystem based model which depends on smart metres using blockchain technology, which will also build a smart contract between citizens and administrations. This paper will show how the reading of electric metres can be stored in the blockchain and how we can protect the privacy of users using blockchain technology. At the end, citizens will make payments without revealing their privacy. At the end of this paper, we will also conclude how we can do energy management using the data stored in the blockchain.

Keywords: Blockchain technology · Energy management · Smart city · Electricity bill payment

1 Introduction

In the 22nd century, we can get an overview of the population living in cities as compared to towns and can guess that in the upcoming 2050, around 68% of the world population will live in smart cities and the remaining 32% will live in towns. And cities will also continue to expand. So, we need to think about digitalization for smart cities so that people can use the resources with no issues and proper feasibility. The importance of long-term development is growing. reliant on effective administration primarily focused on developing countries where urbanisation and digitalization are currently upgrading In this report, we will mainly focus on electricity usage in smart cities.

S. K. Panda et al. (Eds.): CoCoLe 2022, CCIS 1729, pp. 103–114, 2022.
https://doi.org/10.1007/978-3-031-21750-0_9

Currently, electricity monitoring causes a person to record the metre value from house customers, who must then receive and pay a bill without knowing the exact amount of energy consumed by the house owner. The metre figure may not be precise since it was entered by a person, and humans make mistakes all the time. The severe difficulty arises when the personnel must return to the residence and re-enter the metre value in order to rectify it. It's also tough to keep track of a customer's metre value and estimate power usage for vast residential regions. The customer cannot keep track of his or her power use hourly or prepare for it. Without a centralised server, it is also impossible to regulate the price of the customer's used in the meter.

1.1 Bockchain Technology

A blockchain is a decentralised record-keeping platform or open database that keeps a record of all transactions or impacts the operations that are carried out and shared among participants. Every transaction is examined in the public ledger by the consensus of most participants. Once entered, it can not be altered. It is required to define several basic ideas in order to comprehend blockchain technology:

1. **Nodes:** The simplest elements of the blockchain are nodes. Nodes are connected to each other and make a chain. All nodes satisfy the consensus algorithm used in blockchain.
2. **Transactions:** As we all know, the blockchain is immutable, which means we can't make any changes to the blockchain. To make the changes, we need to perform a new transaction which will create a new node and will be added to the blockchain.
3. **Block:**A block is a representation of how a blockchain stores data. A block mainly consists of a self-hash and a previous hash. Along with it, it contains Nonce and Merkle hash. A Merkle hash is basically used to verify the nodes present in a blockchain.
4. **Account:**A blockchain account has two components. The whole system mainly contains two types of keys: one is a private key and the other is a public key. The person who has the private key owns the account. Unlike other centralised solutions, there is no mechanism to claim an account if you somehow lost your private key. Then there is no "I forgot the password" option.

The ledger includes a definite and verifiable record of every transaction that has ever been made. The distributed ledger design combined with blockchain technology protection makes it a much more promising platform for solving current problems. The main pillars of blockchain are:

1. **Immutability:** Any "new entry" added to the ledger has to refer to the previous kind of the hardware wallet. It maintains an irreversible chain, which prevents the credibility of previous entries from being tampered with.

2. **Transparency:** Transparency in the blockchain refers to linked transactions that are openly available to all in the community in key cryptographic form. It will ensure that the user's privacy is protected.
3. **Verifiability:** The database is decentralised and replicated across all locations. This guarantees high consistency (by removing one single failure point) and provides the availability of third-party verifiability as each of all nodes retains the ledger's consensus version.
4. **Decentralization and Distributed Consensus:** Decentralization is the process of blockchain-based verification, maintenance, storage, and transmission of data based on a distributed system structure. Trust between distributed nodes is established in this framework through cryptographic techniques rather than through centralised organizations.

1.2 Motivation

Where anybody who is using electricity, simply pays bills for which they are using. But we can do a lot of things in intermediate which motivates us for this idea. Below are a few points listed.

1. Analyze the usage for every user and show them in which segment they ar usin at ah high rate or low rate.
2. This will help to maintain the balance between users as well as providers.
3. Maintain the anonymity of users as in current time this concept is not in the working model.
4. Provide the transparency of usage and bill payment for the user satisfaction as well as authority also.

We will use the concept of blockchain in our project which is discussed below.

1.3 Scope

The major focus of this project is to provide different feasible facilities to users that allow users to use in an optimal way. The main purpose is to try to build functional as well as non-functional things so that we can fulfil the requirements of users. The online usage system based on Blockchain Technology is simple to grasp. This project is for the creation of an online usage system using Blockchain technology. There will be a website for the providing authority and any user can see the usage data on a regular basis. The user interface will be designed as part of the project, which will contain necessary details at both ends.

1.4 Objectives of the Paper

1. To use Blockchain technology to improve the present usage system.
2. To decrease the time and effort required to go to distribution stations or pay bills in a physical way.
3. Because the bill payment system is entirely online, anybody can access it from anywhere and see their live usage.

4. To reduce usage or wastage by storing the data and analysing it through the latest models so that we can provide appropriate services in specific fields.
5. Maintain the anonymity for users.

1.5 The Significance of Paper

The paper proposes a blockchain-based electric bill payment system in the smart city. By applying this system, the consumer can monitor their electricity usage, pay their bills, and generate incentives using ethereum. The blockchain maintains transparency, immutability, and decentralised data storage. so users can compare the electricity usage of other users with their generated bills. Once the bill is generated, no one can alter it. Since the bill is automatically generated according to the reading of the metre, no one can alter it. Users' personal data is not going to be shared in the proposed system, so the personal identification of the users is secured in the proposed system.

2 Literature Survey

According to [10], the distribution system is interconnected with the data acquisition module, which is an IoT object, through a single IP address that results in a mesh wireless network of devices. They connected the system with the demand response (DR) and the EMS distribution center. Their proposed system is performed on the basis of MATLAB/Simulink. They had not implemented a distributed system using blockchain technology. In [13], a deep investigation of microgrid blockchain is provided with energy community. The concept of "clever towns" is an umbrella term for a utopian city advancement that incorporates data and verbal exchange technology to help citizens, govs, and for-profit and nonprofit organisations create and trade actual facts [7] and enhance the effectiveness of towns' operations in areas such as energy usage, logistics, public transit, and public services. Although there is no agreed definition of "clever town" at this time, there is widespread agreement that a smart city is a city development climate designed to address the challenges of rapid urbanisation through the use of data and verbal exchange technologies, as well as the application of next-generation improvements to all walks of life. In [14], a blockchain-based VPP(virtual power plant) energy management platform is developed to facilitate a rich set of transactive energy activities among residential users with renewables, energy storage, and flexible loads in a VPP. They designed their scheme to be independent and preserve user privacy. Their design includes a decentralised optimization algorithm to optimise the users' energy scheduling, energy trading, and network services. For blockchain implementations references we reviewed the [6] and [5].

3 Proposed Scheme

The scheme is specifically designed for smart cities. It may be applicable in rural areas depending on the availability of internet, smart meters, and the literacy rate of those with access. The proposed system is divided into two parts. The first part is the smart metre and the cloud server connection. In the second part, the cloud servers perform as the blockchain nodes and send transactions to the other servers as well as the authorities. Notations and abbreviations used in this paper are given in the Table 1. The overall proposed model is given in Fig. 1. The subsections divide the explanation of the overall proposed model. Flowchart of the proposed system is shown in Fig. 2.

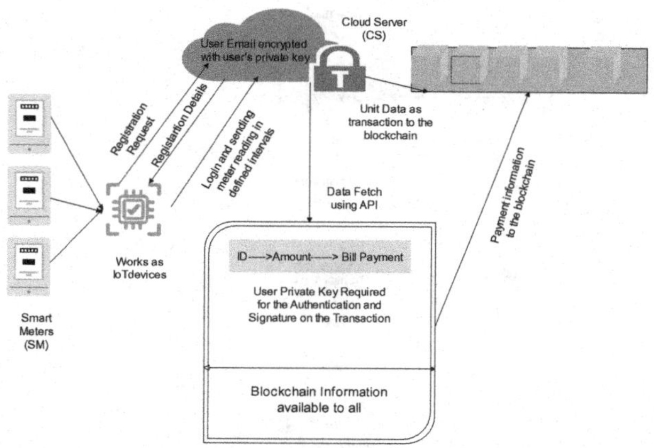

Fig. 1. Overall proposed system

3.1 Smart Meters and Cloud Server

In this part, the smart metres are basically working as IoT(Internet of Things) devices. These devices send metre readings (electricity consumption) every so often (let $\triangle T$). The smart metres choose the cloud server based on the server's availability at the time. Let meter SM_i wants to send reading, the registration phase is required at the first time data sending to any cloud server. Let meter ID is defined as SM_{idx}, want to register with the cloud server CS_j. At the registration phase, secure key exchange is done using the [4].

We have proposed the design of an online bill payment system integrated with Blockchain technology. The proposed system has the following advantages compared to the existing system:

1. Users can pay bills from anywhere in the world.
2. Authenticated by the unique Meter number provided by the Authority to each and every user.
3. Bill payments which are done by users are stored in blockchain technology, which ensures that payments are tamper-proof and we can't change them.
4. It will save a lot of time and decrease the load because there will be no lines for paying bills and all data is stored in the database.

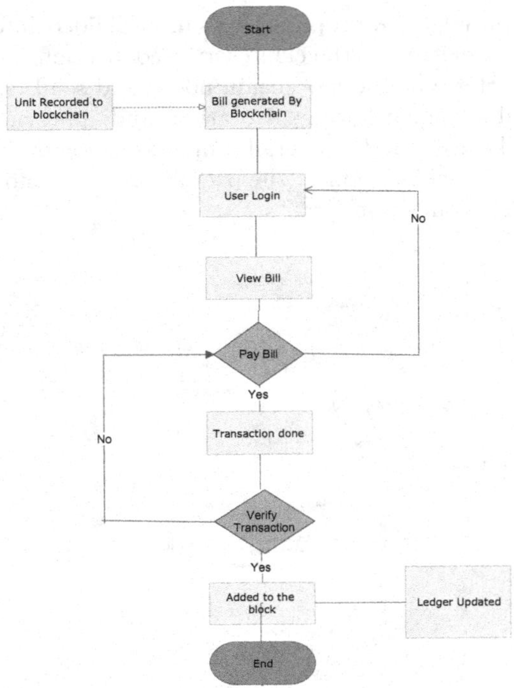

Fig. 2. Flowchart of proposed scheme

Table 1. Symbols and abbreviations used in this paper.

Symbol	Description	Abbreviation	Description
SM_i	Smart meter name as i	BPA	Bill Payment Authority
CS_j	Jth Cloud Server	ETH	Ethereum
EBC	Electricity Blockchain	API	Application Programming Interface
$Read_t$	Reading of unit at t timestamp	IDE	Integrated Development Environment
TX_t	Transaction by Cloud Server at t timestamp	JSON	JavaScript Object Notation

3.2 Cloud Server and Blockchain

In our proposed work, we used a proof-of-work consensus algorithm to create a blockchain. Smart metres are sending data to the cloud server at regular intervals. This data is stored in the blockchain as transactions between cloud servers (transactions from users to authorities). Allow the cloud server CS_j to send the transaction TX_i to the cloud server Cs_k via open channel at the timestamp of T_i. This transaction consists of the registration id of the device within the blockchain. Let universal registration ID of the smart meter is $URID$ and the meter sending the transaction is SM_x(unit of consumption) at time of the instant is n, then the transactions includes data as $[n, URID_x, Sign(n)_{Priv_x}]$, where $Sign(n)_{Priv_x}$ is signature on the data using the private key of the smart meter SM_x. At the time of bill payment, the metre ID works as a unique ID represented as the business partner number. The bill payment methods can be different depending on the selected method by the user.

4 Implementation

We used a python-based blockchain with Metamask as the wallet creator for system implementation. The system enables users to pay their bills from anywhere, and is authenticated by BPA and provided with the ETH wallet address and private key. Security and anonymity are the most crucial fundamentals of this blockchain bill payment system. Below are the list of dependencies which are used in our paper:

1. **Metamask Browser Extension:** It is basically a chrome extension that helps users communicate with blockchain, wallets, and specified keys by preventing them from accessing the different site contexts as well as other features.
2. **Pycryptodome:** A self-contained package built in Python of low-level cryptographic primitives. It mainly supports many Python versions, of which a few are listed here: Python 2.7, Python 3.5 and newer, and PyPy.
3. **NodeJS:** Extended version of Java script and It is a JavaScript runtime built on Chrome's V8 JavaScript engine.

System requirements are given in the Table 2.

Table 2. System requirement for the proposed scheme

Software	Type	Version
Metamask	Ethereum Wallet	10.4.1
Visual Studio Code	Integrated development Environment	1.62
Windows 10	OS	20H2
Django	Framework	3.2.9

4.1 Limitations of the Proposed System

This proposed system is designed for smart cities, where all facilities are available online and network issues, system handling issues, and other network-related issues are neglected. This proposed system is only appropriate for fully developed smart cities and cannot be used in rural areas. This system is also based on the blockchain, so blockchain literacy and using ability are required for the real-time implementation of the proposed system. This system is proposed in the form of ethereum. If any government wants to adopt another currency, then they have to convert the consensus algorithm and platform according to the currency they want to use.

5 Results and Comparisons

A blockchain is a distributed record-keeping system or a public ledger of all transactions or digital events executed and exchanged between interested parties. Every transaction is examined in the public ledger by the consensus of most participants. Once entered, it can never be wiped out. The ledger includes a definite and verifiable record of every transaction that has ever been made. The distributed ledger design combined with blockchain technology protection makes it a much more promising platform for solving current problems. The main pillars of blockchain are:

1. **Immutability.** Any "new entry" added to the ledger has to refer to the previous version of the ledger. It maintains an irreversible chain, which prevents the credibility of previous entries from being tampered with.
2. **Transparency.** Transparency in the blockchain refers to linked transactions that are openly available to all in the community in key cryptographic form. It will ensure that the user's privacy is protected.
3. **Verifiability.** The ledger is decentralized and replicated across multiple locations. This guarantees high consistency (by removing one single failure point) and provides third-party verifiability as all nodes retain the ledger's consensus version.
4. **Decentralization and Distributed Consensus.** Decentralization is the process of blockchain-based verification, maintenance, storage, and transmission of data, based on a distributed system structure. The trust between distributed nodes is established in this framework through cryptographic techniques rather than through centralized organizations.

5.1 Traditional Bill Payment Process:

The traditional bill payment process consists of manual work. The main phases of the bill payment process are discussed below: [3]

1. a. Registration of users: In the traditional bill payment process for registration, users have to come along with their id cards and have to wait in long queues for their turn to be verified according to their age by the Officers and get a manual slip with the information of their electricity usage.
2. Authentication of Users: On bill payment, users must again wait in the long queues for their turn and they must authenticate themselves by showing their id card and registration slip to presiding officers. After validating the users, the presiding officer hands over some registers for the billing system and information regarding the bill.
3. Bill Casting Process : After authentication, the officer gives them a token or unique number after bill amount submitted to the authority and they have to show this token to the authority for the verification.

Graph between number of users and time taken in mining of data in blockchain process is shown in Fig. 3.

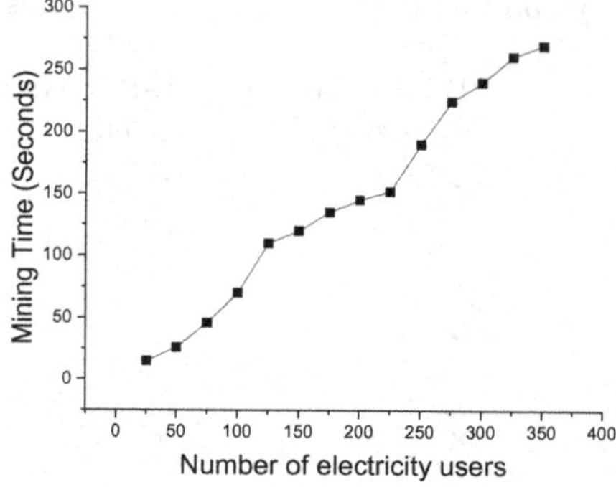

Fig. 3. Number of users vs time taken in mining process

5.2 E-Bill Payment System [3,11]

The electronic bill payment system comes to the rescue from the problems occurring during the traditional bill payment process because, through a communication network, a majority of registered users cast their bill or opinion from provided bill casting devices to provide better solutions. Generally, if we look at the electronic bill payment systems, they comprise three modules on which all the above bill payment phases rely: the first one is for the authorities; the second is the system administrator; and the last one is for the presiding officers. These modules and their roles are discussed below in the main phases of the bill payment process.

1. **Registration of Users and Parties.** Firstly, if any user wants to use the facility of electricity, then he/she must submit an online application from the authority portal. After filling out the application, he must take a print out of that form and submit it to the office for further steps regarding the setup of electric metres at his home.
2. **Authentication of Users.** On the day of bill payment, the officer will be responsible for verifying users based on provided credentials by the system administrator in a registration phase to let them cast bills smoothly within a group.
3. **Bill Verification.** Verification After bill payment, a confirmation message or email is received to the user with all the info regarding the unit usage. After this, the authority verifies the bill and validates whether it is correct or not, and after that, supply starts for the upcoming new interval to users.

Comparison with Existing Systems: The table 3 shows the comparison between the tradistional system and proposed system. It save the time, maintain transparency and fast computation as compared to the traditional system.

Table 3. Symbols and abbreviations used in this paper.

Features	Traditional bill System [11]	E-Bill System [3,11]	Proposed Scheme
Time Consuming	✓	×	×
Fewer Efforts	×	✓	✓
More Efficient	×	✓	✓
Process Overhead	✓	×	×
Bill Tempering	✓	✓	×
Trustworthy System	×	✓	✓
Secure System	×	×	✓
Trust on Third Party	✓	×	×
Privacy Preservation	×	×	✓
Bill Transparency	×	×	✓
Immutability and Verifiability	×	×	✓
Accurate Bill Info	×	✓	✓

5.3 System Security Analysis:

Security is all about managing risks, it's crucial to first know the risks connected with blockchain applications [9]. The risks associated with a blockchain - based system vary depending on the kind of blockchain. Let's take a look at the different types of blockchains, starting with the least risky and working our way up to the most secure:

1. Anyone can join and authenticate on blockchain systems because they are open to the public. They are often more dangerous (for example, cryptocurrencies). It involves the risk of anybody being able to participate in the blockchain without even any control or constraints.
2. Blockchain networks have no limits on processing and are typically confined to corporate networks; registration is governed by a single company (regulator) or consortium.
3. Permissioned blockchain technologies encode the database so that it could only be seen by relevant participants and decrypted by those who satisfy that need for condition.

6 Conclusion and Future Works

6.1 Conclusion

In order to maintain transparency and trust in the various services provided by smart cities, we must adopt new technologies that are constantly evolving. In this paper, we have proposed energy management using blockchain technology in smart cities, in which we have mainly focused on electrical energy. So, based on our implementation and analysis, by adding blockchain technology to existing systems, we have provided transparency in bill payment of electricity usage. Furthermore, we could use AI-based models to analyse electricity usage and predict how many units a user can use in the near future at a specific interval or time. Also, in our paper, we have tried to maintain the anonymity of the user, which means basically not storing any personal data on blockchain. Cities have to turn out to be smart to handle the demanding situations properly. Blockchain has many different capacity programmes in numerous areas, which include metropolis control. A Smart City is predicated on additives that permit statistics collection and storage, supported with the aid of specialised hardware infrastructure.

6.2 Future Scope

Bill payment systems have existed for many years, and although there are differing opinions on their reliability, they have always been regarded as secure because they adhere to several systematic and secrecy criteria different electronic methods have been suggested and implemented. To be efficient, an online bill payment system requires a more reliable and secure method than present systems provide. Along with this, in the future, we will analyse usage by AI-based models and predict, in a specific interval or time, how much energy any user can use in the upcoming future.

References

1. A-khateeb, B.: Regulatory standards and measures: panacea for blockchain technology acceptability, pp. 54–72 (2020). https://doi.org/10.4018/978-1-7998-7110-1.ch003
2. Abdelmaboud, A., et al.: Blockchain for IoT applications: taxonomy, platforms, recent advances, challenges and future research directions. Electronics **11**(4), 630 (2022). https://doi.org/10.3390/electronics11040630. https://www.mdpi.com/2079-9292/11/4/630
3. Casino, F., Dasaklis, T.K., Patsakis, C.: A systematic literature review of blockchain-based applications: Current status, classification and open issues. Telematics Inform. **36**, 55–81 (2019). https://doi.org/10.1016/j.tele.2018.11.006. https://www.sciencedirect.com/science/article/pii/S0736585318306324
4. Chandrakar, P., Sinha, S., Ali, R.: Cloud-based authenticated protocol for healthcare monitoring system. J. Ambient. Intell. Humaniz. Comput. **11**(8), 3431–3447 (2019). https://doi.org/10.1007/s12652-019-01537-2
5. Dewangan, N.K., Chandrakar, P.: Peer-to-peer trade registration process with blockchain in small and medium enterprises (SMEs) in e-governance. In: 2021 4th International Conference on Security and Privacy (ISEA-ISAP), pp. 1–7 (2021). https://doi.org/10.1109/ISEA-ISAP54304.2021.9689760

6. Dewangan, N.K., Chandrakar, P.: Patient feedback based physician selection in blockchain healthcare using deep learning. In: Woungang, I., Dhurandher, S.K., Pattanaik, K.K., Verma, A., Verma, P. (eds.) Advanced Network Technologies and Intelligent Computing. ANTIC 2021. Communications in Computer and Information Science, vol. 1534, pp. 215–228. Springer, Cham (2022). https://doi.org/10.1007/978-3-030-96040-7_17
7. Esposito, C., Ficco, M., Gupta, B.B.: Blockchain-based authentication and authorization for smart city applications. Inf. Process. Manage. **58**(2), 102468 (2021). https://doi.org/10.1016/j.ipm.2020.102468. https://www.sciencedirect.com/science/article/pii/S0306457320309584
8. Huseien, G.F., Shah, K.W.: A review on 5G technology for smart energy management and smart buildings in Singapore. Energy AI **7**, 100116 (2022). https://doi.org/10.1016/j.egyai.2021.100116. https://www.sciencedirect.com/science/article/pii/S2666546821000653
9. Khanna, A., et al.: Blockchain: future of e-governance in smart cities. Sustainability **13**(21), 11840 (2021). https://doi.org/10.3390/su132111840. https://www.mdpi.com/2071-1050/13/21/11840
10. Krishnan, P.R., Jacob, J.: An IoT based efficient energy management in smart grid using dhocsa technique. Sustain. Cities Soc. **79**, 103727 (2022). https://doi.org/10.1016/j.scs.2022.103727. https://www.sciencedirect.com/science/article/pii/S2210670722000580
11. Shi, Q.s., Hao, Y.X., Ren, H.B., Huang, X.H.: Blockchain-based distributed electricity transaction model. Int. J. Energy Res. **46**(8), 11278–11290 (2022). https://doi.org/10.1002/er.7927. https://onlinelibrary.wiley.com/doi/abs/10.1002/er.7927
12. Treiblmaier, H., Rejeb, A., Strebinger, A.: Blockchain as a driver for smart city development: application fields and a comprehensive research agenda. Smart Cities **3**(3), 853–872 (2020). https://doi.org/10.3390/smartcities3030044. https://www.mdpi.com/2624-6511/3/3/44
13. Wu, Y., Wu, Y., Cimen, H., Vasquez, J.C., Guerrero, J.M.: Towards collective energy community: Potential roles of microgrid and blockchain to go beyond p2p energy trading. Appl. Energy **314**, 119003 (2022). https://doi.org/10.1016/j.apenergy.2022.119003. https://www.sciencedirect.com/science/article/pii/S0306261922004123
14. Yang, Q., Wang, H., Wang, T., Zhang, S., Wu, X., Wang, H.: Blockchain-based decentralized energy management platform for residential distributed energy resources in a virtual power plant. Appl. Energy **294**, 117026 (2021)

Design and FPGA Realization of an Energy Efficient Artificial Neural Modular Exponentiation Architecture

C. Pakkiraiah(✉) and R. V. S. Satyanarayana

S.V.University, Tirupati, India
pakkiraiahrssvu19@gmail.com

Abstract. Modular arithmetic computations are used widely in various data security and reliability techniques. Information security systems certainly benefit from the design of energy-efficient modular exponentiation architectures. The use of low-power logic adders to realize modular exponentiation operations is very essential in prospective cryptography contexts. In this paper, various full adder circuit designs are presented which are used in developing an energy efficient modular exponentiation architecture. Here, the full adder is designed using Register Transfer Level (RTL), Standard Logic Cell (SLC), Reversible Logic Gate (RLG), and Artificial Neural Network (ANN) logic methods. All full adder designs are imposed on modular exponentiation circuit to analyze performance metrics in terms of dynamic power dissipation, Figure of Merit, and Energy Delay Product. The Modular Exponentiation architecture is designed based on the above full adders and is simulated and synthesized using Xilinx Vivado Zynq-7000 family configurable device. From the synthesis results, the dynamic power dissipation, Figure of Merit (FOM), and Energy Delay Product (EDP) of the ANN Modular Exponentiation circuit shows an improvement compared to other designs. The total power consumption, dynamic power dissipation, FOM, and EDP of ANN Full Adder and Modular Exponentiation circuit can achieve (8%, 16%), (23.5%, 20.7%), (14.7%, 14%), and (28.5%, 16%) compared to RLG Full adder and Modular Exponentiation circuit.

Keywords: Feynman gate · MLPerceptron · Switching activity · PDP · Modular multiplier · Toffoli gate

1 Introduction

It has been well understood that creating circuitry involves a power-delay tradeoffs. A fast, area efficient modular exponentiation architecture is developed in [1] using look-up table techniques. The industry's expanding use of information communication and technology has heightened the potential of intellectual data theft. Various cryptographic techniques have been developed and verified for overall protection effectiveness in order to obtain trustworthy security. In [2],

S. K. Panda et al. (Eds.): CoCoLe 2022, CCIS 1729, pp. 115–126, 2022.
https://doi.org/10.1007/978-3-031-21750-0_10

the pipelined architecture is designed to implement modular multiplier based on reconfigurable logic proposed. An efficient modular multiplication for large digits is of specific importance since it serves as the foundation for a faster modular exponentiation that is utilized in a variety of cryptosystems. A right shift methodology is introduced in [3] to design array multiplier. Encryption, identification, data security, and non-repudiation are all protection standards in a reliable broadband network, which becomes particularly crucial for electronic transactions and internet privacy. In [4], a parallel modular multiplier design is developed to minimize the complexity of operations.The algorithm's primary function is modular exponentiation, which is accomplished through successive modular multiplications. A modular multiplier with a large throughput architecture is proposed in [5] for RSA crypto systems. Encryption schemes are a major element for establishing data security. Encryption algorithms are frequently implemented in hardware for optimization and practical security implications. The modular exponentiation architecture is proposed in [6] to improve its speed of operation using FPGA devices. The encryption and decryption schemes are used in error correction programming and authentication. Modular multiplications and exponentiation are two basic arithmetic techniques over Galois field. As a result, it's critical to provide rapid exponentiation algorithms that are simple to implement and have low hardware complexity. FPGA based modular exponentiation algorithms are described in [7]. The Internet is being used to process payments, exchange emails, and transfer commodity markets, among many other activities, related to frequent developments in digital technology. In [8], an arithmetic residue multiplier is proposed using the residue number system concept. Modular multiplication structures with less delay and low power have also been investigated, regardless of the intended computer chips. In [9], an innovative approach is described to design modular exponentiation architecture. Using lo power full adders to execute the adding phases of a modular algorithm is one approach to accomplish this. Modularity exponentiation calculation is a widely utilized operation in cryptographic algorithms, including the RSA protocol and the DH key exchange technique. The majorities of modular exponentiation computation techniques are discussed and have demonstrated that such a performance is dependent on repeated modular multiplication calculations. The rest of this paper is organized as follows: Sect. 2 contains a brief discussion on various designs of low power full adders. These full adder designs are imposed on the modular exponentiation circuit and will be discussed in Sect. 3. In Sect. 4, the simulation and synthesis results are presented, followed by conclusion and references.

2 Designs of Various Full Adders

In this section, the design of full adder using various methods such as RTL, SLC, RLG, and ANN methods is discussed.

2.1 RTL Full Adder

The full adder circuit is the primary element to perform additions of three single bit inputs and redirects to two outputs, which are sum and output carry bit. Here, the full adder is designed using standard RTL adder operator. The full adder requires two RTL adders; each RTL adder performs addition between two inputs and produce single output. The output of the first RTL adder is fed to the input of second RTL adder which redirects two outputs such as sum and output carry bit. The schematic of full adder using RTL adders is shown in the Fig. 1.

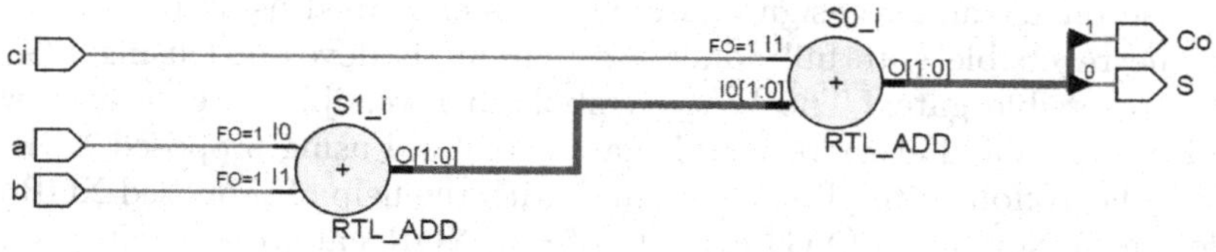

Fig. 1. Schematic of RTL full adder

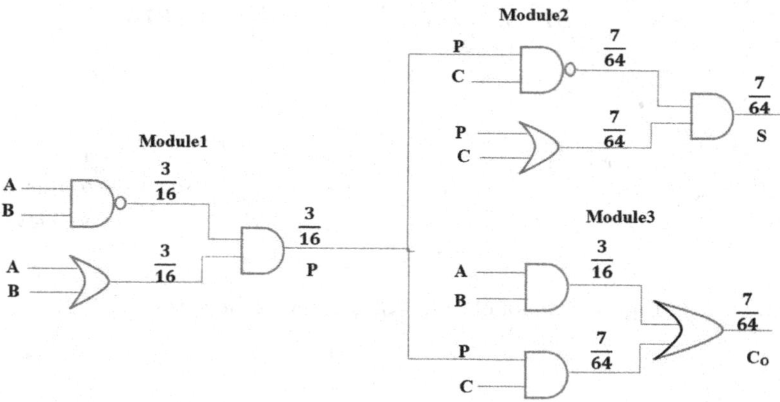

Fig. 2. Logic diagram of PFA [1]

2.2 SLC Full Adder

In [10], the logic minimization technique is used to reduce the gate count of crypto primitives.The minimization of power consumption of binary circuits using a rule-based method is presented in [11]. The SLC full adder(also known as PFA [12]) circuit is developed by applying a logic decomposition method on the conventional full adder circuit which reduces the SA value and gate count of the conventional full adder circuit. The logic diagram of PFA is shown in the Fig. 2 and illustrating each and every gate SA value. The calculation of the total SA value (**1.2968**) of PFA is given as

$$SA = \sum_{i=1}^{9} SA_{gate-i} = 4 * \frac{3}{16} + 5 * \frac{7}{64} = \mathbf{1.2968} \tag{1}$$

2.3 RLG Full Adder

In [13], the binary adder design and analysis is explained using reversible logic gates. The reversible gate full adder logic circuit is developed using FG, TG, and NG reversible gates. The basic symbols of reversible gates are shown in Fig. 3. Here, each and every reversible gate is realized using proposed XOR gate method. The Toffoli Gate (TG) is designed with the help of proposed XOR gate. The design of New Gate (NG) consists of one NOR gate, one NOT gate, one AND gate and two XOR gates. Here, XOR gates are realized using proposed XOR method. The block diagram of reversible full adder is shown in Fig. 4. The first stage of the reversible full adder is having NG and the second stage with TG followed by FG gate.

$$SA = \sum_{i=1}^{9} SA_{gate-i} = 2 * \frac{3}{16} + 12 * \frac{7}{64} = \mathbf{1.6875} \tag{2}$$

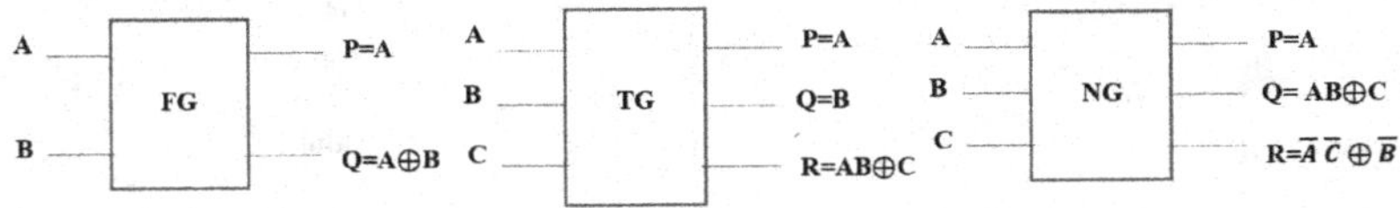

Fig. 3. Symbol of FG, TG, NG reversible gates

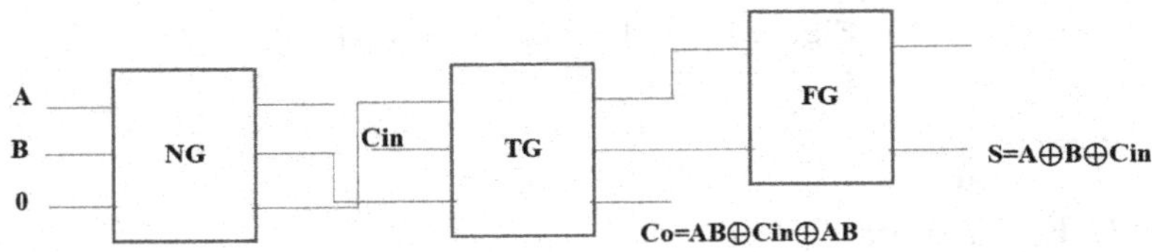

Fig. 4. Block diagram of RLG FA

2.4 ANN Full Adder

An innovative approach is described to design a full adder circuit using a multi-layer concept is proposed in [14]. The design of binary adder using multi-layer perceptron method is broadly described in [15]. In this section, the PFA circuit is designed based on the ANN [16] method. Here, first XOR gate is designed using multi-layer concept and applied same on full adder circuit. The mathematical model of the full adder circuit using an artificial neural network is shown in the Fig. 5.

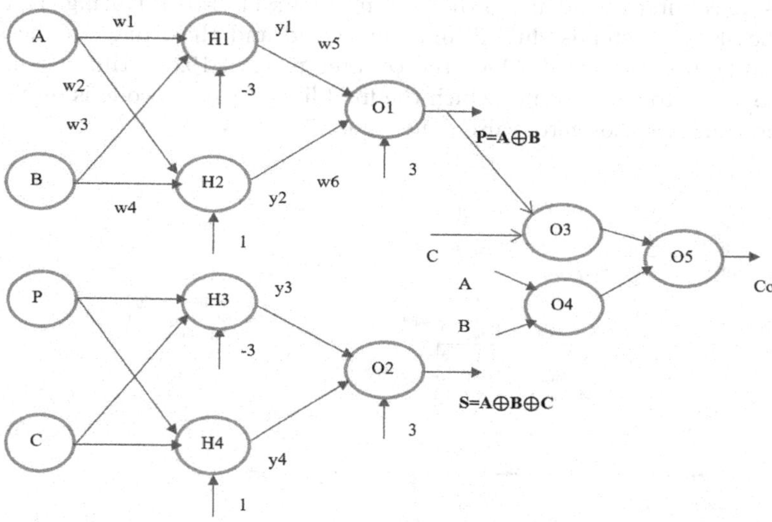

Fig. 5. ANN structure of FA

3 Design of Modular Exponentiation (ME) Architecture

In this section, the design of modular exponentiation architecture and analysis of average switching activity is discussed.

3.1 Introduction

In [17], the design of a modular multiplier based on a scalable radix algorithm is described. The high-speed modular multiplier using a parallel algorithm is proposed in [18]. In [19], a high radix algorithm with a systolic array is used to design Montgomery modular exponentiation on FPGA. Fast and area efficient modular adder architectures are proposed in [20]. In [21], a novel RSA algorithm is described to develop cryptosystems architectures. In [22], high speed realizations of the RSA cryptographic algorithm use PAM's configurability. The modular exponentiation circuit design is realized [23] on a reconfigurable device. The data path architecture of Modular Exponentiation is shown in the Fig. 6. It consists of multiplexers, k-bit registers, k-bit shift registers and modular multiplication units. The important block which is used to perform modular exponentiation is modular multiplication [24]. The data path architecture to perform Modular Multiplication (MM) has several modules, such as two k-bit full adders, k-bit AND logic unit, multiplexers, two (k+1)-bit registers and one shift register. Initially, the modular multiplier was in the default state, the raise start signal followed by the load signal to load x value into the shift register and clear parallel registers. A counter counts up to the bit length of x (192-bit). During each clock cycle, the shift register is shifted and the second and third lines in the above pseudo code are performed. Once the counter reaches 192, a timer is used to make the count to zero, during which the final line of pseudo code is performed. After the timer reaches zero, raise done signal.

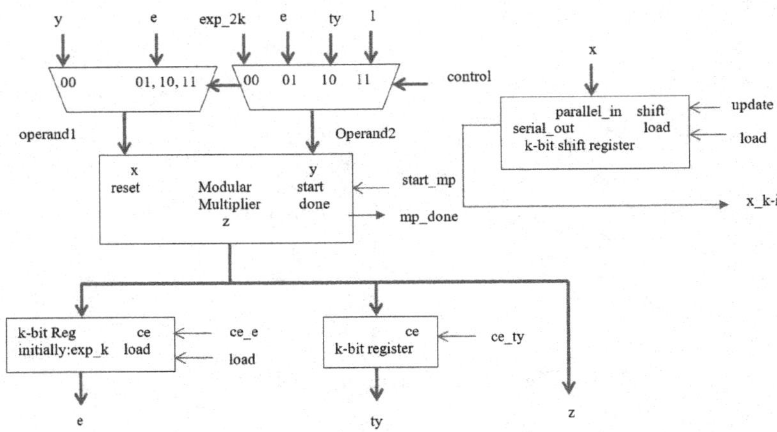

Fig. 6. Data path diagram of ME

3.2 Estimation of Average Switching Activity of ME Circuit Designs

RTL ME. The modular exponentiation circuit design consists of two k-bit full adders and one k-bit AND logic circuit. The generalized expression to estimate Average Switching Activity (ASA) for k-bit RTL ME is given as

$$ASA_{k-bitRTLME} = \sum_{i=1}^{k} \frac{140 * 2^{2\times i} + 312 * 2^{i} - 110}{2^{(i+3)\times 2}} \tag{3}$$

SLC ME. The modular exponentiation circuit design based on SLC FA is known as SLC ME. The SA value of 1-bit SLC ME circuit is calculated as

$$TSA = \frac{3}{16} + 3 * \frac{3}{16} + 3 * \frac{7}{64}] + 3 * \frac{7}{64}] + 3 * \frac{15}{256}] \tag{4}$$

The estimation of Average Switching Activity (ASA) for k-bit SLC ME is as follows:

$$ASA_{k-bitSLCME} = \frac{3}{16} + 3 * \frac{3}{16} + 6 * \frac{7}{64}] + 3 * \frac{15}{256}] + ... \tag{5}$$

$$= \sum_{i=1}^{k} [\frac{3}{16} + 3 * \frac{2^{(i+1)-1}}{2^{(i+1)\times 2}} + 6 * \frac{2^{(i+2)-1}}{2^{(i+2)\times 2}} + 3 * \frac{2^{(i+3)-1}}{2^{(i+3)\times 2}}] \tag{6}$$

The generalized expression to estimate average switching activity for k-bit SLC ME is as follows:

$$ASA_{k-bitSLCME} = \sum_{i=1}^{k} \frac{12 * 2^{2\times i} + 312 * 2^{i} - 110}{2^{(i+3)\times 2}} \tag{7}$$

RLG ME. The modular exponentiation circuit design based on RLG FA is known as RLG ME. The generalized expression to estimate average switching activity for k-bit RLG ME is as follows:

$$ASA_{k-bitRLGME} = \sum_{i=1}^{k} \frac{12 * 2^{2\times i} + 384 * 2^{i} - 112}{2^{(i+3)\times 2}} \tag{8}$$

ANN ME. The modular exponentiation circuit design based on Multi-layer full adder is referred as MME. The generalized expression to estimate average switching activity for k-bit ANN ME is as follows:

$$ASA_{k-bitANNME} = \sum_{i=1}^{k} \frac{12 * 2^{2\times i} + 312 * 2^{i} - 110}{2^{(i+3)\times 2}} \tag{9}$$

Table 1. ASA values of various ME designs

Type of ME	2-bit	4-bit	8-bit	16-bit	$\geq$ 32-bit
RTL	3.2988	2.4854	2.2065	2.18757	2.1875
SLC	1.2988	0.4854	0.2065	0.18757	0.1875
RLG	1.6660	0.5787	0.2123	0.18759	0.1875
ANN	**1.2988**	**0.4854**	**0.2065**	**0.18757**	**0.1875**

Based upon Eqs. 3, 7, 8, and 9, the comparison among ME circuit designs are listed in Table 1 for 2-bit, 4-bit, 8-bit, 16-bit, and above 32-bit. From Table 1, we can observe that the ME design using ANN logic has lowest average switching activity value below 16-bit architecture. Here, the ANN ME circuit consumes less dynamic power even though ME circuit with above 32-bit designs has SA value of 0.1875.

4 Simulation and Performance Results

Here, the simulation results of modular exponentiation architecture followed by synthesis and performance metric evaluation is discussed.

4.1 Simulation Results

The functional behavior of modular exponentiation architecture is verified by using Xilinx Vivado behavioral simulation tool. Here, we are considering inputs
x = 6543210fedcba9876543210fedcba9876543210fedcba987
y = fedcba9876543210fedcba9876543210fedcba9876543210
and m = 2^{192}-2^{16}-1. The modular exponentiation architecture produces an output z=64fbfd16a5607df42ce316e8254f3f81b8ebc19fcd19904d, done = 1. This procedure will be applicable to all possible input vectors The Fig. 7 shows input and output relation when done = 1.

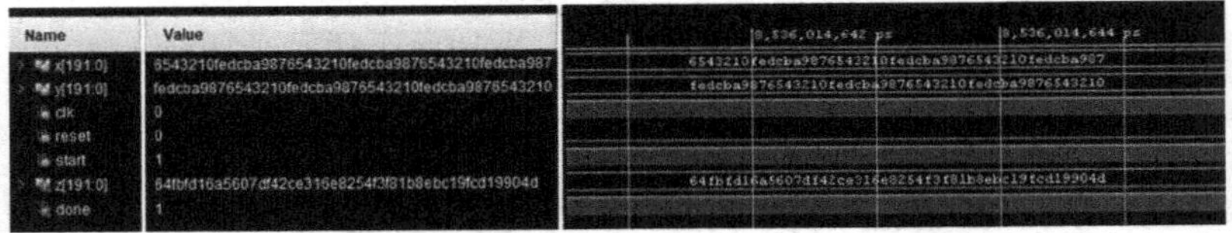

Fig. 7. Simulation results of ME when done = 1

4.2 Synthesis Results

Furthermore, the modular exponentiation architecture is synthesized using Xilinx Vivado synthesis tool and implemented on Zynq-7000 family configurable devices. The implementation results of full adder and modular exponentiation circuit designs using RTL, SLC, RLG, and ANN methods are shown in Figs. 8 and 9. The RTL full adder circuit consumes 0.264 W of dynamic power dissipation with a delay of 6.969 ns.The full adder circuit using RLG method consumes 68 mW of dynamic power dissipation with a delay of 7.203 ns. The full adder circuit design based on ANN dissipates 52 mw of dynamic power followed by a delay of 6.919 ns. The RTL modular exponentiation circuit consumes 2.131 W of

Table 2. Performance metrics of various FA designs

Type of FA design	P_{avg} (W)	$P_{dynamic}$ (W)	Delay (ns)	FOM (nJ)	PDP (nJ)	EDP (*10^{-18} J)
RTL	0.193	0.264	6.969	1.34	1.84	12.8
SLC [12]	0.105	0.090	7.106	0.75	0.64	4.5
RLG	0.094	0.068	7.123	0.68	0.49	3.5
ANN	**0.086**	**0.052**	**6.919**	**0.059**	**0.036**	**2.5**

dynamic power dissipation with a delay of 16.803 ns. The modular exponentiation circuit using SLC method consumes 0.357 W of dynamic power dissipation with a delay of 17.276 ns. The modular exponentiation circuit design based on RLG dissipates 0.439 W of dynamic power followed by a delay of 16.429 ns. The modular exponentiation circuit design based on ANN dissipates 0.348 W of dynamic power followed by a delay of 16.882 ns.

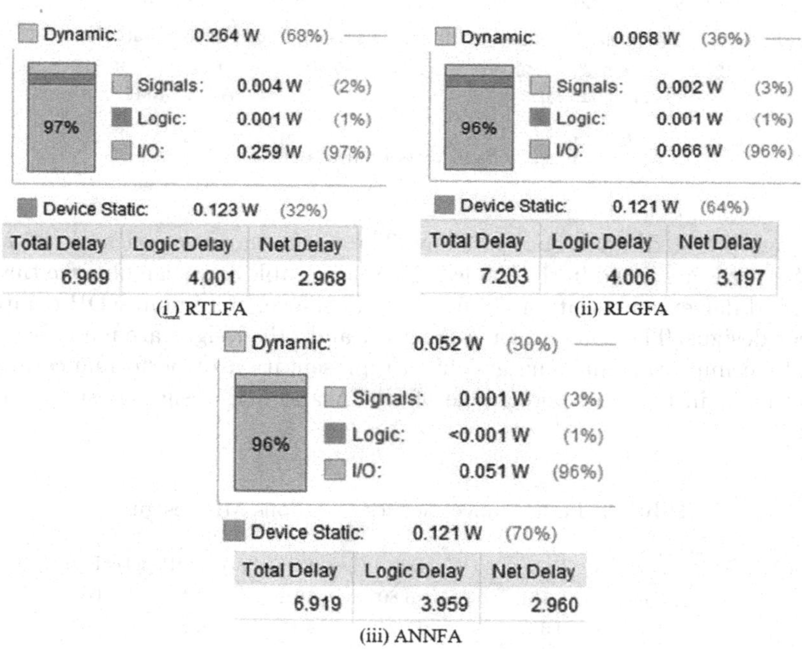

Fig. 8. Synthesis results of FA

4.3 Performance Metrics Evaluation

In order to justify the better performance metrics of all modular exponentiation circuit designs. Here, we are considering three performance metrics, such as FOM, PDP, and EDP. The FOM of a digital circuit is defined as a product

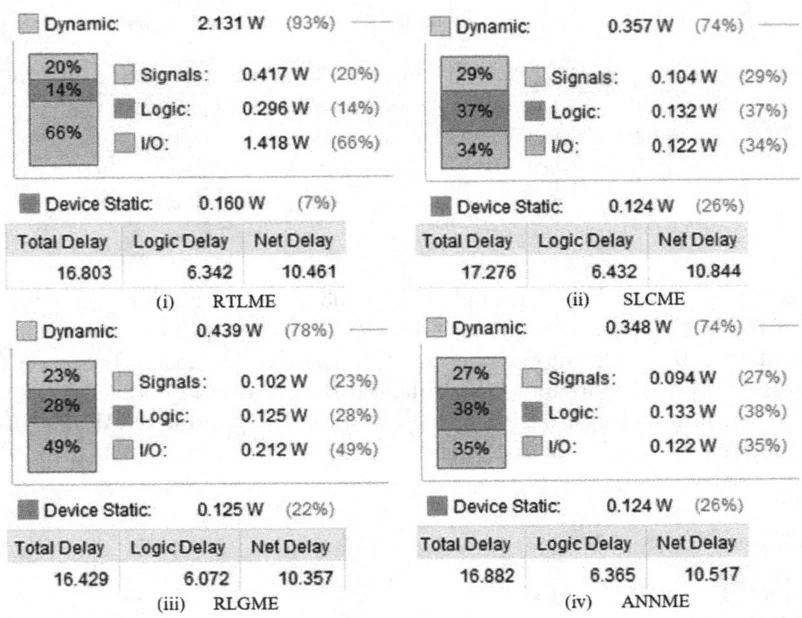

Fig. 9. Synthesis results of ME

of average power dissipation and delay. The performance metrics of full adder circuit designs are listed in the Table 2. From the Table 3, we can observe that the ANN modular exponentiation circuit design achieves minimum EDP compared to other designs. The comparison among FA and ME designs are made based on percentage improvement. The graphical representation of performance metrics improvement in terms of percentage of all FA and ME designs is shown in the Fig. 10.

Table 3. Performance metrics of various ME designs

Type of ME design	P_{avg} (W)	$P_{dynamic}$ (W)	Delay (ns)	FOM (nJ)	PDP (nJ)	EDP (*10^{-18} J)
RTL	1.145	2.131	16.803	19.2	35.8	601
SLC	0.241	0.357	17.276	4.16	6.16	106
RLG	0.282	0.439	16.429	4.63	7.21	118
ANN	**0.236**	**0.348**	**16.882**	**3.98**	**5.87**	**99**

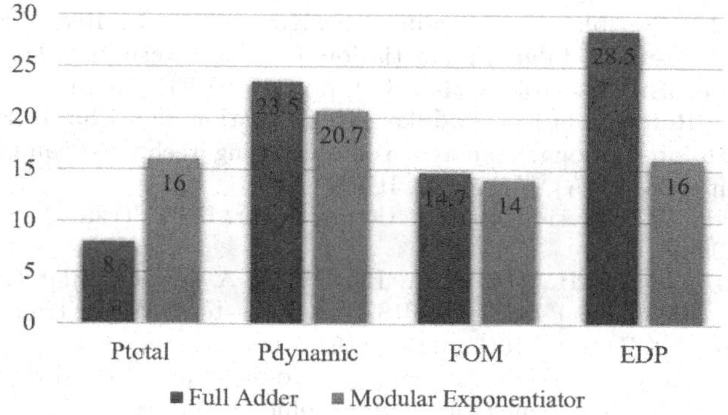

Fig. 10. Improvement in performance metrics of FA amd ME

Conclusion

In future cryptography applications, the employment of low-power logic adders to realize modular exponentiation operations is critical. Various full adder circuit designs are discussed in this work, which can be used to construct energy-efficient modular exponentiation architecture. The full adder is designed using various approaches such as RTL, SLC, RLG, and ANN logic methods. To assess the performance metrics in terms of dynamic power dissipation, Figure of Merit, and Energy Delay Product, all full adder designs are imposed on a modular exponentiation circuit. When compared to RLG full adder and Modular Exponentiation circuit designs, the ANN full adder and Modular Exponentiation circuits attained approximately (28.5% and 16%) in EDP. Thus, the ANN based modular exponentiation circuit is energy efficient and it can be suitable for quantum computing, data security, Artificial Intelligence, Machine Learning, and cryptography applications.

References

1. Reddy, V., Singh, S., Desalphine, V., Selvakumar, D.: A low latency montgomery modular exponentiation. Procedia Comput. Sci. **171**, 800–809 (2020)
2. Daly, A., Marnane, W.: Efficient architectures for implementing montgomery modular multiplication and RSA modular exponentiation on reconfigurable logic. In: Proceedings of the 2002 ACM/SIGDA Tenth International Symposium on Field-Programmable Gate Arrays, pp. 40–49 (2002)
3. Kornerup, P.: A systolic, linear-array multiplier for a class of right-shift algorithms. IEEE Trans. Comput. **43**(8), 892–898 (1994)
4. Hasan, M.A., Wang, M., Bhargava, V.K.: Modular construction of low complexity parallel multipliers for a class of finite fields GF(2^m). IEEE Trans. Comput. **41**(8), 962–971 (1992)
5. Xiao, H., Yu, S., Cheng, B., Liu, G.: FPGA-based high-throughput montgomery modular multipliers for RSA cryptosystems. IEICE Electron. Express **19**, 20220101 (2022)

6. Venkatesh, K., Pratibha, K., Annadurai, S., Kuppusamy, L.: Reconfigurable architecture to speed-up modular exponentiation. In: 2019 International Carnahan Conference on Security Technology (ICCST), pp. 1–6. IEEE (2019)
7. Li, S., et al.: Research in fast modular exponentiation algorithm based on FPGA. In: 2019 11th International Conference on Measuring Technology and Mechatronics Automation (ICMTMA), pp. 79–82. IEEE (2019)
8. Taylor, F.J.: A VLSI residue arithmetic multiplier. IEEE Trans. Comput. **31**(06), 540–546 (1982)
9. Shieh, M.D., Chen, J.H., Wu, H.H., Lin, W.C.: A new modular exponentiation architecture for efficient design of RSA cryptosystem. IEEE Trans. Very Large Scale Integr. (VLSI) Syst. 16(9), 1151–1161 (2008)
10. Raghuraman, S., Nazhandali, L.: Does gate count matter? Hardware efficiency of logic-minimization techniques for cryptographic primitives
11. Das, S., Dasgupta, P., Fiser, P., Ghosh, S., Das, D. K.: A rule-based approach for minimizing power dissipation of digital circuits. In: 2016 IEEE 19th International Symposium on Design and Diagnostics of Electronic Circuits Systems (DDECS), pp. 1–6. IEEE (2016)
12. Pakkiraiah, C., Satyanarayana, D.R.: An innovative design of low power binary adder based on switching activity. Int. J. Comput. Digit. Syst. **11**(1), 861–871 (2022)
13. HOI, H.T.: Design and analysis of full adders using reversible logic (2021)
14. Sabbaghi, R., Dehbozorgi, L., Akbari-Hasanjani, R.: New full adders using multilayer perceptron network. Int. J. Smart Electr. Eng. **8**(03), 117–122 (2019)
15. Pakkiraiah, C., Satyanarayana, R.V.S.: Design of low power artificial hybrid adder using neural network classifiers to minimize energy delay product for arithmetic application. Int. J. Comput. Appl. **184**(12), 1–8 (2022)
16. Pakkiraiah, C., Satyanarayana, R.V.S.: Design of low power full adder using multilayer perceptron to minimize energy delay product of computational logic circuits. IUP J. Electr. Electron. Eng. **15**(2), 42–58 (2022)
17. Tenca, A.F., Todorov, G., Koç, Ç.K.: High-radix design of a scalable modular multiplier. In: Koç, Ç.K., Naccache, D., Paar, C. (eds.) CHES 2001. LNCS, vol. 2162, pp. 185–201. Springer, Heidelberg (2001). https://doi.org/10.1007/3-540-44709-1_17
18. Kawamura, S., Koike, M., Sano, F., Shimbo, A.: Cox-rower architecture for fast parallel montgomery multiplication. In: Preneel, B. (ed.) EUROCRYPT 2000. LNCS, vol. 1807, pp. 523–538. Springer, Heidelberg (2000). https://doi.org/10.1007/3-540-45539-6_37
19. Blum, T., Paar, C.: High-radix montgomery modular exponentiation on reconfigurable hardware. IEEE Trans. Comput. **50**(7), 759–764 (2001)
20. Hiasat, A.A.: High-speed and reduced-area modular adder structures for RNS. IEEE Trans. Comput. **51**(1), 84–89 (2002)
21. Yang, C.C., Chang, T.S., Jen, C.W.: A new RSA cryptosystem hardware design based on montgomery's algorithm. IEEE Trans. Circuits Syst. II: Analog Digit. Sign. Process. **45**(7), 908–913 (1998)
22. Shand, M., Vuillemin, J.: Fast implementations of RSA cryptography. In: Proceedings of IEEE 11th Symposium on Computer Arithmetic, pp. 252–259. IEEE (1993)
23. Nadjia, A., Mohamed, A.: FPGA Implementation of the M-ary Modular Exponentiation. In: 2013 8th IEEE Design and Test Symposium, pp. 1–2. IEEE (2013)
24. Pakkiraiah, C., Satyanarayana, R.V.S.: FPGA realization of low power multi-layer perceptron full adder to minimize EDP of modular multiplier. Int. J. Electron. Eng. Appl. **10**(2), 01-12 (2022)

Comparative Analysis of Power Management System for Microbial Fuel Cell

Soumi Ray[1], Shipra Pandey[2], Madhusmita Mohanty[3], and Subhransu Padhee[4(✉)]

[1] School of Mechanical Engineering, Vellore Institute of Technology, Vellore, India
soumi.ray@vit.ac.in
[2] Department of Electronics and Communication Engineering, Shri Ramswaroop Memorial College of Engineering and Management, Lucknow, India
[3] Odisha Power Transmission Corporation Limited, Bhubaneswar, India
[4] Department of Electrical and Electronics Engineering, Sambalpur University Institute of Information Technology, Burla, Odisha, India
subhransupadhee@gmail.com

Abstract. Microbial Fuel Cell (MFC) is one of the attractive solution to generate electricity from biodegradable organic matter. But there are different technical challenges such as high source impedance, lower specific power density of MFC and ultra low voltage of MFC which limits the usability of the fuel cell. Different energy harvesting schemes to extract energy from MFC are being investigated by the researchers over the past several years. This work provides a comparative analysis of three distinct power management schemes for MFC.

Keywords: Microbial fuel cell · Energy harvesting · Power management system

1 Introduction

The concept of fuel cell is quite old and dates back to 1838. The seminal work by Sir William Robert Grove introduced the concept of hydrogen fuel cell [1]. The actual growth of fuel cell was only in 1990 when fuel cell was actively used in three different segments such as

- Stationary: Power backup for communication and data centers
- Portable: Provides backup power during natural calamity [2] and military operations [3]
- Transportation: Used as power sources in AUV, space vehicle

With advancement of science and technology, there is an exponential growth in research and development of newer fuel cell. Microbial fuel cell (MFC) is a kind of fuel cell that transforms chemical energy in bio-degradable material to electricity using bacteria. The electrical equivalent circuit of MFC proposed by

S. K. Panda et al. (Eds.): CoCoLe 2022, CCIS 1729, pp. 127–133, 2022.
https://doi.org/10.1007/978-3-031-21750-0_11

[4] considers anodic electron flow and dynamic characteristics of output voltage and current. Various challenges of operation of MFC has been discussed in [5]. There are some limitations of equivalent electrical circuit of MFC such as higher input impedance, lower output voltage (0.2 V to 0.5 V), lower power (10 mW) and lower power density (1 mW m^{-2} to 2000 mW m^{-2}). Due to the lower output voltage and higher input impedance, the MFC can not drive a switch on its own. To increase the voltage of MFC, series and parallel configuration of MFC are considered but the main limitation of such connection is the voltage reversal [6].

To extract usable amount of electricity from MFC, power management system (PMS) is required. DC-DC converter is widely used in PMS of fuel cell. A comparative analysis of different DC-DC converter topologies used in hydrogen fuel cell has been discussed in [7,8]. A systematic review of different PMS architecture for MFC has been provided in [9,10]. Energy harvesting from MFC has found specific applications in powering up Internat of Things (IoT) devices [11,12] and powering up of wireless sensor networks [13,14]. Maximum power point transfer scheme for energy harvesting of PMS has been discussed in [15]. PMS comprises of tightly controlled switching power converter which provides desired output voltage and current. But it is observed that the tightly regulated switching converter acts as constant power load and has the capability to destabilize the overall system [16].

This work provides a comparative analysis of three distinct PMS for MFC. These PMS includes charge pump, super capacitor, DC-DC converter and transformer. This paper focuses on the design of PMS using different discrete components.

2 Electrical Equivalent Model of MFC

The modelling of MFC can be categorized in to two broad categories such as [17]

- Mechanism based model
- Application based model

The bioelectrochemical process modelling and validation of the mathematical model of MFC has been discussed in [18]. Ordinary differential equations and partial differential equations have been used for development of mathematical model for MFC.

Figure 1(a) provides the steady-state electrical model of MFC. Figure 1(b) illustrates the dynamic electrical model of MFC where an additional capacitor is connected. Figure 1(c) presents the electrical equivalent circuit of MFC proposed by [4].

To transfer maximum power from MFC (which is considered as a DC voltage V_{MFC} with internal resistance R_{MFC}) to the electrical load denoted as R_L, maximum power transfer concept is used. The power across the load is computed as

$$P_{load} = \left(\frac{V_{MFC}}{R_{MFC} + R_L}\right)^2 R_L \tag{1}$$

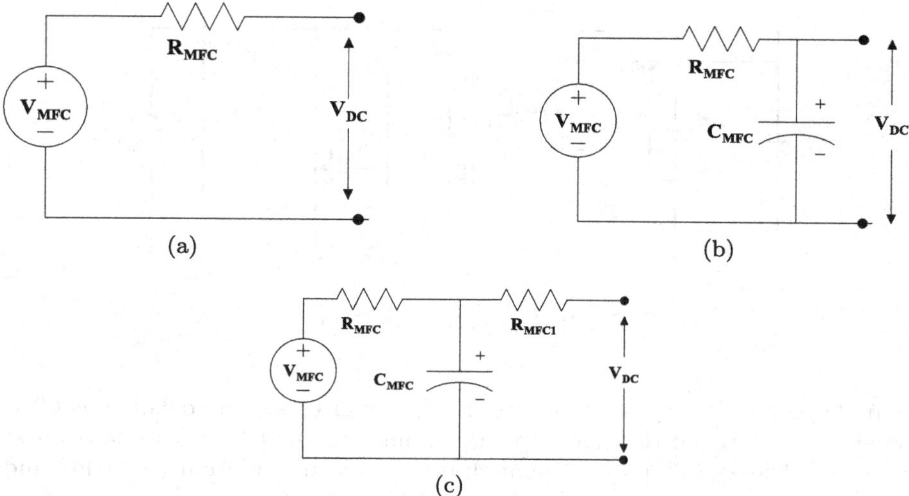

Fig. 1. Electrical equivalent circuit of MFC (a) Steady-state electrical model (b) Dynamic electrical model (c) Circuit proposed by [4]

In order to obtain the maximum power condition, the following condition is considered

$$\frac{dP_{load}}{dR_{MFC}} = 0 \tag{2}$$

The result of differentiation implies

$$\max\left(P_{load}\right) = \frac{V_{MFC}^2}{4R_{MFC}} \tag{3}$$

3 Analysis of PMS for MFC

In literature there are three different type of PMS discussed for MFC i.e.

- Type 1: Capacitor and converter
- Type 2: Charge-pump, capacitor and converter
- Type 3: Capacitor, transformer and converter

In Type 1 PMS, the super capacitor (acting as an energy storage device) is directly connected to the MFC and the MFC is connected to the DC-DC switching regulator. The main limitation of Type 1 PMS is that if the open circuit voltage of the MFC is lower than the required input voltage of converter, than the converter is not able to step up the voltage of MFC. Boost converter requires at least 500 mV to 800 mV to start up and the converter draws a substantially high amount of input current [19]. The output power of the Type 1 PMS is affected by the capacity of the capacitor.

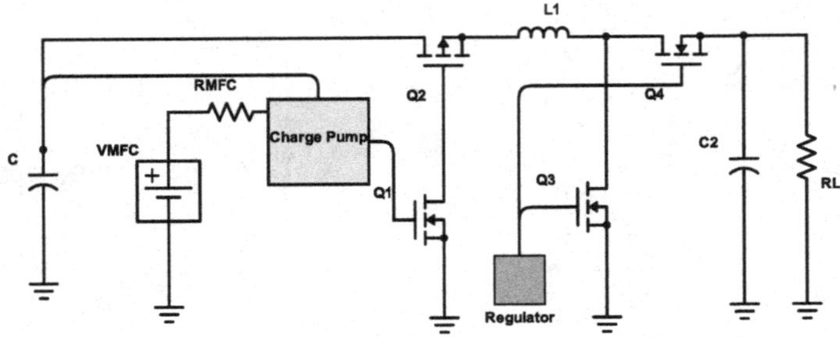

Fig. 2. Type-2 PMS for MFC

In Type 2 PMS (As shown in Fig. 2), the super capacitor (denoted as C) is connected in between the charge pump circuit and DC-DC synchronous boost converter. The charge pump circuit draws a low current from the MFC and uses the low current to charge C. The synchronous boost converter is connected to C via two switches Q_1 and Q_2. When the capacitor charging voltage V_c is lower than the discharging voltage V_d, the switches disconnect the C from the synchronous boost converter and as the super capacitor reaches the discharging voltage, the switch connects C to synchronous boost converter. The switching regulator provides requisite gate pulse to the switches of synchronous boost converter. Average power generated by Type 2 PMS is

$$P_{avg} = \frac{1}{2T_c} C \left(V_d^2 - V_c^2 \right) \tag{4}$$

T_c is the time taken by the super capacitor to charge from V_c to V_d

Comparison of different supercapacitor is provided in Table 1 [20].

Table 1. Comparison of different Supercapacitor

Product Name	Voltage	Rating
EATON-HV08102R7105-R	2.7 V	1 F , 0.2 Ω
EATON-TV10203R0605-R	2.7 V	3 F , 0.08 Ω

The Type 3 PMS is constructed using transformer based converter. In 1957, the concept of blocking oscillator was patented in USA [21]. Blocking oscillator is a very simple energy harvesting circuit which does not require any additional power supply. The blocking oscillator (modified version of Joule Thief Oscillator) shown in Fig. 3 comprises of two transistors (2N3904 and TIP 31), a torodial ferrite core, zener diode and Schottky diode (1N5819). The limitation of the modified version of Joule thief oscillator is that the output voltage is dependent on temperature due to Q_2.

Table 2. Description of different discrete components

Component	Part Number	Specification
Charge Pump	S-882Z	$V_{in} = 0.3\,\text{V}$ to $3\,\text{V}$, $I_{Operation} = 0.6$ μA to 0.5 mA
Charge Pump	S-8880A20	$P_{in(StartUp)} = 26\ \mu\text{W}$, $V_{in} = 0.35\,\text{V}$, $I_{Operation} = 74\ \mu\text{A}$
DC-DC synchronous boost converter	L6920DB	$V_{in} = 0.8\,\text{V}$, $V_o = 1.8\,\text{V}$ to $5\,\text{V}$
DC-DC boost converter	LTC3108	$V_{in} = 20$ mV, $V_o = 2.35\,\text{V}$ to $5\,\text{V}$
DC-DC boost converter	BQ25505	$V_{in} = 0.1\,\text{V}$ to $5.1\,\text{V}$, $V_o = 5.5\,\text{V}$

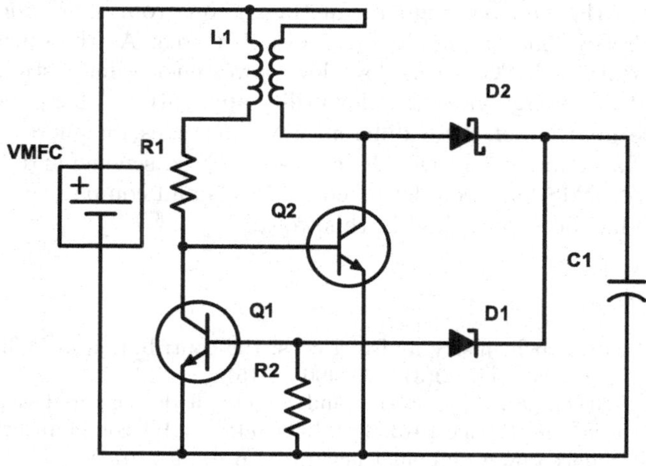

Fig. 3. Type-3 PMS for MFC

Table 2 provides the description of some of the discrete components used in different type of PMS and Table 3 provides the comparative analysis of different discrete implementation of PMS for MFC for Type 2 PMS (i.e. charge pump and boost converter).

Table 3. Comparison of different discrete PMS for MFC using charge Pump and Boost Converter Topology

Parameters	[22]	[23]	[24]	[25]	[26]
Minimum Input Voltage	0.3 V	0.3 V	0.18 V to 0.3 V	0.3 V	0.3 V
Output Voltage	5 V	3.3 V	3.3 V	3.3 V	3.3 V
MPPT	No	No	No	Yes	Yes
Output Power	2.5 W	95 mW	95 mW	N.A	108.9 mW
Super Capacitor	10 F	2.2 F	250 mF	50.94 mF	235 mF

4 Conclusion

MFC is one of the emerging technology where electricity is generated from biodegradable material and bacteria. Extracting power from MFC and design of appropriate PMS is one of the emerging research area. As the output voltage and power density of MFC is very low, low power energy harvesting scheme is required to extract energy and use it for utility application. This paper provides a comparative analysis of three different PMS schemes for energy harvesting from MFC. Charge pump and DC-DC converter based scheme and transformer based scheme of PMS has been discussed in details and comparative analysis of different work has been presented in this work.

References

1. Wisniak, J.: Electrochemistry and fuel cells: the contribution of William Robert Grove. Indian J. Hist. Sci. **50**(3), 476–490 (2015)
2. Spink, S., Saathoff, S.: Superstorm sandy: fuel cell design for disaster recovery vs. backup power. In: Intelec 2013; 35th International Telecommunications Energy Conference, Smart Power and efficiency, pp. 1–6. VDE (2013)
3. Patil, A.S., et al.: Portable fuel cell systems for Americas army: technology transition to the field. J. Power Sources **136**(2), 220–225 (2004)
4. Park, J.-D., Roane, T.M., Ren, Z.J., Alaraj, M.: Dynamic modeling of a microbial fuel cell considering anodic electron flow and electrical charge storage. Appl. Energy **193**, 507–514 (2017)
5. Kim, B.H., Chang, I.S., Gadd, G.M.: Challenges in microbial fuel cell development and operation. Appl. Microbiol. Biotechnol. **76**(3), 485–494 (2007)
6. Koffi, N., Okabe, S.: High voltage generation from wastewater by microbial fuel cells equipped with a newly designed low voltage booster multiplier (LVBM). Sci. Rep. **10**(1), 1–9 (2020)
7. Padhee, S., Pati, U.C., Mahapatra, K.: Comparative analysis of DC-DC converter topologies for fuel cell based application. In: 2016 IEEE 1st International Conference on Power Electronics, Intelligent Control and Energy Systems (ICPEICES), pp. 1–6. IEEE (2016)
8. Padhee, S., Pati, U.C., Mahapatra, K.: Investigation on transient response of fuel cell power conditioning unit during rapid load changes. In: 2015 IEEE International Conference on Computational Intelligence & Communication Technology, pp. 482–487. IEEE (2015)

9. Wang, H., Park, J.-D., Ren, Z.J.: Practical energy harvesting for microbial fuel cells: a review. Environ. Sci. Technol. **49**(6), 3267–3277 (2015)
10. Dutta, A., et al.: A review on power management systems: an electronic tool to enable microbial fuel cells for powering range of electronic appliances. J. Power Sources **517**, 230688 (2022)
11. Veerubhotla, R., Nag, S., Das, D.: Internet of things temperature sensor powered by bacterial fuel cells on paper. J. Power Sources **438**, 226947 (2019)
12. Osorio de la Rosa, E., et al.: Plant microbial fuel cells-based energy harvester system for self-powered IoT applications. Sensors **19**(6), 1378 (2019)
13. Osorío-de-la Rosa, E., et al.: Arrays of plant microbial fuel cells for implementing self-sustainable wireless sensor networks. IEEE Sensors J. **21**(2), 1965–1974 (2020)
14. Yamashita, T., Hayashi, T., Iwasaki, H., Awatsu, M., Yokoyama, H.: Ultra-low-power energy harvester for microbial fuel cells and its application to environmental sensing and long-range wireless data transmission. J. Power Sources **430**, 1–11 (2019)
15. Carreon-Bautista, S., Erbay, C., Han, A., Sánchez-Sinencio, E.: Power management system with integrated maximum power extraction algorithm for microbial fuel cells. IEEE Trans. Energy Convers. **30**(1), 262–272 (2014)
16. Singh, S., Gautam, A.R., Fulwani, D.: Constant power loads and their effects in DC distributed power systems: a review. Renew. Sustain. Energy Rev. **72**, 407–421 (2017)
17. Xia, C., Zhang, D., Pedrycz, W., Zhu, Y., Guo, Y.: Models for microbial fuel cells: a critical review. J. Power Sources **373**, 119–131 (2018)
18. Abul, A., Zhang, J., Steidl, R., Reguera, G., Tan, X.: Microbial fuel cells: control-oriented modeling and experimental validation. In: 2016 American Control Conference (ACC), pp. 412–417. IEEE (2016)
19. Kimball, J.W., Flowers, T.L., Chapman, P.L.: Low-input-voltage, low-power boost converter design issues. IEEE Power Electron. Lett. **2**(3), 96–99 (2004)
20. Poli, F., Seri, J., Santoro, C., Soavi, F.: Boosting microbial fuel cell performance by combining with an external supercapacitor: an electrochemical study. ChemElectroChem **7**(4), 893–903 (2020)
21. Garita-Meza, M.A., Ramírez-Balderas, L.A., Contreras-Bustos, R., Chávez-Ramírez, A.U., Cercado, B.: Blocking oscillator-based electronic circuit to harvest and boost the voltage produced by a compost-based microbial fuel cell stack. Sustain. Energy Technol. Assessments **29**, 164–170 (2018)
22. Donovan, C., Dewan, A., Peng, H., Heo, D., Beyenal, H.: Power management system for a 2.5 W remote sensor powered by a sediment microbial fuel cell. J. Power Sources **196**(3), 1171–1177 (2011)
23. Meehan, A., Gao, H., Lewandowski, Z.: Energy harvesting with microbial fuel cell and power management system. IEEE Trans. Power Electron. **26**(1), 176–181 (2010)
24. Zhang, D., Yang, F., Shimotori, T., Wang, K.-C., Huang, Y.: Performance evaluation of power management systems in microbial fuel cell-based energy harvesting applications for driving small electronic devices. J. Power Sources **217**, 65–71 (2012)
25. Umaz, R.: A two-stage power converter architecture with maximum power extraction for low-power energy sources. Turk. J. Electr. Eng. Comput. Sci. **27**(6), 4744–4755 (2019)
26. Umaz, R.: A power management system for microbial fuel cells with 53.02% peak end-to-end efficiency. IEEE Trans. Circuits Syst. II Express Briefs **67**(11), 2592–2596 (2019)

Communication

Localized Hop-Count Based Routing (LHR) Protocol for Underwater Acoustic Sensor Networks

Sahil Kumar(✉), B. R. Chandavarkar, and Pradeep Nazareth

Wireless Information Networking Group (WiNG),
Department of Computer Science and Engineering, National Institute of Technology Karnataka, Surathkal, Mangalore, India
sahilk4c@gmail.com

Abstract. Underwater Acoustic Sensor Networks (UASNs) is one of the emerging fields in the area of communication due to the number of applications. UASNs face several challenges like limited energy and bandwidth, high bit error rate, packet loss, node mobility, low propagation speed, and routing. Underwater routing is challenging due to the dynamic topology. Many routing protocols used in the UASNs use the hop-count of the neighbor as one of the attributes to select the next-hop. However, due to changes in underwater topology, hop count changes frequently. Obtaining up-to-date hop-count information is one of the major challenges. Many protocols send beacons periodically to update the hop-count, which creates overhead on the network. This paper proposes a Localized Hop-count based Routing (LHR) protocol, which uses a novel mechanism to determine hop-count. Hop-count in LHR is determined based on the local attributes of neighbors. LHR avoids periodic transmission of the beacons from the sink. Thereby, LHR reduces the overhead of transmitting beacons from the sink node periodically. Further, LHR makes use of metrics such as hop-count, depth, and distance for selecting the next-hop.

Keywords: Underwater acoustic sensor networks (UASNs) · Hop-count · UnetStack · Agent

1 Introduction

Water covers the majority of the earth's surface. It is one of the significant sources of various resources useful for human beings. Underwater communication is the core technology, which enables the exploring of underwater resources. In underwater communication, radio frequency (RF) cannot be used, as it consumes more energy to transmit signals for long range. Therefore, acoustic signals are used for underwater communication. Underwater networks that rely on acoustic waves for communication are known as Underwater Acoustic Sensor Networks (UASNs) [1]. UASN comprises of components like surface buoys, data centers, underwater sensors, seabed sensors, etc. [6].

S. K. Panda et al. (Eds.): CoCoLe 2022, CCIS 1729, pp. 137–149, 2022.
https://doi.org/10.1007/978-3-031-21750-0_12

UASNs are used in the fields like underwater monitoring, navigation assistance, military operation, oil spills, and natural calamities like tsunamis [8]. However, there are various issues in UASNs which make their utilization difficult. Routing in underwater acoustic sensor networks is challenging due to various issues which are discussed below [14].

- **Node Mobility:**
  In water, nodes are not stationary like terrestrial networks. The continuous movement of the sensor nodes is there due to the water currents. Different models are used to mimic the movement of nodes in the water and give different results for the same routing protocol.
- **High Energy Consumption:**
  The attenuation of the acoustic wave in an underwater environment is a serious problem. Also due to continuous movement, the link is easily broken. The bit error rate is also higher in the UASNs which results in re-transmissions of the data packets frequently. This leads to the wastage of a large amount of energy.
- **Low Bandwidth and Data Rate:**
  In underwater, power absorption of acoustic waves is a severe problem due to which only limited frequencies can be used for communication. A limited transmission rate is possible. This causes a serious problem for routing in UASNs as a large amount of information flow between nodes is required for route discovery.
- **High Noise and Interference:**
  Interference in underwater is also a major problem which is mainly caused by the reflection due to the surface and the refraction in underwater. Noise is also larger than in the terrestrial networks due to the boats, water currents, and aquatic life present in the water.
- **High Propagation Delay:**
  As RF waves are inoperable in water, acoustic waves are used which increases the transmission time. Other factors like salinity and temperature also affect propagation speed. Deciding on the propagation delay also becomes a challenge as it is highly dynamic in underwater communication.

Hop-count is defined as the number of hops a packet has to make to reach the sink node from the source node. Whenever a packet moves from one node to another node, it is considered as one hop.

There are many existing UASNs routing protocols such as Distance-Vector-based Opportunistic Routing (DVOR), and Location-free Link State Routing (LLSR) they select their next-hop based on hop-count of neighbors. The hop-count information is propagated from the sink and subsequently, other nodes further propagate the information. However, a change in network topology due to water current results in variation in the hop-count. Further, it requires periodic beacons from the sink node to maintain up-to-date hop-count, it requires more number of message transmissions in resource constraint UASNs. To overcome this limitation, this paper proposes a hop-count updation mechanism which eliminates the propagation of messages from the sink node. Based only on the neighbor node's local information, hop-count will be updated. Subsequently, proposes a hop-count based routing protocol referred to as the Localized Hop-count based Routing (LHR) protocol.

The remaining part of this paper is organized as follows: Sect. 2 discusses various hop-count based routing protocols present in the literature. Section 3 provides the design of the proposed Localized Hop-count based Routing (LHR) protocol. Section 4 covers the implementation of LHR protocol in the UnetStack. Section 5 presents the results obtained in the UnetStack simulator. Finally, Sect. 6 covers the conclusion and future work.

2 Related Work

This section elaborates on existing hop-count based UASNs protocol.

Ayaz et al. [2], introduced Hop-by-Hop Dynamic Addressing based routing protocol (H^2-DAB) protocol which has multi-sink architecture. The sink node broadcasts the Hello packets through which nodes can update their HopIDs which indicates how many hops are required to reach the sink node. H^2-DAB disadvantage is that the nodes which are closer to the sink node drain more energy and the void node issue is not addressed in the H^2-DAB [3]. The void node issue is addressed in Void Aware Pressure Routing (VAPR) protocol [17] is a depth-based routing protocol. Beaconing is carried out periodically through the sink node, to update their hop-count and other information like data forwarding direction. Using this information next-hop(s) are selected.

In [4], Location-free Link State Routing (LLSR) protocol is introduced which uses link-state metrics of neighbors to select the best next-hop. Periodic beaconing is done by the sink node so that nodes can update their path quality and hop-count information. The drawback of LLSR is it does not make use of Opportunistic routing. Further, link quality with its neighbor is not considered. This limitation of LLSR is overcome by Channel-Aware Routing Protocol (CARP) [5] protocol. CARP uses hop-count and link quality for next-hop selection. In CARP, the sink broadcasts HELLO packets periodically through which nodes will update their hop-count. In CARP hop-count is considered based on link quality with its neighbor nodes.

Distance-Vector-based Opportunistic Routing (DVOR) [11] protocol is a distance vector-based protocol. The sink node periodically propagates hop-count information through beacons. The beacons are further propagated by nodes that receive the beacon by updating the hop-count. Data forwarding is solely based on the hop-count. A node having data to forward, broadcasts the data packets and only those nodes having a lower hop-count than that of the sender will further forward the packet in a coordinated way. However, DVOR results in duplicate packet transmissions and hidden node problem [15]. Ghoreyshi et al. proposed the Inherently Void-Avoidance Routing (IVAR) protocol [9]. Hop-count and depth information is used in IVAR to determine the data forwarding set. Sink node broadcast beacon periodically after every fixed interval. Further, the receiver of the beacon updates their hop-count and rebroadcasts the beacon.

The sender/forwarder node broadcasts the data packet and only nodes which are having lower hop-count than that of the sender will participate in further packet forwarding in the coordination mechanism. However, IVAR results in duplicate packet transmissions and hidden node problem [13].

The issues of duplicate transmissions and hidden node problem of DVOR are overcome by the Opportunistic Void Avoidance Routing (OVAR) [10]. OVAR protocol is a depth-based routing protocol. The beacons are broadcasted periodically by the sink and subsequently, the receiver will update the hop-count and rebroadcast. All the nodes reachable to the sink update their hop-count. Further, using energy and reliability trade-off clusters of nodes, which are in the vicinity of each other are selected as next-hop(s). Depth based Underwater Opportunistic Routing (DUOR) protocol [16]. Sink broadcasts query packets periodically so that hop-count information can be propagated into the whole network. During data forwarding, the candidate nodes are selected using hop-count and depth information. DUOR has a high end-to-end delay and high energy consumption [12].

In all the above discussed protocols hop-count propagation is carried through the sink node periodically. Periodic beacons waste the energy of the nodes and increase the load on the network. The proposed LHR protocol updates the hop-count information based on neighboring node information and locally obtains the required information.

3 Design of Localized Hop-Count Based Routing (LHR) Protocol

This section presents the design of the proposed LHR protocol. The LHR protocol consists of the following two phases:

- **Phase-I: Initial network setup**
- **Phase-II: Localized hop-count updation and next-hop selection**

3.1 Phase-I: Initial Network Setup

This section elaborates the Phase-I of the proposed LHR protocol. Initially, all the nodes i (except the sink) are unreachable to the sink, and it is indicated by the large hop-count value (Say, 100). The hop-count value of the sink is initialized to 0 to indicate itself as a destination. The sink node triggers the network setup phase by broadcasting the beacon message. Beacon messages contain three fields, node address, hop-count, and depth. Upon receiving the beacon message, the node i compares the hop-count value of the received beacon with that of itself. In the case the hop-count in the beacon is less than that of the node i, it updates its hop-count by incrementing the received hop-count by 1. When node i updates its hop-count, it rebroadcasts the beacon with its updated hop-count. This way, all nodes i reachable to the sink are updated their hop-count.

3.2 Phase-II: Localized Hop-Count Updation and Next-Hop Selection

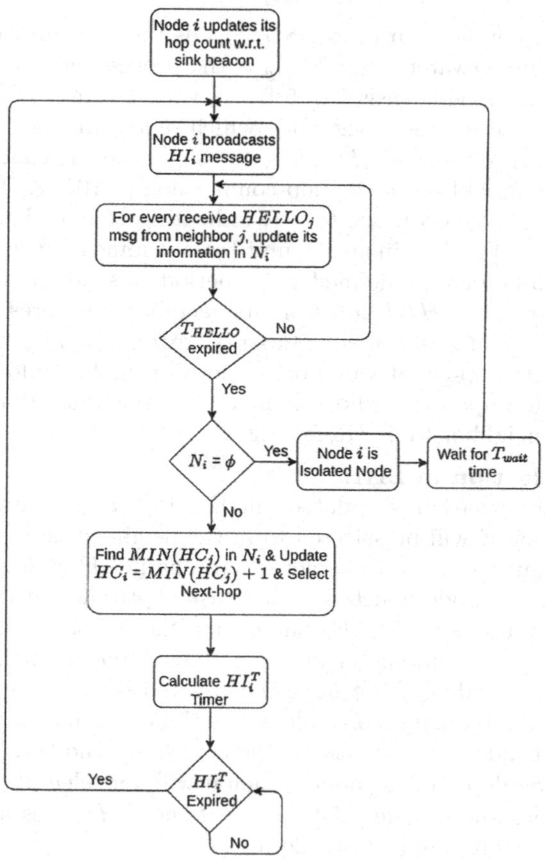

Fig. 1. Phase-II: localized hop-count updation and next-hop selection

This section elaborates the Phase-II of the LHR protocol. Phase II of the LHR is having following steps:

A. Hop-count updation in LHR
B. Next-hop selection in LHR

A. Hop-count updation in LHR
The flowchart for localized hop-count updation is shown in Fig. 1. This phase begins after the completion of Phase-I. Phase-II is triggered by every deployed node i by broadcasting a HI_i message. The HI_i message is a small message consisting of only the node address i. Additionally, node i will wait for T_{HELLO}

period for the $HELLO_j$ messages from those neighbors j which have received HI_i. The T_{HELLO} is computed as per Eq. (1).

$$T_{HELLO} = 2 \times \left(\frac{R}{S_{Medium}} + P_{Delay} \right) \tag{1}$$

where R is the communication range, S_{Medium} is the transmission speed of the acoustic signal in underwater, and P_{Delay} is the processing delay at the node.

The $HELLO_j$ message consists of 5 fields, node address j, hop-count, node depth, and x & y coordinates of the node which sends this message. In the case of a node i is not received any $HELLO_j$ message, then it concludes that it is an isolated node and will retain its hop-count value to 100. As the node i is an isolated node, the next-hop is set to -1, indicating that it does not have any node as its next-hop. Further, in an attempt to determine its neighbors again, the isolated node i waits for a predefined T_{wait} period to send the HI_i message. In the case of node i receives $HELLO_j$ from its neighbor j, i stores the information present in $HELLO_j$ into its neighbor table N_i. After T_{HELLO} timer is expired, node i computes its hop-count value based on its neighbor information present in its N_i. The node i updates its hop-count HC_i to one more than the minimum hop-count in the neighbor table (Refer Fig. 1).

B. Next-hop selection in LHR

Once hop-count information is updated, further node i determines its next-hop. One of the neighbors j will be selected from the neighbor table N_i, which has a minimum hop-count value. In case more than one neighbor has the same hop-count value, then the node which has the least depth among them is selected. If the depth of neighbors is also the same, then the neighbor node that is least distant from the node i among them is selected. After the neighbor selection, the depth of the selected neighbor node is compared with the depth of node i. If the depth of the selected neighbor node is less than or equal to the node i, then only the selected neighbor is assigned as the next-hop of node i. If no neighbor is present at the lower depth of the node i, then it will not select its next-hop. After determining the next-hop, node i determines its next HI_i message transmission time HI_i^T which is computed as per Eq. (2).

$$Hi_i^T = \frac{D_{ij}}{S_{node}} \tag{2}$$

where D_{ij} is the distance between node i & selected neighbor node j, and S_{node} is the average speed at which the node can move and is determined by the environment in which UASN is deployed.

4 Implementation of LHR in UnetStack

This section presents the implementation details of the proposed LHR protocol in the UnetStack simulator. This section mainly focuses on the implementation of various agents in UnetStack are elaborated. Section 4.1 describes various features of UnetStack. Further, Sect. 4.2 elaborates the implementation of additional agents

4.1 UnetStack

UnetStack architecture consists of agents that collaborate together and presents a complete underwater networking framework [7]. A UnetStack agent is a software component that is self-contained and performs a specific function. Agents use messages to communicate with one another which include requests, responses, and notifications. UnetSim is a UnetStack network simulator that empowers us to simulate an underwater network on a single computer system as a discrete event simulation or in real-time.

4.2 User-Defined Agents in LHR

This section elaborates various agents created in the implementation of the LHR protocol. Agents created in the implementation of the LHR protocol are listed below:

A. SinkBeacon agent
This agent is deployed on the sink node. Its organization is shown in Fig. 2. The role of this agent is to send the beacon message which initiates the network setup phase. The function *hcsend()* is responsible for sending the beacon message. Beacon message is sent as a *DatagramReq* by using the *PHY* agent with *USER* protocol.

B. BeaconPropagation agent
This agent is deployed on every node except the sink node. This agent helps with the propagation of beacon messages in the network and its organization is shown in Fig. 2. It listens for *DatagramNtf* messages using the *USER* protocol. Whenever a beacon message is received this agent checks the hop-count and updates hop-count accordingly. Then node rebroadcasts the beacon message with its address, depth, and updated hop-count. The rebroadcast of the message is done after some random delay (0–3 s).

C. PacketTransmit agent
This agent is deployed on the source node. Its function is to transmit the data packets and its organization is shown in Fig. 2. The function *packsend()* handles the data packet transmission and is called after 100 s. The data packet is transmitted after every 30 s by using the *TickerBehavior*. Data packets are sent using the *DATA* protocol by the *router* agent as *DatagramReq*.

D. SinkHello agent
This agent is deployed on the sink node. The structure of the agent is shown in Fig. 2. The main motive of this agent is to reply with a *HELLO* message upon receiving the *HI* message. The values of Address, Xcord, Ycord, and Depth field are obtained using the *node_info* agent. Upon receiving the *HI* message with protocol number 33 it replies with the *HELLO* message with protocol number

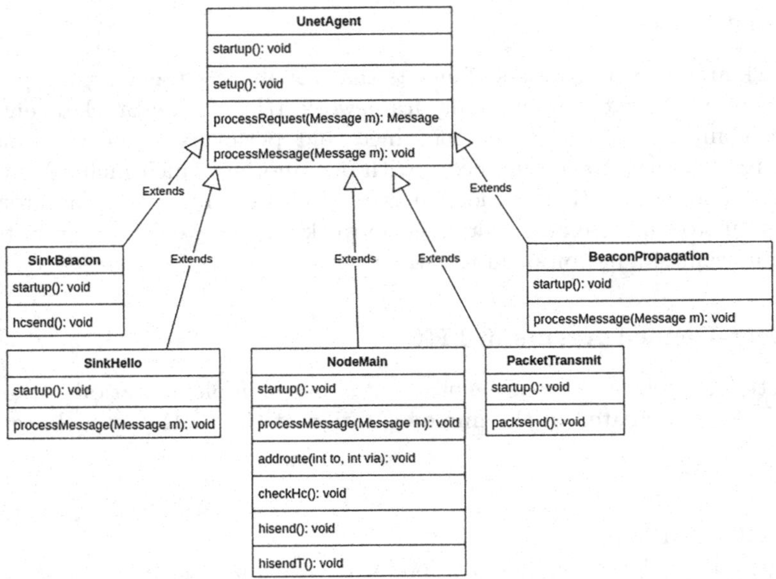

Fig. 2. Organization of agents created

34. $HELLO$ message is sent as a *DatagramReq* by the *PHY* agent after some random delay time (between 0–18 s). The message having protocol number 36 is replied to with the $HELLO$ message using protocol number 37 after some random delay of 0–15 s.

E. NodeMain agent

This agent is deployed on all the nodes except the sink node. This agent is the backbone of the system and carries out the majority of the work. The structure of this agent is shown in Fig. 2.

The function *addroute()* adds the route to the routing table by sending the *RouteDiscoveryNtf* to the *router* agent which updates the routing table.

HI messages transmission is done using 2 functions *hisend()* and *hisendT()*. The *hisend()* function works when a node sends the HI message for the first time. The message is sent with protocol number 33 by the *PHY* agent after some added delay (12–37 s). The function *hisendT()* handles the transmission of the HI message after the initial HI message and used protocol number 36.

The function *checkHc()* is used for calculating the hop-count, next-hop of a node and also HI_i^T timer. If the neighbor table is empty then the hop-count is set as 100 and the next-hop as −1. Then node waits for predefined T_{wait} time (60 s) before sending the HI message. Otherwise, the best neighbor is selected from the neighbor table. If the selected neighbor node's depth is less than or equal to the node's depth then the previous routing entry is deleted using the *EditRouteReq()* and a new route is added.

5 Results and Analysis

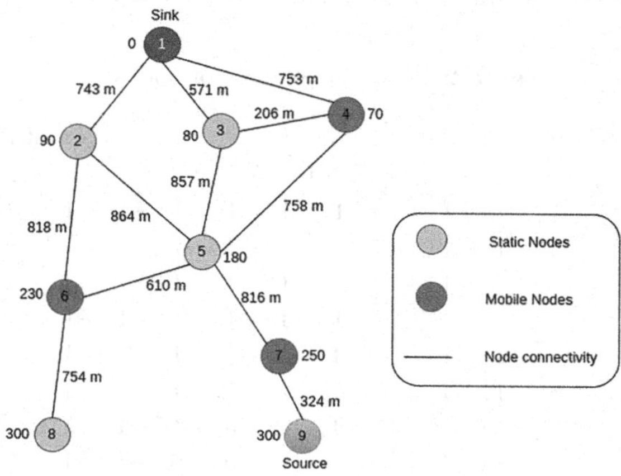

Fig. 3. Simulation topology

The network topology used for the simulation of LHR is shown in Fig. 3. Along with the node, the depth at which they are deployed is mentioned. The line between the nodes indicates that the corresponding nodes are neighbors. The distance between neighboring nodes is shown along the line. For example, nodes 1 and 2 are neighbors, and the distance between them is 743 m. Node 2 is deployed at the depth of 90 m.

Table 1. Node mobility model

Node ID	Mobility model
4	Time 0–300 s → Static
	Time 300–1800 s → Speed: 1 m/s, Angle: 0 w.r.t X-axis
	Time 1800–3300 s → Speed: 1 m/s, Angle: 180 w.r.t. X-axis
	Time 3300–3600 s → Static
6	Time 0–900 s → Static
	Time 900–2100 s → Speed: 1 m/s, Angle: 0 w.r.t X-axis
	Time 2100–3300 s → Speed: 1 m/s, Angle: 180 w.r.t. X-axis
	Time 3300–3600 s → Static
7	Time 0–900 s → Static
	Time 900–2100 s → Speed: 1 m/s, Angle: 180 w.r.t. X-axis
	Time 2100–3300 s → Speed: 1 m/s, Angle: 0 w.r.t X-axis
	Time 3300–3600 s → Static

The simulation period is set to 3600 s. The data packet transmission rate is set to 2 packets/min in the simulation. Packet transmission starts at 130 s. Mobility details of the mobile nodes in the network are provided in Table 1. Angle in mobility represents the direction in which the nodes are moving.

Table 2. Next-hop change of nodes

Time (secs)	Node ID								No. of hops
	2	3	4	5	6	7	8	9	
0	−1	−1	−1	−1	−1	−1	−1	−1	−1
0.844	−1	1	−1	−1	−1	−1	−1	−1	−1
0.959	1	1	−1	−1	−1	−1	−1	−1	−1
0.965	1	1	1	−1	−1	−1	−1	−1	−1
2.183	1	1	1	4	−1	−1	−1	−1	−1
2.632	1	1	1	4	2	−1	−1	−1	−1
3.671	1	1	1	4	2	5	−1	−1	−1
4.921	1	1	1	4	2	5	6	−1	−1
5.351	1	1	1	4	2	5	6	7	4
224.119	1	1	1	4	5	5	6	7	4
270.119	1	1	1	3	5	5	6	7	4
512.785	1	1	1	3	2	5	6	7	4
642.116	1	1	1	2	2	5	6	7	4
761.448	1	1	1	3	2	5	6	7	4
1116.114	1	1	1	3	5	5	6	7	4
1266.764	1	1	−1	3	5	5	6	7	4
1540.113	1	1	−1	3	3	5	6	7	4
1557.926	1	1	−1	3	3	5	7	7	4
1640.69	1	1	−1	3	3	5	7	−1	−1
1720.778	1	1	−1	3	5	5	7	−1	−1
1742.765	1	1	−1	3	5	6	7	−1	−1
1818.022	1	1	−1	3	5	6	7	6	4
1970.764	1	1	−1	3	5	5	7	6	4
2260.11	1	1	−1	3	3	5	7	6	3
2598.015	1	1	−1	3	3	5	7	7	4
2819.438	1	1	−1	3	5	5	7	7	4
2950.769	1	1	−1	2	5	5	7	7	4
3001.922	1	1	−1	2	5	5	6	7	4
3070.101	1	1	−1	3	5	5	6	7	4
3282.751	1	1	1	3	5	5	6	7	4

Table 2 represents the change in the next-hop of the nodes. It conveys the information of the next-hop of the nodes at particular time intervals. The number of hops required to reach the sink node from the source node is also presented in

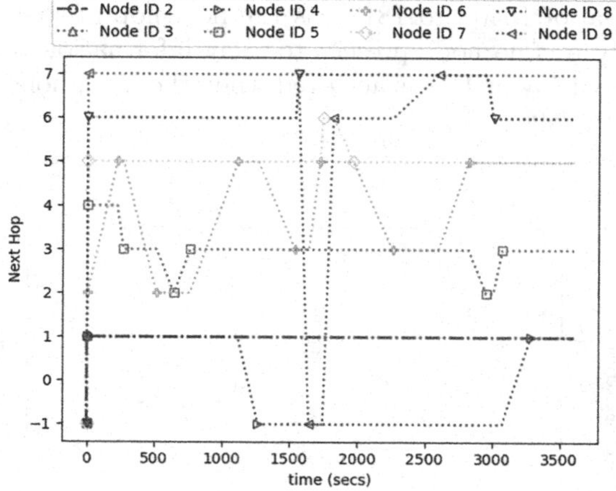

Fig. 4. Next-hop of nodes

the table. In the case a node does not have a next-hop, it is represented by the −1. Initially, all the nodes do not have any next-hop to reach the sink node thus at time 0 s all the nodes have their next-hop set as −1. If the number of hops is set as −1 it represents that currently there is no path present from the source node to the sink node. Change in the next-hop of nodes is shown in Fig. 4.

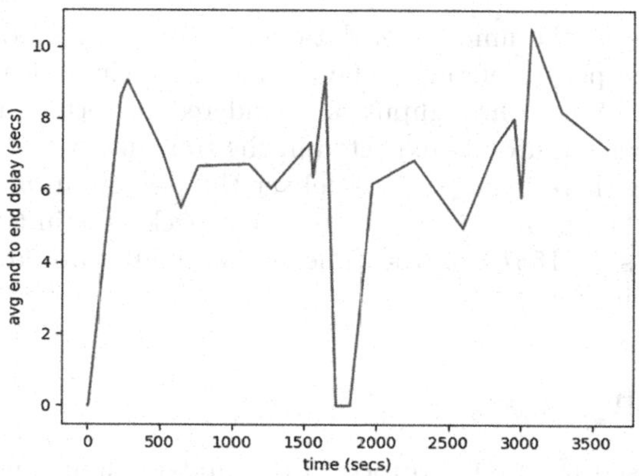

Fig. 5. Average end-to-end delay vs time

End to End Delay:
End to End delay refers to the time taken by a packet to reach from the source node to the sink node. The average end-to-end delay for time intervals is shown in the Fig. 5. Packet transmission starts at 130 s, therefore before 130 s, the end-to-end delay is 0 s. The average delay from time 130 s to 224 s is 8.6 s. The delay

is 0 s in the interval of 1640 s to 1818 s as the next-hop of source node 9 is set to −1 meaning there is no node present to relay information to the sink node. The lowest average delay of 4.9 s is achieved when the no of hops is 3 in the time interval of 2260 s to 2598 s.

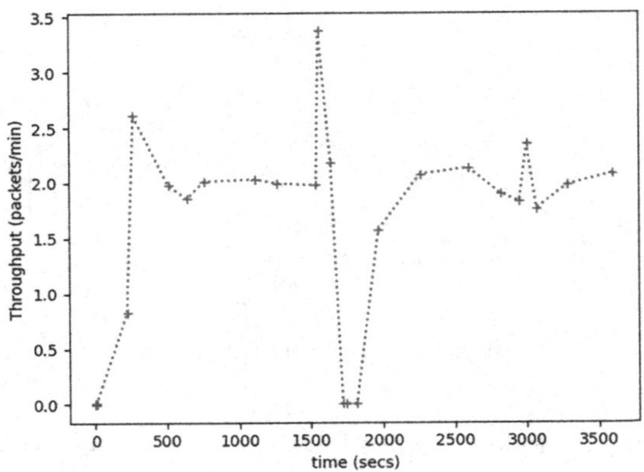

Fig. 6. Throughput vs time

Throughput:
Throughput refers to the amount of data successfully received at the destination over a specific period of time. The throughput achieved in the simulation is shown in Fig. 6. Here, throughput is considered in terms of the number of packets received per minute. As expected in the time interval of 1640 s to 1818 s, throughput is 0 as there is no path to deliver the packets from the source node to the sink node. The highest throughput is 3.36 packets/min for the time interval between 1540 s to 1557 s as the time has a small value due to which the throughput value increased.

6 Conclusion

This paper proposed the LHR protocol. LHR updates hop-count, based on the local neighbor information and avoids periodic beaconing from the sink. Thereby, preventing overhead on the network. Detailed design and implementations of LHR are discussed in this paper. LHR protocol is implemented in UnetStack, further its performance is analyzed in terms of end-to-end delay and throughput. As future work, LHR can be deployed in a test bed environment and thorough actual performance can be analyzed.

References

1. Akyildiz, I.F., Pompili, D., Melodia, T.: Challenges for efficient communication in underwater acoustic sensor networks. ACM SIGBED Rev. **1**(2), 3–8 (2004)
2. Ayaz, M., Abdullah, A.: Hop-by-hop dynamic addressing based (H2-DAB) routing protocol for underwater wireless sensor networks. In: 2009 International Conference on Information and Multimedia Technology, pp. 436–441. IEEE (2009)
3. Ayaz, M., Baig, I., Abdullah, A., Faye, I.: A survey on routing techniques in underwater wireless sensor networks. J. Netw. Comput. Appl. **34**(6), 1908–1927 (2011)
4. Barbeau, M., Blouin, S., Cervera, G., Garcia-Alfaro, J., Kranakis, E.: Location-free link state routing for underwater acoustic sensor networks. In: 2015 IEEE 28th Canadian Conference on Electrical and Computer Engineering (CCECE), pp. 1544–1549. IEEE (2015)
5. Basagni, S., Petrioli, C., Petroccia, R., Spaccini, D.: CARP: a channel-aware routing protocol for underwater acoustic wireless networks. Ad Hoc Netw. **34**, 92–104 (2015)
6. Boukerche, A., Sun, P.: Design of algorithms and protocols for underwater acoustic wireless sensor networks. ACM Comput. Surv. (CSUR) **53**(6), 1–34 (2020)
7. Chitre, M., Bhatnagar, R., Soh, W.S.: UnetStack: an agent-based software stack and simulator for underwater networks. In: 2014 Oceans-St. John's, pp. 1–10. IEEE (2014)
8. Felemban, E., Shaikh, F.K., Qureshi, U.M., Sheikh, A.A., Qaisar, S.B.: Underwater sensor network applications: a comprehensive survey. Int. J. Distrib. Sens. Netw. **11**(11), 896832 (2015)
9. Ghoreyshi, S.M., Shahrabi, A., Boutaleb, T.: An inherently void avoidance routing protocol for underwater sensor networks. In: 2015 International Symposium on Wireless Communication Systems (ISWCS), pp. 361–365. IEEE (2015)
10. Ghoreyshi, S.M., Shahrabi, A., Boutaleb, T.: A novel cooperative opportunistic routing scheme for underwater sensor networks. Sensors **16**(3), 297 (2016)
11. Guan, Q., Ji, F., Liu, Y., Yu, H., Chen, W.: Distance-vector-based opportunistic routing for underwater acoustic sensor networks. IEEE Internet Things J. **6**(2), 3831–3839 (2019)
12. Ismail, N., Mohamad, M.M.: Review on energy efficient opportunistic routing protocol for underwater wireless sensor networks. KSII Trans. Internet Inf. Syst. (TIIS) **12**(7), 3064–3094 (2018)
13. Khasawneh, A., Latiff, M.S.B.A., Kaiwartya, O., Chizari, H.: Next forwarding node selection in underwater wireless sensor networks (UWSNs): techniques and challenges. Information **8**(1), 3 (2017)
14. Li, N., Martínez, J.F., Meneses Chaus, J.M., Eckert, M.: A survey on underwater acoustic sensor network routing protocols. Sensors **16**(3), 414 (2016)
15. Luo, J., Chen, Y., Wu, M., Yang, Y.: A survey of routing protocols for underwater wireless sensor networks. IEEE Commun. Surv. Tutor. **23**(1), 137–160 (2021)
16. Ma, Z., Guan, Q., Ji, F., Yu, H., Chen, F.: An efficient and low-signaling opportunistic routing for underwater acoustic sensor networks. In: Kim, K., Joukov, N. (eds.) ICISA 2017. LNEE, vol. 424, pp. 22–29. Springer, Singapore (2017). https://doi.org/10.1007/978-981-10-4154-9_3
17. Noh, Y., Lee, U., Wang, P., Choi, B.S.C., Gerla, M.: VAPR: void-aware pressure routing for underwater sensor networks. IEEE Trans. Mob. Comput. **12**(5), 895–908 (2012)

Underwater Acoustic Sensor Networks' Performance Evaluation Tool (UASN-PET) for UnetStack

Harendra Singh Kushwaha and B. R. Chandavarkar(✉)

Department of Computer Science and Engineering, National Institute of Technology Karnataka, Surathkal, Mangalore, India
brcnitk@gmail.com

Abstract. An underwater sensor network simulator is an analytical tool used to analyze the network performance of a WSN (Wireless Sensor Network). There are various underwater network simulators such as NS2-MIRACLE, SUNSET, Aqua-Net/Mate, DESERT, and UnetStack. However UnetStack is more compatible to real modems from the deployment point of view in comparison with other. UnetStack creates a log-0.txt file and a trace.json file after compiling a groovy file. These trace files are analyzed to get data for per- performance study of a new protocol. To make the process of getting data for performance studies easier, the Underwater Acoustic Sensor Networks Performance Evaluation Tool (UASN-PET) for UnetStack is proposed. This tool helps in extracting and presenting a performance study of a network topology through an interactive GUI. UASN-PET for UnetStack is written in Python so that researchers can spend more time and attention on developing new protocols rather than analyzing trace files. This paper also discusses UnetStack's trace file format

Keywords: Underwater network simulation · Unetstack · Simulation trace · Performance analysis

1 Introduction

In underwater network research [1], Implementing a complete testbed to evaluate a complex network topology protocol is extremely expensive, time-consuming, and requires additional manpower. This realistic challenge emphasizes the need for a simulation environment capable of accurately simulating underwater networks. The underwater network simulation tool [2] allows users to create network topologies similar to that found in advanced computer network systems. Before the implementation, simulation results can be used to evaluate performance, identify issues, determine the root cause, and resolve issues. The output of each simulation is recorded in the log files. Extracting the simulation result from log

National Institute of Technology Karnataka Surathkal.

S. K. Panda et al. (Eds.): CoCoLe 2022, CCIS 1729, pp. 150–161, 2022.
https://doi.org/10.1007/978-3-031-21750-0_13

files will be time-consuming and difficult. Evaluating the simulation results and presenting that efficiency is important to save time and effort. The goal of an automated trace analyzer tools [3] is to display the simulation results graphically and provide a more intuitive way to show the performance metrics.

Various underwater network simulators are NS2-MIRACLE [4], SUNSET [5], Aqua-Net/Mate [6], DESERT [7], and UnetStack [8]. NS2-MIRACLE is a group of packages that enhance the functionality of the NS-2 Network Simulator. For managing cross-layer communication [9], it offers a strong algorithm. SUNSET underwater network simulator is based on the ns2-MIRACLE. It is capable of using previously written code for simulations. A virtual channel simulator that operates in real-time is called Aqua-Net/Mate. DESERT is another open-source tool for simulating underwater networks. Its goal is to become a useful tool for replicating, following, and interpreting underwater network protocols for research. UnetStack is an agent-based configurable framework for software-defined underwater networks that enables the rapid design, simulation, testing, and deployment of software-defined underwater networks.

For any simulation run in UnetStack, it generates a trace and a log file, which should be further processed to extract the performance metrics of the simulation. In the log file, simulation scripts or the agents can do custom logging and that logged information can be used to analyze the performance metrics. Look at the messageID of the response messages and find the equivalent stimulus message (same messageID) on the next node in the trace file to trace an event across nodes. Then repeat the process from that node to the next one until reaches the destination. However, the task of processing the simulation traces for extracting and analyzing the desired network performance metrics is an additional overhead that incurs significant time and effort. The UnetStack Trace Analyzer is created so that researchers could simply focus on the design of new protocols rather than wasting time analyzing trace files.

In this paper, Underwater Acoustic Sensor Networks' Performance Evaluation Tool (UASN-PET) is created which reads the trace.json file, and traverses it to extract the data for computing performance metrics like packet sent, the packet received, throughput, packet delivery ratio, and end-to-end delay, and then represents it in a simplified graphical manner. It simplifies the post-processing of the trace.json file.

Section 2 of the paper provides a brief introduction to UnetStack and its output files, Sect. 3 describes the design details of UASN-PET, Sect. 4 describes the development of the UASN-PET, Sect. 5 present result analysis using UASN-PET with one example topology, and Sect. 6 concludes the paper and discusses future improvements that can make UASN-PET more robust and user-friendly.

2 Introduction to UnetStack and Its Simulation Output

UnetStack is an underwater network simulator. In 2004, the Acoustic Research Lab at the National University of Singapore developed UnetStack as a component of the Unet project. UnetStack is the foundation for an underwater network simulator. Simulation in the UnetStack can be performed in real-time or discrete event simulation.

UnetStack is based on the Fjage agent framework [8], rather than a conventional protocol stack of layers. UnetStack is a collection of software agents that represent different layers of the network stack and run predefined services. This technique is defined as service-oriented architecture [10], enabling information sharing, service delivery, and behavior negotiation between different agents. Researchers can create, test, and add new functions to a process that would not have been possible with traditional layer-based network architecture. Agents can be written in Groovy, Java, Python 3, Julia, C, and JavaScript, as UnetStack provides API bindings for these programming languages. The protocol can be simulated and the performance of the implemented protocol can be tested by deploying it in different scenarios.

2.1 Output Files of a Simulation in UnetStack

1. **logs/log-0.txt file**
   The logs/log-0.txt trace file contains the Java logging framework text logs. The simulation code and the contents of the Agents may log additional data to this document using log.info() or log.fine() methods. This provides a flexible and configurable method for logging in simulation for letter research.
2. **logs/trace.nam file**
   When the UnetStack system was built, the UnetStack community decided to use the same trace document design as NS2 for logging because people were already familiar with it. The tracer calculates important details like the numbers of queued packets, transmitted packets, received packets, lost packets, offered load, and true load. It also contains details about node migration. This concept is not the default in UnetStack 3.3.0, but it can be utilized in simulation successfully.
   Note. The trace file can be set up in simulation by using the following commands:
   - trace = new NamTracer().
   - trace.open('logs/trace.nam').
3. **logs/trace.json file**
   A JSON trace file is used to track the progress of a simulation. In the logs folder, trace.json is generated automatically. This file includes a complete trace of each and every activity in the network, on each node. The trace is divided into several groups, each of which describes a simulation or the performance of a set of commands. A group is made up of a series of events, each of which contains data on the event's timing, component (agent operating on a node), threads ID, response, and stimulus. The stimulus is usually a message from another agent, and the response is usually a message sent back. The thread ID connects several events that may occur across many agents and nodes but all have the same root cause.
   It's easy to integrate the activity tracer architecture into own agents. Use a

trace() call to capture information that is produced in response to a stimulus. For examples

- send trace(stimulus, new DatagramDeliveryNtf(stimulus))
- request trace(stimulus, req), timeout

Note. The JSON event logging framework is now supported by all default agents in UnetStack 3.3.*

3 Design of UASN-PET

Tool design is the process of planning, creating, and analyzing tools. The design of a tool is determined by the function that the tool will perform.

3.1 Approach Taken

UnetStack typically generates the logs/log-0.txt and the logs/trace.json file for any simulation which should be further processed to extract the desired results. Starting from UnetStack 3.3, the UnetStack simulator generates trace files in rich JSON format with the default name logs/trace.json. This file includes a complete trace of each and every activity in the network on each node. In the logs folder, trace.json is generated automatically. Figure 1 shows the high-level approach taken by the tool to extract the information from the trace.json file and plot the graphs. The user creates a simulation script which is run in the UnetStack simulator. As an output of the simulation, UnetStack produces log-0.txt and trace.json files. Our tool takes the trace.json file as an input and the process is for extracting the useful data. Letter it plots the various performance metrics graphs.

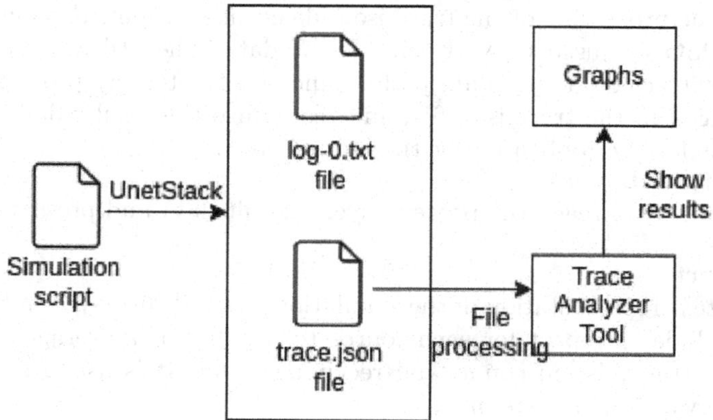

Fig. 1. UnetStack simulation process

3.2 Architecture of UnetStack Trace Analyzer

The architecture of the UnetStack [8] trace analyzer is partitioned into three layers as shown in Fig. 2. An input layer, a processing layer, and then an output layer. The first layer is the input layer which handles the inputs required for the tool. The processing layer is the second layer. This layer traverses the trace.json file to extract the useful data and format it for the presentation layer. The output layer is the third layer. This layer presents network performance results like throughput, average end-to-end delay, and packet delivery ratio in the form of a graph and report.

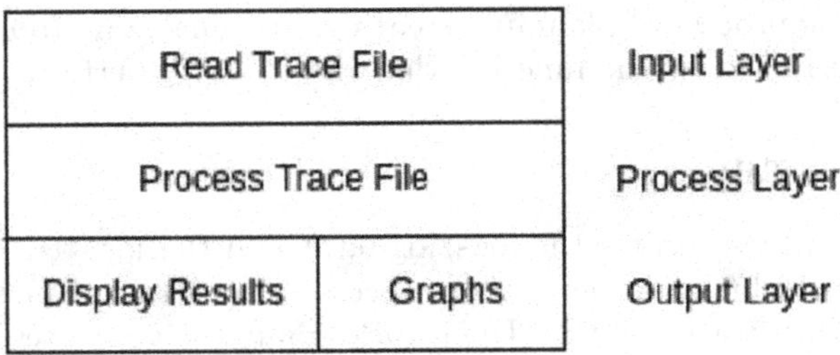

Fig. 2. UnetStack trace analyzer layers

3.3 Layers Are Described Briefly Below

1. **The Input Layer**
   The data in the Input Layer comes from the trace.json file generated by the UnetStack simulation. A GUI has been created with python's Tkinter library which allows the UnetStack trace analyzer to select the trace.json.
2. **The Processing Layer**
   The trace file of UnetStack is in JSON formate. Since the process layer involves the processing of the trace.json file event by event, Python's built-in package JSON is used to work with JSON data. The utility is used in this layer to extract data, calculate performance parameters by processing every event logged in the trace.json file, and reorganize the results data so that it is suitable for the tools used for the output layer.
3. **The Output Layer**
   The output layer reads the process layer's result data and presents it in two formats:
   - **Report**
     The text representation of the simulation result is displayed in the report. It includes a report for each source to destination's average end-to-end delay, transmission count, and receiving count. It is useful to know the exact value of the outcome.
   - **Graph**
     The Trace Analyzer uses the Matplotlib library [11] for graph plotting. Graphs are useful for comparing the results of different sources. As a result, three graphs will be produced. One is for the average end-to-end delay, another for packet delivery ratio, and a third for throughput

4 Implementation of UASN-PET

The UASN-PET is built with open-source tools [12]. The operating system used is Linux. The Python programming language is used for coding the logic of the tool and python's Tkinter library [13] is used to create the GUI of the tool.

The main challenge in extracting the performance metrics from trace.json is tracing a data packet from source to destination. The packet ids in UnetStack change with each hop. This occurs because the packet forwarded from the intermediate node is treated as a new packet, resulting in the generation of a new id for the same packet, which is then sent to the next hop or destination. In single-hop communication, if the sender sends a packet with some id it remains the same at the destination. So tracing a data packet in single-hop communication is not a problem. The issue arises during multi-hop communication [14]. The packet ids in multihop communication change at each hop. When we try to track a data packet from source to destination, this will cause a problem. Because the packet id changes at each node, it is impossible to trace the packet because the packet id is unique to each hop, making it difficult to trace the packet.

4.1 Tracing a Data Packet on Multi-hop Communication

The logs/trace.json file keeps a complete trace of all network activity in the form of a JSON object known as an event. Each event includes information about the event's timing, component (agent running on a node), thread ID, response, and stimulus. The stimulus is a message from another agent, and the response is a message sent back. An instance of an event is shown Fig. 3 with the explanation of their fields.

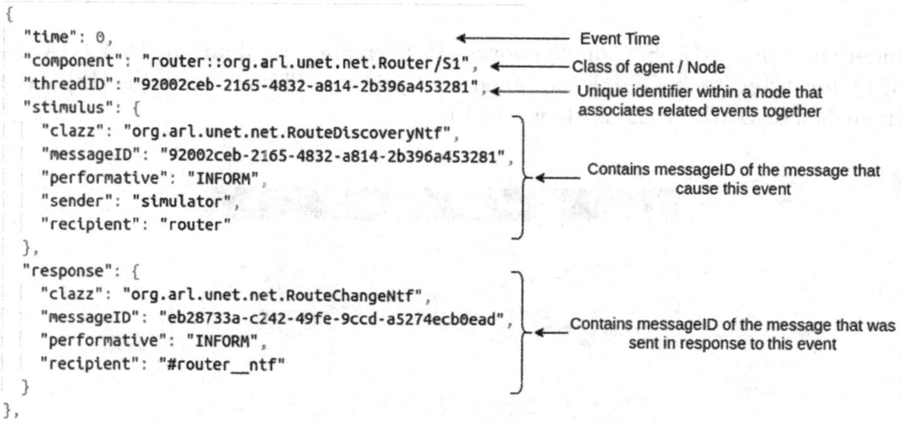

```
{
  "time": 0,
  "component": "router::org.arl.unet.net.Router/S1",
  "threadID": "92002ceb-2165-4832-a814-2b396a453281",
  "stimulus": {
    "clazz": "org.arl.unet.net.RouteDiscoveryNtf",
    "messageID": "92002ceb-2165-4832-a814-2b396a453281",
    "performative": "INFORM",
    "sender": "simulator",
    "recipient": "router"
  },
  "response": {
    "clazz": "org.arl.unet.net.RouteChangeNtf",
    "messageID": "eb28733a-c242-49fe-9ccd-a5274ecb0ead",
    "performative": "INFORM",
    "recipient": "#router__ntf"
  }
},
```

Event Time
Class of agent / Node
Unique identifier within a node that associates related events together
Contains messageID of the message that cause this event
Contains messageID of the message that was sent in response to this event

Fig. 3. Various fields of an event in trace.json file

The thread ID connects several events that may occur across many agents and nodes but all have the same root cause. Tracing an event through the agents in the node involves collating the events with the same threadID. Since the threadID is internal to the stack and is not transferred across nodes, the threadID on each node is typically unique. By analyzing the TX messages in a simulation and identifying the threadID on the sending and receiving sides of each, it is still possible to link the threadIDs on different nodes. Datagram timing details for all network stack layers are contained in the trace.json file. All messages connected to a datagram from which they originated are individually identified by the threadID field. Look at the messageID of the response messages and find the equivalent stimulus message (same messageID) on the next node in the trace file to trace an event across nodes. From that node to the next, repeat the procedure until the destination.

Suppose a scenario where source Node-A sent a data packet to Sink Node-C via Node-B. To traverse the data packet from source to destination, the following event in trace.json file will be looked up.

DatagramReq from router@A to uwlink@A → TxFrameReq from uwlink@A to phy@A → TX from phy@A to phy@B → RxFrameNtf from phy@B (publish on topic) → DatagramReq from router@B to uwlink@B → TxFrameReq from uwlink@B to phy@B → TX from phy@B to phy@C → RxFrameNtf from phy@C (publish on topic)

It is noticeable that the response.messageID of each event JSON entry corresponds to the stimulus.messageID of the next JSON entry. This allows following the sequence of events.

5 Result and Analysis of UASN-PET

Underwater Acoustic Sensor Networks' Performance Evaluation Tool (UASN-PET) for UnetStack GUI is designed in Python's Tkinter package [13]. GUI screenshot of UASN-PET is shown in Fig. 4

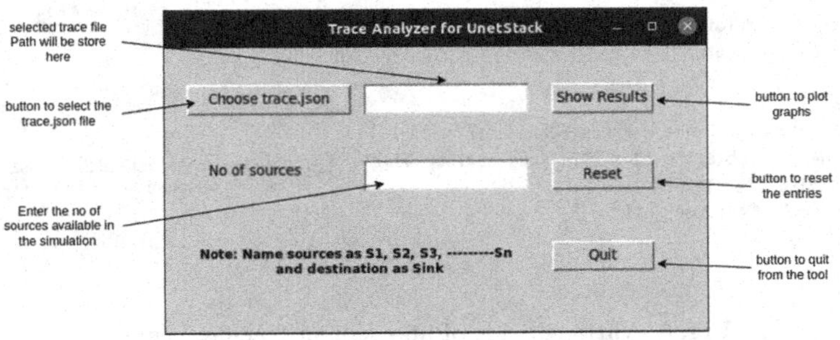

Fig. 4. (GUI SCREENSHOT)

UASN-PET has two entries. The first is to store the trace.json and the second is to enter the no of sources available in the simulation. UASN-PET has four buttons. The first is used to select the trace.json, the second is used to show results. The third is to reset the entries and the fourth is to quit the tool. When the user clicks the show results button after selecting the trace.json file and entering the number of sources, UASN-PET checks whether the number of sources entered is correct or not. If it is found that the no of sources entered by the user is not the same as the no of sources available in the simulation, an error message will appear. Otherwise, it will plot graphs for throughput (packets per minute), average end-to-end delay (milliseconds), and packet delivery ratio.

5.1 Result Analysis on Network Topology

The UASN-PET has been tested for many standard network topologies. The tool has been tested for various scenarios. Here two network topologies and their performance metrics graphs have been presented which are simulated in UnetStak and its trace file is analyzed using UASN-PET.

1. **Simulation Topology-1**
   Figure 5 represent a network topology consists of total eleven nodes. There are four senders in the simulation. Sender S1 and S2 are five hops away from the Sink and following path as $sourc \rightarrow A \rightarrow B \rightarrow C \rightarrow D \rightarrow Sink$. Sender S3 and S4 are four hops away from the Sink and following path as $source \rightarrow F \rightarrow E \rightarrow D \rightarrow Sink$ as shown in the Fig. 5. The communication range of the Channel is 1000 m. And the simulation is set to run for 60 min. Performance metrics are computed every four minutes.

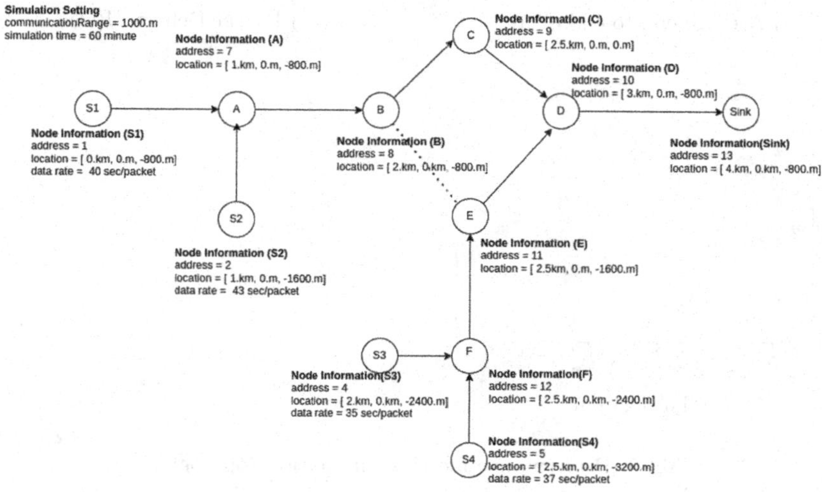

Fig. 5. Simulation topology-1

After simulation of the network topology given in Fig. 5 UnetStack generate a trace.json file as the output of the simulation which is given to the UASN-PET to calculate the simulation result. The UASN-PET extracts three performance metrics Average end-to-end delay, Packet Delivery Ratio, and Throughput for the simulation and plot graph for each. The average end-to-end delay (milliseconds) is calculated by averaging the time taken by all packets received every four minutes. Figure 6a represents the average end-to-end delay for all sources available in the simulation. On X-axis, there are 15 points representing every four minutes average delay calculation of simulation. The Y-axis shows the average delay in milliseconds. Figure 6b represents packet delivery ratio for each sources. On X-axis, there are 15 points representing every four minutes calculation of simulation. The Y-axis shows the packet delivery ratio in percentage. The throughput is calculated by the number of packets received per minute. Figure 6c represents the throughput plot for every source. On X-axis, there are 15 points representing every four minutes of simulation. The Y-axis shows the throughput in packets per minute.

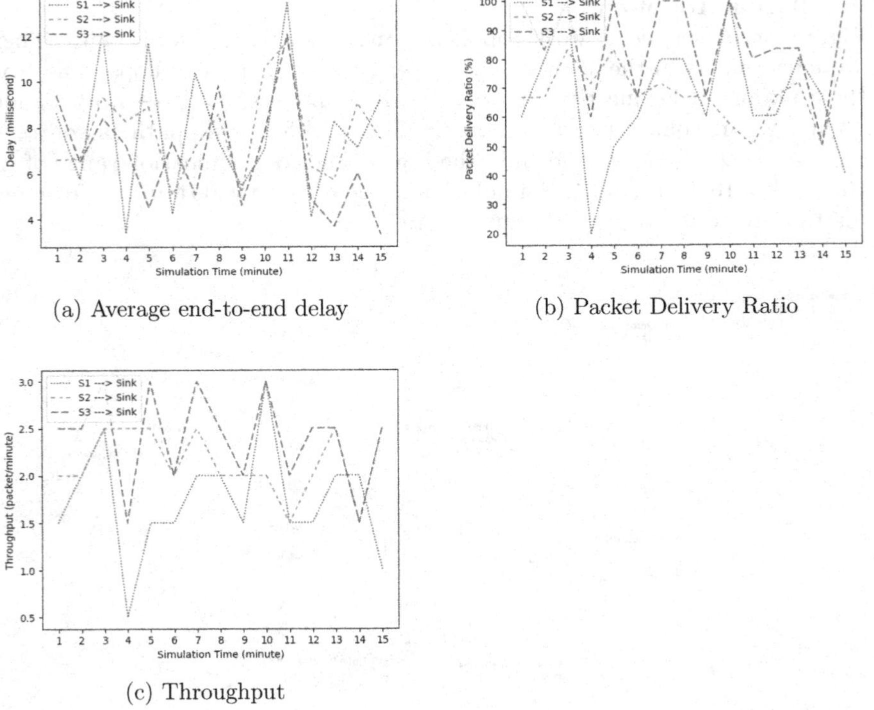

(a) Average end-to-end delay

(b) Packet Delivery Ratio

(c) Throughput

Fig. 6. Performance metrics: simulation topology-1

2. **Simulation Topology-2**
Figure 7 represent a network topology consists of total six nodes. There are three senders in the simulation network. Sender S1 and S2 are three hops away from the Sink and following path as $sourc \rightarrow A \rightarrow B \rightarrow Sink$. Sender S3 is two hops away from the Sink and following path as $source \rightarrow B \rightarrow Sink$ as shown in the Fig. 7. The communication range of the Channel is 100 m. And the simulation is set to run for 30 min. Performance metrics are computed every two minutes.

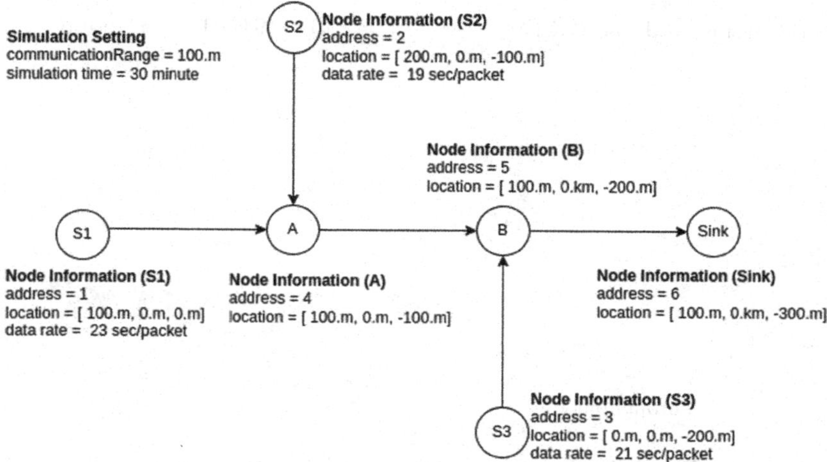

Fig. 7. Simulation topology-2

After simulation of the network topology given in Fig. 7 UnetStack generate a trace.json file as the output of the simulation which is given to the UASN-PET to calculate the simulation result. UASN-PET extracts three performance metrics Average end-to-end delay, Packet Delivery Ratio, and Throughput for a simulation and plot graph for each. The average end-to-end delay (milliseconds) is calculated by averaging the time taken by all packets received for every two minutes. Figure 8a represents the average end-to-end delay for all sources available in the simulation. On X-axis, there are 15 points representing every two minutes calculation of simulation. The Y-axis shows the average end-to-end delay in milliseconds. The packet delivery ratio is calculated by the ratio of the received count and the transmit count for every two minutes and presented in percentage. On X-axis, there are 15 points representing every two minutes of simulation. The Y-axis shows the packet delivery ratio in percentage. Figure 8b represent packet delivery ratio for each sources. The throughput is calculated by the number of packets received per minute. Figure 8c represents the throughput plot every source. On X-axis, there are 15 points representing every two minutes of simulation. The Y-axis shows the throughput in packets per minute.

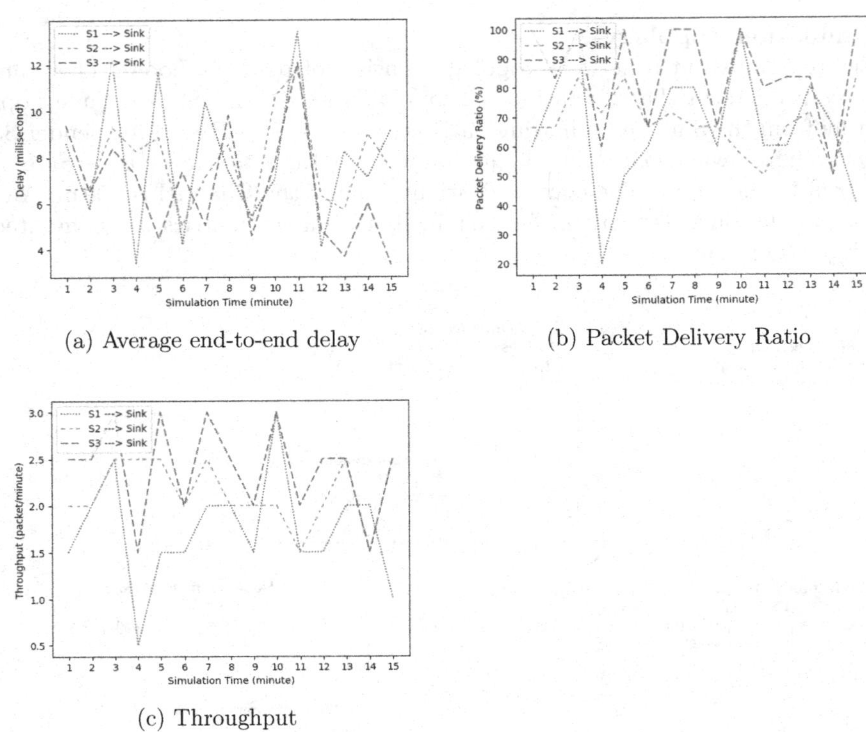

(a) Average end-to-end delay

(b) Packet Delivery Ratio

(c) Throughput

Fig. 8. Performance metrics: simulation topology-2

5.2 Prerequisites for the Tool

While designing the tool it has been taken care that the tool is less error-prone. That's why there are some prerequisites to use the tool.

1. Sources name should be in the sequence of S1, S2, S3, ———-Sn.
2. Destination should be named - "Sink"
3. Reliability should be set to false.

6 Conclusions and Future Work

The UASN-PET is a trace analyzer tool developed to make it easier to analyze network performance after simulation on UnetStack. The tool serves the needs of users through an easy-to-use GUI and eliminates the manual processing task with the click of a button. This could increase user productivity by allowing them to spend more time and attention to networking studies while reducing the burden of performance analysis. This tool can be further developed by adding more network parameters to make it more robust.

References

1. Partan, J., Kurose, J., Levine, B.N.: A survey of practical issues in underwater networks. ACM SIGMOBILE Mobile Comput. Commun. Rev. **11**(4), 23–33 (2007)
2. Ovaliadis, K., Savage, N.: Underwater sensor network simulation tool (USNeT). Int. J. Comput. Appl. **71**(22) (2013)
3. Kemper, P., Tepper, C.: Automated trace analysis of discrete-event system models. IEEE Trans. Software Eng. **35**(2), 195–208 (2008)
4. Baldo, N., Maguolo, F., Miozzo, M., Rossi, M., Zorzi, M.: ns2-MIRACLE: a modular framework for multi-technology and cross-layer support in network simulator 2. In: Proceedings of the 2nd International Conference on Performance Evaluation Methodologies and Tools, pp. 1–8 (2007)
5. Petrioli, C., Petroccia, R., Potter, J.R., Spaccini, D.: The sunset framework for simulation, emulation and at-sea testing of underwater wireless sensor networks. Ad Hoc Netw. **34**, 224–238 (2015)
6. Zhu, Y., et al.: Aqua-net mate: a real-time virtual channel/modem simulator for aqua-net. In: 2013 MTS/IEEE OCEANS-Bergen, pp. 1–6. IEEE (2013)
7. Masiero, R., et al.: Desert underwater: an ns-miracle-based framework to design, simulate, emulate and realize test-beds for underwater network protocols. In 2012 Oceans-Yeosu, pp. 1–10. IEEE (2012)
8. Chitre, M., Bhatnagar, R., Soh, W.-S.: UnetStack: an agent-based software stack and simulator for underwater networks. In: 2014 Oceans-St. John's, pp. 1–10. IEEE (2014)
9. Liu, P., Tao, Z., Lin, Z., Erkip, E., Panwar, S.: Cooperative wireless communications: a cross-layer approach. IEEE Wirel. Commun. **13**(4), 84–92 (2006)
10. Akyildiz, I.F., Pompili, D., Melodia, T.: State-of-the-art in protocol research for underwater acoustic sensor networks. In: Proceedings of the 1st ACM International Workshop on Underwater Networks, pp. 7–16 (2006)
11. Ari, N., Ustazhanov, M.: Matplotlib in python. In: 2014 11th International Conference on Electronics, Computer and Computation (ICECCO), pp. 1–6. IEEE (2014)
12. Koranne, S.: Handbook of open source tools. Springer Science Business Media. Springer, New York (2010). https://doi.org/10.1007/978-1-4419-7719-9
13. Beniz, D., Espindola, A., et al. Using tkinter of python to create graphical user interface (GUI) for scripts in LNLS. WEPOPRPO25 **9**, 25–28 (2016)
14. Dingde Jiang, X., Ying, Y.H., Lv, Z.: Collaborative multi-hop routing in cognitive wireless networks. Wireless Pers. Commun. **86**(2), 901–923 (2016)

Zero Watermarking Scheme Based on Polar Harmonic Fourier Moments

Alina Dash(✉) and Kshiramani Naik

Department of IT, VSSUT, Burla, Odisha, India
alinadash_cse@vssut.ac.in

Abstract. Various research on digital watermarking has developed great significant progress in recent years but image copyright protection remains a major issue that must be addressed due to the growth and popularization of computer technology. In zero watermarking algorithms, the main tool is continuous orthogonal images for images. Ongoing orthogonal continuous activity is used, consistent in rotation and measurement, and highly improved. Polar Harmonic Fourier Moments (PHFMs) have the ability to define a solid image with excellent performance among the defined continuous orthogonal moments before. PHFM is therefore proposed to deal with images to make a robust image of zero watermarking image suitable for embedding watermark on this paper. Watermarking systems can help with identification and integrity; the importance of the medical image on the other hand should not be altered. Any changes within the cover image may have an impact on the process of decision-making. So, the features of medical images, collected as a set of data will be extracted. We use the Arnold modification of binary sequencing images to be generated for a selected moment to improve security objectives. Then the watermark is embedded in a special function between the scrambled logo image and the binary element of the cover image. A watermarked image abstracted from the PHFMs value without actively embedded to the host image.

Keywords: Zero watermarking · Polar Harmonic Fourier Moment (PHFMs) · Arnold transformation · Cosine transform-based chaotic system (CTBCS)

1 Introduction

Zero watermarking algorithms perform great work in real-world problems, but according to research, the least work is done by considering different types of zero watermarking algorithms to avoid watermarking limitations in medical science. Zero watermarking techniques don't change the original image, it means that the technique has good imperceptibility, and the image will remain the same throughout the process. These strategies effectively balance the relationship between invisibility, durability, and embedded watermark information. A third party known as copyright protection authority involves in the scheme independently and holds the owner's private key, the copyrighted watermark, and copyright-protected image information.it addresses various image security requirements. Unlike watermarking, the zero-watermark strategy does not implant any data into the

S. K. Panda et al. (Eds.): CoCoLe 2022, CCIS 1729, pp. 162–171, 2022.
https://doi.org/10.1007/978-3-031-21750-0_14

host picture. Advanced zero-watermarking development [1] incapacitates the constraint of watermarking innovations. In zero watermarking "zero" indicates the almost zero or least modification of original image during embedding process. A high-level method of zero-watermarking generates a zero-watermark without changing the cover image during the watermark process. The data or information used by the algorithms should not change in the zero watermarking processes. So, the zero watermarking concepts motivate us to go for research on it.

The remaining sections of this proposed model is listed here. Section 2 discusses about literature survey. Section 3 elaborates the enhanced model of medical image zero watermarking along with preprocessing of model, embedding and extraction process based on Polar Harmonic Fourier Moments (PHFMs). Section 4 discusses the results which ensures the authenticity and integrity in proposed medical image zero watermarking system. Section 5 contain conclusion of the whole work.

2 Literature Survey

2.1 Related Work

The initial idea of zero watermarking concept was presented by Wen et al. [2]. They calculated high-performance cumulants using discrete cosine transform. The proposed algorithm shows robustness against different attacks like jpeg compression, separating, and point turning. Chen et al. [3] introduced an algorithm based on a zero-watermarking concept within the wavelet space for digital rights validation. This algorithm uses the element of the host picture matrix obtained from the curvelet domain's minimal-frequency band. It has sent an encoded watermark sequence to a third party along with a timestamp. Waleed et al. [4] used a genetic algorithm in their experiment for the creation of the zero-watermark in Discrete cosine transform domain to safeguard intellectual property rights. Here the secret watermark sharing concept is being proposed which is very robust in nature. A copyright protection scheme was proposed by Asha rani et al. [5] based on SVD and DWT, where secret image was encrypted within the original image. The concept of master share and ownership share was elaborated in the paper and the algorithm was able to resist geometrical and other image processing attacks. Chun Peng et al. [6] developed an algorithm for color images by applying Quaternion exponent moments (QEMs). Zero watermarks are generated from the feature image created by selected QEMs of the original cover picture and scrambled watermark picture. This algorithm is resistant to both geometric and some image processing damages. A novel zero watermarking approach considering polar complex exponential transform (PCET) and logistic chaotic mapping was designed by Wang et al. [7]. An XOR operation is applied to get the watermarked image and copyright validation is being performed. Chen et al. [8] developed an effective and distortion-free zero watermarking method for copyright protection of color images, based on hyperchaotic encryption and majority voting pattern. The featured image was extracted using singular value decomposition and foremost voting patterns. In order to achieve security, the binary copyright logo defuses with a hyperchaotic system and the model is highly resistant to geometric and non-geometric threats. To deal with copyright protection of stereo images, Yang et al. [9] presented a method based on zero watermark concept, using Fast Quaternion Generic Polar Complex Exponential Transform (FQGPCET). It solves the moment computing problem and uses a tent map. This algorithm provides a decent result between robustness and discriminability. Xiayao et al. [10] apply a multi-slice feature for a zero-watermarking scheme. The scheme improves the distinguishability and attack resistance property in volumetric medical images. Logistic system based chaotic mapping is also used and it satisfies the lossless quality requirement. The numerical instability problem faced by the Integer-order Radial Harmonic Fourier moments (IoRHFMs), Zhiqiu et al. [11] proposed fractional-order radial harmonic Fourier moments (FoRHFMs) based zero watermarking method for medical images. The proposed algorithm not only achieves lossless copyright protection, but also robust to different geometric attacks and common attacks.

2.2 Existing Problem

From the above analysis, some issues are existing in zero watermarking methods which are known as:

(1) The equalization signifies the dispersal of 0 and 1 between signals from zero watermarks to original images, which are rarely discussed. The number allocation of '0' and '1' is used to equalize the zero-watermark signal should be uniform.
(2) The discriminant and the low discriminability of watermarking signals from zero watermarking led to false positives for security purposes.
(3) Due to a regular encryption algorithm, the security of the algorithm is not satisfying.

3 Proposed Methodology

This proposed model aims to adapt original medical image watermarking using Polar Harmonic Fourier Moments (PHFMs) based master share creation to ensure the integrity, authenticity and robustness. The process consists of two phases that is embedding, and extraction. Proposed zero watermarking model is depicted in Fig. 1.

In the initial state, different types of images like CT Scan X-RAY of brain are gathered for experimental process. Host image and watermark image taken for experiment is the medical related image. The feature points are the points where value will be calculated that reflect all the original images feature. Here, amplitudes of image moments are taken as feature points which will calculate by PHFMs. Most accurate feature points among them are calculated. After that a binary image sequence is created which is undergoes scrambling binary image sequence by Arnold transformation. Following that we can perform an XOR operation on binary features of both cover and logo image, generated by Cosine mapping based chaotic system (CTBCS) to generate a zero watermarked image. The algorithm ensure that the watermarked features are distributed evenly in space and improves the watermark resistance to various attack.

3.1 Embedding

Embedding process involve the formation of zero watermark by adding the extracted feature of cover image with the logo image. The process goes under different types of

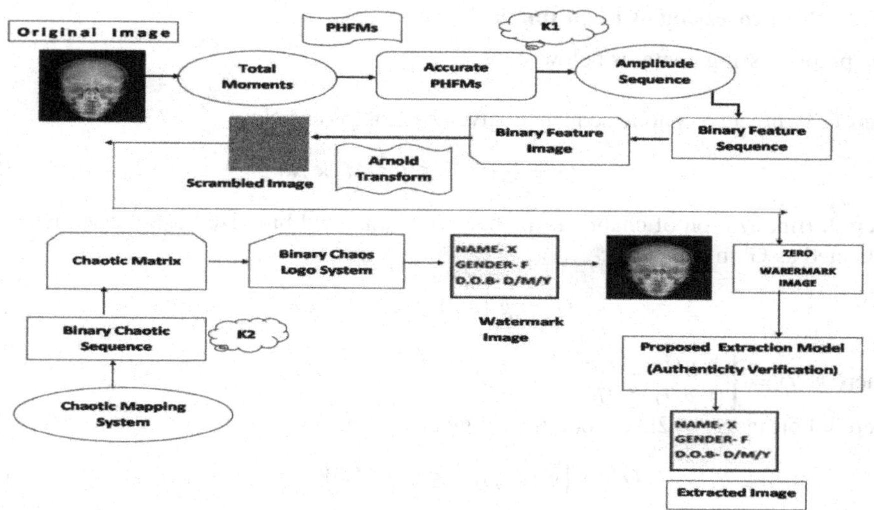

Fig. 1. The proposed work model of zero watermarking algorithm

phases to create the watermarked image. Embedding phase is again divided into three main processes.

3.1.1 Generation of Feature Image from Original Image

This includes following phases:

Step 1. Calculation of Polar Harmonic Fourier Moments (PHFMs). $n_{\max}$ order of PHFMs i.e. Q_{nm} is given in Eq. (1) as below.

$$Q_{nm} = \frac{2}{\pi} \int_0^{2\pi} \int_0^1 f(r, \theta)\overline{P_{nm}(r, \theta)} r dr d\theta \tag{1}$$

Step 2. Calculation of Accurate PHFMs from PHFMs. The sequence of accurate PHFMs is recorded in P with coefficient value $(1 + n_{max})(1 + 2n_{max})$ is mentioned in Eq. (2) as:

$$\text{P} = \{p_1, p_2, p_3 \ldots\ldots. p_{n_{max}}\} \tag{2}$$

where, $\text{P} = \{Q_{nm}, n + |m| \leq N, m \neq 4i, i \in z\}$
Step 3. Creation of Amplitude sequences as in Eq. (3) given by

$$A^k = \left\{a^k(i), 1 \leq i \leq M \times N\right\} \tag{3}$$

Step 4. Binarization of sequence, which is defined in Eq. (4) as:-

$$h(i) = \begin{cases} 1, a^k(i) \geq Th_1 \\ 0, a^k(i) \leq Th_1 \end{cases} \tag{4}$$

where Th1 is known as the threshold value computed by mean of A^k values.
Step 5. Creation of 2D binary feature image.
Step 6. Scrambling of feature image.

3.1.2 Pre-processing of Logo Image

The preprocessing contains below steps:

Step 1. To create a chaotic sequence, given by Eq. (5) as below

$$G = \{g(i), 1 \leq i \leq M \times N\} \tag{5}$$

Step 2. Binarization of chaotic sequence. The generated binarized chaotic sequence is collected as G′ in Eq. (6) as:-

$$G' = g'(i), 1 \leq i \leq M \times N \tag{6}$$

where $g'(i) = \begin{cases} 1, g(i) \geq Th_2 \\ 0, g(i) \leq Th_2 \end{cases}$

Step 3. Formation of 2D chaotic matrix given by Eq. (7)

$$G'' = \{g''(I, j), 1 \leq i \leq M, 1 \leq j \leq N\} \tag{7}$$

Step 4. Equation (8) represent the generation of chaotic logo image:

$$W_g = XOR(W, G'') \tag{8}$$

3.1.3 Zero Watermark Evaluation

The resultant of this operation evaluates the zero-watermark image I_z. So, the constructed zero watermark is defined in Eq. (9) as follows:

$$I_z = XOR(S_h, W_g) \tag{9}$$

The proposed zero watermarking process of embedding system is provided in Fig. 2 as below:-

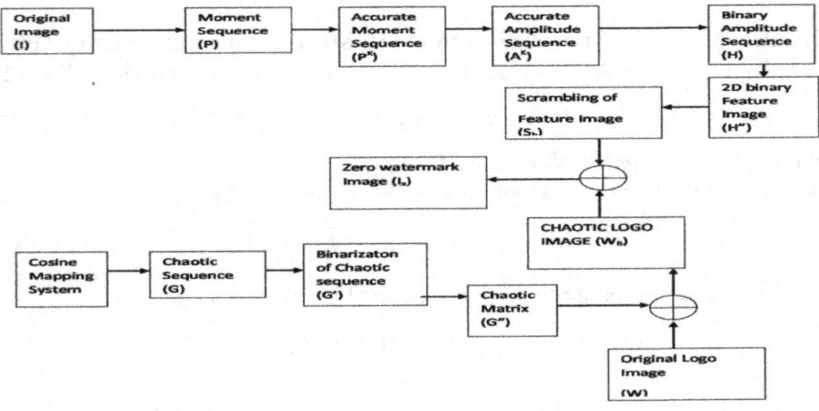

Fig. 2. Embedding phases of proposed zero watermark algorithm

3.2 Extraction Process

Extraction process involves recovery of original watermark from the attacked/untacked watermarked image. Here the attacked image is I'. The process passes through different phases of watermarked image to extract the original logo data So, the watermark image w to be extracted from the image given by Eq. (10) and the extraction process is depicted in Fig. 3 as below.

$$I' = f'(p, q) \quad \{0 \le p \le M, 0 \le q \le N\} \tag{10}$$

The extraction process is further done in three sub processes.

3.2.1 Preprocessing of Images

Step 1. Calculation of Polar Harmonic Fourier Moments (PHFMs) of image to be verified.
Step 2. Selection of accurate PHFMs coefficient.
Step 3. Amplitude sequence generation.
Step 4. Generation of binarized sequence.
Step 5. Creation of 2D binary image.
Step 6. Creation of Scrambled binary feature image.

3.2.2 Extraction of Binary Chaotic Watermark Image

A XOR operation is conducted among zero watermarked image I_z, and the binary feature image $\widehat{S_h}$. The result of operation gives the binary chaotic logo image $\widehat{W_g}$ is mentioned as follows in Eq. (11) as below.

$$\widehat{W_g} = \text{XOR}(\widehat{S_h}, I_z) \tag{11}$$

It includes following steps further.

Step 1. Generation of chaotic sequence using key k2.
Step 2. Binarization of sequence.
Step 3. Generation of two-dimensional binarized chaotic matrix.
Step 4. Selection of accurate PHFMs coefficient.

3.2.3 Extraction of Watermark Images

After getting the required two-dimensional chaotic sequence and the extracted chaotic binary logo image is obtained. So, here a XOR operation will be conducted between both two-dimensional chaos matrix and chaotic watermark image to find the host watermark. The extracted watermark image is obtained by the Eq. (12), mentioned as below.

$$(\text{W}) = \text{XOR}(\widehat{W_g}, \widehat{\widehat{G''}}) \tag{12}$$

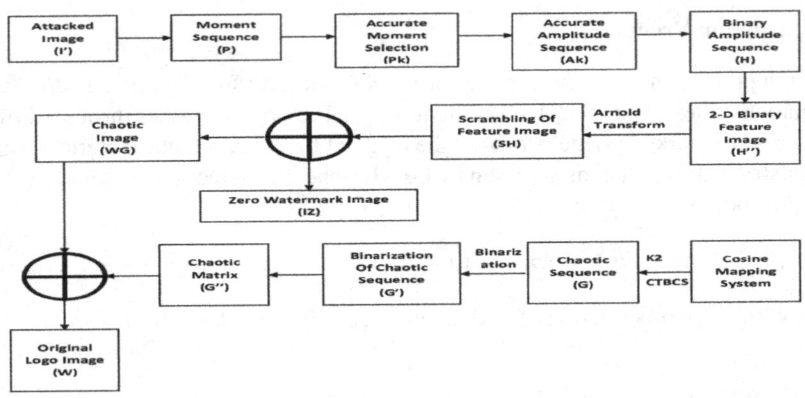

Fig. 3. Block diagram of proposed zero watermarking Extraction process.

4 Experimental Results

For experiment purpose, medical images like CT and X-RAY image of brain are taken as host image of size 128 × 128. A 32 × 32 size image containing patient's information is considered as logo and is shown in Fig. 4. All these testing images are collected from a Kaggle dataset. MATLAB environment of R2020a is being used as experimental tool.

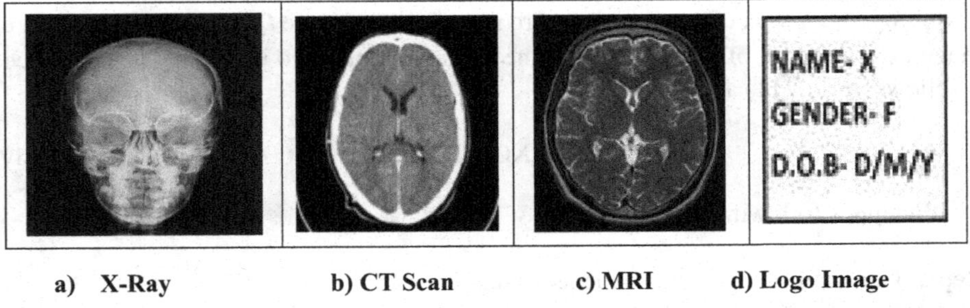

a) X-Ray **b) CT Scan** **c) MRI** **d) Logo Image**

Fig. 4. a, b, c, d as Host images and d represents logo image containing patient information.

4.1 Experimental Result on Reconstruction of PHFMS

In this process, a limited condition is set for calculation of used moment number. The number of moments found in the reconstruction process is being used for calculating the minimal frequency.

The limited condition set for PHFMs is mentioned in Eq. (13) as:-

$$n + |m| \leq K(0 \leq n \leq n_{max},\ 0 \leq m \leq m_{max}) \tag{13}$$

The number of moments is calculated as: $(k+1)^2$ So, the image reconstruction is written in Eq. (14) as:-

$$F(r,\theta) = \sum\sum Q_{nm}K_n(r)\exp(jm\theta)\ \ n+|m| \le K \tag{14}$$

For experimental purpose, a grey scale medical images like X-Ray and CT scan are taken. Further X-Ray images under goes image reconstruction process with $n_{max} = 5$, 10, 15, 20, 25. The reconstructed images of X-Ray images are shown in Fig. 5. From the experiment we can observe that by increasing the order value, the reconstructed images give more accurate picture. By increasing the good quality of images, the Mean Square Reconstruction Error (MSRE) value decreases. The MSRE value is calculated at each node which is define in Eq. (15) as:-

$$\varepsilon = \frac{\sum_{x=0}^{M-1}\sum_{y=0}^{N-1}\left|f(x,y) - \overline{f(x,y)}\right|^2}{\sum_{x=0}^{M-1'}\sum_{y=0}^{N-1} f^2(x,y)} \tag{15}$$

where, ε is represent to MSRE value.

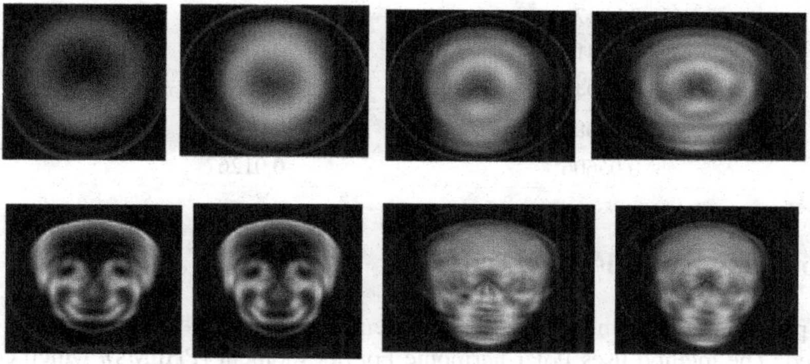

Fig. 5. Reconstructed X-ray images

Comparison of harmonic Fourier moments of Radial Harmonic Fourier Moments (RHFMs) and Polar Harmonic Fourier Moments (PHFMs) are shown in Fig. 6, where $n_{max} = 5,\ 10,\ 15,\ 20,\ 25$. A comparison table of MSRE value of RHFMs and PHFMs are stored in Table 1. The images state that value at $n_{max} = 5,\ 10,\ 15,\ 20,\ 25$.

From the table it is clearly visible that PHFMs exhibits better performance than that of RHFMs. By increasing order of K value, MSRE of RHFMs also increases with high disturbance where the MSRE of PHFMs decreases.

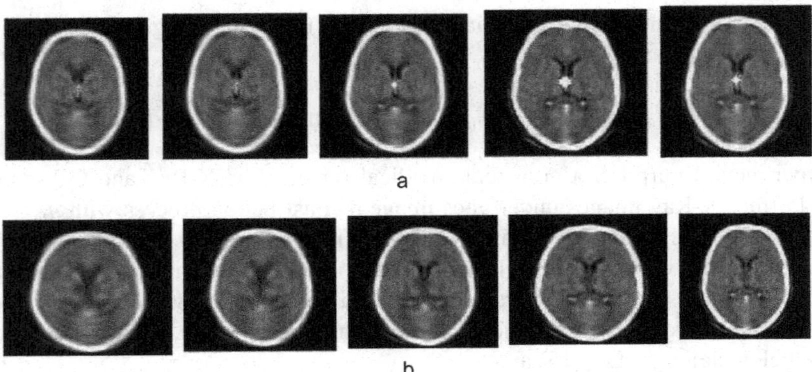

Fig. 6. a: Reconstruction of image at $n_{max} = 5, 10, 15, 20, 25$ for RHFMs. b: Reconstruction of image at $n_{max} = 5, 10, 15, 20, 25$ for PHFMs.

Table 1. A comparison table of MSRE value of RHFMs and PHFMs

n_{max}	MSRE (RHFMs)	MSRE (PHFMs)
5	0.0847	0.08426
10	0.03412	0.0398
15	0.02944	0.02613
20	0.0408	0.0184
25	0.06606	0.01267

5 Conclusion and Future Scope

In this paper a medical image watermark system based on zero watermarking is being proposed. The method uses Polar harmonic Fourier moment (PHFMs), which consist of radial basic function (RBFs). In PHFMs, the moments are orthogonally continuous having the invariant properties. The experimental value results the reconstruction of image that is highly stable as compared to RHFMs and rotationally invariant in nature. We found the Mean square rotation error value of PHFMs is quite low (0.01267) as compared to RHFMs (0.06606) indicating the better image quality. The experimental result shows that our proposed PHFMs based zero watermarking shows intense robustness for both common and geometrical images.

References

1. Jalil, Z., Mirza, A.M., Iqbal, T.: A zero-watermarking algorithm for text documents based on structural components. In: 2010 International Conference on Information and Emerging Technologies, pp. 1–5. IEEE (June 2010)
2. Wen, Q., Sun, T.F., Wang, S.X.: Concept and application of zero-watermark. Acta Electonica Sinica **31**(2), 214 (2003)

3. Chen, T.H., Horng, G., Lee, W.B.: A publicly verifiable copyright-proving scheme resistant to malicious attacks. IEEE Trans. Industr. Electron. **52**(1), 327–334 (2005)
4. Waleed, J., Jun, H.D., Hameed, S.: A robust optimal zero-watermarking technique for secret watermark sharing. Int. J. Secur. Appl. **8**(5), 349–360 (2014)
5. Rani, A., Bhullar, A.K., Dangwal, D., Kumar, S.: A zero-watermarking scheme using discrete wavelet transform. Procedia Comput. Sci. **70**, 603–609 (2015)
6. Wang, C.P., Wang, X.Y., Xia, Z.Q., Zhang, C., Chen, X.J.: Geometrically resilient color image zero-watermarking algorithm based on quaternion exponent moments. J. Vis. Commun. Image Represent. **41**, 247–259 (2016)
7. Wang, C.-P., Wang, X.-Y., Chen, X.-J., Zhang, C.: Robust zero-watermarking algorithm based on polar complex exponential transform and logistic mapping. Multimed. Tools Appl. **76**(24), 26355–26376 (2016). https://doi.org/10.1007/s11042-016-4130-7
8. Wang, C., Wang, X., Xia, Z., Zhang, C.: Ternary radial harmonic Fourier moments based robust stereo image zero-watermarking algorithm. Inf. Sci. **470**, 109–120 (2019)
9. Yang, H.Y., Qi, S.R., Niu, P.P., Wang, X.Y.: Color image zero-watermarking based on fast quaternion generic polar complex exponential transform. Signal Process.: Image Commun. **82**, 115747 (2020)
10. Liu, X., et al.: A novel zero-watermarking scheme with enhanced distinguishability and robustness for volumetric medical imaging. Signal Process.: Image Commun. **92**, 116124 (2021)
11. Xia, Z., et al.: A robust zero-watermarking algorithm for lossless copyright protection of medical images. Appl. Intell. **52**(1), 607–621 (2021). https://doi.org/10.1007/s10489-021-02476-2

Dual Image Watermarking Technique Using IWT-SVD and Diffie Hellman Key Exchange Algorithm

Priyanka Priyadarshini(✉) and Kshiramani Naik

Veer Surendra Sai University of Technology Burla, Sambalpur 768018, Odisha, India
ppriyadarshini398@gmail.com

Abstract. One of the most serious issues in today's information systems is data security when communicating over an open network. Digital watermarking is a technology which is rapidly evolving from the recognition of ownership to the recovery of altered information. This work presents dual image watermarking approach formulated on Diffie-Hellman key Exchange (DHKE) algorithm to enhance the secure technique such as: confidentiality, authenticity and non-repudiation. The present dual watermarking technique is intended for safe keeping of copyright by utilizing Integer wavelet transform (IWT) and Singular Value Decomposition (SVD). Before embedding both logos, host images are transformed by IWT. Again, SVD has been applied on selected bands of both the transformed logos. Singular Values (SVs) of both the converted watermark logos are embedded to the sub bands which are transformed by SVD of the original image. The proficiency of present technique has been analyzed in respect of performance parameters such as MSE, SSIM, PSNR, NC. Also, simulation results signify the high embedding capacity of the proposed work.

Keywords: Dual image watermarking · IWT · SVD · DHKE · Security

1 Introduction

Along with the progression of advanced innovation, use of digital image has been popular as information carrier. The major concern during the transmission is the protection of digital information. Watermarking is a technique to keep confidential digital images safe from unauthorized copying or manipulation. The process of digital watermarking technique involves embedding digital data in other cover media like images, audios, videos or text file to ensure the protection of the content. The data embedded into the cover media is called as watermark. According to various embedding techniques digital watermarking can be specified into spatial domain and transform domain. Spatial domain is quite easy and trouble free but this technique is unable to achieve more robustness. Use of transform domain scheme can procure more robust than spatial domain. Recently many transform domain-based research works have been implemented. In this domain Discrete Cosine Transform (DCT) [3], Discrete Wavelet Transform (DWT), IWT [4],

S. K. Panda et al. (Eds.): CoCoLe 2022, CCIS 1729, pp. 172–183, 2022.
https://doi.org/10.1007/978-3-031-21750-0_15

Contourlet transform (CT) and combination of DWT-SVD [2, 4] schemes have been widely used.

In this projected work, a dual image watermarking technique for copyright protection to attain the following objectives.

- To protect the copy right of the cover work.
- To achieve high robustness.
- Generating the watermarked image with high imperceptibility.
- Extracting the watermark with zero loss.
- Enhancing the security by generating embedding key.

This paper work categorized such as: - Sect. 1: introduction, Sect. 2: description of connected existing works, Sect. 3: contribution of present technique, Sect. 4: fundamental concepts about IWT, SVD and DHKE, Sect. 5: present method, Sect. 6: deals with the simulation results and conclusion is presented in Sect. 7.

2 Related Works

P. Sivananthamaitrey et al. [1] Presented a "Dual watermarking" technique using SWT (stationary wavelet transform) for ownership authentication, tamper detection and high embedding capability. In the embedding process, stationary wavelet transform is performed on original image and secret image. Watermark inserted in the Green part with a scaling factor 'α' and another binary watermark is embedded in Blue part of original image using LSB substitution. Embedded image is divided into separate parts i.e. Red, Gwm and Bwm in extraction part of the proposed work. SWT is applied on green component Gwm to get one watermark. Another Binary watermark has been extracted from Blue part of the image. This existing technique has been applied to different images and also this algorithm has considerably less complexity.

Priyank Khare et al. [2] Proposed a dual image watermarking for protection by utilizing HT (homomorphic transform), DWT, SVD and Arnold transform. Embedding procedure of this paper describes that, firstly the cover image divided into two parts i.e. reflectance and brightening part. By utilizing HT and DWT on reflectance part of cover image brings recurrence sub groups i.e. HL sub part and LH sub part which are decomposed by singular value decomposition. For embedding process two secret images are choose whereas security of existed technique is reinforced by executing shuffling of second secret image across Arnold Transform (AT). Use of DWT and SVD changed two watermarks. SVs of both modified watermark inserted into SVs of cover media. Reproduction results obviously implies for highly protectable and imperceptible.

Zhenyu Li et al. [3] developed blind watermarking calculation in light of RHFMs (radial harmonic Fourier moments) and DWT-DCT to accomplish copyright security. Initially a zero-watermark has been provided by performing DCT on the first picture. In the mean time, heading data of the beginning was determined and embedded in the RHFM area. In the proposed technique, one-level DWT is used to get the modified watermark. Subsequently low-recurrence sub-band has been separated into 8 × 8 separated blocks. All the above separated blocks were changed by using DCT, again two low-recurrence sub-bands were chosen to insert watermark. Exploratory outcomes exhibited the well protected calculation in opposition to various attacks.

Chunlin Song et al. [4] developed a robust watermarking system a region based watermarking technique with enhance measures. On different locations of the cover image Watermark data has been embedded by applying the composition of DWT & SVD technique. This procedure is derived from a previous speculation to improve the strength of watermarking cycle by utilizing watermark information which recurrence range is not unlike that of the original information. Proposed method uses double watermarking advances and implant portions of watermark pictures into chosen districts in the host picture. The results show that this procedure is stronger to assaults than the first DWT-SVD strategy.

Tien-You Lee et al. [5] presented a dual watermarking technique for integrity verification and recuperation. This plan gives the capacity to distinguish the altered areas and double opportunity for alter recuperation progressively. To extract the watermark for damage revival a confidential key which is transmitted with the watermarked image and public chaotic algorithm are used. Exploratory outcomes show that this calculation is better than the thought about strategies, particularly when the altered region is huge.

Aparna J R et al. [6] developed an algorithm for watermarking technique using Diffie Hellman key exchange. This is a block separation computation which applied cryptographic concept (DHKE) to figure out embedding places in the cover media by which the watermark can embed securely. Asymmetric key cryptography (Diffie Hellman Key Exchange) used to find different keys and utilizing these keys the watermark pieces are to be inserted into cover media. Exploratory outcomes demonstrate the way that this strategy can endure different mathematical assaults and have high robustness than different techniques.

From the related existing methods we acquire that most of the watermarking techniques are dealing with tamper detection, increasing the data payload for storing more secret information inside the cover image and recovery of poor visual quality watermark. The sole purpose of our work is to procure excellent output data with a high embedding capacity. A portion of the highlights of our proposed work are described in Sect. 3.

3 Contribution of Our Work

This paper commences a new scheme for watermarking images. This technique provides advantages such as security in communication, storage reduction and requirements of bandwidth. In the proposed method, IWT is performed on the host image, resulting in a high peak histogram, supporting high embedding capacity. Using IWT provides a multi-resolution analysis that enhances imperceptibility. The method of selecting HL and LH sub-bands used to find out embedding place in cover media, which accomplished imperceptibility as well as robustness, while applying of SVD enhances the robustness of the algorithm since singular values is not affected more by different signal processing steps. Integer wavelet transformation of images increases the computational complication of the technique. In the proposed method, one of the watermark logo is transformed by IWT and producing result in an HL sub-band whose SV is calculated using SVD. Similarly, another Watermark logo is transformed by IWT, resulting in an LH sub-band and subsequently SVD is put in the same band to procure SVs. Additional SVs from the above both sub-bands of cover image are converted with both watermark's SVs. The 'C' logo is stand for watermark-1, and 'Institute' logo for watermark-2. Even if the watermark is tampered with, the confidentiality of the information content can be guaranteed another watermark provides the correct information. Hence some main features of this proposed work are:

Combining IWT and SVD offers better execution and cost efficient functional execution than DCT, DWT [8] and SVD [7, 10] and avoid expensive floating point memory required. In this manner, the proposed calculation utilizing IWT & SVD might be utilized in various applications such as- intellectual property right protection [9] through communication channel in which copyright protection, proprietary advantages also licenses credible to cover up in confidence. Moreover as different survived techniques, this present technique is not only can be used for gray scale images but also can be use for color images, and can safely execute substandard pictures from unwanted access, furthermore their characteristics and comparison may be progressed concurrently. Execution time of the proposed method is minimized as the use of IWT and SVD combination scheme provides fast calculation. Simulation results demonstrate that when compared the result with existing spatial domain; the proposed technique have better imperceptibility and robustness in addition with high data payload for embedding more data into the cover media which is also independent of the size of the watermark data and decreases burden on bandwidth and storage requirements.

4 Fundamental Concepts

4.1 IWT

IWT is a basic change of linear transformation, where the output is adjusted to the closest integer value. It is also implemented for hardware operations, to circumvent the utilization of floating point which is an expensive activity. IWT can be utilized to have a result of combined lossy and lossless backup of original data. In programming executions, numerous processors presently offers multimedia guidelines which can do parallel execute on different integer value operations. The utilization of IWT is likewise a way to reduce the memory demands of the compression techniques as integer numbers are utilized rather than floating point numbers. IWT is exceptionally providing direct result of the recently work done. Evaluating this distinction in a hypothetical framework is significant and this is done by accepting that adjusting is same or equivalent to some type of quantization. Their fundamental concern is the deficiency of the ideal reproduction properties after filter operation. This decomposition of original data into sub bands can be expanded to various times to get higher sub-bands. The main advantages of using IWT are: it provides lossless result and efficient data payload which provides better imperceptibility because multiple watermarks can be embedded into any preferred sub-band.

4.2 SVD

The SVD of a data set is a particularization of that matrix element into three sub matrices. It has interest logarithmic properties and conveys significant mathematical and hypothetical bits of knowledge about linear transformation. SVD of matrix M is given by the formula: $M=U\sum V^T$, Where M is the original matrix which we need to decompose. U is the left singular columns consisting eigenvectors of MM^T, W is the diagonal matrix containing singular values (Eigen values) and VT represents right singular values which contains eigenvectors of M^TM.

SVD can be used as a compression method. In a more complex methodology, for specific classes of pictures one could utilize a proper premise with the goal that the best hundred particular vectors are adequate to roughly address any image [10]. This implies that the space crossed by the main hundred singular vectors isn't excessively not the same as the space traversed by the main 200 singular vectors of a given grid in that class. Compressing these matrices by this standard premise can save considerably since the standard premise is communicated just a single time and a matrix is derived by sending the best hundred singular values for the standard operation. In watermarking procedures SVD is habitually utilized as singular values shows unique strength towards different changes made in images by unauthorized access. Hence robustness of watermarking technique is expanded with utilization of SVD.

4.3 DHKE

Cryptographic techniques give confidentiality to the security policies. In general two types of cryptographic concept are used i.e. symmetric and public key cryptology. In symmetric key cryptosystem identical key is used to encode and decode information, whereas asymmetric key cryptology uses two different key to encrypt and decrypt data. Hence Asymmetric key cryptography is more secure that symmetric key cryptography. In this proposed method we use DHKE to find the confidential key value before embedding the information into cover media. This gives high Robustness for the proposed technique.

Public key cryptosystem uses two keys, one is private key 'K_{pr}' and another one is public key 'K_{pu}'. Public key is available to both users (sender and receiver) but private key of sender side is only known to the sender and private key of receiver side is only known to the receiver. In public key cryptosystem sender makes cipher data using public key of receiver and the receiver gets the original information by decrypting the cipher text using private key. In DHKE, using private and public key of both authorized users it defines a secret key which can be shared between both the users. Figure 1 projects the detail operation and algorithm of DHKE are given below.

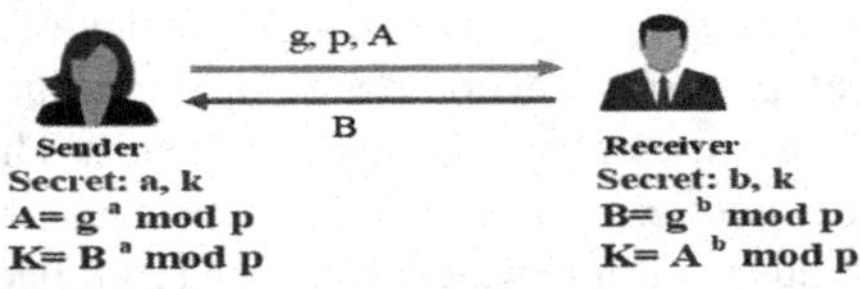

Fig.1. Process of DHKE

Using the DHKE protocol two hosts can derive a secret key without exchanging the secret key as it is. From Fig: 1, Let sender's Private Key and Public key is 'a', 'A' like that receiver's Private key and Public key is 'b', 'B' respectively. If one of the users selects prime numbers 'g' & 'p' where 'g' is the primitive root of 'p' and exchange the same with other user both the user can know the value of 'g' and 'p'. Since users already know their private key so both the users can determine the value of their public key and exchange with each other.

Public key of sender as defined by the formula given in Eq. (1):

$$A = g^a mod\ \ p \tag{1}$$

Public key of Receiver as defined by the formula given in Eq. (2):

$$B = g^b mod\ \ p \tag{2}$$

Both users receives public key of each other and using that public key and their own private key both the users determine the secret key. Here both the users acquire a similar secret key.

Secret key of sender as defined by the formula given in Eq. (3):

$$K = B^a mod\ \ p \tag{3}$$

Secret key of receiver as defined by the formula given in Eq. (4):

$$K = A^b mod\ \ p \tag{4}$$

5 Proposed Method

In this part the proposed method is described i.e. embedding and extraction algorithm of watermarking. Embedding procedure makes use of transformation by IWT and SVD and DHKE is also used to enhance the security. Commonly in watermarking algorithms the data bits are directly inserted into the bits of cover media which results the attacker to find out secret data from watermarked media easily. So in this work the positions of embedding are selected by taking singular values of sub band HL and LH of host image which is transformed by Integer wavelet transform. This proposed embedding technique use a key value to encrypt the watermark data before embedding into the cover media and that key is defined by DHKE to embed the watermark more securely. Embedding of watermark in sub bands provides imperceptibility and use of the DHKE gives robustness for which the proposed method simultaneously attained a prime requirement for any watermarking algorithm. Figure 2 describes detail procedure about the embedding algorithm and Fig. 3 shows the steps of extraction process of the projected technique. Algorithm and mathematical formulae are given in the embedding and extraction algorithm section.

5.1 Embedding Algorithm

Step 1: Apply IWT on the cover image, 'I' resulting HL and LH sub-bands; then SVD is applied to these particular sub-bands.

$$SVD\ (\mathrm{I}_{HL}) = U_{HL} S_{HL} V_{HL}^T \tag{5}$$

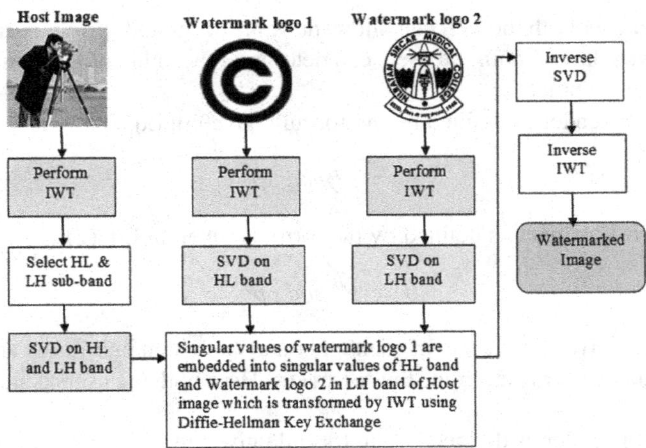

Fig. 2. Embedding algorithm

$$SVD\,(\mathrm{I}_{LH}) = U_{LH} S_{LH} V_{LH}^{T} \tag{6}$$

Step 2: Apply IWT on watermark logo 1 and choose HL sub-band whose SVs are evaluated using SVD.

$$SVD\,(W_{L1}) = U_{L1} S_{L1} V_{L1}^{T} \tag{7}$$

Step 3: Apply IWT on watermark logo 2 and select LH sub-band where SVs are determined using SVD.

$$SVD\,(W_{L2}) = U_{L2} S_{L2} V_{L2}^{T} \tag{8}$$

Step 4: Generate the secret key **'K'** by applying DHKE algorithm which is described in Eq. (1), (2), (3) and (4).

Step 5: Watermark logo1 and watermark logo 2, both are embedded with the cover image, using the following Eqs.: (9) and (10) respectively.

$$Ew1 = \mathrm{S_{HL}} + K * S_{L1} \tag{9}$$

$$Ew2 = \mathrm{S_{LH}} + K * S_{L2} \tag{10}$$

Inverse process of SVD is applied to derived altered coefficients 'Ew1' and 'Ew2', and then inverse IWT is applied to get the watermarked image 'Wm'.

5.2 Extraction Algorithm

To get both the watermark logo we need to follow the extraction algorithm which is described in the Fig. 3 and step wise procedure given in below section. In this procedure watermarked image 'Wm' taken as input and after the whole process it gives output as two extracted watermark logo EXw1 and EXw2.

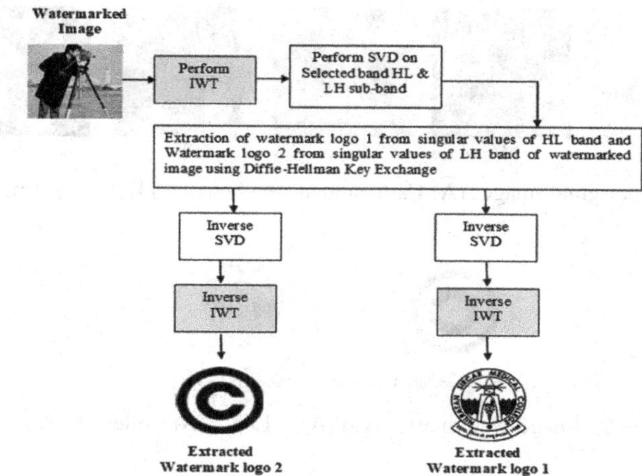

Fig. 3. Extraction algorithm

Step 1: Apply IWT on 'Wm' to recover components and SVD to get HL and LH sub-bands.

$$SVD\ (\mathrm{Wm}_{HL}) = U_{WMHL} S_{WMHL} V_{WMHL}^{T} \tag{11}$$

$$SVD\ (\mathrm{Wm}_{LH}) = U_{WMLH} S_{WMLH} V_{WMLH}^{T} \tag{12}$$

Step 2: *EXw1 and EXw2* (modified coefficients of SVD) of both image watermarks are recovered by applying the following Eqs. (13) and (14) respectively.

$$EXw1 = (S_{WMHL} - S_{HL})/\ K \tag{13}$$

$$EXw2 = (S_{WMLH} - S_{LH})/\ K \tag{14}$$

Step 3: Inverse SVD individually enforced on *EXw1, EXw2* to determine revised wavelet factor of watermark logo 1 & 2.
Step 4: Inverse IWT is performed to recovery watermark logo 1 and watermark logo 2 by decrypting both watermark logo.

6 Simulation Result and Analysis

The experimental work has done in MATLAB-16 and the different images have taken from SIPI image database and Kaggle dataset which are shown in Fig. 4 and two different types of watermark logos shown in Fig. 5. Various performance measures have considered and compared with the existing works to evaluate the efficiency of the proposed method.

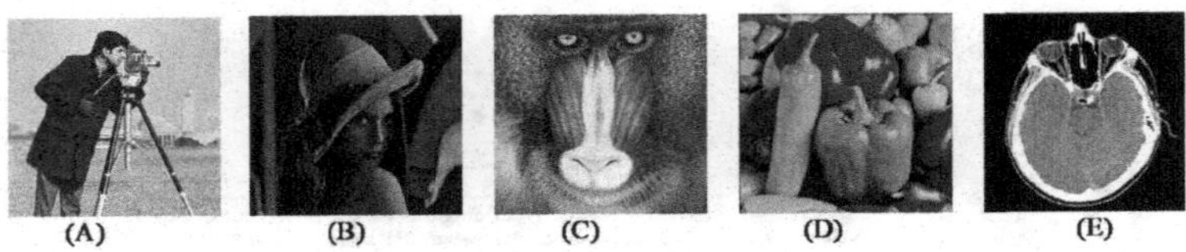

Fig. 4. Different original Images (A) Camera man, (B) Lena, (C) Bob, (D) Pepper, (E) MRI

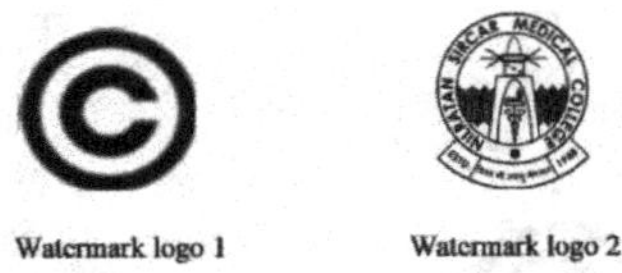

Fig. 5. Image Watermarks used (A) C Logo, (B) College Logo.

Figure, Fig. 6 shows that there is no visual degradation in the watermarked images and the extracted logos which indicates good performance of the proposed method. For more clarification and the performance of the proposed method, the performance measures i.e. Mean square error (MSE), Peak signal to noise ratio (PSNR) and Structural similarity index (SSIM) are calculated for all experimental images taken and shown in Table 1.

MSE is one, which is used to check the quality of extracted information. Numerically it can be defined in Eq. (14) where n is the size of image, Xi is the cover image, Yi is the watermark image.

$$MSE = \frac{1}{n}\sum\nolimits_{i=1}^{n}(Xi - Yi)^2 \tag{15}$$

PSNR is an accurate parameter which is used to assess the dissimilarity among the watermark image and the extracted watermark image. It may be clarified that, where the quality of the PSNR value is low the extracted image is not so qualitative. Hence high PSNR value provides better result. Mathematically it can be defined in Eq. (16) Where 'P' is maximum value of the signal.

$$PSNR = 10 * log10\frac{P^2}{MSE} \tag{16}$$

The SSIM defines distinction between two comparative pictures one is reference picture and the other is processed picture. Since the ideal worth of SSIM is '1', it shows the better comparison between these two pictures. The formula to calculate SSIM value is defined in Eq. (17) where μX is the cover image and μy is the watermark image.

$$SSIM\,(x, y) = \frac{(2\mu_x\mu_y + c_1)(2\sigma_{xy} + c_2)}{(\mu_1^2 + \mu_2^2|c_1) + (\sigma_1^2 + \sigma_2^2|c_2)} \tag{17}$$

In the above experimental result, it has been observed that the present method provides high PSNR value and low MSE value and most of the SSIM value calculation

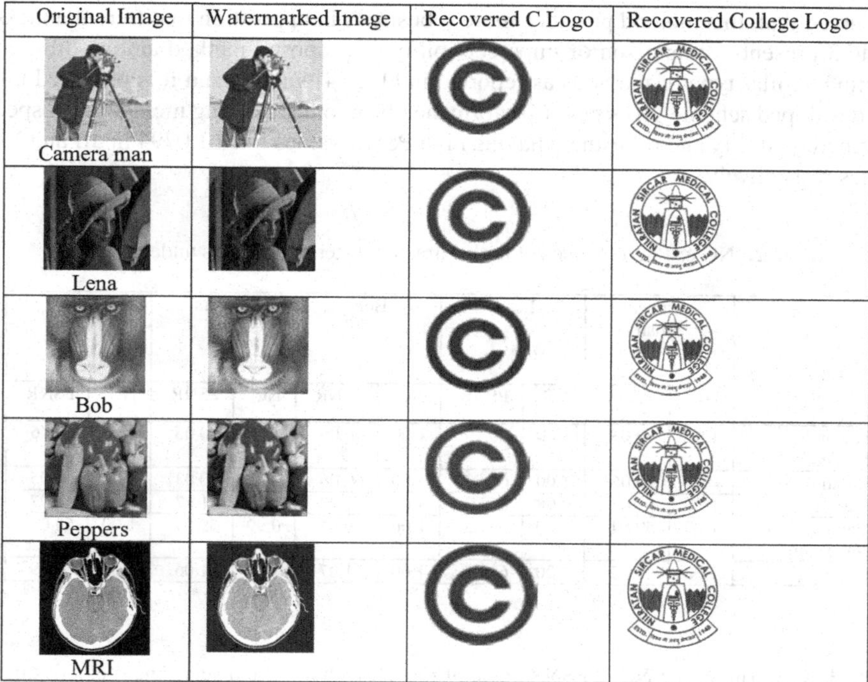

Original Image
Watermarked Image
Recovered C Logo
Recovered College Logo
Camera man
Lena
Bob
Peppers
MRI

Fig. 6. Original images, Watermarked Images, and the extracted logos

Table 1. Performance measures of proposed method

Experimented Images	MSE	PSNR1 (Wm1)	PSNR2 (Wm2)	NC_1	NC_2	SSIM
Camera man	1.0358×10^{-6}	60.0667	60.0659	1.00	1.00	1
Lena	1.0266×10^{-6}	60.0666	60.0644	1.00	1.00	0.9997
Bob	1.0335×10^{-6}	61.0746	61.0798	1.00	1.00	1
Peppers	1.0098×10^{-6}	59.0419	60.0419	1.00	1.00	1
MRI	1.0165×10^{-6}	61.0689	61.0684	1.00	1.00	0.9995

gives the ideal value 1, which clarify that this method is highly imperceptible and robust in nature.

Various attacks such as Salt and Pepper, Rotation, Median, Gamma correction, Scaling are likewise put-in to the present method for analyzing the robustness. Table 2 shows the NC and PSNR value of different images experimented under attack. Table 2 contains the NC values and PSNR values of both the watermarks experimented on different images. From the result it proves that PSNR values are high in the present method than the surviving methods. Hence this study specifies our proposed technique achieved good imperceptibility as well as robust in nature. Hence most of the NC values are 1 and nearest to 1 NC value is considered as better result, so it can undoubtedly be presumed that, this method provides more robustness in opposition to different attacks. Table 3 presents comparison of imperceptibility of proposed method among different existing similar type of methods as reported in [1, 3, 4] and [5] and it is observed that our developed scheme gives better performance from other existing methods in respect to imperceptibility and robustness having high PSNR values like 61.0794 in dB and NC values respectively.

Table 2. NC & PSNR Values of both extracted watermark Logos under Attacks

Attacks	Camera man		Lena		Bob		Peppers		MRI	
	NC	PSNR	NC	PSNR	NC	PSNR	NC	PSNR	NC	PSNR
Salt and Pepper	1.00	60.05	1.00	60.19	1.00	60.06	1.00	60.06	1.00	60.06
Rotation	0.99	60.06	1.00	60.03	1.00	60.06	0.99	60.03	1.00	60.05
Median	1.00	61.07	0.98	61.09	1.00	61.07	1.00	61.07	1.00	61.07
Gamma correction	1.00	59.04	1.00	59.03	1.00	59.04	0.99	59.04	1.00	59.05
Scaling	1.00	61.05	1.00	61.08	1.00	61.07	1.00	61.06	1.00	61.09

Table 3. Compare of the NC & PSNR value of present technique and surviving methods under attack

Attacks	P. Sivananthamaitreyet *al.* 1		Zhenyu Li *et al.*[3]		Nasir N. Hurrah *et al.* [4]		Tien-You Lee *et al.* [5]		**Proposed method**	
	NC	PSNR	NC	PSNR	NC	PSNR	NC	PSNR	**NC**	**PSNR**
Salt & pepper	0.99	59.09	0.93		0.49	-	0.99	-	**1.00**	**60.06**
Rotation	0.99	59.98	0.96	41.16	0.51	40.45	0.99	40.68	**0.99**	**60.05**
Median	1.00	-	0.99	-	0.48	40.09	1.00	-	**1.00**	**61.07**
Gamma correction	1.00	60.23	0.93	41.27	0.49	41.5	0.99	30.69	**1.00**	**59.05**
Scaling	1.00	-	1.00	-	0.59	-	0.99	-	**1.00**	**61.09**

7 Conclusion

This work presents a dual image watermarking method by using IWT and SVD. The secret key used for embedding process is generated by the DHKE algorithm by using the private key and public key of both sender and receiver.IWT gives better perceptual imperceptibility by selecting the significant embedding area of the cover image.SVD transformation of the selected sub bands of IWT transformed image enhance the robustness of the proposed technique against unauthorized access and modification. The benefits of embedding two watermarks into single cover media to get back the data exact information after extraction and against any attacks. This method also provides efficient data payload which is very significant in watermarking algorithm. Experimental result demonstrates that our proposed technique gives better PSNR result from the exciting methods. The dual image watermarking using IWT and SVD for standard test images with a secret key performs both robustness and imperceptibility.

References

1. Sivananthamaitrey, P., Rajesh Kumar, P.: High embedding capacity dual digital watermarking using stationary wavelet transform. Materials Today: Proceedings (2021)
2. Priyank, K., Srivastava, V.K.: A novel dual image watermarking technique using homomorphic transform and DWT. J. Intell. Syst. **30.1**, 297–311 (2021)
3. Li, Z., et al.: Blind and safety-enhanced dual watermarking algorithm with chaotic system encryption based on RHFM and DWT-DCT. Digital Signal Process. **115**, 103062 (2021)
4. Song, C., Sud, S., Merabti, M.: A robust region-adaptive dual image watermarking technique. J. Visual Commun. Image Represent. **23.3**, 549–568 (2012)
5. Lee, T.-Y., Lin, S.D.: Dual watermark for image tamper detection and recovery. Pattern Recogn. **41**(11), 3497–3506 (2008)
6. Aparna, J.R., Ayyappan, S.: Image watermarking using Diffie Hellman key exchange algorithm. Procedia Comput. Sci. **46**, 1684–1691 (2015)
7. Asha, D., Patidar, V.: Development and analysis of IWT-SVD and DWT-SVD steganography using fractal cover. J. King Saud Univ. Comput. Inform. Sci. **34** (2020)
8. Qiang, S., Zhang, H.: Image tamper detection and recovery using dual watermark. In: 2010 6th International Conference on Wireless Communications Networking and Mobile Computing (WiCOM). IEEE (2010)
9. Fares, K., et al.: A DWT based watermarking approach for medical image protection. J. Ambient Intell. Human. Comput. **12.2**, 2931–2938 (2021)
10. Zurinahni, Z., et al.: Hybrid SVD-based image watermarking schemes: a review. IEEE Access **9**, 32931–32968 (2021)

A Communication-Efficient Federated Learning: A Probabilistic Approach

Chaitanya Thuppari(✉) and Srikanth Jannu

Department of Computer Science and Engineering, Vaagdevi Engineering College, Bollikunta, Warangal 506 005, Telangana, India
chaitu786chaitanya@gmail.com, j.srikanth@live.com

Abstract. Federated learning (FL) empowers edge gadgets, similar to the IoT gadgets, servers, and industries that cooperatively prepare a model in the absence of respective privacy information. It expects gadgets that they trade their ML parameters. Subsequently, it expects to be together get familiar with a solid model relies upon the quantity of preparing ventures and boundary time for transmission per each step. Practically, It's transmissions are regularly overseen at a large number of partaking gadgets on asset-restricted correspondence organizations, for example, remote organizations with restricted data transfer capacity and power. Along these lines, the rehashed FL boundary transmission from edge gadgets instigates a remarkable postponement, which might be bigger than the ML model preparation time by significant degrees. Thus, correspondence delay establishes a genuine issue in FL. A correspondence proficient FL system is proposed to together further develop the FL union time, hence the preparation misfortune. During this system, a probabilistic gadget choice plan is implied such as the gadgets which will altogether further develop the union speed and prepare misfortune to get the high probabilities to choose for the transmission model. We propose a novel technique to additionally decrease the transmission time and to downsize the amount of the model boundaries traded by gadgets, and an effective remote asset designation conspire is created. Reproduction results show that the proposed FL system can further develop identification exactness.

Keywords: Federated learning · Machine Learning · Communication-efficient · Energy consumption · Deep learning

1 Introduction

Machine Learning (ML) utilizes information to acknowledge shrewd and free decision making what's more decision. ML calculations used with in a wide assortment regions, comparative as PC vision, normal language handling, clinical imaging, and dispatches [1,2]. Information are habitually gathered on predisposition at the edges of organizations Images and course book dispatches are as often as possible produced and put away on advanced cells; biomedical signs are

S. K. Panda et al. (Eds.): CoCoLe 2022, CCIS 1729, pp. 184–192, 2022.
https://doi.org/10.1007/978-3-031-21750-0_16

gathered by clinical and wearable inclination, and regularly put away on asylum servers; vivid types of signs are recorded by IoTs frameworks and identifiers. In certain activities, comparable to the preparation an ML assessment framework for clinical information, the edge inclination may not share their information, because of sequestration undertakings and guidelines. Similarly, conveying huge volumes of amassed information by various versatile predispositions might prompt an outstanding weight on the correspondence structure. These contemplations brought about the requirement for calculations which trains a model in a disseminated design, comparative edge predisposition adds to the learning methodology without taking an interest of their respective information which is known as Federated Learning (FL).

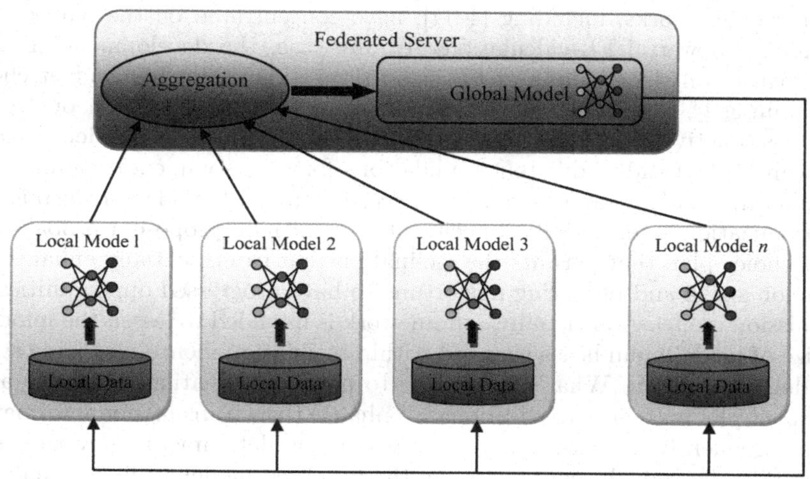

Fig. 1. An architecture of federated learning

All things considered, the execution of FL in sensible tasks faces a few difficulties which come from its circulated activity, which is unnaturally different from conventional unified ML calculations [3]. These difficulties incorporate i) correspondence outflow persuaded by the dull model boundary trades; ii) gadget tackle variety, as every gadget might have different computational capacities; iii) information variety, as every gadget can penetrate a minuscule and individualized dataset; iv)sequestration and security issues. With these difficulties, the correspondence outflow comprises a significant right-back because of the accompanying reasons. Firstly, method is prepared with interaction among the gadgets, consequently, the confluence time, relies upon the streamlining method, for representation, the quantity and the transmission detainment per iteration. Second, method preparation done possibly developed by a huge number of edge predisposition, and every gadget should share its enormous size FL boundaries continuously on to CC. Hence, method developed over a reasonable organization by restricted computational, correspondence uploads, its FL boundary transmission confinement is greater than the time of predisposition. Subsequently, it is important to plan a correspondence outline that can significantly improve the confluence speed and model delicacy, along these lines permitting its activity to preparing huge scope ML models north of millions of edge inclination. The overall architecture of the federated learning is given in Fig. 1.

The rest of the paper is coordinated as follows: the related work is introduced in Sect. 2, trailed by proposed framework in Sect. 3. In Sect. 4, results and investigation is illustrated. At last, the paper finishes up in Sect. 5.

2 Related Work

Various related works, including [4–11], have concentrated on the plan of correspondence powerful FL calculations. In any case, the development of these works focuses on streamlining of FL in a solitary viewpoint like gadget choice and planning [4–6], FL model boundary update, and transmission or organization asset activity [7–9]. In this review, we propose a correspondence viable FL outline that handles different foundations for correspondence confinement, by deliberately enhancing the gadget choice, FL model boundary transmission, and organization asset activity. Specifically, we initially propose a probabilistic gadget choice plan that permits the inclination that can essentially enhance the conversion speed and preparing misfortune to have progressed opportunities for transmission model. Additionally, a framework is intended to lessen the information size of model boundaries changed within inclination, hence idealizing speed of model conjunction. What's more, due to named inclination, a remote asset assignment plot is created to additionally enhance their transmission information rates, consequently decreasing the FL transmission detainment at every education step. In the end, the conjunction of the proposed model outline is analysed. Recreation results grounded on genuine information exhibit the presentation of the proposed model outline and to permit exact and quick agreeable preparation of various edge predisposition in a unified way.

Federated learning (FL) proposed in [5] is a dispersed education calculation that empowers edge inclination to deliberately prepare a typical model without expectation of their private information. It's strategy depends on the ability of every gadget to prepare a private FL model, grounded on their personal information, iterative predisposition uploading and concurring their unique model boundaries with one another coordinated with a CC unit [6]. Because of their exceptional highlights, model is applied in a wide assortment of pragmatic activities comparable as portable console vaticination [7], speaker and order acknowledgment [8], and information storehouses for insurance agencies [9].

Mills et al., have proposed an adapted FedAvg to use a distributed form of Adam optimisation which reduces the convergence time to produce Communication-Efficient FedAvg [10]. Popovoski et al. have proposed blockchained FL architecture which updates the local models that are usually exchanged and verified. The authors have also analyze an end-to-end latency

BlockFL to optimize the rate of block generation [11]. An effective federated frame work called MOON has been designed to utilize the similarity between model representations. This process is used to correct the local model of distinct users that includes conducting in the level of contrastive learning model [12]. A decentralized scheme [13] has been proposed for reliable device selection using FL in blockchain. This scheme has been proposed for the purpose of attaining efficient reputation of the users.

3 Communication-Efficient FL

3.1 Basic Concepts of FL

Federated learning is a genuinely new sort of education that stays away from incorporated information assortment and model preparation. Then, at that point, FL is tied in with preparing different AI models on portable inclination (which are applied to as visitors) and furthermore joining the aftereffects of all comparative models into a solitary model that lives at a garçon. Hence, a model is prepared on inclination themselves utilizing ground-verity information and simply the prepared model partakes with a garçon. This way the stoner's information is mishandled to make machine/profound proficiency models while keeping information hidden. For this situation, FL benefits from the stoner's information without uncovering their sequestration. The crude information is accessible at the stoner's inclination and noway moved to a server farm, however, a model out of this information is made, which thus is moved to the garçon. The FL can be exemplified in an accompanying manner

1. A general (took an interest) model is prepared garçon-side.
2. Various visitors are named for preparing on top of the overall model.
3. The named visitors download the model.
4. The overall model is prepared on the inclination, utilizing the addicts' private information, grounded on a streamlining calculation like the stochastic grade drop.
5. A synopsis of the progressions made to the model.
6. The garçon summations the updates from all inclinations to enhance the took part model. Update accumulation is finished utilizing another calculation called the unified averaging calculation.

The most common way of moving the overall model to versatile predisposition and smoothing out them as indicated by the entered rundown of updates is rehashed. Allow b be boundaries of the model, ideal case of the model is

$$\min_{b} \frac{1}{N} \sum_{i=1}^{U} \sum_{n \in S_i} f(b, x_{i,n}, y_{i,n}) \tag{1}$$

where, S_i represents a bunch of N_i preparing information tests of every gadget i. Each preparing information test gadget i in n that comprises information vector

$x_{i,n}$ and yield vector $y_{i,n}$, f representing the function of capacity, and N denotes the complete number of preparing tests.

This typical model advancement calculation is the first stochastic gradient descent framework [15]. At each iteration, every gadget i utilizesτ SGD rounds to prepare its unique model o_i. Specifically, the update cycle at replication t starts at CC taking part of worldwide model b_t, that first sets the unique models to $o_{i,t+1} = b_t$, trailed by τ nearby SGD way,

$$q_{i,t+1}^{k} = q_{i,t+1}^{k-1} - \frac{\beta_{t+1}^{k}}{N_{i,t+1}^{k}} \sum_{n \in S_{i,t+1}^{k}} \nabla f\left(q_{i,t+1}^{k-1}, x_{i,n}, y_{i,n}\right) \tag{2}$$

where, $q_{i,t+1}^{k}$ represents the nearby model of gadget i at k updations of neighborhood FL model iterations $t+1$, β_{t+1}^{k} represents the rate of learning, $S_{i,t+1}^{k}$ denotes the dataset preparation of stoner i at unique step k of iteration i that comprises of $N_{i,t+1}^{k}$ preparing tests capriciously named from the first preparation dataset S_i, and $\nabla f(\cdot)$ is the genuine capacity regarding the model boundaries.

Whenever every gadget finishes τ method of unique FL preparing by means of Eq. 2 that sends their prepared the parameters of unique model, $q_{i,t+1}^{\tau} - b_t$. The CC summations entered unique model boundaries of the sharing predisposition to a global model as

$$b_{t+1} = \frac{1}{N} \sum_{i=1}^{U} N_i \left(q_{i,t+1}^{\tau} - b_t\right) + b_t \tag{3}$$

The local SGD method of local and global models update based on Eq. 2 and Eq. 3 respectively. At confluence, $b = q_1 = \cdots = q_U$.

3.2 Probability Based Gadget Selection Method

Because of a restricted organization asset and energy-obliged inclination, just a subset of predisposition can partake in FL at every replication. Consequently, it's important to plan a gadget determination framework that chooses the predisposition that can essentially improve confluence speed and preparing misfortune to run the model. To present our proposed gadget choice plan, we initially characterize

$$g_{i,t} = \sum_{k=1}^{\tau} \sum_{n \in S_{i,t+1}^{k}} \nabla \left(q_{i,t+1}^{k-1}, x_{i,n}, y_{i,n}\right) \tag{4}$$

here, d_i denotes the distance from device i to the CC. $\alpha \in [0,1]$. $g_{i,t}$ determines the participation probability of each device. The proposed model is to anticipate whether to increase the confluence speed of the global model to the optimal global model and compared to invariant selection as in [14]. Moreover, d_i is the model parameter that determines the distance of the transmission which affects the transmission delay. As a result, right hand side of the equation Eq. 4 gives the transmission delay per learning step. The CC model updates the probability connection of devices $p_{i,t}$ is given by

$$p_{i,t} = \frac{\alpha \left\| g_{i,t} \right\|}{\sum_{i=1}^{U} \left\| g_{i,t} \right\|} + (1-\alpha) \frac{\max_{j \in \mu} d_j - d_i}{\sum_{i=1}^{\mu} \left(\max_{j \in \mu} d_j - d_i \right)} \tag{5}$$

Here, the Eq. 5, the probability $p_{i,t}$ of gadget i at round t depends on the contribution and its transmission delay to the model. Additional term which affects the convergence speed that device carryout respective local update.

4 Simulation Results

We simulate our proposed FL framework for written by hand number ID and object acknowledgment. For correlation purposes, an FL calculation that utilizes the proposed gadget choice and asset assignment plans without the construction of unique FL model boundaries; and a standard FL calculation [15], that erratically decides gadget determination and asset designation without compacting the first FL model boundaries of every gadget. All approved settings are definite in equipments and Styles. We first gauge the proposed correspondence powerful FL plot by relating written by hand numbers from 0 to 9, as displayed in Fig. 1. Then, at that point, the dark whole numbers are the distinguishing proof aftereffects of the proposed FL plot, while the red number is some unacceptable identification result. From Fig. 2, we can see that the proposed FL algorithm can rightly identify the handwritten integers.

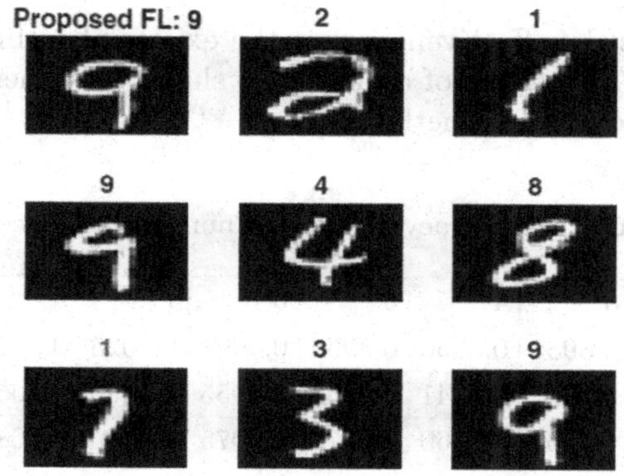

Fig. 2. An example of implementing FL for handwritten digit identification

Figure 2 shows how the distinguishing proof precision changes as the quantity of chosen gadgets differs. From Fig. 2, we can see that pattern a can accomplish preferable execution over baseline a i.e., FedAvg [16] and baseline b as FedProx [17]. This is on the grounds that gauge a utilizations the proposed gadget determination plot, subsequently further developing ID precision. Figure 2 likewise shows that, as the quantity of chosen gadgets expands, the hole between the proposed FL and benchmark diminishes. This is because of the way that, as the quantity of chosen gadgets builds, the effects of pressure blunders on the worldwide FL model update decline.

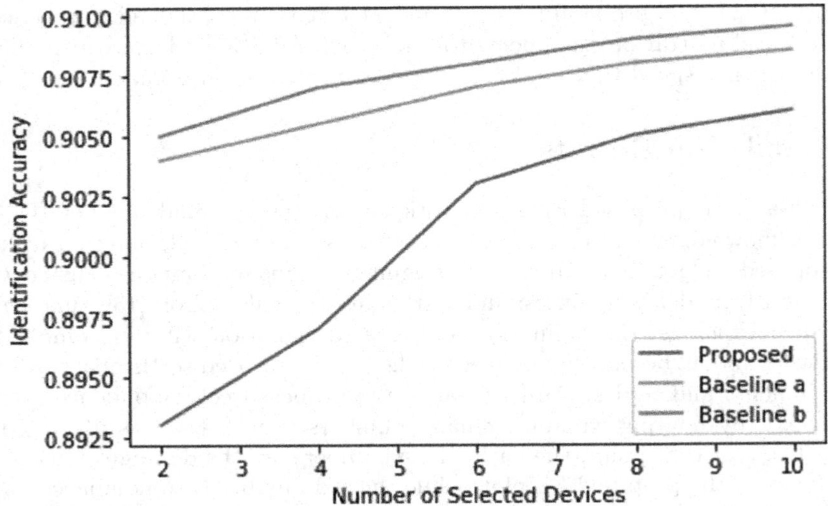

Fig. 3. Accuracy with respect to variable number of devices

The Fig. 3 shows the effectiveness over the existing baseline models FedAvg [16] and FedProx [17] in terms of accuracy. It shows that the proposed method outperforms over the existing methods.

Table 1. Accuracy by varying number of devices

	2	3	4	5	6	7	8	9	10
Proposed	0.8925	0.8937	0.8950	0.8963	0.9001	0.9025	0.9028	0.9033	0.9038
Baseline a	0.9035	0.9037	0.9041	0.9050	0.9055	0.9060	0.9065	0.9068	0.9070
Baseline b	0.9050	0.9057	0.9060	0.9070	0.9075	0.9080	0.9085	0.9089	0.9095

Table 1 demonstrates the efficacy of the proposed method over the existing baseline algorithms FedAvg [16] and FedProx [17] in terms of accuracy.

Table 2. Energy Consumption by varying number of devices

	2	3	4	5	6	7	8	9	10
Proposed	0	10	30	70	100	130	200	250	270
Baseline a	250	350	450	550	600	800	1000	1500	1800
Baseline b	260	400	500	800	1200	1400	1600	1800	2000

Table 2 demonstrate the results of the proposed method and its efficacy over the existing methods in terms of energy.

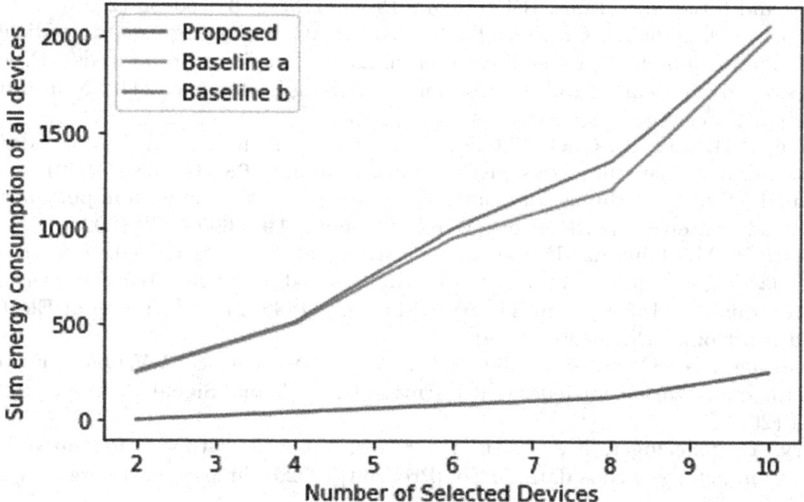

Fig. 4. Energy consumption with respect to number of devices

From Fig. 4, we see that the proposed FL altogether decreases the energy that every one gadgets utilized for FL boundary transmission. This is on the grounds that we mutually upgrade remote asset assignment and gadget determination.

5 Conclusion and Future Scope

We proposed a communication-efficient FL framework. In that frame work, we proposed probabilistic device selection algorithm is designed. We have shown that even though the number of selected devices varies, our proposed method performs better than the baseline algorithms. Moreover, we decrease the transmission time and to downsize the amount of the model boundaries traded by gadgets, and an effective remote asset designation conspire is created. Reproduction results show that the proposed system can further develop identification exactness.

A future direction is to distinct the model classes as well as model heterogeneity. Also, the proposed methods may be emulated to address heterogeneous few-shot learning, multi-modal learning, and multi-task learning.

References

1. Voulodimos, A., Doulamis, N., Doulamis, A., Protopapadakis, E.: Deep learning for computer vision: a brief review. Comput. Intell. Neurosci. **2018**, 1–13 (2018)
2. Jurafsky, D., Martin, J.H.: Speech and Language Processing: An Introduction to Speech Recognition, Computational Linguistics and Natural Language Processing. Prentice-Hall, Upper Saddle River (2008)
3. Li, T., Sahu, A.K., Talwalkar, A., Smith, V.: Federated learning: challenges, methods, and future directions. IEEE Signal Process. Mag. **37**, 50–60 (2020)
4. Chen, T., Giannakis, G., Sun, T., Yin, W.: LAG: lazily aggregated gradient for communication-efficient distributed learning. In: Bengio, S., et al. (eds.) Proceedings of Advances in Neural Information Processing Systems, p. 2440. Neural Information Processing Systems Foundation (2018)
5. Yang, H.H., Liu, Z., Quek, T.Q.S., Poor, H.V.: Scheduling policies for federated learning in wireless networks. IEEE Trans. Commun. **68**, 317–333 (2020)
6. Ren, J., et al.: Scheduling for cellular federated edge learning with importance and channel awareness. IEEE Trans. Wirel. Commun. **19**, 7690–7703 (2020)
7. Amiri, M.M., Gunduz, D.: Machine learning at the wireless edge: distributed stochastic gradient descent over-the-air. In: Proceedings of 2019 IEEE International Symposium on Information Theory (ISIT), pp. 1432–1436. Institute of Electrical and Electronics Engineers (2019)
8. Shlezinger, N., Chen, M., Eldar, Y.C., Poor, H.V., Cui, S.: UVeQFed: universal vector quantization for federated learning. IEEE Trans. Signal Process. **69**, 500–514 (2021)
9. Sery, T., Shlezinger, N., Cohen, K., Eldar, Y.C.: Over-the-air federated learning from heterogeneous data. arXiv [Preprint] (2020). https://arxiv.org/abs/2009.12787
10. Mills, J., Jia, H., Min, G.: Communication-efficient federated learning for wireless edge intelligence in IoT. IEEE Internet Things J. **7**(7), 5986–5994 (2019)
11. Popovski, P., et al.: Wireless access for ultra-reliable low-latency communication (URLLC): principles and building blocks. IEEE Netw. **32**, 16–23 (2018)
12. Acar, D.A.E., et al.: Federated learning based on dynamic regularization. arXiv preprint arXiv:2111.04263 (2021)
13. Kang, J., et al.: Reliable federated learning for mobile networks. IEEE Wirel. Commun. **27**(2), 72–80 (2020)
14. McMahan, B., Moore, E., Ramage, D., Hampson, S., y Arcas, B.A.: Communication-efficient learning of deep networks from decentralized data. In: Proceedings of Machine Learning Research, vol. 54, pp. 1273–1282 (2017)
15. Bonawitz, K., et al.: Towards federated learning at scale: System design. In: Proceedings of the 2019 11th International Conference on Systems and Machine Learning. Association for Computing Machinery (2019)
16. McMahan, B., Moore, E., Ramage, D., Hampson, S., y Arcas, B.A.: Communication-efficient learning of deep networks from decentralized data. In: Artificial Intelligence and Statistics, pp. 1273–1282 (2017)
17. Li, T., Sahu, A.K., Zaheer, M., Sanjabi, M., Talwalkar, A., Smith, V.: Federated optimization in heterogeneous networks. arXiv preprint arXiv:1812.06127 (2018)

Learning

Pavement Distress Detection Using Deep Learning Based Methods: A Survey on Role, Challenges and Opportunities

Ankit Khatri(✉), Ravi Khatri, Abhishek Kumar, and Kuldeep Kumar

Dr B R Ambedkar National Institute of Technology Jalandhar, Jalandhar, Punjab, India
{ankitk.cs.21,ravik.cs.21,abhishekk.cs.21,kumark}@nitj.ac.in

Abstract. Roadways have always been one of the most used modes of transportation, and their contribution to the nation's economy is also huge. To meet the demands of the growing global population and an increase in urbanization, there has been an exponential rise in the number of vehicles plying on the roads as well as the length of the roads. With this increase in traffic, coupled with other issues like heavy rainfall, the material used for the construction of the road, etc., the condition of the roads deteriorates with cracks and potholes developing on them, which may lead to serious accidents. For effective maintenance of roads and to reduce the associated risks, these defects must be detected. With the advent of Deep Learning (DL) in the recent past and its applications in various sectors, we have comprehensively explored various approaches, particularly using DL in this study, along with the associated challenges in adopting such techniques and future opportunities in this domain. Based on our analysis, using object detection-based models turned out to outperform other approaches.

Keywords: Pavement distress · Deep learning · CNN · Object recognition

1 Introduction

India, with 11% of the world's share of fatalities due to road accidents, sadly tops this list [1]. According to Ministry of Road Transport and Highways data, the majority of these deaths occur between the ages of 18 and 60 [1], which is the most economically productive age. Thus, it leads to a great loss to the country in the form of its most precious asset, i.e., human resources. The World Health Organization has stated that among the major causes of deaths in the world, road accidents stand at the eighth position. These deaths incur a huge burden in the form of treatment costs as well as hamper the productivity of the dead, impaired, and even their family members. Although there are a variety of causes that lead to such accidents, which include overspeeding, driver's negligence, bad condition of roads, the existence of cracks and potholes, lack of strong vehicle standards in the country, etc. [36]. Out of these, one of the major reasons for this massive number of fatalities is the poor condition of roads with multiple defects, which are caused by heavy rainfall, which results in inundation of water over the pavements,

S. K. Panda et al. (Eds.): CoCoLe 2022, CCIS 1729, pp. 195–207, 2022.
https://doi.org/10.1007/978-3-031-21750-0_17

the rising number of vehicles plying on them, the lack of quality construction material used and unstable soil. The significance of our study is as follows:

For the efficient maintenance of the roads and to ensure the safety of people on these roads, the magnitude of such road damage must be known. There are multiple ways to assess the extent of road damage, which may be broadly classified into manual, semi-automated, and fully automated.

In the case of manual assessment, the assessors ply the road using a vehicle moving slowly. They note down the extent of such defects by visual assessment. But this approach takes a lot of time and requires extensive human interference.

In the case of semi-automated assessment [2–4], the evaluation of road damage is done through the collection of images using automated systems. These images are collected using a swift-moving vehicle. These are then sent for manual defect detection, which again requires human intervention.

In fully automated road damage assessment, complex and modern sets of sensors [3–5] are installed on the moving vehicle. These sensors gather the images of the roads, which are then sent for automated defect detection. But this kind of fully automated system is very costly and many countries lack the funds to implement such systems. However, in today's world, mobile phone devices have very good cameras and impressive computation power, which presents an economical and efficient solution to the above problem. For example, Mertz et al. [6] have used mobile phone devices to collect images of roads that were positioned on various frequently plying vehicles. Mobile phone devices with sensors were used by Casas-Avellaneda and Lopez-Parra [7] to detect potholes on the roads. A mobile application was developed by Maeda et al. [8] for automatic road evaluation in Japan.

Motivation for this Study: Roads and infrastructure are crucial to national growth. Metaled or unmetalled roads drive economic growth. Natural disasters, environmental causes, human interference, inexpensive building materials, and normal wear and tear degrade roads, causing cracks, potholes, and other deformations that cause accidents, human and animal deaths, economic slowness, etc. It's important to repair these problems and identify them first. There have been manual and automated approaches to achieve it. After DL's excellent performance in image issues, various research has analyzed its ability to automatically recognise road damage. Our paper includes all significant and state-of-the-art methodologies implemented in this domain, together with their advantages, limitations, and performance over key evaluation measures. This study aims to help future scholars obtain a complete source of important studies in this field.

This study includes all recent and state-of-the-art road damage identification solutions presented by different authors. We've also included the benefits, cons, and challenges of these studies.

The remainder of the paper is organized as follows: First, we have discussed a few basic concepts and terminologies in Sect. 2. In Sect. 3, we have reviewed research articles comprehensively related to the problem domain. In Sect. 4, we have included the challenges in this domain and the contributions made by our study. Finally, we have concluded the paper in Sect. 5 along with future scope.

2 Basic Concepts and Terminologies

In this section, we will discuss some relevant concepts and terminologies using which the problem of pavement distress detection has been solved by most of the studies in the literature survey. The concept of deep learning is the baseline for proposing solutions to the problem. Various architectures, including CNN, region-based CNN, YOLO, etc., have been used by various studies to propose their solutions. These architectures have been explained in brief in this section.

2.1 Deep Learning

This type of learning tries to mimic the workings of the human brain. There are billions of neurons present inside a human brain that operate using electrical impulses [42]. In DL, we try to create a similar network of neurons, which is known as a neural network that consists of multiple layers. The first layer accepts the inputs, the last layer outputs the results, and in between the network may contain hidden layers. As the data is growing at a very fast rate and with the advancements in the computation power of the systems, the capacity of handling such large data has drastically improved. Deep Learning techniques coupled with this improved processing power have achieved significant results in problems involving big data. Deep learning is used in different areas, such as natural language processing, optical character recognition, recommendation systems, etc. It has proven to be extremely effective, particularly in the identification of objects in images, and it is also used to identify road damage using images of defects.

2.2 Convolutional Neural Networks

It is used in a variety of image processing applications. It extracts important information from an image through a four-layered process that includes a convolution layer, a pooling layer, a ReLU layer, and a fully connected layer [43]. This type of neural network works on data that is in grid format. An example of this kind of data is images. Hence, for image processing tasks, convolutional neural networks are preferred.

2.3 Object Detection Algorithms

With the emergence of the concept of the self-driving car, there has been a significant increase in the field of object detection. The main aim of this task is to locate the entity of interest in the given input image. As a conventional CNN cannot be used for the efficient implementation of such tasks, advanced algorithms have been developed. These architectures are briefly described below:

R-CNN: [37] Using the selective search algorithm, a set of 2000 regions is drawn out from the image and the task of finding the objects is performed.

Fast R-CNN: [38] It is quicker than the R-CNN algorithm, as the convolution phase is performed just once for each input and a corresponding feature map is produced from it.

Faster R-CNN: [39] It outperforms the above algorithms by using a different network to forecast the region's proposals instead of using the selective search algorithm.

You Only Look Once (YOLO): [40] This object detection algorithm creates bounding boxes along with the class probabilities using only a single CNN. Then, to find the thing of interest, the box with a likelihood estimate above a certain threshold is chosen.

Single Shot Detection: [41] Similar to the YOLO algorithm, the Single Shot Detection algorithm is also capable of detecting the object of interest in a single scan of the image. It is faster and more accurate than R-CNN's as it gets rid of the region proposals used in the latter.

3 Literature Review

There has been a significant amount of research in the domain of pavement distress detection. In this section, we have summarized different methodologies used by researchers. We have also listed the datasets used by the authors for the implementation process in Table 1. We have explored various machine learning techniques which use advanced detection algorithms for the above problem domain. Table 2 is a summary of the articles we looked at, which brings this section to a close.

Du et al. [9] have used a huge dataset of 45,788 images that were collected using a camera mounted on a dedicated vehicle covering almost 200 km at a rate compared with fewer than 80 km per hour for assessing road damage. They have used the YOLO algorithm to project the position of the fault as well as its category in a given input image. However, they have not used the cost-effective approach of using mobile phone devices for image collection. Instead, they have used advanced high-resolution cameras for this purpose. The YOLO-based model used has a very high level of accuracy and doesn't require any manual work during detection.

Majidifard et al. [10] have proposed a solution using a labelled dataset that consists of images collected from different camera views, which consists of both top-down and wide-view for the classification purpose. They have gathered street-view images using the Google API and have manually labelled them into nine different categories of road damage. They have also collated the outcomes of the Faster R-CNN model with the YOLO-based model, which shows that the latter performs much better. However, they used a small dataset consisting of 7,237 images only. The advantage of their approach is the easy availability of Google street-view images.

The solution presented by Patra et al. [11] uses a CNN based model which achieves the task of pothole detection using a dataset consisting of images collected using the Google API. They have also compared their model with six other conventional models. Their suggested framework delivers a significant accuracy of around 97.6%. The area under the curve value (AUC) is also greater than that of those other models.

According to Goodfellow et al. [12], to achieve sufficiently good results, a dataset consisting of at least 5,000 images of each category must be used for the task of image classification. Although the techniques used for image collection using the Google API by the above authors have the advantage of the images being easily accessible, and free of cost, this advantage comes with the tedious task of manually labeling each collected image which is very time-consuming.

Smartphones were used for collecting the images in a methodology developed by Maeda et al. [8] for the task of pavement distress detection. This study was a major breakthrough and served as a starting point for future studies. It categorized the road defects in Japan's road network into eight different classes. They developed a dataset which was called the Road Damage Dataset-2018, which was also made open-source for easy accessibility. They also developed a mobile application for instantaneous road damage evaluation. This application was adopted by multiple townships in Japan. The IEEE Big Data Conference, which was held in the USA in 2018, conducted a challenge named Big Data Cup [1], in which several teams submitted solutions to the problem of road damage type detection. Although the solutions provided were novel and better in terms of accuracy than the model proposed by Maeda et al. [8], the dataset used by these teams was the same as developed by [8].

The solution proposed by Alfarrarjeh et al. [13] uses Deep Learning methodologies for performing the task of finding the entity of interest in a given input image. They have used the YOLO object detection algorithm. The model was trained on a dataset that had different categories of damage as defined by the Japan Road Association.

[14] gave a solution that was again a part of the IEEE Big Data Cup challenge organized in 2018 in which they improved the accuracy of the model proposed by [8] by performing certain hyperparameter tuning. They also presented the approaches to enhancing the available dataset. Some modifications were also proposed to the dataset provided by [8], which contained 9,053 images.

The model proposed by Wang et al. [15] was again submitted as a solution to the IEEE Big Data Cup challenge-2018. They used Faster R-CNN and SSD algorithms for the task of object recognition. They used VGG-16 and ImageNet pre-trained ResNet-101 as the underlying basis of these object detection models. For better accuracy, they have used ensemble techniques. Wang et al. [16] have used Faster R-CNN for classifying the types of road damage, training their model on the dataset provided by [8]. The parameters were tuned based on the examination of the area of the location of the damage as well as the aspect ratio. A few data augmentation techniques were also applied before training.

Angulo et al. [17] augmented the dataset provided by [8] by the addition of more images gathered from Mexico and Italy. Their dataset contained 1,803,454 images collected using mobile phone devices. Various publicly available datasets supplemented with crowdsourced images are the sources of this huge dataset. The labelling of the dataset was done manually and the location, damage type, as well as the extent of damage were marked for each image. Both the conventional and deep learning-based models were trained on this dataset, and their performance was compared. The conventional model used was LBP-Cascaded Classifier, and the deep learning models used were RetinaNet and MobileNet.

More images were gathered from Italy by Roberts et al. [18] using the mobile application developed by [8]. They have classified the type of road damage as well as the intensity of the damage. Biçici and Zeybek [19] used UAV photogrammetry to generate point clouds for detecting road distress, which is considered to be a high-accuracy, efficient, automated method for detection. The SFM pipeline was used to generate a high-density 3D model from UAV images. After that, a vertically based algorithm was used to get rid of unrelated parts of the environment in a 3D point cloud.

Zhang et al. [20] presented a CNN-centered methodology for correctly detecting pavement cracks, which is called CrackNet. It works on over one million parameters during the learning process and has over five layers. It was trained over multiple three-dimensional road images under various conditions and was tested successfully. Using a gradient-based optimization function for training to minimize the cost is the main objective. They have used Mini-batch Gradient Descent in their study. Cracks were detected at a pixel level by their proposed model. However, in this version of CrackNet, it requires considerable processing time and has a lot of difficulties in detecting hairline cracks.

Another study [21] uses a dataset of 500 images to categorize each image using supervised deep CNN for training purposes. The images were collected by a mobile phone. Their proposed model outperforms other models used in this problem domain. The Drop out methodology is used for reducing the overfitting of their proposed model by using a threshold value of 0.5. Silva and Lucena [22] are aimed at detecting cracks on concrete surfaces using a model centered upon machine learning that is intended to increase automation by combining with UAV (unmanned aerial vehicles). As a result, the transfer learning technique was employed. For the development of this model, the opensource model VGG16 was used.

Anand et al. [23] have proposed an approach to detect potholes and cracks using texture and spatial features centered upon Deep Neural Networks. Their proposed model uses the image texture to categorize damaged roads. They have combined two separate datasets, of which the first one consists of grayscale images collected using a mobile phone device and the second one consists of images collected using sensors. They have achieved very good accuracy over other models.

In [24], Fan et al. developed a technique for learning crack structure without altering unprocessed photos to analyze different pavement conditions. The model used two datasets, which consisted of images collected using a mobile phone device. The performance of their model was collated with different other models. Their approach in terms of dealing with different pavement textures shows a better performance. Without any preprocessing, the network is able to learn from the images that are unprocessed.

Zhu et al. [44] came up with a way to find potholes on roads by using three cutting-edge methods: Faster R-CNN, YOLOv3, and YOLOv4. These were trained on a set of data that was made by unmanned aerial vehicles. With an average accuracy of 56.62%, YOLOv3 was better at making predictions than the other methods.

With a cost-efficient video data collection technique, Zhang et al. [45] proposed a pavement distress detection technique using convolutional neural networks. In this work, the detectors are put into different groups. The F1-score for all kinds of flaws was compared, but the score went up when two kinds of cracks were combined into one.

Guerrieri et al. [46] used multiple public datasets to find pavement damage and created a new dataset for stone pavement damage. They then used deep learning and YOLOv3 to train a model to find pavement damage. Different parameters, such as loss, precision, recall, and RSME, are used to measure performance. For different kinds of flaws, the rate of finding them was between 91.0% and 97.3%.

Wen et al. [47] came up with a good deep learning model that was trained on both 2D and 3D images. The model's performance was judged based on a parameter called "interaction over union," which gives a detection accuracy of 83.7%.

Table 1 describes the databases utilized in various investigations. The sizes of these datasets are classified into three categories: less than (<) 1000 images; greater than (>) 1000; less than 5000 images; and greater than 5000 images. In Table 1, NK refers to Not Known, which means that the location from where the dataset was collected is unknown.

Table 1. Datasets available for road damage detection.

Dataset name	Collected from (Location)	Size of the dataset
CrackIT [25]	NK	<1000
CrackTree200 [31]	NK	<1000
SDNET2018 [30]	USA	<1000
Crack500 [33]	USA	<1000
GAPs v1 [3]	Germany	Between 1000–5000
GAPs v2 [32]	Germany	Between 1000–5000
Majidifard et al. [10]	USA	>5000
Maeda et al. [8]	Japan	>5000
Angulo et al. [17]	Italy, Japan, Mexico	>5000
RDD-2020 [35]	India, Japan, Czech Republic	>5000
Du et al. [9]	China	>5000

Table 2. Summary of the works related to the role of Deep Learning and Object detection algorithms for road damage detection.

Author Name	Techniques used	Dataset collected using	Collection procedure	Captured vision	Performance
Oliveira and Correia [25], 2017	KNN algorithm	Ocular equipment	–	Vertical	F score: 0.97, Precision: 0.98, Recall: 0.95
Shi et al. [26], 2016	Random Forest algorithm	Mobile Phone	Static	Vertical	F score: 0.939, Precision: 0.945, Recall: 0.936

(*continued*)

Table 2. (*continued*)

Author Name	Techniques used	Dataset collected using	Collection procedure	Captured vision	Performance
Majidifard et al. [10], 2020	Faster R-CNN and YOLOv2	Google API	–	Vertical and Wide	F score: 0.84, Precision: 0.93, Recall: 0.77
Maeda et al. [8], 2018	Single Shot detection algorithm, MobileNet	Mobile Phone	Mobile Application	Wide	Precision and recall greater than 71% and 77% in MobileNet and InceptionV2 respectively
Angulo et al. [17], 2019	RetinaNet	Mobile Phone	–	Wide	mAP: 0.91522
Cui et al. [27], 2015	Random Forest Algorithm	Mobile Phone	Static	Vertical	F score: 0.79, Precision: 0.78, Recall: 0.81
Mei et al. [28], 2020	GAN	GoPro camera device	–	Wide	F score: 0.92, Precision: 0.97, Recall: 0.88
Li et al. [29], 2014	Deep Learning	Mechanized pavement assessor	–	Vertical	Alligator, transverse, and longitudinal crack accuracy rates are 97.5 percent, 100 percent, and 88 percent, respectively
Eisenbach et al. [3], 2017	ASINVOSNet	High-tech Industrial Camera	Mobile Vehicle	Vertical	BER: 0.071, Accuracy: 94%, F score: 0.88
Dorafshan et al. [30], 2020	AlexNet Deep CNN	Camera	–	Vertical	Accuracy: 95.52% using transfer learning with 10 training epochs
Zou et al. [31], 2012	Minimum spanning Trees	Camera	–	Vertical	F score: 0.85, Precision: 0.79, Recall: 0.92

(*continued*)

Table 2. (*continued*)

Author Name	Techniques used	Dataset collected using	Collection procedure	Captured vision	Performance
Stricker et al. [32], 2019	ASINVOSNet, ResNet	High-tech Industrial Camera	Mobile Vehicle	Vertical	F score: 0.90, BER: 0.08, GME: 0.91
Yang et al. [33], 2020	Hierarchical Boosting Architecture	Mobile Phone	–	Vertical	AIU: 0.17, ODS: 0.68, OIS: 0.70
Weng et al. [34], 2019	Edge Identification and Morphological Functioning	-	–	Vertical	Reconstruction accuracy: 93.7% and the coefficient of correlation between breadth assessment findings and actual results is 0.97
Zhu et al. [44], 2021	Faster RCNN, YOLOv3 and YOLOv4	Unmanned Aerial Vehicle	–	Vertical	The prediction performance of YOLOv3 outperformed the other techniques with an average precision of 56.62%
Zhang et al. [45], 2021	CNN	GOPRO hero 7	–	–	The F1 score for the crack class increased when two classes of cracks were merged together and tested
Guerrieri et al. [46], 2022	YOLOv3	Digital Camera	–	–	The detection rate for several types of defects was in the range 91.0% to 97.3%

(*continued*)

Table 2. (*continued*)

Author Name	Techniques used	Dataset collected using	Collection procedure	Captured vision	Performance
Wen et al. [47], 2022	PDSNet	Camera and lasers	–	–	The model gives a detection accuracy of 83.7%

4 Challenges in This Domain and Contributions of Our Study

In this arena, problems include road distress detection and comparing existing solutions. Effective damage estimation, including more cracks and defect types for detection, installing and mounting developed systems on vehicles, performing efficiently on road images in different lighting conditions, complex crack topology, and including more images of roads from various countries remain challenges in this area. Low contrast between damages and surrounds, inhomogeneity of concentration along fissures, potential reflections identical to cracks, and real-time distress identification also offer obstacles in developing sophisticated pavement fault detection systems. Traditional, semi-automated, and completely autonomous operations are ineffective in terms of cost, time, and labor. The organizations responsible for maintaining decent road conditions still struggle to cope with this problem due to a lack of finances for pricey image-capturing devices and a unified dataset that is not limited to photographs from certain nations and damages in those countries.

This paper reviews studies on cost-effective road defect identification. Several state-of-the-art investigations on this issue domain included using deep learning architectures. These strategies must be explored to reduce road fatalities and preserve their condition because they automate pavement inspection, are cost-effective, need less human intervention, and save time. We've also summarized relevant datasets. Future researchers can utilize this information to construct a standard dataset to compare model results. This can also help government agencies employ a holistic database for detection. This study will give scholars a rundown of previous works and their shortcomings. Future researchers can expand on our extensive work. We've listed the authors' datasets, which will be beneficial for future research in this area.

5 Conclusion and Future Scope

This paper has explored the role of various techniques that use advanced models to detect damage on roads using images collected at various geographical locations. The techniques using state-of-the-art object detection models fared better than other approaches in our analysis. Although there are several ways to perform this task using advanced devices, these techniques are not cost-effective as many countries lack the finance required to implement such sophisticated systems. Therefore, to overcome the above constraint, researchers have come up with alternative cost-effective strategies that mostly deal with the data collection phase. As the problem of road accidents is universal in nature, the dataset used must be made more inclusive with images from the world over. A video input would also help to improve the functionality of existing techniques. To expand the coverage of a model, other sensor data from mobile phones can be integrated. We have surveyed these approaches along with their advantages, which will be handy for any future research in this field.

References

1. Road Accidents in India: Ministry of Road Transport and Highways, Transport Research Wing, Govt. of India (2018). https://morth.nic.in/sites/default/files/Road_Accidednt.pdf
2. McGhee, K.: Automated Pavement Distress Collection Techniques, National Cooperative Highway Research Program, NCHRP Synthesis 334 Report, Transportation Research Board, Washington DC (2004). https://doi.org/10.17226/23348
3. Eisenbach, M.: Gross, How to get pavement distress detection ready for deep learning? A systematic approach. In: International Joint Conference on Neural Networks (IJCNN), pp. 2039–2047 (2017). https://doi.org/10.1109/IJCNN.2017.7966101
4. Zhang, D., et al.: Automatic pavement defect detection using 3D laser profiling technology. Autom. Constr. **96**, 350–365 (2018). https://doi.org/10.1016/j.autcon.2018.09.019
5. Guan, J., Yang, X., Ding, L., Cheng, X., Lee, V.C., Jin, C.: Automated pixel-level pavement distress detection based on stereo vision and deep learning. Autom. Constr. **129**, 103788 (2021). https://doi.org/10.1016/j.autcon.2021.103788
6. Mertz, C., Varadharajan, S., Jose, S., Sharma, K., Wander, L., Wang, J.: City-wide road distress monitoring with smartphones. In: Proceedings of ITS World Congress, pp. 1–9 (2014). https://www.ri.cmu.edu/pub_files/2014/9/road_monitor_mertz_final.pdf. Accessed 28 July 2021
7. Avellaneda, D.A.C., López-Parra, J.F.: Detection and localization of potholes in roadways using smartphones. DYNA **83**(195), 156–162 (2016). https://doi.org/10.15446/dyna.v83n195.44919
8. Maeda, H., Sekimoto, Y., Seto, T., Kashiyama, T., Omata, H.: Road damage detection and classification using deep neural networks with smartphone images. Comput. Aided Civ. Infrastruct. Eng. **33**, 1127–1141 (2018). https://doi.org/10.1111/mice.12387
9. Yuchuan, D., Pan, N., Zihao, X., Fuwen Deng, Y., Shen, H.K.: Pavement distress detection and classification based on YOLO network. Int. J. Pavement Eng. **22**(13), 1659–1672 (2020). https://doi.org/10.1080/10298436.2020.1714047
10. Majidifard, H., Jin, P., Adu-Gyamfi, Y., Buttlar, W.G.: Pavement image datasets: a new benchmark dataset to classify and densify pavement distresses. Transp. Res. Rec. **2674**, 328–339 (2020). https://doi.org/10.1177/0361198120907283
11. Patra, S., Middya, A.I., Roy, S.: PotSpot: Participatory sensing based monitoring system for pothole detection using deep learning. Multimedia Tools Appl. **80**(16), 25171–25195 (2021). https://doi.org/10.1007/s11042-021-10874-4
12. Goodfellow, I., Bengio, Y., Courville, A.: Deep Learning. MIT press, (2016). http://www.deeplearningbook.org
13. Alfarrarjeh, A., Trivedi, D., Kim, S.H., Shahabi, C.: A deep learning approach for road damage detection from smartphone images. In: 2018 IEEE International Conference on Big Data (Big Data), pp. 5201–5204. IEEE (2018). https://doi.org/10.1109/BigData.2018.8621899

14. Kluger, F., et al.: Region-based cycle-consistent data augmentation for object detection. In: 2018 IEEE International Conference on Big Data (Big Data), , pp. 5205–5211. IEEE (2018). https://doi.org/10.1109/BigData.2018.8622318
15. Wang, Y.J., Ding, M., Kan, S., Zhang, S., Lu, C.: Deep proposal and detection networks for road damage detection and classification. In: 2018 IEEE International Conference on Big Data (Big Data), pp. 5224–5227. IEEE (2018). https://doi.org/10.1109/BigData.2018.8622599
16. Wang, W., Wu, B., Yang, S., Wang, Z.: Road damage detection and classification with faster R-CNN. In: 2018 IEEE International Conference on Big Data (Big Data), pp. 5220–5223. IEEE (2018). https://doi.org/10.1109/BigData.2018.8622354
17. Angulo, A., Vega-Fernández, J.A., Aguilar-Lobo, L.M., Natraj, S., Ochoa-Ruiz, G.: Road damage detection acquisition system based on deep neural networks for physical asset management. In: Martínez-Villaseñor, L., Batyrshin, I., Marín-Hernández, A. (eds.) MICAI 2019. LNCS (LNAI), vol. 11835, pp. 3–14. Springer, Cham (2019). https://doi.org/10.1007/978-3-030-33749-0_1
18. Roberts, R., Giancontieri, G., Inzerillo, L., Di Mino, G.: Towards low-cost pavement condition health monitoring and analysis using deep learning. Appl. Sci. **10**, 319 (2020). https://doi.org/10.3390/app10010319
19. Biçici, S., Zeybek, M.: An approach for the automated extraction of road surface distress from a UAV-derived point cloud. Autom. Constr. **122**, 103475 (2021). https://doi.org/10.1016/j.autcon.2020.103475
20. Zhang, A., et al.: Automated pixel-level pavement crack detection on 3D asphalt surfaces using a deep-learning network. Comput. Aided Civ. Infrastruct. Eng. **32**, 805–819 (2017). https://doi.org/10.1111/mice.12297
21. Zhang, L., Yang, F., Zhang, Y.D., Zhu, Y.J.: Road crack detection using deep convolutional neural network. In: 2016 IEEE International Conference on Image Processing (ICIP), pp. 3708–3712. IEEE (2016). https://doi.org/10.1109/ICIP.2016.7533052
22. Silva, W.R.L.D., Lucena, D.S.D.: Concrete cracks detection based on deep learning image classification. In: Multidisciplinary Digital Publishing Institute Proceedings, vol. 2, p. 489 (2018). https://doi.org/10.3390/ICEM18-05387
23. Anand, S., Gupta, S., Darbari, V., Kohli, S.: Crack-pot: autonomous road crack and pothole detection. In: 2018 Digital Image Computing: Techniques and Applications (DICTA), pp. 1–6. IEEE (2018). https://doi.org/10.1109/DICTA.2018.8615819
24. Fan, Z., Wu, Y., Lu, J., Li, W.: Automatic Pavement Crack Detection Based on Structured Prediction with the Convolutional Neural Network. arXiv preprint arXiv:1802.02208 (2018)
25. Oliveira, H., Correia, P.L.: CrackIT—an image processing toolbox for crack detection and characterization. In: 2014 IEEE International Conference on Image Processing (ICIP), pp. 798–802. IEEE (2014). https://doi.org/10.1109/ICIP.2014.7025160
26. Shi, Y., Cui, L., Qi, Z., Meng, F., Chen, Z.: Automatic road crack detection using random structured forests. IEEE Trans. Intell. Transp. Syst. **17**, 3434–3445 (2016). https://doi.org/10.1109/TITS.2016.2552248
27. Cui, L., Qi, Z., Chen, Z., Meng, F., Shi, Y.: Pavement distress detection using random decision forests. In: Zhang, C., et al. (eds.) ICDS 2015. LNCS, vol. 9208, pp. 95–102. Springer, Cham (2015). https://doi.org/10.1007/978-3-319-24474-7_14
28. Mei, Q., Gül, M.: A cost effective solution for pavement crack inspection using cameras and deep neural networks. Constr. Build. Mater. **256**, 119397 (2020). https://doi.org/10.1016/j.conbuildmat.2020.119397
29. Li, L., Sun, L., Ning, G., Tan, S.: Automatic pavement crack recognition based on BP neural network. PROMET-Traffic Transp. **26**, 11–22 (2014). https://doi.org/10.7307/ptt.v26i1.1477
30. Dorafshan, S., Thomas, R.J., Maguire, M.: SDNET2018: an annotated image dataset for non-contact concrete crack detection using deep convolutional neural networks. Data Brief. **21**, 1664–1668 (2018). https://doi.org/10.1016/j.dib.2018.11.015

31. Qin Zou, Y., Cao, Q.L., Mao, Q., Wang, S.: CrackTree: automatic crack detection from pavement images. Pattern Recogn Let **33**(3), 227–238 (2012). https://doi.org/10.1016/j.patrec.2011.11.004
32. Stricker, R., Eisenbach, M., Sesselmann, M., Debes, K., Gross, H.-M.: Improving visual road condition assessment by extensive experiments on the extended gaps dataset. In: International Joint Conference on Neural Networks (IJCNN), pp. 1–8 (2019). https://doi.org/10.1109/IJCNN.2019.8852257
33. Yang, F., Zhang, L., Yu, S., Prokhorov, D., Mei, X., Ling, H.: Feature pyramid and hierarchical boosting network for pavement crack detection. IEEE Trans. Intell. Transp. Syst. **21**, 1525–1535 (2020). https://doi.org/10.1109/TITS.2019.2910595
34. Weng, X., Huang, Y., Wang, W.: Segment-based pavement crack quantification. Autom. Constr. **105**, 102819 (2019). https://doi.org/10.1016/j.autcon.2019.04.014
35. Arya, D., et al.: Deep learning-based road damage detection and classification for multiple countries. Autom. Construct. **132**, 103935 (2021). ISSN 0926-5805, https://doi.org/10.1016/j.autcon.2021.103935
36. Hatmoko, J., Setiadji, B., Wibowo, M.: Investigating causal factors of road damage: a case study. MATEC Web Conf. **258**, 02007 (2019). https://doi.org/10.1051/matecconf/201925802007
37. Ross, B.G., Donahue, J., Darrell, T., Malik, J.: Rich feature hierarchies for accurate object detection and semantic segmentation. In: 2014 IEEE Conference on Computer Vision and Pattern Recognition, pp. 580–587 (2014)
38. Ross, B.G.: Fast R-CNN. In: 2015 IEEE International Conference on Computer Vision (ICCV), pp. 1440–1448 (2015)
39. Ren, S., He, K., Girshick, R.B., Sun, J.: Faster R-CNN: towards real-time object detection with region proposal networks. IEEE Trans. Pattern Anal. Mach. Intell. **39**, 1137–1149 (2015)
40. Joseph, R., Divvala, S.K., Girshick R.B., Farhadi, A.: You only look once: unified, real-time object detection. In: 2016 IEEE Conference on Computer Vision and Pattern Recognition (CVPR), pp. 779–788 (2016)
41. Liu, W., et al.: SSD: single shot multibox detector. In: Leibe, B., Matas, J., Sebe, N., Welling, M. (eds.) ECCV 2016. LNCS, vol. 9905, pp. 21–37. Springer, Cham (2016). https://doi.org/10.1007/978-3-319-46448-0_2
42. Schmidhuber, J.: Deep learning in neural networks: an overview. Neural Netw. **61**, 85–117 (2015)
43. Zeiler, M.D., Fergus, R.: Visualizing and understanding convolutional networks. In: Fleet, D., Pajdla, T., Schiele, B., Tuytelaars, T. (eds.) Computer Vision – ECCV 2014. ECCV 2014. LNCS, vol. 8689. Springer, Cham (2014). https://doi.org/10.1007/978-3-319-10590-1_53
44. Zhu, J., Zhong, J., Ma, T., Huang, X., Zhang, W., Zhou, Y.: Pavement distress detection using convolutional neural networks with images captured via UAV. Autom. Constr. **133**, 103991 (2022). https://doi.org/10.1016/j.autcon.2021.103991
45. Zhang, C., Nateghinia, E., Miranda-Moreno, L.F., Sun, L.: Pavement distress detection using convolutional neural network (CNN): a case study in Montreal, Canada. Int. J. Transp. Sci. Technol. **11**(2), 298–309 (2022). https://doi.org/10.1016/j.ijtst.2021.04.008
46. Guerrieri, M., Parla, G.: Flexible and stone pavements distress detection and measurement by deep learning and low-cost detection devices. Eng. Failure Anal. **141**, 106714 (2022). https://doi.org/10.1016/j.engfailanal.2022.106714
47. Wen, T., et al.: Automated pavement distress segmentation on asphalt surfaces using a deep learning network. Int. J. Pavem. Eng. 1–14 (2022). https://doi.org/10.1080/10298436.2022.2027414

Performance Enhancement of Animal Species Classification Using Deep Learning

Mahendra Kumar Gourisaria[1(✉)], Utkrisht Singh[1], Vinayak Singh[1], and Ashish Sharma[2]

[1] School of Computer Engineering, KIIT Deemed to be University, Bhubaneswar 751024, Odisha, India
mkgourisaria2010@gmail.com

[2] Department of Computer Engineering and Applications, GLA University, Mathura 281001, Uttar Pradesh, India

Abstract. Automatic recognition of animal classes by their imageries is an imperative and perplexing task, especially with different animal breeds. Many image classification systems have been projected in the literature but they involve some disadvantages like accuracy deterioration or exhaustive confined calculation. This paper focuses on two methodologies: Transfer Learning and Convolutional Neural Network (CNN) for image-based species identification for distinct animal classes and categorized around twenty-eight thousand animal images from Google Images into ten diversified animal classes. For transfer learning, we have implemented VGG16 (Visual Geometry Group), Efficient NetB2, ResNet101 (Residual Network), Efficient NetB7, and Resnet50 networks that are pre-trained and equated the results of the 5 custom-built CNN networks with these networks using various evaluation metrics that can assist practitioners and research biologists in accurately recognizing various animal species. In terms of performance, VGG-16 attained a maximum accuracy of 0.99 and a Least Validation Cross Entropy Loss of 0.044 for the classification of different species of animals.

Keywords: Animal species · Image detection · Deep learning · CNN · VGG16 · Transfer Learning

1 Introduction

Despite being one of the oldest computer techniques, image categorization remains vital for categorizing different animal classes. From Fourier transforms to neural systems, an extensive distance in the field of image cataloging has been traveled. However, it remains a challenging computation process due to hindrances in the photos, such as obstruction, posture variabilities, lighting, concealment, and more.

Cataloging photographs into one of many prearranged modules are referred to as image classification. Physically inspecting and classifying photographs may be laborious, especially when there is a hefty amount of the present, thus computerizing the process with Machine Learning (ML) would be advantageous. Using Deep Learning one

S. K. Panda et al. (Eds.): CoCoLe 2022, CCIS 1729, pp. 208–219, 2022.
https://doi.org/10.1007/978-3-031-21750-0_18

may create a system that can conduct categorization on its own [1]. Therefore, we need to transmute the photographs to numbers so that the computer can easily deduce them. Pre-processing is used to advance image information by overturning unwanted falsifications or augmenting certain image characteristics that are imperative for additional handling of the image dataset.

Accurate species recognition is the groundwork for all facets of phylogenetic exploration and is a vital component of workflows in organic research, including ecology, medicine, and evolutionary studies. While image labeling is utilized universally, it is not fully instigated in some businesses or industries. Animal species classification is one such region because of the complexities of photographs, the automated classification of animal shots remains an unresolved issue. They are the most difficult to label and recognize when it comes to imagery.

Convolutional Neural Networks are generally used for image categorization. Image Classification is the process of extracting characteristics from an image to identify configurations in an image collection because of the large number of trainable restrictions, using an Artificial or Simulated Neural Network (ANN) or CNN to categorize photos would be extremely time-consuming. Therefore, training neural networks necessitates a significant amount of computing power. In such cases, Deep Learning (DL) can be beneficial, it contributes several powerful algorithms for optimizing and simplifying complex tasks [2]. DL is a subset of ML that allows the classifier to consistently characterize data using training sources such as text, images, or voice recognition. Implementing a classifier with several layers can produce better results, but it is more time-consuming and complex. Consequently, we may sporadically use the Transfer Learning principle to develop very effective Neural Networks (NNs).

Despite considerable effort, earlier studies have several drawbacks. To begin with, traditional methods typically retrieve several features before employing machine learning classifiers such as Support Vector Machine (SVM) or K-Nearest Neighbors (KNN) to discern animal species. Further to that, both extraction of features and classification techniques necessitate a large number of adjustments. This is because the performance of traditional classifiers like SVM and KNN [3, 4] strongly depends on the quality of the extracted features. A Bilinear CNN approach was recommended [5] for extracting features that combine two CNN architectures. Another [6] novel technique is defined as the Multi-Attention CNN for fine-grained classification processes. Channel grouping, convolutional layers, and a sub-network for part categorization consist of the whole network. Another prevalent error in present classification works is that it disregards the relationship between the parts as well as the association between the characteristics collected from various imageries. The spatial relationship among the fragments of the imageries and the relationship among the images & their fragments are enormously valued in removing discriminating parts and making image categorization easier.

Machine learning has led to several improvements in the medical realm, such as sperm assessment [7], and tuberculosis detection [8] as well as research works including improved illness detection techniques [9–11]. Convolutional neural networks (CNN) trained on multiple photos of 10 distinct animal classes were implemented to accurately evaluate if the custom CNN architecture can recognize the correct breed of animal classes. The remainder of the paper is laid out as follows: 2. Related Works determining the different works done in the literature by various researchers 3. Dataset and Methods used include the dataset description, techniques used for enhancing the results, and explains us the various technologies used for classification 4. Results and Discussion part helps us understand and analyze the predictions made by the NNs, 5. Conclusions and Future Work summarizes the paper's work and some aspects that could be covered in the future. Several CNN architectures were thoroughly analyzed to determine the optimum architecture for the animal classification dataset used.

2 Related Work

There have been several studies on categorizing animal imagery, each of which has achieved a different degree of accuracy in its datasets. To address the difficulty of separating diverse animal groups, several researchers have previously stressed the use of various DL Algorithms, notably CNN and Transfer learning models. Nonetheless, the majority of the research in this field focuses on feature identification using contemporary CNN architectures.

Norouzzadeh et al. [12] (2018) demonstrated a technique that divides classification into two components: trying to detect an image containing animals (VGG best model) and their classification. Their method ranks the animals the same as an audience volunteer team. After pre-training their models on Open Images Dataset V4, they were able to identify the highest taxonomic classification rank with European wild mammal species with 93% accuracy. Using CNNs, Willi et al. [13] (2019) distinguished different animal species. They reached an accuracy score of 92.5% for the Snapshot Serengeti dataset and 91.4% for the Snapshot Wisconsin data - set. In an image database of 2500 images, Parham et al. [14] (2021) utilized the YOLO model to detect or identify zebras, creating bounding boxes for Plains Zebras with an accuracy score of 55.6% and Grevy's Zebras with an accuracy score of only 56.6%. Villa *et al.* [15] (2017) significantly improved the accuracy of the same dataset by incorporating the Snapshot Serengeti dataset to identify 20 distinct animal species using a convolutional neural network. Using ResNet architecture, they attained an accuracy of around 0.889 in the Top-1 category and about 0.981 in the Top-5 category. Many people have had success recognizing animals using camera-trap pictures. However, their models were based on feature extraction that was explicitly built for different purposes, and they only functioned with just a few thousand photographs. Although extraction of features is amongst the first steps in image processing, its usage in automatic image categorization is limited, resulting in poor accuracy rates in the studies.

CNN was utilized for the classification of different breeds of dogs in yet another investigation by Hsu [16] (2015). For categorization, two prominent architectures, LeNet and GoogleNet, had being used. With LeNet, the model accuracy was 0.95, while with GoogleNet it was 0.89. Various breeds of dogs were categorized using landmark-based shape-identifying techniques for animals in a comparatively equivalent job by Liu *et al.* [17] (2012). The Grassmann manifold is used to represent the dog's form as pixels. The model has been tested on 133 different dog breeds and 8,351 photos, with a detection accuracy Of 0.965.

Yu et al. [18] (2013) individually photo-shopped and picked images that only showed the animal's full body. They utilized a dataset with over 7000 Infrared (IR) photos taken by a motion sensor camera from 2 distinct field sites. They used a support vector machine (linear kernel) to categorize 18 different species of animals to achieve 82% accuracy.

A two-layered machine learning architecture was presented by Rathor *et al.* [4] (2021) to accomplish creature detection utilizing the local binary pattern (LBP) and histogram-oriented gradients (HOG) approach. On different layers, Support Vector Machine and Gradient Boosting classifiers were employed to accurately categorize the image. The examination of the results demonstrates that our suggested model is productive and efficient, with a 95.15% accuracy.

ML has a wide variety of applications sectors, including the medical industry, picture or speech recognition, gene detection for selecting the best cattle, dog breed detection, and identifying other types of endangered species to save them from extinction. Liver disease prediction [19–21], Diabetes mellitus diagnosis [22], and Gall bladder detection [23] are some of the approaches based on machine learning algorithms used in the healthcare business.

3 Data Preparation

In this part, the techniques used for classifying different animal breeds by using various Transfer Learning Models and CNN architecture have been explained in detail. Before training the architecture, a variety of tactics were employed to balance, normalize, and regulate the image dataset. This segment plots out the contents of the paper as follows: 3.1 Dataset used, 3.2 Image Augmentation, 3.3 Artificial Neural Network (ANN), 3.4 Convolutional Neural Network (CNN), 3.5 Transfer Learning, and 3.6 Software and hardware used.

3.1 Dataset Used

The animal dataset [24] comprises 28K standard quality animal imageries from 10 different categories: dog, spider, cat, cow, sheep, butterfly, squirrel, horse, chicken, and elephant which were deployed by Corrado Alessio to the Kaggle website. All of the photographs were gathered via Google Photos and manually reviewed. To imitate real-world settings, some incorrect data has been used. Each class was separated into its subfolder in the root directory. The number of images in each genre range from 2K to 5K. Table 1 gives the image count for all of the animal species in detail.

3.2 Image Augmentation and Pre-processing

Deep learning models often demand a large quantity of data to learn about working properly. Thousands of images are required in the case of CNN, which is a challenging task. Therefore a photo enhancement approach is utilized to tackle this problem. The path to the image database is saved in a variable, and a function in Python code is written for stacking folders with photos into an array formation. Because the pictures in the training dataset were of varying sizes, they had to be resampled before being utilized as

Table 1. Image count for different animal species

S.no	Species	Scientific name	Image count
1	Dog	Cane	4863
2	Spider	Ragno	4821
3	Cat	Gatto	1668
4	Cow	Mucca	1866
5	Sheep	Pecore	1820
6	Butterfly	Farfalla	2112
7	Squirrel	Scoiattolo	1862
8	Horse	Cavallo	2623
9	Chicken	Gallina	3098
10	Elephant	Elephante	1446

the model's input. The images are then smoothened to remove any unwanted noise. This is accomplished through the use of Gaussian blur, also known as the Gaussian function. The image is then segmented, by isolating the background from the neighboring pixels.

Whitening transformations, Calibration of features (pixel values), random rotations and shifts, zooming, rescaling, flipping, shearing, and other techniques used in image augmentation also aid in effectively increasing the quality of the existing dataset. In our approach, we have used Zoom range (0.2), Rotational range (10), Horizontal flip (True), Shearing (10 Degrees along X and Y-axis), Rescaling (1.0/255), Width shift range (0.1), and Height shift range (0.1).

3.3 Artificial Neural Network (ANN)

The mainstay of deep NNs and the deep learning framework is ANN. ANNs are strong algorithms utilized in a variety of domains, including classification and problems, as well as certain unique applications such as audio recognition, character recognition, and face recognition. ANNs are commonly paired with specialized layers like as deconvolutional and convolutional layers. They are divided into three layers: input, concealed, and output. An ANN's construction is seen in Fig. 1(a). Weights are modified throughout the training phase to connect every layer's nodes in a directed way to each of the nodes in the following layer. They are frequently combined with specialized layers like as deconvolutional and convolutional layers.

Let $M = \{M_1, M_2, \ldots, M_Q\}$ depict the established assortment of layers of the ANN containing an aggregate of Q layers along with (Q-2) hidden layers. Then the number of nodules (nodes) $N = \{Ni_1, Ni_2, \ldots, Ni_{P(i)}\}$, $1 \leq i \leq Q$ and P_i denote the number of nodules in layer *Li*. The relation between the nodules is denoted as weights by set $V = \{V_2, V_3, \ldots, V_Q\}$ whose initial constituent is V_2 because the beginning layer M_1 (input layer) lacks weights from a prior layer that does not present. Each element in V is defined by $V_i = Vi_{1,1}, Vi_{1,2}, \ldots, Vi_{1,P(i)}, Vi_{2,P(i)}, \ldots, Vi_{P(i-1),P(i)}\}$. Every nodule inside an ANN is meant to look like a neuron, with the ability to fire and spread a stimulus or disregard it entirely. Each nodule accepts input values from all other nodules in the preceding layer that is multiplied by their corresponding weights, resulting in Eq. (1).

$$S = \sum_{j=1}^{pi-1} V_i^{j,k} N_{i-1}^{j}, 1 \leq \mathrm{k} \leq P_i \tag{1}$$

Insertion of the dataset through the initial layer leads to the broadcasting via a system with some randomly initialized weights, and each nodule has an initiation function φ(S) that determines when to send the input value forward. Sigmoid, rectified linear unit (ALU), softmax, leaky reLU, and other forms of activation functions $\varphi(S)$ exist. Figure 1(a) explains the concept of input, hidden, and output layers for ANN Models.

3.4 Convolutional Neural Network (CNN)

CNNs are mostly used to categorize entities using visual data. Face detection, Activity identification, scene labeling, and other tasks have all been accomplished with CNNs. Dense layers (here ANN layers are stated as dense layers) and Convolutional layers are the two major principal layers in the CNN models. The basic idea here is to locate structures from an image using certain detectors that are 2D matrices (kernels). Due to this, it produces a feature map that contains the spatial connections among pixels in the supplied picture. Thus CNN's primary component is a convolutional layer, consisting of a set of filters (or kernels), the characteristics of which must be learned throughout the training process. The filters are typically smaller in size than the actual picture. Each filter interacts with the image to produce an activation map.

Following the convolution, a max-pooling layer is implemented to downsample the discovered characteristics, allowing the algorithm to determine if the picture is stretched, slanted, or rotated, giving spatial invariance. Pooling decreases the number of parameters by 75% as well as eliminates overfitting. To organize all of the pooled values, they get structured into a vertical arrangement of layers that will be implemented into an ANN. Finally, the values are transmitted through the ANN to the output layer, where they are displayed as the output at the output layer. A complete convolutional neural network for 3 CNN layers is shown in Fig. 1(b). A convolution operation of two functions a(t) and b(t) can be given as,

$$a(t) * b(t) \triangleq \int_{-\infty}^{\infty} a(\tau) b(t-\tau) d\tau \tag{2}$$

3.5 Transfer Learning

Transfer learning is a very good alternative for Convolutional Neural Networks. More precisely, training models for a single job incorporate data class associations that may be reused for other tasks in a related sector. Using the reprocessed characteristics of an originally trained model, the learning process might be comparable to the parameters of the most likely approach for the given problem. Depending on the area of the system, the

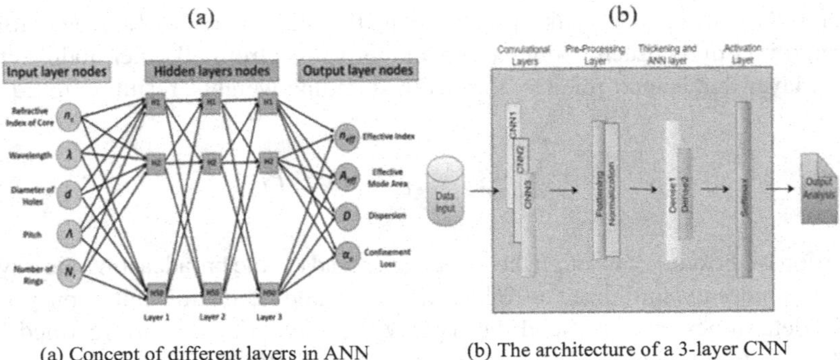

(a) Concept of different layers in ANN (b) The architecture of a 3-layer CNN

Fig. 1. (a) Concept of different layers in ANN (b) The architecture of a 3-layer CNN

job at hand, and the accessibility of data, different TL algorithms and approaches are used. E.g. AlexNet, ImageNet, and Inception. Researchers using deep learning techniques for image classification devised the TL approach to get beyond the limitations of traditional ML models and get better results. Natural language processing and image identification are two key aspects of the TL field. For transfer learning, VGG-16, Efficient NetB7 (NETB7), ResNet101, Efficient NetB2 (NETB2), and Resnet50 model. Comparison of different Transfer Learning Models.

3.6 Software and Hardware Used

Intel i7 10th generation CPU and 8 GB RAM workstation system were used for the implementation process, all of the CNN architectures along with Transfer Learning Models were trained using Python 3 and the Keras library (which utilizes TensorFlow as a backend) high-level API for neural network development.

4 Experimentation and Results

This part describes the numerous evaluations conducted using the Animal Class dataset using some CNN architectures and Transfer Learning Models as we choose the best one to achieve more precise results. This subsection is divided into two parts: Experiments and analysis, and 4.2. Results of the Models Used.

4.1 Experiments and Analysis

Different CNN models and TL Models for a multitude of convolutional layers, a multitude of dense layers, incorporation, and expulsion of regularisation layers like Batch Normalization, and digital image dimensions, Dropout, pooling sequence sizes, kernel sizes, and were equated on the efficiency of each architecture's maximum accuracy and other assessment metrics during training the models. A convolutional layer consists of kernels which frequently have the same depth as the input. The pooling layer serves two purposes. The first is to lower the number of computations performed in the system along with spatial dimension representations. The second goal is to alleviate the overfitting issue. Another alternative is to use the dropout layer. The components in this particular type of layer are picked at random, and their weights are neutralized thus the output does not affect the backpropagation or forward pass. Batch normalization is the process of adding more layers to a deep neural network that makes it quicker and much more reliable. The standardizing and normalizing procedures are performed by the new layer on the input given by the previous layer. Table 2 defines the different abbreviations used in Tables 3 and 4, which include the predictions of five CNN architectures and TL Models with the different parameters used.

Table 2. Abbreviations used

Abbreviations	Meaning
IS	Input Size of image
TT	**Training Time for the Model (in seconds)**
TL	Training Loss
LVCEL	Least Validation Cross Entropy Loss (test set)
TACC	Training Accuracy
MVA	Maximum Validation Accuracy
VR	Recall on Test Set
VFS	F1 Score on Test Set
TFS	F1 Score on Training Set
VPR	Precision on Test Set
TPR	Precision on Training Set
CL	Number of CNN Layers in a specific architecture
AL	Number of ANN Layers in a specific architecture
BN	Batch Normalization
DP	Dropout

Table 3. Performance of 5 different CNN architectures

Model	IS	**TT**	TACC	TL	MVA	LVCEL	TFS	Total Recall	TPR	VFS	VR	VPR	**AL**	**CL**	**BN**	**DP**
CNN1	(256,256)	**634**	0.906	0.781	0.865	0.710	0.893	0.858	0.918	0.896	0.861	0.922	2	5	Yes	Yes
CNN2	(256,256)	**659**	0.837	0.892	0.792	0.757	0.818	0.796	0.851	0.827	0.825	0.873	3	3	Yes	No
CNN3	(256,256)	**647**	0.777	0.869	0.712	0.862	0.829	0.807	0.792	0.739	0.813	0.721	1	3	No	No
CNN4	(256,256)	**653**	0.867	0.801	0.828	0.780	0.846	0.827	0.873	0.858	0.837	0.912	2	4	Yes	Yes
CNN5	(256,256)	**628**	0.924	0.931	0.855	0.690	0.908	0.879	0.947	0.911	0.889	0.951	4	5	Yes	Yes

Table 4. Performance of different Transfer Learning Models

Model	IS	TT	TACC	TL	LVCEL	MVA	Average F1 Score	Average Recall	Average Precision
VGG-16	(256,256)	**946**	0.990	0.029	0.044	0.984	0.982	0.979	0.988
EfficientNETB7	(256,256)	**749**	0.962	0.284	0.173	0.954	0.961	0.957	0.959
RESNET101	(256,256)	**689**	0.964	0.146	0.277	0.894	0.924	0.891	0.885
EfficientNETB2	(256,256)	**896**	0.988	0.175	0.280	0.974	0.978	0.980	0.976
RESNET50	(256,256)	**797**	0.896	0.453	0.245	0.764	0.863	0.856	0.784

Figure 2(a) and (b) plot the confusion matrix for the best CNN Architecture and Transfer Learning Model respectively. It can be assessed from Tables 3 and 4 that CNN architectures 1, 5 as well as VGG-16, and NetB2 performed exceedingly well respectively, particularly the Transfer Learning Models as they were able to form better relationships with the dataset and thus gave good results. It is mostly due to the fact of different convolutional and dense layers are being added with the correct amount of filters. The training time for the VGG-16 model was the highest among all TL Models due to the complex architecture involved in the framework and NetB2 took the second most time for the classification of animal species. Consequently, these 2 models were the best performing models for the animal species dataset. Additionally, CNN architectures 2 and 3 were unable to predict well due to the fact they were light architectures so forming a relationship with the dataset was limited. Ultimately, we can conclude from Tables 3 and 4 that MVA and LVCEL need not improve much with rising architectural size, although the time spent running the models continued to increase. Approximately time for all CNN architectures wss moreover same but due to different configurations (layers), CNN architecture 2 got the most time to train the epochs, which was followed by CNN architecture 4. CNN architecture predictions were the least accurate which came out to be 0.777. This leads us to the straightforward premise that if the design for a particular dataset is uncomplicated and simpler, the better will be the results. Incorporating more layers to the NN may lead it to underfit the dataset as it attempts to find characteristics that do not exist. Figure 2(a) summarizes the Training Accuracy, Training Loss, and Maximum Validation Accuracy for VGG-16 and CNN-5 models.

Additionally, CNN architectures 2 and 3 were unable to predict well due to the fact they were light architectures so forming a relationship with the dataset was limited. Ultimately, we can conclude from Tables 3 and 4 that MVA and LVCEL need not improve much with rising architectural size, although the time spent running the models continued to increase. This leads us to the straightforward premise that if the design for a particular dataset is uncomplicated and simpler, the better will be the results. Incorporating more layers to the NN may lead it to underfit the dataset as it attempts to find characteristics that do not exist.

4.2 Results of Selected Model

The analysis step was completed by computing precision, recall, and F1-score, where TP denotes true positives, FP denotes false positives, and FN denotes false negatives.

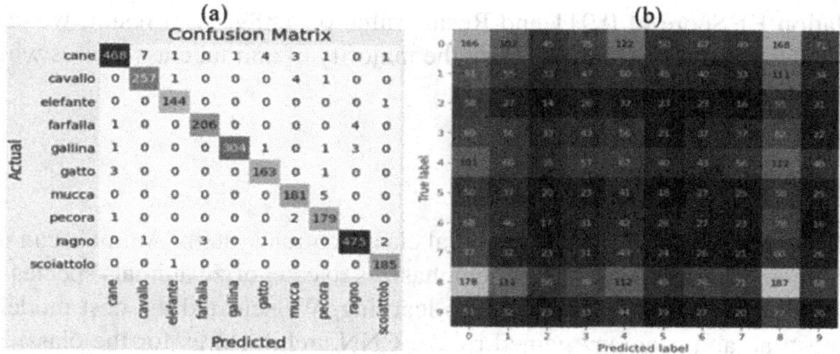

Fig. 2. (a) Confusion Matrix for CNN architecture 5, and (b) Confusion Matrix for VGG-16 model

The recall relates directly to how often real positives are found in other words however many right hits were discovered. Precision is the percentage of received hits that were true positives, or accurate hits. The F1-score aggregates a classifier's accuracy score and recall into a single statistic by calculating their harmonic mean. Its primary objective is to evaluate the results of multiple classifiers. Figure 3(b) describes the comparison of some evaluation metrics used for the prediction of animal classes accurately for all the models.

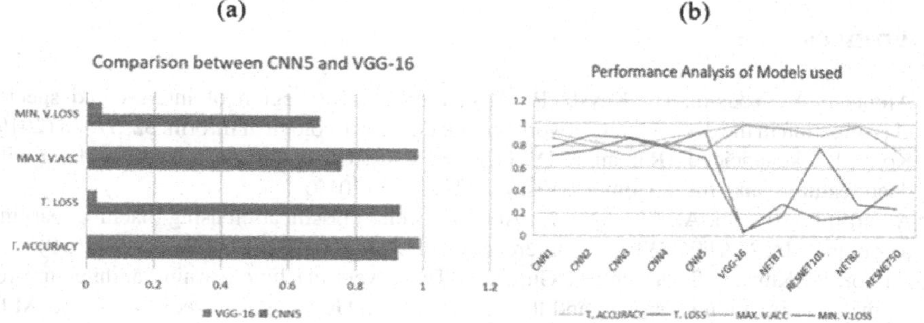

Fig. 3. Performance analysis of different models (b) Comparison between best CNN and VGG-16 models

During our implementation, VGG-16 achieved the average F1 score of 0.982 and Recall score of 0.979 outperforming all other neural networks, followed by Efficient-NetB2 which had the average F1 Score of 0.978 and Recall score of 0.98, both of these assessment metrics are more than 0.95 which indicates that the NN performed efficiently and correctly labeled the various images for different animal classes.

The precision score for the VGG-16 model was found to be 0.988 and for Efficient NetB2 it came out to be 0.959. The results obtained via Transfer Learning Models were better since they were able to form a close relationship with the dataset, and since they leverage information from prior trained NNs, they already know the features of the dataset well. The best CNN architecture 5 had the best results while evaluating achieving the validation F1 Score of 0.911 and Recall value of 0.889. As a result, we can state that these NNs can accurately categorize the majority of animal class photos while also ruling out negative occurrences.

5 Conclusion and Future Work

Animal Species classification is an essential classification system. Animals can be classified into thousands of species. Paper emphasizes to categorize animals species into 10 major classes by using the power of deep learning. We selected the best model based on training time and accuracy gained by the CNN architectures for the classification. Transfer Learning Models were also trained, demonstrating that keeping CNN architectures and NN's simple is crucial for maintaining accuracy and efficiency. As a result of these findings, greater emphasis was placed on achieving an even higher accuracy score. We admit that further more fine-tuning can enhance the performance of these CNN architectures.

Future research with the animal class picture classification may potentially be done utilizing multimodal learning or Object Detection Techniques. Principle Component Analysis can also be used for data filtering purposes. Some limitations in this study are better usage of processor and GPU could be done. Since CNN and Tl were used in this study hence training time was comparatively more. More dataset a with more classes can be used for this classification task.

References

1. Ahmeda, A., Yousifa, H., Kaysb, R., Hea, Z.: Semantic region of interest and species classification in the deep neural network feature domain. Ecological Inform. **52**, 57–68 (2019)
2. Kong, B., Supancic, J., Ramanan, D., Fowlkes, C.C.: Cross-domain image matching with deep feature maps. Int. J. Comput. Visions **127**, 1–13 (2019)
3. Alharbi, F., Alharbi, A., Kamioka, E.: Animal species classification using machine learning techniques. In: MATEC Web of Conferences, vol. 277, p. 02033, EDP Sciences (2019)
4. Rathor, S., Kumari, S., Singh, R., Gupta, P.: Two layers machine learning architecture for animal classification using hog and lbp. In: Goyal, V., Gupta, M., Trivedi, A., Kolhe, M.L. (eds.) Proceedings of international conference on communication and artificial intelligence. LNNS, vol. 192, pp. 445–453. Springer, Singapore (2021). https://doi.org/10.1007/978-981-33-6546-9_42
5. Lin, T.Y., RoyChowdhury, A. Maji, S.: Bilinear CNN models for fine-grained visual recognition. In: Proceedings of the IEEE International Conference on Computer Vision (ICCV), pp. 1449–1457 (2015)
6. Zhang, L., Yang, Y., Wang, M., Hong, R., Nie, L., Li, X.: Detecting densely distributed graph patterns for fine-grained image categorization. IEEE Trans. Image Process. **25**(2), 553–565 (2016)
7. Chandra, S., et al.: Prolificacy assessment of spermatozoan via state-of-the-art deep learning frameworks. IEE Access **10** (2020)
8. Singh, V., Gourisaria, M.K., Harshvardhan GM, Singh, V.: Mycobacterium tuberculosis detection using CNN ranking approach. In: Gandhi, T.K., Konar, D., Sen, B., Sharma, K. (eds.) Advanced Computational Paradigms and Hybrid Intelligent Computing. AISC, vol. 1373. Springer, Singapore (2022). https://doi.org/10.1007/978-981-16-4369-9_56

9. Das, H., Naik, B., Naik, H.S., Jaiswal, S., Mahato, P., Rout, M.: Biomedical data analysis using a neuro-fuzzy model with post-feature reduction. J. King Saud Univ. Comput. Inform. Sci. **34** (2020)
10. Singh, V., et al.: Diagnosis of intracranial tumors via the selective CNN data modeling technique. Appl. Sci. **12**, 2900 (2021)
11. Liang, Y., Li, Q., Chen, P., Xu, L., Li, J.: Comparative study of backpropagation artificial neural networks and logistic regression model in predicting poor prognosis after acute ischemic stroke. Open Med. **14**(1), 324–330 (2019)
12. Norouzzadeh, M.S., et al.: Automatically identifying, counting, and describing wild animals in camera-trap images with deep learning. Proc. Natl. Acad. Sci. **115**, E5716–E5725, USA (2018)
13. Willi, M., et al.: Identifying animal species in camera trap images using deep learning and citizen science. Methods Ecol. Evol. **10**, 80–91 (2019)
14. Parham, J., Stewart, C.: Detecting plains and Grevy's Zebras in the realworld. In: Proceedings of the 2016 IEEE Winter Applications of Computer Vision Workshops (WACVW). Lake Placid, NY, USA (2016)
15. Villa, A.G., Salazar, A., Vargas, F.: Towards automatic wild animal monitoring: identification of animal species in camera-trap images using very deep convolutional neural networks. Ecological Informat. **41**, 24–32 (2017)
16. Hsu, D.: Using convolutional neural networks to classify dog breeds. CS23 1n Convolutional Neural Networks for Visual Recognition, vol. 2 (2015)
17. Liu, J., Kanazawa, A., Jacobs, D., Belhumeur, P.: Dog breed classification using part localization. In: Fitzgibbon, A., Lazebnik, S., Perona, P., Sato, Y., Schmid, C. (eds.) ECCV 2012. LNCS, vol. 7572, pp. 172–185. Springer, Heidelberg (2012). https://doi.org/10.1007/978-3-642-33718-5_13
18. Yu, X., Wang, J., Kays, R., Jansen, P.A., Wang, T., Huang, T.: Automated identification of animal species in camera trap images. EURASIP J. Image Video Process. **2013**(1), 1 (2013). https://doi.org/10.1186/1687-5281-2013-52
19. Dutta, K., Chandra, S., Gourisaria, M.K.: Early-stage detection of liver disease through machine learning algorithms. In: Tiwari, S., Trivedi, M.C., Kolhe, M.L., Mishra, K., Singh, B.K. (eds.) Advances in Data and Information Sciences. LNNS, vol. 318. Springer, Singapore (2022). https://doi.org/10.1007/978-981-16-5689-7_14
20. Kuppili, V., et al.: Extreme learning machine framework for risk stratification of fatty liver disease using ultrasound tissue characterization. J. Med. Syst. **41**(10), 1–20 (2017)
21. Singh, V., Gourisaria, M.K., Das, H.: Performance analysis of machine learning algorithms for prediction of liver disease. In: 2021 IEEE 4th International Conference on Computing, Power and Communication Technologies (GUCON), pp. 1–7 (2021)
22. Gourisaria, M.K., Jee, G., Harshvardhan, G.M., Singh, V., Singh, P.K., Workneh, T.C.: Data science appositeness in diabetes mellitus diagnosis for healthcare systems of developing nations. IET Commun. (2022)
23. Muneeswaran, V., Pallikonda Rajasekaran, M.: Gallbladder shape estimation using tree-seed optimization tuned radial basis function network for assessment of acute cholecystitis. In: Bhateja, V., Coello, C.A., Coello, S.C., Satapathy, P.K. (eds.) Intelligent engineering informatics. AISC, vol. 695, pp. 229–239. Springer, Singapore (2018). https://doi.org/10.1007/978-981-10-7566-7_24
24. Alessio, C.: Animals-10 dataset from https://www.kaggle.com/datasets/alessiocorrado99/animals10/code. 15th May 2021

Intelligent Intrusion Detection System Using Deep Learning Technique

Azriel Henry[1] and Sunil Gautam[2(✉)]

[1] Department of Computer Sciences and Engineering, Institute of Advanced Research, Gujarat Gandhinagar, India

[2] Department of Computer Science and Engineering, Institute of Technology, Nirma University Ahmedabad, Gandhinagar, Gujarat, India

gautamsunil.cmri@gmail.com

Abstract. There is constant growth in the digitization of information across the world. However, this rapid growth has raised concerns over the security of the information. Today's internet is made up of nearly half a million different networks. Network intrusions are very common these days which put user information at high risk. An intrusion detection system (IDS) is a software/system to analyze and monitor the data for the detection of intrusions in the host/network. An intrusion Detection System competent in detecting zero-day attacks and network anomalies is highly demanded. Researchers have used different methods to develop robust IDS. However, none of the methods is exceptionally well and meets every requirement of IDS. Machine learning/Deep learning (ML/DL) are among the widely used methods to develop IDS. This proposed technique uses a DL model, Recurrent Neural Network (RNN) with Gated Recurrent Unit (GRU) framework. There are several datasets to evaluate the performance of the learning techniques. CICIDS 2017 is the dataset that contains a variety of cyber-attacks. The proposed technique will use the same to evaluate the deep learning technique. Moreover, the study will also showcase the comparison between the results of existing machine learning algorithms and the proposed algorithm. The comparison would be done on different matrices such as True positive (TP) and False positive (FP) rates, accuracy, precision, etc.

Keywords: Cyber security · CICIDS 2017 · ML/DL · Neural networks

1 Introduction

The advancements in network technology have proved beneficial to various sectors as it allows users, companies, and industries to enhance their capacity and scope. Although these advancements have also brought cyber threats to the end-users. There is a parallel advancement seen from the attacker's side. They have developed a variety of ways to intrude the network and hence abuse it. Several traditional approaches are taking the responsibility to handle such intruders. However, these approaches are inefficient when it comes to a zero-day attack. IDS is the key component in the field of network security. IDS is a tool or software which is capable of detecting potential attacks in the network

S. K. Panda et al. (Eds.): CoCoLe 2022, CCIS 1729, pp. 220–230, 2022.
https://doi.org/10.1007/978-3-031-21750-0_19

by applying detection algorithms. It can be compared with the burglar alarm. If a thief tries to open a car the alarm in the car will start to ring. Similarly, the IDS will alert the owner about any potential intrusions. It monitors and analyses the host system or the network for possible hostile attacks. This system protects the networks from attackers by detecting any potential threats. The IDS can be classified into two groups based on its architecture i.e. Host and Network-based IDSs. HIDS is the IDS that is installed on the host machine itself. It monitors the host's activities. It can detect attacks that the NIDS is unsuccessful to detect. It can verify the success or failure of an attack. Moreover, it does not necessitate supplementary computer hardware. Unlike HIDS, NIDS is installed on the network. It can detect attacks that are based on the network. It is easier to deploy as it is directly installed on the network and not on every host system. It can detect real-time attacks and send a quick response. Moreover, it can also detect failed attacks i.e. attacks that are failed to intrude the system [1].

The approach to developing an IDS can be parted into two classes namely Signature and Anomaly based IDSs. SIDS detects intrusions in the network using known patterns, sequences, or a set of rules. SIDS is more accurate for previously known attacks. It generates detailed log files which ease down the process of tracking the cause of the alarm. Also, the administrators need to spend less amount of time dealing with false-positive attacks. 'However, a database needs to be constantly updated. Also, it takes developers a few days or hours to update the signature database. Anomaly-based IDS detects any change in the network traffic pattern by comparing it with the regular traffic. Anomaly-based IDS does not require updating the database. It observes the network behaviour and creates a network activity profile. Moreover, it is efficient with larger systems compared to signature-based IDS. However, there are higher chances of false-positive in anomaly-based IDS. Also, developing a suitable method for selecting the features for each category of attacks is a challenge [2].

Anomaly-based IDS approach has proven more efficient than signature-based IDS as it can detect a zero-day attack. Zero-day attacks are attacks that are not previously known to the victim or the system. As AIDS detects an anomaly in the network it can detect such zero-day attacks accurately. However, different approaches are developed on the same detection method. These approaches have three classes namely learning, knowledge, and statistical based approaches. Machine Learning-based approach uses training data to train the model for the classification of attacks. After training, the model is then evaluated on a testing dataset.

This approach is classified into three classes namely supervised, semi-supervised, and unsupervised learning. There are Different ML algorithms such as Random Forest-RF, KNearest Neighbour-KNN, Decision Tree-DT, Naive Bayes-NB, etc. are used to develop an IDS. Moreover, different neural networks are also used to develop an IDS which are capable to classify more accurately. One of these neural networks, Recurrent Neural Network is discussed in this paper. Secondly, the Knowledge-based approach uses human knowledge to generate a set of rules for the attacks. Finite State Machines, Description languages, and Expert Systems are the methods used to develop Knowledge-based IDS. Thirdly, the statistical-based approach uses statistical parameters such as mean, median, mode, standard deviation, etc. to detect the intrusion. Time series models,

Univariate, Multivariate, etc. are the models used to develop a statistical-based IDS [3, 4].

DL models such as NeuralNetworks, Deep Neural networks (DNN), Deep Boltzmann Machine (DBM), Deep Belief Networks (DBN), Restricted Boltzmann Machine (RBM), RNN, etc. are mostly used as it detects zero-day attack as well as it outperforms the existing machine learning models. We have used DL model, RNN to develop an IDS that can efficiently detect the attacks.

The remainder of the paper is planned as follows. Second section exhibits appropriate background information. Third section presents the proposed model. Fourth section discusses and analyses the experiments and outcomes of the proposed algorithm on several metrics. Finally, fifth section concludes the research work and sightsees the directions for future work (Fig. 1).

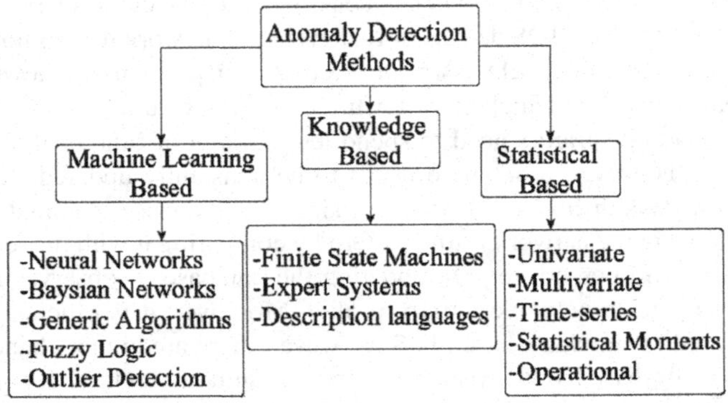

Fig. 1. Anomaly-based IDS techniques

2 Related Work

There are various methods proposed to develop an efficient Intrusion Detection System which is discussed in this section. Researchers have used different techniques such as traditional, machine learning, deep learning, immune system-based method, etc. These techniques solve many issues for IDS, however, they have their limitations.

Dutt I. et al. [5] demonstrate an Immune system like a model with two layers of the algorithm. The first stage is the anomaly detection based on Statistical Modelling. To find the vulnerability this layer will capture the preliminary traffic of the network. Adaptive Immune is the second layer that determines the attributes of the suspicious network package. They have conducted experiments both in the real-time environment as well as on existing datasets KDD99 and UNSW-NB15. They claim that their model SMAD shows 96.04% and approximately true positive rate of 97% for actual traffic and datasets respectively. Significantly apprehensive traffic is tested with the second layer, AIAD, which shows a positive rate closer to 99%.

Wisanwanichthan T. et al. [6] proposed a Hybrid Approach that contains double layers with Naive Bayes as the first classifier and Support Vector Machine (SVM) as the second algorithm. The Naive Bayes classifier is used to detect Probe and DoS attacks whereas, SVM distinguishes U-2-R and R-2-L from usual instances. The classifier is tested on the NSL-KDD dataset. They claim to achieve results with a classification rate-93.11%, in addition, a 96.67% classification rate of R-2-L, and 100% of U-2-R. However, this proposed model needs to be evaluated for more types of attacks.

Tama B. et al. [7] proposed a model with two sections namely, hybrid attribute optimization and ensemble classifier. The feature selection technique is combined using three methods: genetic algorithm, particle swarm, and ant colony model. They have used two standard datasets namely KDD (updated version) and UNSW-NB15 to test the performance of their algorithm. They claim that their algorithm outdoes other state-of-the-art Meta as well as individual classifiers.

Pu G. et al. [8] demonstrate the use of unsupervised anomaly detection methods by combining two techniques i.e. clustering based on sub-space and SVM with one class. They have used the NSL-KDD dataset for evaluation. They claim that their proposed algorithm outperforms three other existing clustering algorithms. However, an efficient feature selection method can improve the existing results.

Aleesa A. et al. [9] have showcased three deep learning techniques to develop an IDS namely Artificial Neural Network, DNN, and RNN with LSTM. They have evaluated these models on the UNSW-NB15 dataset. They claim that their proposed models ANN and DNN show superior results when compared to other related models.

Mendonca R. et al. [10] proposed an IDS using Tree with CNN classifier with the activation function called SRS. They claim that their proposed model with SRS shows decent results for metrics such as sensitivity, accuracy, F-measure, and precision. The time complexity was also low with SRS when compared with other algorithms. However, other activation functions may result in better performance.

Zhong M. et al. [11] demonstrates an IDS using Text-CNN (Convolution Neural Network) and GRU (Gated Recurrent Unit). Text- CNN has decent efficacy in solving problems that are at character-level, and to adapt to sequence modeling they can be altered. They have used GRU to solve issues such as related to the gradient. To test the performance of their model they have used two datasets namely. KDD and ADFA-LD dataset. They claim that their model can provide a more accurate signal about malicious behaviour when compared with traditional algorithms like C4.5, NB, SVM, the SVM-RBMS, etc.

Zhang R. et al. [12] proposed an IDS for an unmanned aerial system with multifractal analysis to detect spoofing attack in unmanned aerial systems (UAS). They claim that their proposed model can detect commonly observed intrusions such as Man-in-the-Middle attacks in UAS. They also claim that the classifier achieves high classification accuracy with a slight false-positive rate.

Ullah I. et al. [13] proposed an IoT (Internet of Things) network based anomaly-based IDS. They have used CNN (Convolution Neural Network) to create a multi-class classification model. They have implemented the CNN model in one, two, and three dimensions. Their model is evaluated using datasets namely, BoT-IoT, IoT NI,

MQTT-IoT-IDS2020, and IoT-23 ID. They claim that their proposed classification model exhibited high metrics scores when compared with other classification techniques.

Yao R. et al. [14] proposed an IDS with cross layer feature mixture of CNNs and long short-term memory (LSTM) networks. The KDDCup99 and KDD (Updated version) datasets were used to test their proposed model. They claim that their model achieves better results than other DL classifiers in earlier studies which are based on only one component.

This section presents a variety of proposed models to develop an IDS. The majority of these research areas intersect learning techniques such as machine learning, deep learning, etc. Moreover, these techniques have proved to be more effectual and accurate when compared to various other old methods. Deep learning algorithms are widely used as it provides more flexibility. Also, most of the studies use early datasets such as KDD, NSL-KDD, etc. This study uses the CICIDS 2017 (Canadian Institute of Cybersecurity IDS) dataset which offers various categories of cyber-attacks.

3 Proposed Method

Key components of the proposed technique are discussed here in this section. Figure 2 displays that the technique is classified into two main stages. The beginning stage involves the removal of redundant data and selecting optimum features from the CICIDS 2017 dataset. The correlated features are calculated using Pearson's Correlation Coefficient function. As shown in the flowchart, the second stage is the classification of cyber-attacks. The classification is performed using the proposed model called RNN-GRU.

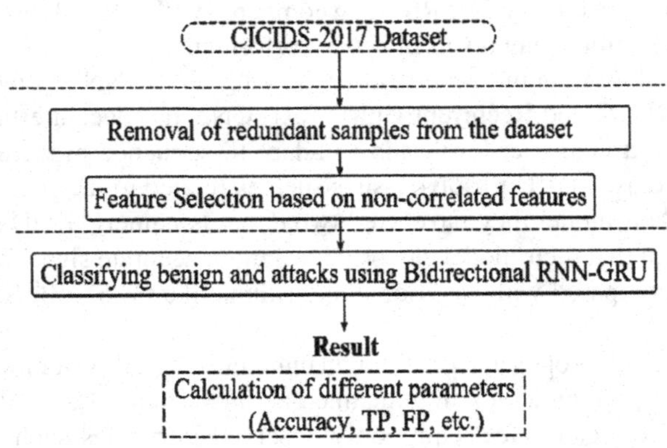

Fig. 2. Proposed model layout

3.1 Dataset Pre-processing

In this study, we have used a dataset created by a research crew in the Canadian Institute of Cybersecurity i.e. CICIDS 2017. This dataset covers more variants of features and metadata compared to traditional datasets. However, to remove the redundancy in the dataset and to find the optimum feature subset, pre-processing is performed. Table 1 shows the details of the CICIDS 2017 dataset before and after removing the redundant features. The filter method called Pearson's Correlation Coefficient finds the optimum subgroup of attributes from the attribute set. It measures the degree of linear correlation or similarity of the features in the dataset and delivers a correlation coefficient value that ranges between −1 to 1 i.e. [−1, 1]. The equation of Pearson's Correlation Coefficient is as follows [15, 16].

$$\rho_{X,Y} = \frac{cov(X, Y)}{\sigma_X \sigma_Y}$$

which can be derived as,

$$\frac{E((X - \mu_X)(Y - \mu_Y))}{\sigma_X \sigma_Y}$$

$$\frac{E(XY) - E(X)E(Y)}{\sqrt{E(X^2) - E^2(X)}\sqrt{B(Y^2) - E^2(Y)}} \quad (1)$$

where '$cov(X, Y)$' is a covariance function for 'X' and 'Y', whereas 'σ_X' and 'σ_Y' are the standard deviation of X and Y respectively, and '$E(X)$' is the expected value of 'E'.

Table 1. Data Distribution in CICIDS-2017 dataset.

Sub-dataset	Number of instances	
	With redundancy	Without redundancy
Tuesday Samples	445909	425240
Wednesday	692703	613287
Thursday Morning	170366	164300
Thursday Afternoon	288602	254625
Friday Morning	191033	184145
Friday Afternoon-DDoS	225745	223666
Friday Afternoon-PortScan	286467	214114

Table 2 shows the number of features for each sub-dataset after using Pearson's Correlation Coefficient function. The features were reduced to less or equal to 43 features from a total of 77 features.

3.2 RNN-GRU (Recurrent Neural Network-Gated Recurrent Unit)

This paper proposes a model using a neural network algorithm called Recurrent Neural Network (RNN). RNN provides the ability to resolve issues such as long term dependencies and variable correlations that are seen in other neural networks. RNN enables the

Table 2. Selected features

Sub-dataset	Total
Tuesday	43
Wednesday	41
Thursday Morning	39
Thursday Afternoon	40
Friday Morning	37
Friday Afternoon-DDoS	39
Friday Afternoon-PortScan	37

network to add feedback on the outputs of the previous time step in the current time step. Gated Recurrent Unit (GRU) framework is designed to combat exploding or vanishing gradient problems. GRU is the improved version of the LSTM framework. GRUs has a gate structure having two gates namely the reset and update gates. We have used a bidirectional RNN where two GRU layers are stacked on top of each other. Both layers are kept in opposite directions. As shown in Fig. 3, one GRU layer moves in the forward direction whereas the other GRU layer moves in the backward direction. Equations (2), (3) and (4) show the mathematical expressions of RNN and GRU respectively [17–19].

RNN

$$
\begin{aligned}
a^t &= b_1 + Wh^{(t-1)} + Ux^t h^t \\
&= A\left(a^{(t)}\right) y^t \\
&= b_2 + Vh^{(t)}
\end{aligned}
$$

where 'b_1' and 'b_2' are the biases whereas, 'W', 'U', and 'V', and are the weights of layer connections namely hidden-hidden, input-hidden, and hidden-output, and respectively and 'A' is an Activation function.

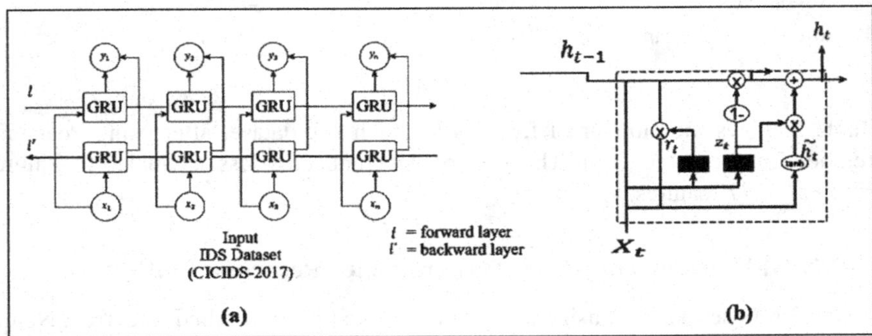

Fig. 3. (a) RNN Architecture (b) GRU Architecture

GRU

$$r_t = sigm(W_{xr}x_t + W_{hr}h_{t-1} + b_r) \tag{3}$$

$$z_t = sigm(W_{xz}x_t + W_{hz}h_{t-1} + b_z) \tag{4}$$

$$h_t = z_t \odot h_{t-1} + (1 - z_t) \odot \widetilde{h_t} \tag{5}$$

where 'r_t', and 'z_t', 'x_t', and 'h_t' are the reset gate, update gate, input vector, and output vector respectively. Like LSTM, '*b*' denotes the baises and '*W*' denotes the weight matrices.

4 Experiments and Results

To assess the algorithm we considered metrics such as true positive rate (TPR), false-positive rate (FPR), precision, and accuracy. The proportion of correct matches amongst factual true instances is TPR. Whereas, the proportion of the incorrect matches amongst non-factual instances is FPR. Precision is the proportion of accurate or incorrect guesses made by the algorithm. Finally, accuracy is used to measure the efficacy of the proposed algorithm. Equations (6), (7), (8), and (9) show the mathematical expressions of TPR, FPR, Precision, and Accuracy respectively [20–22].

$$TPR = \frac{TP}{(TP + FN)} \tag{6}$$

$$FPR = \frac{FP}{(FP + FN)} \tag{7}$$

$$Precision = \frac{TP}{(TP + FP)} \tag{8}$$

$$Accuracy = \frac{(TP + TN)}{(TP + TN + FP + FN)} \tag{9}$$

where FP, FN, TP, and TN are False Positive, False Negative, True Positive, and True Negative respectively.

The experiments were performed using python on the Google Colab platform. Python libraries such as sklearn, keras, tensorflow were used to classify and analyse the data. To test the technique, the CICIDS 2017 dataset is classified into training set and testing set i.e. 67% - training set and 33% - testing set. As discussed in the previous section, the correlation-based feature selection technique reduced the feature set to less or equal to 43 features for all sub-datasets. Table 3 shows the TPR, FPR, and precision values for all the attacks in the dataset. The results show that most of the attacks are classified with higher accuracy. However, attacks such as Heartbleed and XSS are not predicted accurately by the proposed model. One of the reasons behind this is the lesser amount

Table 3. Statistical parameters of each attacks

Attacks	TPR	FPR	Precision
FTP-Patator	0.9846	0.0002	0.9817
SSH-Patator	0.9216	0.0004	0.9398
Goldeneye	0.8394	0.0045	0.7593
Hulk	0.9615	0.0136	0.9652
Slowhttptest	0.7515	0.0028	0.6912
Slowloris	0.7886	0.0030	0.6947
Heartbleed	0	0.0008	0
Brute Force	0.5933	0.0032	0.6317
Sql Inj	0.5446	0.0033	0.4
XSS	0.25	0.0002	0.0666
Infiltration	0	0.0002	0
Bot	0.6172	0.0036	0.6354
DDoS	0.9809	0.0101	0.9923
PortScan	0.9934	0.0036	0.9950

of training data for these attacks. Moreover, the results show a very less FPR value for most of the attacks. As a result, the precision values are higher.

Table 4 shows the accuracy values for each sub-dataset of the CICIDS 2017 dataset. The outcomes exhibit that the proposed algorithm gives more than 96% accurate predictions for each sub-datasets. Thursday-Afternoon sub-dataset which contains Infiltration attacks shows the highest accuracy value among the other sub-datasets. Our proposed model has an average accuracy value of 98.99%. Table 5 compares our proposed model with other related approaches for IDS. Naïve Bayes is a machine learning algorithm based on probability. Along with the Bidirectional RNN-GRU model we have also tested the NB classifier. However, it shows the least accuracy among other classifiers. Moreover, the proposed model is also compared with other techniques namely Random Forest [23], Artificial Neural Network [23] and AdaBoost based IDS [24]. These techniques are also evaluated on CICIDS 2017 dataset. Our proposed model outperforms these techniques with the highest accuracy.

Table 4. Accuracy

Sub-dataset	Accuracy (%)
Tuesday	0.9984
Wednesday	0.9676
Thursday Morning	0.9923
Thursday Afternoon	0.9995
Friday Morning	0.9923
Friday Afternoon-DDoS	0.9847
Friday Afternoon-PortScan	0.9951

Table 5. Performance of classifiers

Classifier	Accuracy (%)
Naïve Bayes	64.49
Random Forest [23]	96.24
ANN(50 iterations) [23]	87.79
ANN(500 iterations) [23]	96.53
AdaBoost-based IDS [24]	81.83
Bidirectional RNN-GRU	98.99

5 Conclusion

In the research we discussed here, we have developed an IDS with a DL technique - RNN with GRU framework. Several pieces of research are presenting traditional as well as deep learning techniques to develop an IDS. However, issues such as inaccurate or inefficient data, longer dependency, etc. create a scope or need to further research in this space. The proposed model RNN-GRU resolves a longer dependency issue that prevails in other deep learning techniques. Moreover, the technique is assessed on the CICIDS 2017 dataset that provides a variety of cyber-attacks. The comparison shows that our technique outperformed other techniques in accurately predicting the attacks.

References

1. Mahendra, P., et al.: An efficient feature selection based bayesian and rough set approach for intrusion detection. Appl. Soft Comput. **87**, 105980 (2020)
2. Ansam, K., et al.: Survey of intrusion detection systems: techniques, datasets and challenges. Cybersecurity **2**(1) (2019)
3. Nasrin, S., et al.: Survey on SDN based network intrusion detection system using machine learning approaches. Peer-to-Peer Network. Appl. **12**(2), 493–501 (2018)

4. Jyothsna, V., et al.: A review of anomaly based intrusion detection systems. Int. J. Comput. Appl. **28**(7), 26–35 (2011)
5. Inadyuti, D., et al.: Immune System Based Intrusion Detection System (IS-Ids): a proposed model. IEEE Access **8**, 34929–34941 (2020)
6. Wisanwanichthan, T., Thammawichai, M.: A double-layered hybrid approach for network intrusion detection system using combined naive bayes and SVM. IEEE Access **9**, 138432–138450 (2021)
7. Adhi, T.B., et al.: Tse-Ids: a two-stage classifier ensemble for intelligent anomaly-based intrusion detection system. IEEE Access **7**, 94497–94507 (2019)
8. Guo, P., et al.: A hybrid unsupervised clustering-based anomaly detection method. Tsinghua Sci. Technol. **26**(2), 146–153 (2021)
9. Aleesa, M., et al.: Deep-intrusion detection system with enhanced UNSW-NB15 dataset based on deep learning techniques. J. Eng. Sci. Technol. **16**(1), 711–727 (2021)
10. Robson, V.M., et al.: Intrusion detection system based on fast hierarchical deep convolutional neural network. IEEE Access **9**, 61024–61034 (2021)
11. Ming, Z., et al.: sequential model based intrusion detection system for IOT servers using deep learning methods. Sensors **21**(4), 1113 (2021)
12. Zhang, R., et al.: A multifractal analysis and machine learning based intrusion detection system with an application in a UAS/Radar system. Drones **6**(1), 21 (2022)
13. Ullah, I., Mahmoud, Q.H.: Design and development of a deep learning-based model for anomaly detection in IOT networks. IEEE Access **9**, 103906–103926 (2021)
14. Yao, R., et al.: Intrusion detection system in the advanced metering infrastructure: a cross-layer feature-fusion CNN-LSTM-based approach. Sensors **21**(2), 626 (2021)
15. Zhu, H., et al.: Multiple ant colony optimization based on pearson correlation coefficient. IEEE Access **7**, 61628–61638 (2019)
16. Feng, W., et al.: An expert recommendation algorithm based on pearson correlation coefficient and FP-growth. Cluster Comput. **22**(S3), 7401–7412 (2018)
17. Nesma, M.R., et al.: Recurrent neural networks: an embedded computing perspective. IEEE Access **8**, 57967–57996 (2020)
18. Wei, X., et al.: An RNN-based delay-guaranteed monitoring framework in underwater wireless sensor networks. IEEE Access **7**, 25959–25971 (2019)
19. Apeksha, S., et al.: Performance evaluation of deep neural networks applied to speech recognition: RNN, LSTM and Gru. J. Artif. Intell. Soft Comput. Res. **9**(4), 235–245 (2019)
20. Fredrik, W., et al.: Spotting words in medieval manuscripts. Studia Neophilologica **86**(sup1), 171–186 (2014)
21. Elise, A., et al.: Machine learning for cross-gazetteer matching of natural features. Int. J. Geograph. Inform. Sci. **34**(4), 708–734 (2019)
22. Zhang, Q., et al.: A new road extraction method using sentinel-1 SAR images based on the deep fully convolutional neural network. Eur. J. Remote Sens. **52**(1), 572–582 (2019)
23. Pelletier, Z., et al.: Evaluating the CIC IDS-2017 dataset using machine learning methods and creating multiple predictive models in the statistical computing language R". Int. Res. J. Adv. Eng. Sci. **5**(2), 187–191 (2017)
24. Arif, Y., et al.: Improving AdaBoost-Based Intrusion Detection System (IDS) performance on CIC Ids 2017 dataset. J. Phys. Conf. Ser. **1192**, 012018 (2019)

Rice Leaf Disease Detection and Classification Using a Deep Neural Network

Subasish Mohapatra(✉), Chandan Marandi, Amlan Sahoo, Subhadarshini Mohanty, and Kunaram Tudu

Odisha University of Technology and Research, Bhubaneswar, India
{smohapatra,sdmohantycse}@outr.ac.in

Abstract. In the 21st-century crop complaint is a serious concern for food security. In this period, utmost of the husbandry support centers and numerous growers use different technologies to ameliorate productivity in farming, but still concerned about plant safety and fast detection of plant leaf diseases which remains difficult in different parts of the regions. Rice plants are frequently infected with diseases that can result in social and financial damage. Many rice crop diseases manifest themselves first on the leaves of the plants. As we say, automated rice plant disease diagnosis is an important aspect of food security, yield loss estimate, and disease management. As a result, computer vision and image processing are utilized to identify infected leave. With the proliferation of digital cameras and ongoing advancements in the computer vision area, automated disease detection techniques are in great demand in precision agriculture, high-yield agriculture, smart greenhouses, and other fields. This study uses an open dataset with 4 types of leaf infections, namely brown spot, blast, bacterial blight, and tungro. In this research, automatically identify plant leaf infection and classify whether the leaf is healthy or diseased, instead of the traditional overlong manual disease diagnostic method, deep CNN models may obtain the best accuracy. We have compared our suggested model (custom-CNN) against pre-trained deep CNN models i.e. VGG19, DensNet121, InceptionV3, as well as ResNet152 deep learning models, and with a learning rate of 0.001, the custom-CNN model obtained greater accuracy of 97.47%. This paper is willing to support and help the farmer Community of the world.

Keywords: Rice leaf disease · Convolutional neural network · Deep learning · ResNet-152 · InceptionV3 · Custom-CNN

1 Introduction

In India, rice is a significant element of the national economy. Paddy is the main nutriment in India and has more rice-cultivated land than China. In the Eastern tract of Odisha, the residents of the Balasore District rely on agriculture frugality husbandry. Here, the rice planter supports growing rice in the District of Balasore for two agricultural seasons at a time. The Kharif season is based on the monsoon and the Rabi season is dependent upon the water regarding the Borewell Shallow Water Pump. Every time it has been disclosed,

S. K. Panda et al. (Eds.): CoCoLe 2022, CCIS 1729, pp. 231–243, 2022.
https://doi.org/10.1007/978-3-031-21750-0_20

paddy fields have been damaged by numerous infections and various pest attacks. The majority of young farmers with less knowledge in agriculture are unable to recognize the types of infections and diseases. Pesticide application is useless when they don't have any idea about the disease types [1]. These situations encourage us to continue our study on rice leaf disease that appear in Odisha's eastern region.

In Eastern Odisha, four varieties of crop diseases have been commonly identified: bacterial blight, brown spot, blast, and tungro. Detection manually is exciting work as it involves varieties of features. In most cases, rice condition diagnosis is monitored by either visual observation or laboratory testing. The visually observable is time-consuming and scarcely handled by a specialist. A laboratory trial necessitates the use of chemical reagents as well as a lengthy process.

The goal of agricultural disquisition is to enhance crop yield and quality while decreasing expenses and boosting production. For efficient management over some aspect that impacts the product and quality of the crops, the crop is commonly managed effectively with early assessments of the issue and performance of the potential result within the current possible timeframe. As a result, the performance of Automated Systems may be a fundamental requirement for farmers to prosper, assisting them with improved delicacy in the early detection of situations. The modern approaches of machine knowledge play a major character in the complaint type procedure throughout this process. The primary motive of this research is to do a relevant examination of Deep Neural Network models to improve the accuracy of infected rice leaf categorization using images of diseased rice leaves. This method consists of:

- Images of infected rice leaves from a publicly available internet site.
- Implementing an automated detection technique to identify infected rice leaf images from healthy paddy leaf images.
- To compare the outcomes of deep CNN models to increase the accuracy of the whole system.

The remnants of the paper are organized as follows. Section 2 summarizes all the literature surveys for this paper. Section 3 contains the methodology and flow diagram of the proposed model. Section 4 depicts various types of rice disease types and data descriptions. The implementation of the custom-CNN model, simulation environment, data acquisition, image pre-processing, and feature extraction using CNN are being described in Sect. 5. Section 6 contains results analysis along with the error analysis. Similarly, the conclusion and future work of this paper has been described in Sect. 7.

2 Literature Survey

Recently, a lot of practitioners have used many types of deep neural network models for the distinct types of crop and vegetable plant leaf classification.

Yibin Wang et al. [2] proposed a model which uses Bayesian optimization (ADSNN-BO) with an attention-based neural network to classify or detection of diseases of rice from images of rice leaves. This proposed Bayesian optimization, model was based on the augmentation attention mechanism and MobileNet architecture. To tune its hyper-parameters ADSNN-BO techniques were applied. The performance of this research shows that the method compatible with Bayesian optimization achieves 94.65% accuracy.

In another article, Vasantha et al. [3] show that LS, BLB, and BS are the three common diseases of plants of rice and for these diseases, the detection solution with test results exhibiting 1.0 and CNN model with a high-level fusion techniques are considered as the best solution. The second-best technique is AlexNet_Neural Network outperforms with 0.99 accuracies standing over other contemporary exhibiting better F1-score along with deep feature based SVM method having better Accuracy.

Rehman et al. [4] suggested a paper that helps farmers in reduction of the loss of their economy substantial by timely diagnosis and the pests perfectly applied to rice plants. Recently image classification performance is improved by the development of CNN in deep learning. In this research, rice plant images were created from the inspiration of image categorization of CNN's success which is deep learning-based for identifying diseases and pests. The proposed architecture achieves 93.3% of accuracy without reducing model size significantly.

Gugan et al. [5] describe a proposition model for the detection of early-stage diseases of rice leaves. Their proposed material includes a transfer learned model with high accuracy which provides a mobile solution for farmers. For balancing the samples of no of diseases a generative adversarial network is utilized.

Tawde et al. [6] verified that paddy infection is the big primary problem come across by most farmers; hence early detection is the only remedial. This research section gives an overview of several methodologies and a compact discussion of key features of different techniques and classifiers for detecting the diseases of rice.

Islam et al. [7] have worked on four disease types and one healthy rice leaf of class. For automatic detection of rice leaf disease, it uses CNN models of deep learning instead of the manual or traditional way of detection disease process where the performance is also considerable contentious. In this paper the highest result achieved is 92.68% from Inception-ResNet-V2 outperformed the other models are Xception, VGG-19, and ResNet-101.

Sethy et al. [8] have shown the deep feature of the predictive model which evaluate based on ResNet50 plus SVM and the results were found to be performed far enhanced with an F1 score of 0.9838 compared to the transfer learning counterpart as well. AlexNet outperforms other classification models such as LBP plus SVM, and bag-of-features plus SVM in terms of classification contributions.

Kumar et al. [9] describe in their article that there is a need for yield loss estimation, food security, and management of the disease for automatic identification of different kinds of plant diseases. These automation methods are at the peak for smart greenhouses, highly productive plants, and precision agriculture. Working with an open dataset acquires an accuracy of 99.40% on an evaluation set with the proposed ResNet34 model.

Harpale et al. [10] classified both healthy and ill-health leaf images. For classification and automated feature extraction, CNN is used and with the help of shape, size, and color diseases are getting distinguishable. It outperforms with a minimum number of parameters with 88% accuracy and this architecture is utilized for mobile efficiency or on embedded applications.

In the above literature review many studies on rice leaf disease detection describe a comparison analysis utilizing different deep learning models but there are limitations of there model. In this given proposed model, we not only present a comparison of the workings of a basic and sophisticated model, but we also strive to provide explanations for the model's predictions. This model used deep feature extraction which is automatically extracted the image feature from input data, where existing model are using manual feature extraction method.

Motivation. Previously, the only way to diagnose disease was to examine the leaf manually. This was done by inspecting plant leaves manually or consulting a book to detect the condition. This approach has three key drawbacks: first, it is inaccurate; second, it is impossible to analyze every leaf; and third, it is a lengthy procedure. Rice farming creates jobs and contributes significantly to the stabilization of the Gross Domestic Product (GDP). This research gives an overview of several methodologies and briefly discusses key features of various classifiers and methods for identifying crop diseases. As a result, the effectiveness of Automated Systems may become a requirement for farmers to thrive, assisting them in the early identification of conditions with more sensitivity. The fundamental goal of this research is to perform a relevant analysis of Deep Neural Network models to improve rice leaf classification accuracy from unhealthy rice leaf images.

3 Methodology

In the multilayer architecture of convolutional neural networks (CNNs), the complete network determines its performance over certain criteria. In most cases, it includes three basic layers as convolution layer, the fully connected layer, and the pooling layer. The feature extractor is formed by the convolutional and pooling layer, whereas the connected layer works as a classifier. The convolutional layer's features are reduced in dimensionality by the pooling layer. In the process of classifying the images, the fully connected layer, the feature extraction approach is then used by softmax, and the convolution layer uses a series of learnable filters to extract features from an input image. The 2-D feature map is created by taking a sliding window technique, the dot products of each filter with the raw picture pixel.

Much work has been done in the last several years on machine learning is being used to identify diseases on rice leaves and deep learning convictions adopting various methods. The flowchart depicts a benchmarked technique using a personalized deep learning model via Fig. 1. The image pre-processing phase began following the capture of infected leaf images, and pre-processed images were fed into a deep CNN. The models' convolutional blocks the major feature out of the acquired input images. The DNN model begins each node's weights based on the considered attributes of the images. Four neural nodes compensate the model's final dense layer, and an activation function like softmax assists in predicting the data's class.

The computer takes one image from the dataset and pre-processes it by rotating, zooming, flipping, shuffling, and resizing it. This will propose five deep CNN models: custom-CNN, VGG-19, ResNet-152, InceptionV3, and DenseNet121, which were designed to extract and classify features. Finally, use the best model to predict the outcome. In the result section, the comparison of the same has been mentioned in Table 2.

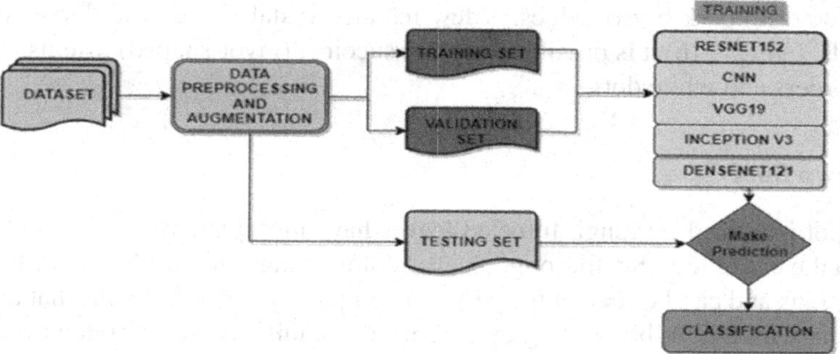

Fig. 1. Flowchart of the proposed methodology

4 Rice Disease Type and Dataset Description

The disease images were gathered from the agricultural areas during the last few months from the local area of Balasore District, belonging to the state of eastern Odisha and some of the disease images were collected from web sources. There are 5932 images of infected rice leaves in the dataset, with the most prolific diseases like bacterial blight, blast, brown spot, and tungro types among them. The afflicted portion's patches were taken from the original images. All four categories of rice leaf diseases were scaled to 300 × 300 pixels and processed as data samples.

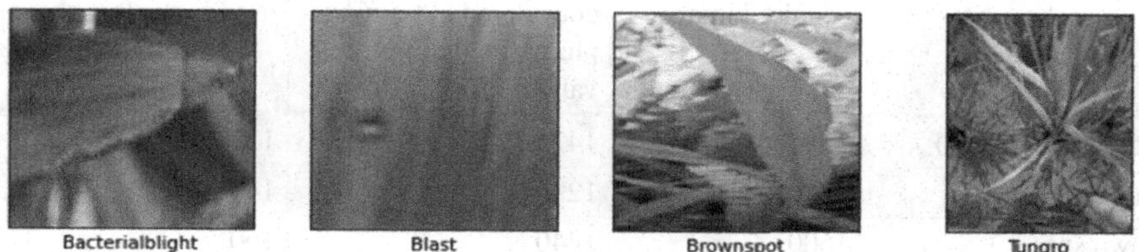

Fig. 2. Rice leaf disease image dataset

4.1 Bacterial Blight

"Xanthomonas oryzae" bacteria cause a bacterial disease in rice plants. The diseased leaf turns grey-green and rolls up, straw-colored, yellow, and eventually dies succeeding withering. Lesions are having curvy borders and spread to the bottom. Bacterial ooze that looks like morning dew drop can be seen on young lesions. Leaves affected by Leaf Blight showed in Fig. 2 (a).

4.2 Blast

Magnaporthe oryzae causes this type of fungal disease in rice plants. The first sign is that it turns to grey-green patches from white which is succinct (pivot-shaped) and has dark-red color to dark-brown edges. A few feature crystal shapes with large cores and sharp ends. In Fig. 2 (b) it is possible to notice succinct (pivot-shaped) lesions with dark brown borders and white dots.

4.3 Brown Spot

Brown spot is caused by fungi. Infected leaves have multiple large spots on them that can harm the entire leaf. Small, round, leaves color changes to purple-brown from dark brown lesions and can be seen in the early on completely formed lesions that are round to elliptical with a light brown to grey core near a reddish-brown perimeter created by the fungi's blights. Figure 2. (c) shows the Brown Spot damaged leaves with tiny dark brown blemishes.

4.4 Tungro

Tungro is caused by the interaction of two viruses which are spread by leafhoppers. It results in slowed development, leaf discoloration, sterile or partially filled grains, and fewer tillers. It infects the rice that is cultivated, certain wild rice cousins, and other grassy weeds and is typically seen in rice paddies. As shown in Fig. 2 (d) tungro-infected plants have a yellow or orange-yellow discoloration (Table 1).

Table 1. Data description.

Rice leaf disease class	Total number of acquired images	Number of images considered in training phase (including validation)	Number of images used in the test phase
Bacterial Blight (a)	1584	1425	159
Blast (b)	1440	1296	144
Brown spot (c)	1600	1440	160
Tungro (d)	1308	1176	132
Total	5932	5337	595

5 Implementation

This is a quantitative application of deep learning research. Discuss the procedures used in these studies in this field.

5.1 Simulation Environment

The experimental performance of rice leaf disease classification models is based on five deep Neural Network models. This study was conducted using the python 3.8 Anaconda environment and Keras 2.2.4 deep learning. All of the programs were tested on an ASUS ROG with Intel Core i5 9th Gen Processor with 16 GB RAM along with Windows 11 Pro as an Operating System and an NVIDIA GeForce GTX 1650/60 Hz graphics card.

5.2 Image Acquisition

The dataset was collected from a web source and the local area in eastern Odisha. There are 5932 images of infected rice leaves in the dataset, with bacterial blight, blast, brown spot, and tungro types among them. The patches on the affected part were taken from the original images. Some photographs of crop infections were gathered in my town's neighborhood. All of the patches were scaled to 300 × 300 pixels and processed as data samples. The four types of rice leaf diseases are presented in Fig. 2.

5.3 Image Preprocessing and Augmentation

In our instance, all of the pictures in the dataset have been downsized to meet the needs of the various DNN models [14, 15]. The ResNet model requires input photos with dimensions of 240 × 240 × 3, whereas CNN, VGG19, InceptionV3, and DenseNet121 all require an image of size 224 × 224 × 3. As per the prerequisite for ResNet, all images are scaled down to 240 × 240, and CNN [13], VGG19, InceptionV3, and DenseNet121 all received 224 × 224. ImageDataGenerator library in Keras is being used in the simulation process to generate augmented images by using various image augmentation techniques like zoom, rotation, horizontal, vertical shift, etc.

The convolutional layer first aligns the selected feature pixels from the acquired pictures before multiplying each input image pixel by matching the corresponding feature pixel. It computes in a way that divides by the total number of pixels in the feature after the addition of each pixel value. After the computation process is over the resultant values are stored inside a matrix called a feature map, which allows the filter to be moved over the whole image. The feature map is being used to reverse all the computed values. In a very similar way, all of the selected features go through the procedure, resulting in various feature matrices. The Eq. (1) for obtaining the customized convolutional layer is mentioned as follows,

$$u_{ijm} = \sum_{K=0}^{K-1} \sum_{p=0}^{H-1} \sum_{q=0}^{H-1} z_{i+p,j+q,k}^{(l-1)} h_{pqkm} + b_{ijm} \quad (1)$$

Here the evaluation model bias is commonly set as b_{ijm} which is independent of the positional value of the pixels present in an image. h_{pqkm} is considered the uniform value of the weighted pool used for every pixel $z_{i+p,j+q,k}^{(l-1)}$. Where z is obtained a result from previous layer input data, l is number of layers, k is number of channels and $i + p$ and $j + q$ is representing feature map of the input data.

As an Activation function, the Rectified Linear Unit (ReLu) is being used in the very next steps which help in eliminating all negative values from the feature index and replacing them with zeros. Equation (2) shows the formula for the activation ReLu function.

$$f(x) = \max(0, x) \tag{2}$$

The max-pooling layer scaled the input image size to a reduced state by extracting the maximized value out of the correlation or heat map of the features of the convolutional layer. The resulting max-pooling layer equation is mentioned as follows in Eq. (3),

$$u_{ijk} = \max_{p,q \epsilon P_{i,j}} z_{pqk} \tag{3}$$

Here, $P_{i,j}$ define a set of pixels including the area. A pixel value, u_{ijk} is a particular pixel value obtained by the use every z_{pqk} pcs of pixel value with every k channel that is being considered.

Finally, in the process of building the model, the interlinked layer transforms the reduced pixels from the model's final extracting or pooling layer into a single list array vector. The procedure involved in the classification process is considered to be fully connected and irreversible.

5.4 Deep Neural Network Model Training

First of all, dividing the whole dataset into training and testing classes of the infected rice leaf images. For training, the class labels and images are kept in separate arrays. The train is to test ration has been set to 90:10. The 90% data is then separated again, with 10% going to use for validation. Integers are used to encode the class labels, and then one-hot encoding is applied to them, resulting in every label being represented as a vector instead of an integer. Following that, all of the other DNN models are loaded from Keras, the final completely connected layers are dropped, and made the remaining layers are non-trainable. Then, with categorical cross-entropy as the classification loss function, the proposed model has been built with the help of the Adam optimizer. As the results were steady after 30 epochs, we set an early stop at 30 epochs.

6 Result Analysis

6.1 Simulation Environment

To identify and diagnose leaf diseases, this study used five Deep Neural Networks using four pre-trained algorithms from Keras and one custom-CNN developed from scratches, as shown in Table 3. The study discovered that the custom-CNN model had the greatest accuracy of all of them, at 0.9747, and that custom-CNN was also ahead of all of them in precision, recall, and F1 score. VGG19 has a 0.96 accuracy after custom-CNN. The ResNet-152 model has a precision of 0.70, whereas DensNet121 and InceptionV3 have precisions of 0.66 and 0.69, respectively. It has the lowest results in comparison with various performance matrices like accuracy, precision, recall, and F1 Score. For all training procedures, the number of epochs was taken to be 30. Table 2 provides an analytical study of various models which covers all other aspects.

Accuracy. The ratio of properly identified leaf classes (True Positive (TP) + True Negative (TN)) to the cumulative leaf classes (True Positive (TP) + True Negative (TN) + False Positive (FP) + False Negative (FN)) represents an algorithm's accuracy. If the dataset contains a major class imbalance, then using accuracy as the main metric will not do well, but it performs better in the case of the equal samples belonging to each class.

Table 2. Analysis of different pre-trained keras model and custom-CNN model.

Models	Precision	Recall	F1 Score	Accuracy
CNN	0.97	0.97	0.97	0.97
VGG19	0.96	0.96	0.96	0.96
DenseNet121	0.66	0.66	0.65	0.66
InceptionV3	0.69	0.68	0.68	0.69
ResNet-152	0.70	0.70	0.70	0.70

The accuracy is determined as follows:

$$Accuracy = \frac{(\mathrm{TP} + \mathrm{TN})}{(\mathrm{TP} + \mathrm{FP} + \mathrm{TN} + \mathrm{FN})} \tag{4}$$

Precision. The precision of an algorithm is given as the ratio of properly diagnosed plant leaf classes with the disease (True Positive (TP)) to the total number of leaf classes projected to have the disease (True Positive (TP) + False Positive (FP)). The precision is calculated as:

$$Precision = \frac{\mathrm{TP}}{(\mathrm{TP} + \mathrm{FP})} \tag{5}$$

Recall. The recall measure is defined as the segment correctly concerning classifying feature classes (True Positive (TP)) in consideration of the total number of leaf classes with the disease. The computed formula is presented in Eq. (6). The concept behind the recall is the number of leaf classes who have been diagnosed with the ailment. It is otherwise named sensitivity.

$$Recall = \frac{\mathrm{TP}}{(\mathrm{TP} + \mathrm{FN})} \tag{6}$$

F1 Score. It is often referred to as the F Measure. The F1 score represents the balance of accuracy and recall. This statistical benchmark is used to analyze the enactment of the classifier. F1 score can be utilized when there is an unequal class distribution and we need to balance precision and recall. It is calculated as:

$$F1\,Score = \frac{2 \times \mathrm{Recall} \times \mathrm{Precision}}{\mathrm{Recall} + \mathrm{Precision}} \tag{7}$$

From the experimented model outcomes, the customized-CNN model eclipsed the other four models in terms of various performance matrices. The performance matrix comparison is depicted in Table 3. As shown in Table 3, bacterial blight, leaf blast, brown spot, and tungro, all scored more than 0.90 for precision, although recall was 1.00 for tungro and 0.90 for the other classes. Finally, for the F1 score, the brown spot scored the most at 0.99, while the Leaf blast scored the lowest at 0.94. Table 3 contains all of this information as well as some additional data (Fig. 3).

Table 3. Performance evaluation for each class of custom-CNN model.

Classes	Bacterial blight	Leaf blast	Brown spot	Tungro
Precision	0.96	0.95	0.97	1.00
Recall	0.99	0.93	1.00	0.96
F1 Score	0.97	0.94	0.99	0.98

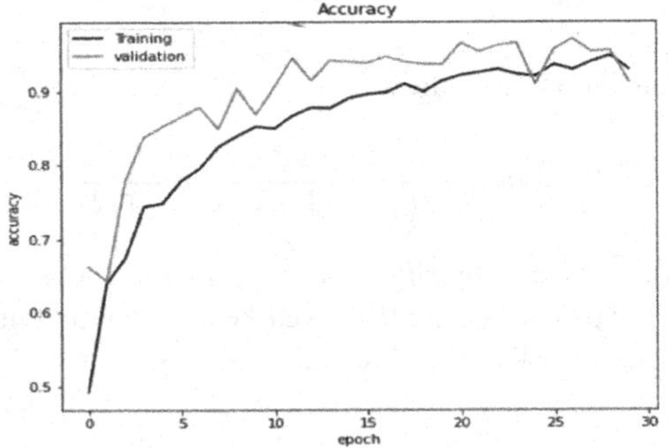

Fig. 3. Training and validation accuracy graph.

6.2 Error Analysis

Manually detecting disease is challenging; however, technology has greatly simplified the process. Even said, technology will never be able to achieve the same level of perfection as humans, and there will always be certain limits.

When it comes to disease detection, the machine might be a bit confused. Following the selection of the best model, an error occurred. In Fig. 4, there are 6 data conflicts between Leaf Blast and Bacterial Blight, 4 data Brown Spot, 5 data Tungro with Leaf Blast, and 2 data Bacterial Blight with Leaf Blast. Even though the number is insignificant.

This part will explore several approaches for recognizing and categorizing diseases of rice and its leaves, as well as how to diagnose rice using various machine learning and deep learning tools and technologies. There have been a lot of studies done on this

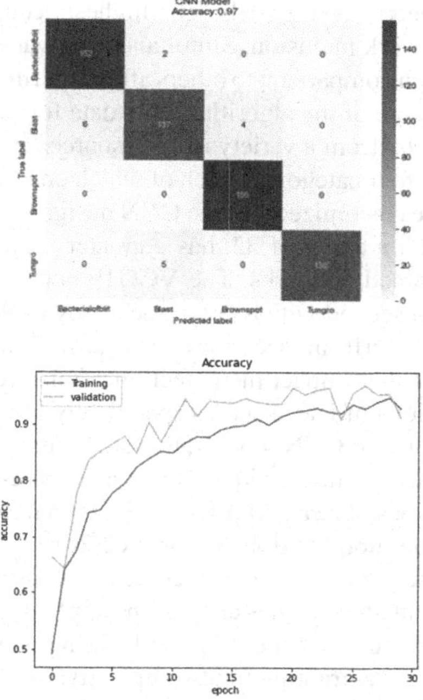

Fig. 4. Confusion matrix of custom-CNN model

topic in the past, and it continues to be done now. In Table 4, various findings regarding to some of the comparisons have been noted.

Table 4. Statistical analysis comparison of related works.

References	Diseases	Technologies	Accuracy
Wang et al. [2]	Brown spot, Rice Hispa Damage, Leaf Blast, Healthy	ADSNN-BO	94.65%
Rahman et al. [4]	BLB, BHP, BS, FS, Hispa, NB, SBR, Stm, Others	Simple CNN	93%
Ghosal et al. [12]	Leaf Blast, Leaf Blight, Brown spot	VGG-16, CNN	92%
Proposed Model	**Bacterial Blight, Brown spot, Tungro, Leaf Blast**	**Custom-CNN**	**97.47%**

7 Conclusion and Future Scope

This research assessed the performance of five benchmark deep CNN architectures, one of which was developed from the ground up (custom-CNN), while the others were simply

Keras pre-trained based deep CNN models. The highest accuracy obtained is 97.47% with the custom-CNN network inclusion. Simultaneously various performance metrics are considered to be better in comparison to others after experimenting with the accuracy, precision, recall, and F1 score of the algorithm. The data for model training and testing in this research was gathered from a variety of web sources as well as local farm areas. The dataset is divided into four categories, each of which contains four rice leaf diseases that are often afflicted. The customized-unique CNN design, which includes a reduction and deep CNN blocks with a depth of 32, has a greater influence on adapting to tiny datasets than other pre-trained networks. The VGG19 network which is a pre-trained model from Keras came in second with a testing accuracy of 96.52%.

Considering the model performance, a proper rigorous examination is required to understand the parameters that impact the detection of plant diseases. With the inclusion of many more variations of leaf diseases specifically in rice plants along with the consideration of very fine-tuned CNN models, this study may be expanded in the hopes of improving accuracy and speeding up identification. This research might be extended by the insertion of more types of rice leaf diseases, larger datasets, and other Deep Neural Network models. Furthermore, custom-greatest CNN's obtained accuracy motivates this work to learn about the same and make a detailed comparison with other deep CNN models. Transfer learning methodologies can also be applied to generate a more precise prediction of rice leaf diseases, and this transfer learning adaptation improved model accuracy while reducing model training time complexity.

This proposed model has taken some reparation in image processing:

i. It would be nice if there is less time to trained the proposed model.
ii. It required fine tune of image for greater accuracy and recognition.

References

1. Singh, A.K., Sreenivasu, S.V.N., Mahalaxmi, U.S.B.K., Sharma, H., Patil, D.D., Asenso, E.: Hybrid feature-based disease detection in plant leaf using convolutional neural network, bayesian optimized SVM, and random forest classifier. J. Food Qual. **2022** (2022)
2. Wang, Y., Wang, H., Peng, Z.: Rice diseases detection and classification using attention based neural network and bayesian optimization. Expert Syst. Appl. **178**, 114770 (2021)
3. Vasantha, S.V., Kiranmai, B., Krishna, S.R.: Techniques for rice leaf disease detection using machine learning algorithms. Int. J. Eng. Res. Technol. **9**(8), 162–166 (2021)
4. Rahman, C.R., et al.: Identification and recognition of rice diseases and pests using convolutional neural networks. Biosys. Eng. **194**, 112–120 (2020)
5. Kathiresan, G., Anirudh, M., Nagharjun, M., Karthik, R.: Disease detection in rice leaves using transfer learning techniques. J. Phys. Conf. Ser. **1911**(1), 012004 (2021). IOP Publishing
6. Tawde, T., Deshmukh, K., Verekar, L., Reddy, A., Aswale, S., Shetgaonkar, P.: Identification of rice plant disease using image processing and machine learning techniques. In: 2021 International Conference on Technological Advancements and Innovations (ICTAI), pp. 102–108. IEEE (2021)
7. Islam, M.A., Shuvo, M.N.R., Shamsojjaman, M., Hasan, S., Hossain, M.S., Khatun, T.: An automated convolutional neural network based approach for paddy leaf disease detection. Int. J. Adv. Comput. Sci. Appl. **12**(1), 280–288 (2021)

8. Sethy, P.K., Barpanda, N.K., Rath, A.K., Behera, S.K.: Deep feature based rice leaf disease identification using support vector machine. Comput. Electron. Agric. **175**, 105527 (2021)
9. Kumar, V., Arora, H., Sisodia, J.: Resnet-based approach for detection and classification of plant leaf diseases. In: 2020 International Conference on Electronics and Sustainable Communication Systems (ICESC), pp. 495–502. IEEE (2020)
10. Harpale, D., Jadhav, S., Lakhani, K., Thyagarajane, K.: Plant disease identification using image processing. Int. Res. J. Eng. Technol. (IRJET) **7**, 3571–3573 (2020)
11. Kaur, S., Pandey, S., Goel, S.: Plants disease identification and classification through leaf images: a survey. Arch. Comput. Methods Eng. **26**(2), 507–530 (2019)
12. Ghosal, S., Sarkar, K.: Rice leaf diseases classification using CNN with transfer learning. In: 2020 IEEE Calcutta Conference (CALCON), pp. 230–236. IEEE (2020)
13. Hossain, S.M.M., et al.: Rice leaf diseases recognition using convolutional neural networks. In: Yang, X., Wang, C.-D., Islam, M.S., Zhang, Z. (eds.) ADMA 2020. LNCS (LNAI), vol. 12447, pp. 299–314. Springer, Cham (2020). https://doi.org/10.1007/978-3-030-65390-3_23
14. Li, L., Zhang, S., Wang, B.: Plant disease detection and classification by deep learning—a review. IEEE Access **9**, 56683–56698 (2021)
15. Pothen, M.E., Pai, M.L.: Detection of rice leaf diseases using image processing. In: 2020 Fourth International Conference on Computing Methodologies and Communication (ICCMC), pp. 424–430. IEEE (2020)

Training Scheme for Stereo Audio Generation

Padmaja Mohanty(✉)

Vinoba Bhave University, Hazaribag, India
mohantyp.7@gmail.com

Abstract. The Voice substitution and audio generation are being used more and more often in a variety of computer listening applications. Furthermore, state-of-the-art perceptual synthesis is allowing richer music without the need for expensive equipment. True audio immersion is when the listener feels what they are listening to, they become part of the story being told. True stereo audio must be generated differently to make use of two channels rather than just one. However, generating stereo audio has not been a popular topic in literature despite being an important component of a listener's experience. Some great tools for generating stereo audio are Sharp Beta Point or Audacity. This research is focused on developing a generative model for stereo audio generation. It also presents new forms of representation that effectively capture stereo image of stereo audio. It is evident from results that the proposed method improves audio quality to significant degree.

Keywords: Generative model · Multi-channel audio · Learning representation

1 Introduction

From classical acoustics research to the modern music industry, spatiality is one of the most important acoustical features. Classical acoustic studies deal with spatiality (ASW) [12], but in the two-channel digital audio environment most familiar to the public. Stereo image control is one of the most important tasks for satisfying modern audiences in the music industry.

There have been several works in the literature relevant to audio generative model proposing the use of neural networks to synthesize instrumental sounds and voices. For example, there is the well-known WaveNet [16] that generates audio in an autoregressive manner in the time domain with a network, and GAN-Synth [4], which generates audio by image-learning based on audio converted to spectrogram with Generative Adversarial Network. Discussions on performance improvements for earlier audio generative models continued, but while there are studies to improve the fidelity of generated audio, such as NSF (Neural source-filter) [17], no serious discussion has been conducted on multi-channel audio generation. Conventional neural audio synthesis models, including the aforementioned models, generate plausible quality audio, but only mono audio can

S. K. Panda et al. (Eds.): CoCoLe 2022, CCIS 1729, pp. 244–253, 2022.
https://doi.org/10.1007/978-3-031-21750-0_21

be generated, or support multi-channel audio generation [3], but they do not consider inter-channel coherence, resulting in low-quality spatiality. Since at least a two-channel environment must be provided to satisfy the modern audience, the need for discussion of the multi-channel audio generation with plausible spatiality is emphasized [8].

Overall, this research propose a methodology that allows a two-channel audio generative network to learn stereo images of a target audio set. The problem is approached from a channel split perspective to enable the network to learn stereo images. The conjecture is applied to an architecture based on GANSynth [4] to verify the proposed methodology. The research shows promising results on the stereo audio generation problem with the new dataset [10].

Some of the major contributions of this paper are **1)** The ease-of-use and adaptability it offers to future audio generation research and applications. **2)** The introduction of a new public dataset composed of two-channel stereo audios that have high-fidelity and rich stereo images. **3)** The introduction of a proper representation of the stereo image, namely *'Side distance'* and *'STSD'*, and definition of the distance metric between them, enabling quantitative evaluation of the stereo image generation model.

2 Literature Review

2.1 Audio Generative Model

The most prominent models for audio generation were created to mimic human speech. In this case, models require handling variable length, and WaveNet [16] used the autoregressive method for variable-length inputs and outputs. A flow-based WaveGlow [13] has emerged that compensates for slow speed of autoregressive models. Currently, music is still being generated by a mixture of speech. However, this is just a temporary stage in the development of audio generation for music. NSynth [5] proposed generation of a single musical note to use WaveNet, but it is still slow, and global latent conditioning was impossible. GANSynth [4] helps solve these issues; it is created by using a class of artificial neural networks called GANs together with Convolutional Variational Autoencoders. It is a piece of software for Generative Adversarial Networks which includes GANs and variational autoencoders - two neural networks for generating images. The purpose of this software is to help people visualise and understand why certain pictures are generated in image generation. Priyanka et al. [15] also proposes similar innovative usage of GAN in animal biometrics based cattle identification. As a result of the research to date, it is possible to learn a single note of a variety of instruments to convincingly describe the sound of real instruments and to create a variety of synthesizers by interpolation between two instruments. Despite such breakthrough development, the reason that the generated musical notes cannot be used for commercial music is that the generated result is a single channel.

2.2 Multi-channel Audio

There are many uses of machine listening in the community, like speech separation and enhancement and speech recognition. It is because they are able to analyze different sounds in light of a particular location [2,11,18].

On the other hand, [6] proposed an upmixing conversion of the mono signal to pseudo-stereo in order to enhance the audio effect. However, to the best of my knowledge, there are still no attempts to generate high-fidelity multi-channel audio with a neural network. It is necessary to learn the difference while maintaining the coherency of both channels to form a spatiality of sound. Stereo Side coding involves summing up and subtracting each channel, depending on the perceived direction of the sound it is desired to manipulate. ([7] described the concept of mid-side coding of using the interchannel redundancies.) Therefore, for a high-performance multi-channel audio generative model, this research trains the state-of-the-art audio generative model ([4], so-called GANSynth) through the mid-side coding to verify whether this attempt can effectively learn stereo image.

3 Proposed Method

3.1 Training Scheme

As mentioned above, channel coherency is an important property for the plausible spatiality formation in two-channel audio. However, when the network generates two-channel audio, if left and right channels are created without a guide of channel coherency, the spatiality of the generated audio will not be appropriate. Since creating additional networks associated with channel coherence caused overhead, it is recommended to find a different method to avoid burdening the network. Therefore, it is valid to make the following conjecture: Network will learn stereo image better when using the mid-side (M-S) channel than using the left-right (L-R) channel. When y is stereo audio and y_M and y_S are mid and side channel of stereo audio y, y_M and y_S as following:

$$y_M = \frac{y_L + y_R}{2}, \quad y_S = \frac{y_L - y_R}{2}$$

where y_L and y_R are left and right channel of stereo audio y.

3.2 Custom Dataset

To validate the aforementioned methodology for the stereo image learning for the network, a new dataset was needed. Since the focus of this research is on a stereo audio generation model, an audio set with the drastic and various stereo images was needed for the conjecture, but none of the conventional datasets were appropriate. Inspired by the NSynth dataset, which is mainly used by previous studies on neural audio synthesis [4,5], a new dataset was composed using the stab, which is a single staccato note or chord that adds dramatic punctuation

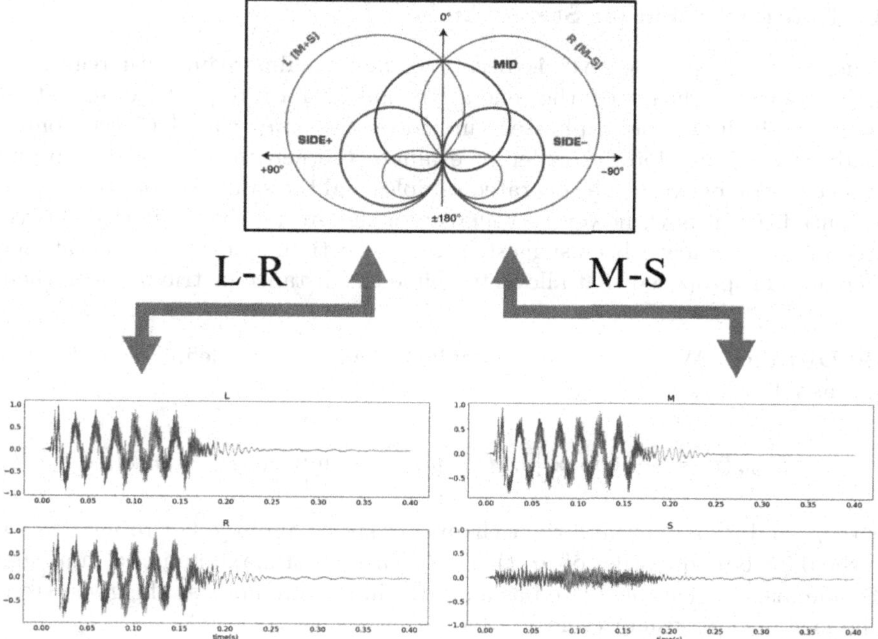

Fig. 1. Example of channel representation for two-channel audio. The left one is the L-R channel representation, and the right one is the M-S channel representation.

to a composition, used in modern electronic music. For clarity of the task, the length of each sample was adjusted to 400 ms (Fig. 1).

Due to the lack of a large number of sources, the data was augmented in three ways to obtain a sufficient amount of data. The augmentations performed are as follows: L-R channel change, time-stretching without pitch shift, and FIR filtering. A total of 11,520 data points were produced that maintain the characteristics of the original data through these augmentations. Note that variations on the pitch were not added because the data often have atonal properties.

4 Experiments

In this section, first the novel representation of stereo audio, *'Side distance' (D_{side}) and 'Short-time Side Distance (STSD)'* is proposed. Next, the existing metrics for evaluating sample generation are introduced, then the new metrics for evaluating stereo image generation by combining existing metrics with side distance and STSD is proposed. Then the proposed method using M-S channels is compared with the previous method(GANSynth [4]) which consumes L-R channels by both quantitative and qualitative methods.

4.1 Representation for Stereo Audio

Artificial Intelligence or "AI" is becoming more mainstream with regards to content creation. The goal of the generative model is for it to produce suggestions that might include words, phrases, and ideas that are related to the content already there. Therefore, in order to evaluate the generative model, a proper distance metric between the generated samples and the samples from the dataset is essential. Until now, however, a metric for measuring the similarity between stereo images has never been suggested. In this section, a novel representation of stereo audio is proposed that allows to define the distance metric between them.

Side Distance. When y is a stereo audio of length T, we define *'side distance'* D_{side} as following:

$$D_{side}(y) = \frac{\sqrt{2}}{2}\left(\max_{t\in[0,T)}[y_L(t) - y_R(t)] - \min_{t\in[0,T)}[y_L(t) - y_R(t)]\right) \tag{1}$$

where y_L and y_R are left and right channel of stereo audio y. For robustness, we use the 0.95, 0.05 quantiles of $y_L(t) - y_R(t)$ instead of maximum and minimum. The side distance can be viewed as an index indicating how far the given stereo audio is spread as visualized in Fig. 2a

Short-Time Side Distance (STSD). Although side distance is an indicator of how wide the given stereo audio is spread in the auditory space, it cannot express the change of the stereo image over time. Therefore, the concept of *'Short-time Side Distance (STSD)'* is introduced in this research to capture the characteristics of the stereo image over time. The STSD is a sequence of side distance of a windowed signal. STSD is a concept involving the measuring of distances on multiple shorter segments of the signal. In this concept, it's important to segment your signal into different amounts so that you can evaluate the worthiness and quality of each segment individually. Formally,

$$STSD(y(t)) = D_{side}(y(\tau)w(t)) \tag{2}$$

where $w(t)$ is a window function which is nonzero for short period of time. As depicted in Fig. 2b, STSD contains the change in the side distance of the windowed short fragment of signal over time.

4.2 Evaluation Metrics

Following prior work, earth mover's distance (EMD), proposed by [14], is used in this research to measure the similarity between two stereo audios' STSDs. Formally, EMD is defined as follows:

$$\mathrm{EMD}(s_1, s_2) = \min_{\phi: s_1 \to s_2} \sum_{x\in s_1} \|x - \phi(x)\|_2$$

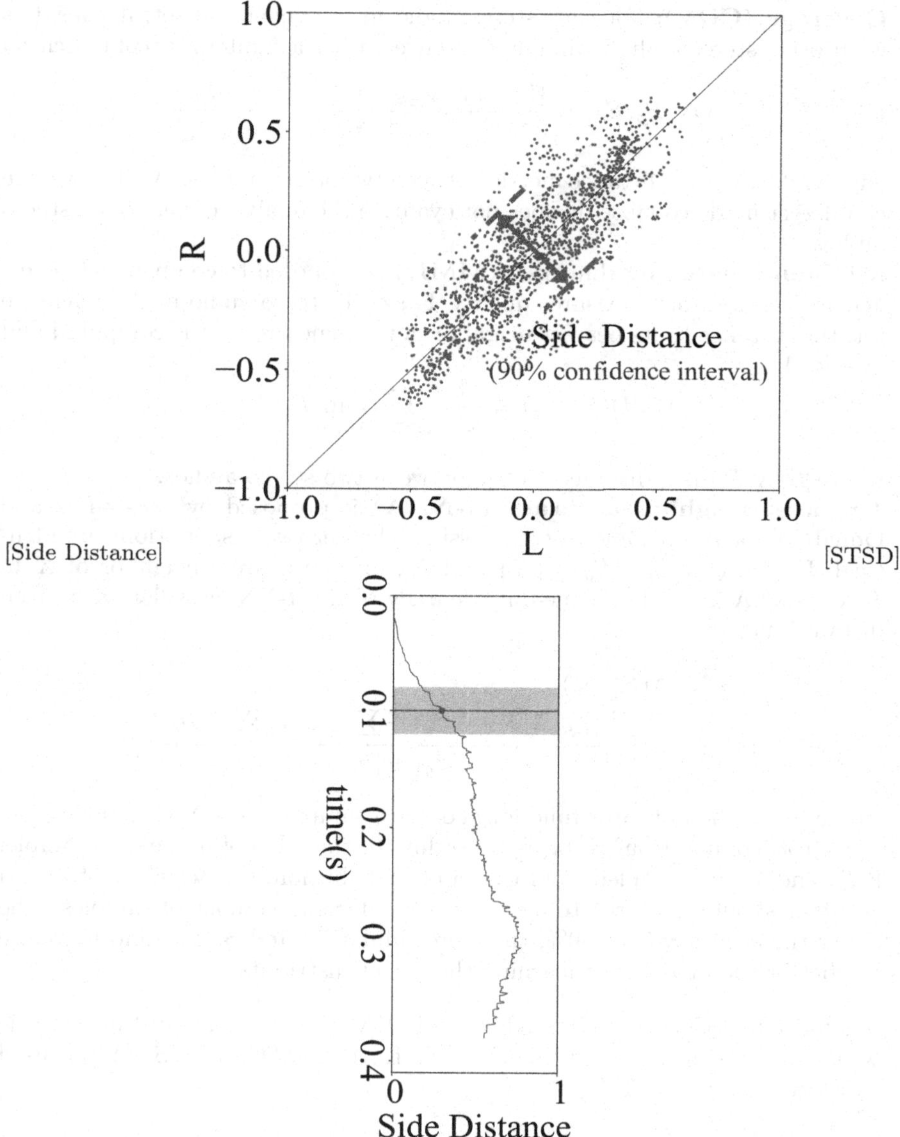

Fig. 2. Stereo audio representation. (a) shows the Lissajous figure and side distance, (b) shows the STSD.

where s_1 and s_2 are two distributions and ϕ is a bijection between them. Note that s_1 and s_2 can be any distribution. One can use STSD of stereo audio as s_1 and s_2.

Let S_g be the set of generated stereo audios and S_r be the set of reference audios with $|S_g| = |S_r|$. For assessing the model MMD, COV are taken into account which are introduced by [1] and 1-NNA proposed by [9].

- **Coverage (COV):** For each stereo audio in the generated set, it considers what other stereo audio within its reference set has a similar ratio of matches.:

$$\mathrm{COV}(S_g, S_r) = \frac{|\{\arg\min_{Y \in S_r} D(X,Y) | X \in S_g\}|}{|S_r|},$$

  where $D(X,Y)$ is a distance metric between two stereo audios. While coverage can detect mode collapse, it does not evaluate the quality of generated stereo audios.
- **Minimum matching distance (MMD)** is proposed to complement coverage as a metric that measures quality. For each stereo audio in the reference set, the distance to its nearest neighbor in the generated set is computed and averaged:

$$\mathrm{MMD}(S_g, S_r) = \frac{1}{|S_r|} \sum_{Y \in S_r} \min_{X \in S_g} D(X,Y),$$

  where $D(X,Y)$ is a distance metric between two stereo audios.
- **1-nearest neighbor accuracy (1-NNA)** is proposed by Lopez-Paz and Oquab [9] for two-sample tests, assessing whether two distributions are identical. Let $S_{-X} = S_r \cup S_g - \{X\}$ and N_X be the nearest neighbor of X in S_{-X}. 1-NNA is the leave-one-out accuracy of the 1-NN classifier with given distance metric:

$$\begin{aligned} &\text{1-NNA}(S_g, S_r) \\ &= \frac{\sum_{X \in S_g} \mathbb{1}[N_X \in S_g] + \sum_{Y \in S_r} \mathbb{1}[N_Y \in S_r]}{|S_g| + |S_r|}, \end{aligned}$$

  where $\mathbb{1}[\cdot]$ is the indicator function. For each sample, the 1-NN classifier classifies it as coming from S_r or S_g according to the label of its nearest sample. If S_g and S_r are sampled from the same distribution, the accuracy of such a classifier should converge to 50% given a sufficient number of samples. The closer the accuracy is to 50%, the more similar S_g and S_r are, and therefore the better the model is at learning the target distribution.

As a definition of COV, MMD, 1-NNA, and $D(X,Y)$ can be any distance metric between two audio samples. In this research, EMD(STSD(X), STSD(Y)) is used as a distance metric $D(X,Y)$.

4.3 Experimental Results

Quantitative Results. For a fair comparison, both the proposed model and GANSynth [4] were trained with exactly same hyperparameters (including network architectures, learning rate, epochs) in the training set. The only difference during the training scheme between GANSynth [4] and the proposed method is the channel encoding. The proposed method consumes two-channel audio that is reparameterized from L-R representation to M-S representation while GANSynth [4] takes input as raw L-R represented stereo audios. The quantitative

Table 1. Quantitative comparison results of stereo audio generation on the proposed dataset. The best results are marked in bold. Note that MMD is multiplied by 10^3.

	COV (↑)	MMD (↓)	1-NNA (↓)
GANSynth [4]	34.55	1.42	76.22
Ours	**45.31**	**1.05**	**68.66**

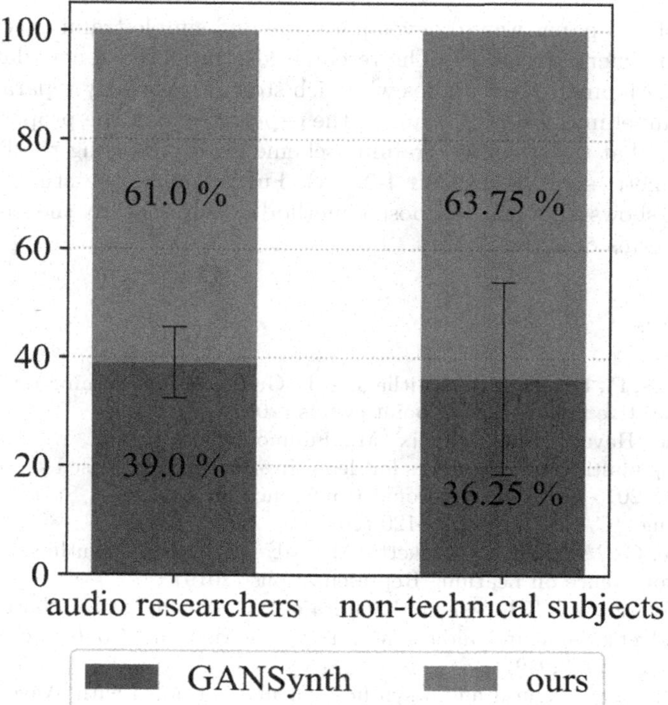

Fig. 3. Listening evaluation for audio quality to concurrent work. The proposed method received better results on both subject group, especially it is quite significant for audio researchers group ($p < 0.01$).

results are reported in Table 1. It is observed that there is significant improvement by simple reparameterization of the stereo audio in terms of every evaluation metrics (COV, MMD, 1-NNA).

Comparing Audio Quality to Concurrent Work. To better compare the proposed method with concurrent work, a subjective analysis is performed over the stereo audios generated by both methods. Figure 3 shows the percentages of participants based on how they voted for the plausibility comparisons between the proposed method and GANSynth [4]. The study employed 15 participants with different backgrounds - 5 audio researchers, 10 non-technical subjects. The participants were asked to choose the better audio between the proposed method and other work. It can be observed that the proposed method received better results on both the audio researcher group and the non-technical subject group.

5 Conclusion

The focus of this paper was to develop a novel and simple training scheme for a stereo audio generative model. The research also proposed a new dataset composed of two-channel stereo audios with rich stereo images. By reparameterizing the L-R channel into the M-S channel, the experiments on the proposed dataset demonstrate that the proposed training scheme gives promising results on every evaluation metrics (MMD, COV, 1-NNA). Furthermore, the study on human evaluations shows that the proposed method is superior to the conventional method in terms of audio quality.

References

1. Achlioptas, P., Diamanti, O., Mitliagkas, I., Guibas, L.J.: Learning representations and generative models for 3D point clouds (2017)
2. Araki, S., Hayashi, T., Delcroix, M., Fujimoto, M., Takeda, K., Nakatani, T.: Exploring multi-channel features for denoising-autoencoder-based speech enhancement. In: 2015 IEEE International Conference on Acoustics, Speech and Signal Processing (ICASSP), pp. 116–120 (2015)
3. Donahue, C., McAuley, J., Puckette, M.: Adversarial audio synthesis. In: International Conference on Learning Representations (2019)
4. Engel, J., Agrawal, K.K., Chen, S., Gulrajani, I., Donahue, C., Roberts, A.: GANSynth: adversarial neural audio synthesis. In: International Conference on Learning Representations (2019)
5. Engel, J., et al.: Neural audio synthesis of musical notes with WaveNet autoencoders. In: Precup, D., Teh, Y.W. (eds.) Proceedings of the 34th International Conference on Machine Learning, International Convention Centre, Sydney, Australia. Proceedings of Machine Learning Research, vol. 70, pp. 1068–1077. PMLR (2017)
6. Fink, M., Kraft, S., Zölzer, U.: Downmmix-compatible conversion from mono to stereo in time-and frequency-domain. In: Proceedings of the 18th International Conference on Digital Audio Effects (2015)
7. Johnston, J.D., Ferreira, A.J.: Sum-difference stereo transform coding. In: Proceedings of ICASSP 1992: 1992 IEEE International Conference on Acoustics, Speech, and Signal Processing, vol. 2, pp. 569–572 (1992)
8. Liu, T., Yan, D., Yan, N., Chen, G.: Anti-forensics of fake stereo audio using generative adversarial network. Multimed. Tools Appl. **81**, 17155–17167 (2022). https://doi.org/10.1007/s11042-022-12448-4
9. Lopez-Paz, D., Oquab, M.: Revisiting classifier two-sample tests (2016) arXiv:1610.06545
10. Menéndez González, V., Gilbert, A., Phillipson, G., Jolly, S., Hadfield, S.: SaiNet: stereo aware inpainting behind objects with generative networks. arXiv-2205 (2022)

11. Nugraha, A.A., Liutkus, A., Vincent, E.: Multichannel audio source separation with deep neural networks. IEEE/ACM Trans. Audio Speech Lang. Process. **24**, 1652–1664 (2016)
12. Okano, T., Beranek, L.L., Hidaka, T.: Relations among interaural cross-correlation coefficient ($IACC_E$), lateral fraction (LF_E), and apparent source width (ASW) in concert halls. Acoust. Soc. Am. **104**, 255–265 (1998)
13. Prenger, R., Valle, R., Catanzaro, B.: WaveGlow: a flow-based generative network for speech synthesis. In: ICASSP 2019 - 2019 IEEE International Conference on Acoustics, Speech and Signal Processing (ICASSP), pp. 3617–3621 (2019)
14. Rubner, Y., Tomasi, C., Guibas, L.J.: A metric for distributions with applications to image databases. In: Sixth International Conference on Computer Vision (IEEE Cat. No.98CH36271), pp. 59–66 (1998)
15. Singh, P., Devi, K.J., Varish, N.: Muzzle pattern based cattle identification using generative adversarial networks. In: Tiwari, A., Ahuja, K., Yadav, A., Bansal, J.C., Deep, K., Nagar, A.K. (eds.) Soft Computing for Problem Solving. AISC, vol. 1392, pp. 13–23. Springer, Singapore (2021). https://doi.org/10.1007/978-981-16-2709-5_2
16. van den Oord, A., et al.: WaveNet: a generative model for raw audio (2016)
17. Wang, X., Takaki, S., Yamagishi, J.: Neural source-filter-based waveform model for statistical parametric speech synthesis. In: ICASSP 2019 - 2019 IEEE International Conference on Acoustics, Speech and Signal Processing (ICASSP), pp. 5916–5920. IEEE (2019)
18. Xiao, X., et al.: Deep beamforming networks for multi-channel speech recognition. In: 2016 IEEE International Conference on Acoustics, Speech and Signal Processing (ICASSP), pp. 5745–5749 (2016)

A Machine Learning Approach for Classification of Lemon Leaf Diseases

Soumya Ranjan Sahu[1](✉), Sudarson Jena[2], and Sucheta Panda[1]

[1] VSSUT, Burla, India
{srsahu_phdca,suchetapanda_mca}@vssut.ac.in
[2] SUIIT, Sambalpur University, Jyoti Vihar, Burla, India
sjena@suiit.ac.in

Abstract. Automated classification of plant leaf diseases is one of the complex concerns in robotics and machine learning fields. Several models have been introduced for detecting and classifying leaf diseases with high classification performance. With the advancement of image processing and machine learning, predicting diseases is the most significant research in recent years. This paper aims to classify lemon leaf diseases by segmenting the diseased part. The lemon leaf dataset is split into training and testing folders. The presented classification method consists of segmentation, feature extraction, and classification steps. For the classification of lemon leaf disease, at first, segmentation is done by using the K-mean clustering algorithm. The infected part of the lemon leaf can be partitioned by the above algorithm. The feature extraction is performed using Gray Level Co-occurrence Matrices (GLCM) method, to extract the texture features from the image. The GLCM method generates the statistical features from the image. The features are passed to the Support Vector Machine (SVM) for the classification of lemon leaf disease. Experiments are conducted for the lemon leaf dataset by taking some samples and the results demonstrate high classification accuracy at a faster speed than other traditional classification methods.

Keywords: Image processing · Segmentation · K-mean clustering · Gray level co-occurrence matrices (GLCM) · SVM

1 Introduction

In recent years, agriculture has become much more important than it is used to feed humans as well as animals. Efficient farming in agriculture is growing rapidly by introducing new technology and methods to fulfill the demand of food industries. The technology takes care of all the needs required by the industries and also plants. Agriculture becomes the most important part of social life as they produce oxygen for living organism and balances the environment. Disorders in the plant leaves affect the plant so it becomes difficult to make their own food and this led to damage to the plant. Diseases in the plant are also harmful to social life as all living organisms depend upon the plant for oxygen and food. So, early detection of plants is so necessary to protect them. In the

S. K. Panda et al. (Eds.): CoCoLe 2022, CCIS 1729, pp. 254–265, 2022.
https://doi.org/10.1007/978-3-031-21750-0_22

past decade, some classical methods were used to take care of it, which were very time-consuming and less accurate. It is quite hard to detect various diseases in wide-range crop fields; hence it is a complex task, which involves optical observation of leaves and expert manpower [1–3]. So, it is very difficult for farmers and non-expert to find out about the disease. So, disease classification and prediction undertake the researchers to observe by introducing new methods and technology.

To overcome the above problem, image processing techniques [4–8] are very helpful for recognizing and classifying diseases. Recently, a number of research carried out using the application of machine learning and deep learning. Machine learning algorithm provides feature extraction to extract various kinds of features like shape, color, point, and texture. Feature analysis is a very necessary part of the field of classification and detection because the accuracy and computational complexity of the system are much more dependent on it. After the extraction of features, a classification method like Support Vector Machine (SVM) is used to detect and predict the disease. In this paper, the lemon leaf dataset is taken for research which was collected from various lemon trees. To detect and predict the disease, we have designed a model using K-mean clustering, GLCM feature extraction, and SVM methods.

The organization of this paper is as follows. Section 2 of this paper presents related works. In Sect. 3, the classification method for lemon leaf diseases was proposed. In Sect. 4, results and analysis are discussed. Section 5 of this paper describes the conclusion of the research.

2 Related Works

Classification and detection of plant diseases is a very important research area in recent times. Many types of research have been conducted for the early detection of plant diseases. Modern methods are introduced for this purpose. As machine learning is an advanced technology as compared to the classical method which can overcome the problem of expert judgment and manual observation. Automatic detection can be possible with the emerging technology of machine learning. In this section, some existing research work with their proposed algorithm and method are discussed.

K. Singh et al. [9] proposed a method for pea plant's rust disease and healthy leaves to classify them. They used Gaussian filters on leaf images for smoothing and removing the noise, in pre-processing part. For better visualization they used log transform to the preprocessed image. Then they performed Binary threshold segmentation to partition images in the form of black and white. They remove the structuring element by using erosion operation. After using all the methods, they extracted the feature component by discrete wavelet transformed and stored the features in a 2D matrix form and then they classified the image by using SVM with 89.6% accuracy. FT. Pinki et al. [10] introduced a method for paddy leaves for classification of three types of diseases using SVM. They separate the affected part of the leaf by k-mean clustering and then extracted the features and finally applied the SVM classifier to classify the leaf disease. In their experiment, they achieved the accuracy of 92%. R. Meena Prakash et al. [11] used citrus leaf to identify various diseases using GLCM texture feature extraction. Firstly, they performed color space conversion for better visualization and then they applied clustering method. Finally, they applied SVM classifier and got a result of 90% accuracy.

In the other work, Sagar Vetal et al. [12] used segmentation method and multi-class svm to identify several diseases. They used several algorithms like; Multiclass SVM algorithm, Histogram matching method, genetic programming, and ANN to achieve their aim. They found the accuracy of 92.94% with Artificial Neural Network and a 90% of accuracy obtained by using Eigen regularization and extraction the accuracy was 90% and 93.75% of accuracy was calculated by using multi-class SVM. Saradhambal, et al. [13] used K-mean clustering algorithm and Otsu's classifier to detect the plant disease automatically. They used neural network-based classifier for classification of disease. R. Ronnel et al. [14] used 600 rice plant images and suggested a model to classify the rice diseases. They classified three types of rice diseases. For this work, they used transfer learning method and achieved the accuracy of 91.23%. X. Xie et al. [15] introduced improved DCNN for grape leaves to classify four types of disease. They implemented the method in real-time environment. The dataset they used consists of 4449 grape leaves. They concluded that Inception-ResNet-v2 gave a good result with 81.1% of mean average precision. J. Liu et al. [21] introduced an improved YOLOv3 model to detect the location of the tomato plant disease and classify the disease under natural conditions. Ferentinos et al. [22] used VGGNet model to classify 58 diseases of 25 crops and gain a classification accuracy of 99.5%.

As per the above studies, this is clearly known many research has been carried out in the field of plant disease detection and classification with different types of datasets. The combination of some machine learning algorithms is very helpful to obtain good accuracy. The summary of all reviews is presented in Table 1.

Table 1. The summary of the classification and segmentation techniques with benefits and limitations

Source	Year	Techniques	Benefits	Limitations
K. Singh et al. [9]	2018	Binary threshold, wavelet, SVM	Binary threshold techniques divide the image into two parts so that the diseased part can be easily identified	Time-consuming
FT.Pinki et al. [10]	2018	K-mean clustering, shape, texture and color feature extraction, SVM	A simple and fast method to segment a large number of datasets by K-mean clustering	Difficult to predict K with a fixed number of clusters
Meena Prakash et al. [11]	2018	Texture feature extraction, SVM	Eliminates noisy spots	Computationally expensive

(*continued*)

Table 1. (*continued*)

Source	Year	Techniques	Benefits	Limitations
Sagar Vetal et al. [12]	2017	Histogram matching method, genetic programming, ANN	Neural network can extract the feature automatically	Time-consuming
Saradhambal, et al. [13]	2018	K-mean clustering, Otsu's classifier, Neural Network	Homogeneous regions are obtained	Difficult to implement on a minimum number of resources
R. Ronnel et al. [14]	2018	Transfer learning method	Gives high accuracy	Architecture design is too difficult
X. Xie et al. [15]	2020	Inception-ResNet-v2	Good potential for training the dataset	Feature Information can be lost due to the hidden layer
J. Liu et al. [21]	2020	Improved YOLOv3	Gives good training accuracy	Failed to localize tiny spot
Ferentinos et al. [22]	2018	VGGNet	Easy to implement	Overfitting problem

3 Proposed Method for Classification of Lemon Leaf Disease

This section describes the methodologies used to detect and classify lemon leaf disease. The proposed method for classification includes image acquisition, enhancement, segmentation, feature extraction, and classification. All the steps used for classification are shown in a block diagram in Fig. 1.

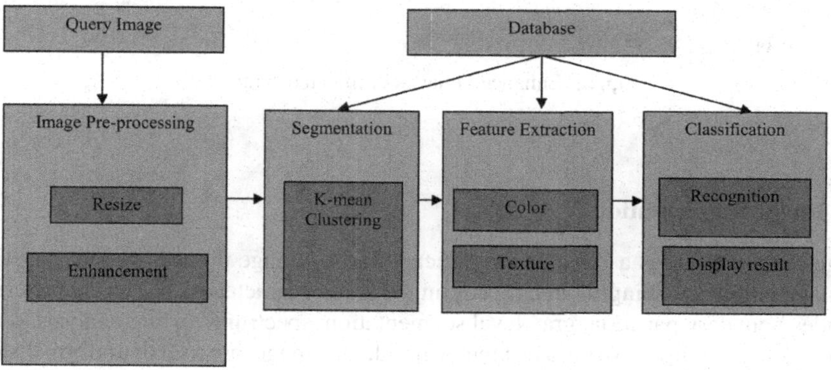

Fig. 1. Proposed method for classification of lemon leaf disease

The research work was conducted by using lemon leaf dataset. The dataset contains 140 numbers of samples. Image resizes is performed to make all the image uniform in rows and column. The images are resized into 256*256. The dataset was split into training and testing at a ratio of 80:20. Figure 2 shows some samples of the infected lemon leaf images.

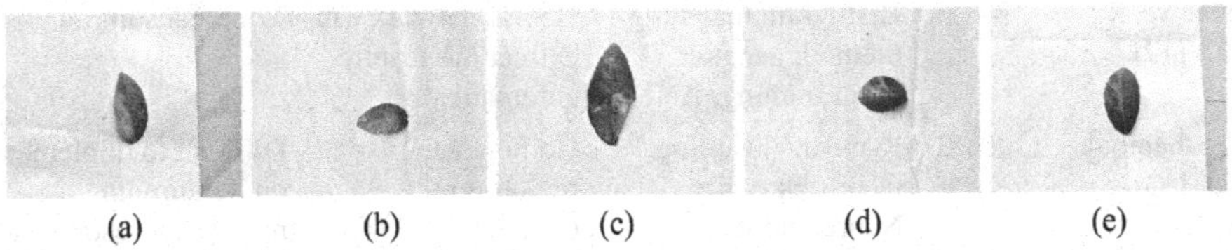

(a) (b) (c) (d) (e)

Fig. 2. Samples of infected lemon leaf

3.1 Image Pre-processing

Image acquisition is the first step of digital image processing where the image is taken to perform various operations to fulfill the objectives of the study. It is also an act of retrieving an image from hardware, so it can be passed through further processes [16]. After acquisition images need to be preprocessed for better visualization. Image enhancement is the method, used to make the graphic display more useful by improving the features like contrast, brightness, sharpness, and others. The following Fig. 3 shows the enhanced image of our samples.

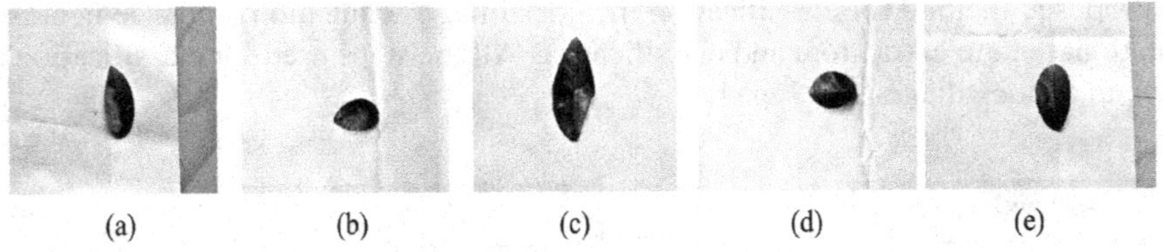

(a) (b) (c) (d) (e)

Fig. 3. Enhanced images of infected samples

3.2 Image Segmentation

Image segmentation is a basic and significant part of image processing that partitions an image into its meaningful areas according to some characteristics. The characteristic includes boundary partition, gray level segmentation, spectrum, texture analysis, color-based segmentation, and so on. The method divides an image into a set of uniform disjoint regions. Segmentation can be used for two purposes. The first purpose is to separate the image components for further study. The second goal is to apply representation changes in the image.

3.2.1 K-mean Clustering

Clustering is an unsupervised machine learning algorithm that divides a set of data into a specific number of groups [17]. This is a region-based portioned method that divides the object into similar types of components according to their feature. The clustering algorithm classifies the item into k groups of similarity. For this calculation, Euclidian distance is used as a measurement.

$$(L)^2=\sum_{i=1}^{n}(x_i - y_i)^2 \tag{1}$$

where L indicates the Euclidian distance

x and y are the two vectors between which actual distance can be calculated.

n is the number of dimensions components of vectors x and y.

The K-means clustering algorithm computes the centroid of the given data and repeats until the optimal centroid is found. In this algorithm, the clusters are assigned by data points in this manner that the sum of the squared distances between data points and the centroid is probably very small. Hence it reduced the diversity within the cluster that leading to similar data points in each cluster.

3.3 Feature Extraction

Feature extraction is a process of dimensionality reduction by which an initial set of raw data is reduced to more manageable groups for processing. Feature extraction involves simplifying the number of resources required to describe a large set of data accurately. In classification problems, the feature extraction method gives the details about the object. The extraction method includes color, shape, texture, and many more. In this paper, the GLCM feature extraction method is used to extract the texture features of the image.

3.3.1 Gray Level Co-occurrence Matrices (GLCM)

The co-occurrence matrix is a 2D array in which both row and column are denoted by a set of possible image values [18]. In the GLCM method, features are calculated in the form of statistics which includes energy, entropy, contrast, Inverse Difference Moment (IDM) and etc.

Energy

Energy is also known as the uniformity of an image. Homogeneity of an image is measured by energy. The homogeneity is depended on the image clarity and its pixel. It is high when the image is good in clarity and the pixels are similar. It is calculated by.

$$\text{Energy}(E) = \sqrt{\sum_{i=0}^{N-1}\sum_{J=0}^{N-1} M^2(i,j)} \tag{2}$$

Entropy

Entropy is the amount of information needed to compress an image. It measures loss of information of an image. It can be calculated by,

$$\text{Entropy}(\text{ent}) = \sum_{i=0}^{N-1}\sum_{J=0}^{N-1} M(i,j)(-\ln(M(i,j)) \tag{3}$$

Contrast

Contrast can be measure by intensity of a pixel and is calculated by,

$$\text{Contrast}(\text{con}) = \sum_{i=0}^{N-1}\sum_{J=0}^{N-1} (i-j)^2 M(i,j) \tag{4}$$

IDM

IDM feature obtains the measures of the closeness of the distribution of the GLCM elements to the GLCM diagonal. IDM has a range of values so as to determine whether the image is textured or non-textured.

$$\text{IDM} = \sum_{i=0}^{N-1}\sum_{J=0}^{N-1} \frac{1}{1+(i-j)^2} M(i,j) \tag{5}$$

3.4 Classification

For classification of the lemon leaf disease, Support Vector Machine (SVM) is used. The SVM classifier classifies the data by finding the best hyperplane that separates all data points of one class from those of the other class. The dimensions of the hyperplane depend on the features present in the dataset, which means if there are 2 features then the hyperplane will be a straight line. SVM algorithm works by finding the similarities between the classes. The plane makes a group of similar type of class by separating them into their corresponding features. The following figure shows the working principle of Support Vector Machine (Fig. 4).

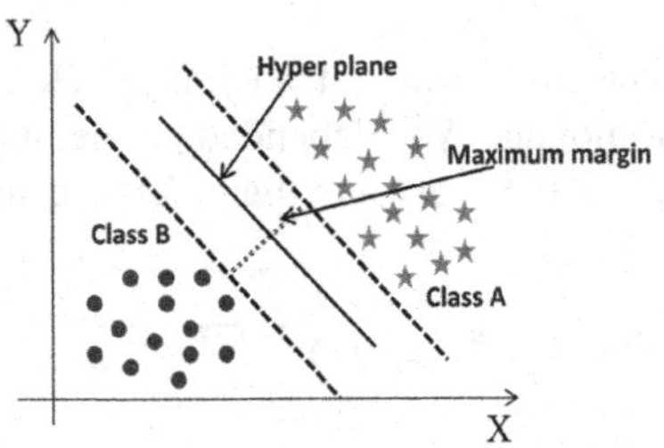

Fig. 4. Working principle of SVM algorithm

Algorithm for proposed classification method for detection of infected lemon leaves

Input -: *Query lemon leaf image*

Output-: *Classification of disease, calculate the diseased area in percentage, evaluate the accuracy*

Start

Step 1:- input the query lemon leaf image.
Step 2:- image processing
Step 2.1:- Image resizing and Enhancement
Step 3:- Segmentation of Image.
*Step 3.1:- Convert the image into l*a*b* color space from RGB image.*
*Step 3.2:- Classifying the color a*b* color space using K-mean cluster.*
Step 3.3:- Measure Euclidian Distance.
Step 4:- Select the disease part cluster.
Step 5:- Feature extraction using GLCM.
Step 6:- If training?
Step 6.1:- Yes, classification of image and stop.
Step 6.2:-No, Testing the image.
Step 7:- If, disease image?
Step 7.1:- Yes, Show the predicted diseases name and go to step 8.
Step 7.2:- No, Healthy image, and go to step 9.
Step 8:- Calculate the percentage of diseased Area.
Step 9:- Evaluating accuracy.

End

4 Results and Analysis

In the research work, lemon leaf disease detection consists of three major phases which are segmentation, feature extraction and classification. K-mean clustering algorithm is applied for segmenting the diseased part of the leaf. The GLCM method is used for texture feature extraction. For the classification of disease, SVM method is used and performance of the model is evaluated. GLCM matrix properties of the infected lemon leaf are shown in Table 2.

Table 2. GLCM matrix properties of infected part of lemon leaf

Sample image	Energy	Entropy	Contrast	IDM	Co-relation
a	0.9745	0.1761	0.0275	255	0.8834
b	0.9717	0.1898	0.0167	255	0.9241
c	0.9782	0.1529	0.0143	255	0.8835
d	0.9932	0.0432	0.0106	255	0.6847
e	0.9877	0.0900	0.0084	255	0.7706

The infected part of the lemon leaf with classification results of the sample images are shown in Fig. 5.

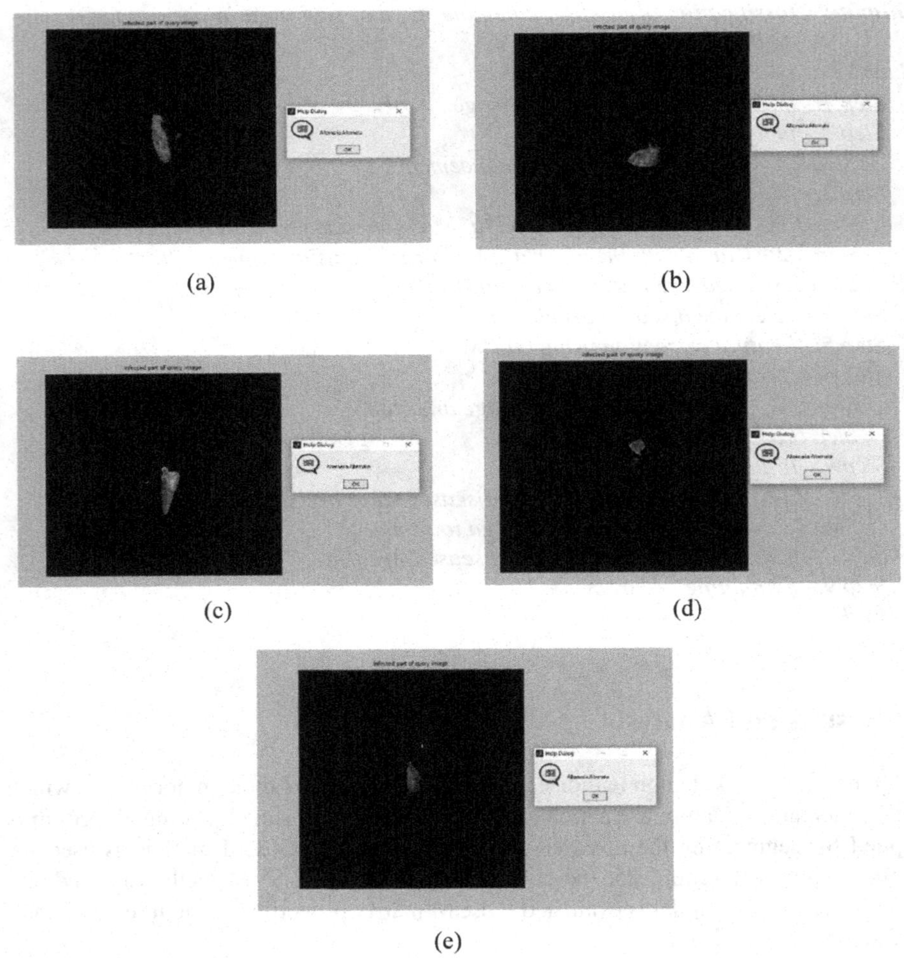

Fig. 5. Classification result of infected lemon leaf

Measuring the diseased area can be calculated by the following formula.

Let P_a be the affected area of the leaf and P_u be the unaffected area of the leaf.

Let P_L be the total pixel of the image, then the total pixel can be calculated by the following formula

$$P_L = P_a + P_u \quad (6)$$

Then the percentage of the diseased area of the lemon leaf can be calculated by following the formula

$$P_D = \frac{P_a}{P_L} \times 100 \quad (7)$$

The percentage of affecting area of the lemon leaf sample is shown in Table 3.

Table 3. Percentage of affected area

Sample image	Percentage of affecting area (in %)
a	15.0015
b	16.2592
c	15.9991
d	15.2398
e	15.5530

The performance of the method can be determined by the parameters, TP (True positive), TN (True negative), FP (False positive), and FN (False negative).

The accuracy indicates the closeness of the test that is taken in different samples, results to the true value and repeatability of the test. The accuracy of the test can be calculated by the formula:

$$\text{Sensitivity} = (TP/(TP + FN)) * 100 \quad (8)$$

$$\text{Precision} = (TP/(TP + FP)) * 100 * 100 \quad (9)$$

$$\text{Accuracy} = ((TP + TN)/(TP + TN + FP + FN)) * 100 \quad (10)$$

Table 4 shows the performance metrics of the proposed classification method for lemon leaf disease.

Table 4. Performance metrics using classification method

Sample images	Sensitivity	Precision	Accuracy
a	75%	52.94%	82.25%
b	66.66%	80%	90.32%
c	100%	50%	80.64%
d	75%	52%	82.25%
e	66%	80%	90%

5 Conclusion

In this paper, an effective classification method is derived to detect and classify the lemon leaf disease with maximum detection rate. The classification method includes different sub-process based on image enhancement, segmentation, feature extraction and classification. K-mean clustering is used to segment the infected part accurately and the GLCM method extracts the feature component of the image. Finally the accuracy of the classification model for lemon leaf disease gives better accuracy as compared with existing system.

References

1. Vishnoi, V.K., Kumar, K., Kumar, B.: Plant disease detection using computational intelligence and image processing. J. Plant Dis. Prot. **128**, 19–53 (2021)
2. Verma, S., Chug, A., Singh, A.P.: Prediction models for identification and diagnosis of tomato plant diseases. In: International Conference on Advances in Computing, Communications and Informatics, pp. 1557–1563 (2018)
3. Poojary, H., Shabari, S.B.: A survey on plant disease detection using support vector machine. In: International Conference on Control, Power, Communication and Computing Technologies, pp. 292–295 (2018)
4. Nagaraju, M., Chawla, P.: Systematic review of deep learning techniques in plant disease detection. Int. J. Syst. Assur. Eng. Manag. **11**(3), 547–560 (2020). https://doi.org/10.1007/s13198-020-00972-1
5. Kaur, S., Pandey, S., Goel, S.: Plants disease identification and classification through leaf images: a survey. Arch. Comput. Methods Eng. **26**(2), 507–530 (2018). https://doi.org/10.1007/s11831-018-9255-6
6. Rehman, T.U., Mahmud, M.S., Chang, Y.K., Jin, J., Shin, J.: Current and future applications of statistical machine learning algorithms for agricultural machine vision systems. Comput. Electron. Agric. **156**, 585–605 (2019)
7. Muhammad, H.S., Johan, P., Khalid, M.A.: Plant disease detection and classification by deep learning. Plants, 1–22 (2019)
8. Kamilaris, A., Prenafeta-Boldu, F.X.: Deep learning in agriculture: a survey. Comput. Electron. Agric. **147**, 70–90 (2018)
9. Singh, K., Kumar, S., Kaur, P.: Support vector machine classifier based detection of fungal rust disease in pea plant (Pisamsativam). Int. J. Inf. Technol. (2018)
10. Khatun, N., Islam, S.M.M.: Content based paddy leaf disease recognition and remedy prediction using support vector machine. In: 20th IEEE International Conference Computer science Information Technology, pp. 1–5 (2018)
11. Prakash, R.M., Saraswathy, G.P., Ramalakshmi, G., Mangaleswari, K.H., Kaviya, T.: Detection of leaf diseases and classification using digital image processing. In: Proceedings of 2017 IEEE International Conference Innovation Information Embedded Communication System, pp. 1–4 (2018)
12. Vetal, S., Khule, R.S.: Tomato plant disease detection using image processing. Int. J. Adv. Res. Comput. Commun. Eng. (IJARCCE) **6**(6), 293–297 (2017)
13. Saradhambal, G., Dhivya, R., Latha, S., Rajesh, R.: Plant disease detection and its solution using image classification. Int. J. Pure Appl. Math. **119**(14), 879–884 (2018)
14. Ronnel, R., Daechul, P.: A multiclass deep convolutional neural network classifier for detection of common rice plant anomalies. Int. J. Adv. Comput. Sci. Appl., 67–70 (2018)

15. Xie, X., Ma, Y., Liu, B., He, J., Li, S., Wang, H.: A deep-learning-based real-time detector for grape leaf diseases using improved convolutional neural networks. Frontiers in Plant Science, 1–14 (2020)
16. Raut, S., Fulsunge, A.: Plant disease detection in image processing using matlab. Int. J. Innovative Res. Sci. Eng. Technol. (IJIRSET) **6**(6), 10373–10381 (2017)
17. Dhanachandra, N., Manglem, K., Yambem, J.C.: Image segmentation using K-means clustering algorithm and subtractive clustering algorithm. In: Eleventh International Multi-Conference on Information Processing (IMCIP) (2015)
18. Ramakrishnan, M., Sahaya, A.N.: Groundnut leaf disease detection and classification by using back propagation algorithm. In: IEEE ICCSP Conference, pp. 978–1–4 799–8081–9/15 (2015)
19. Pallavi, S.M., Raisoni, G.H., Phule, S.: Plant disease detection using digital image processing and GSM **7**(4) (2017)
20. Vidyashanakara, N.M., Kumar, G.H.: Leaf classification based on GLCM texture and SVM. Int. J. Future Revolution Comput. Sci. Commun. Eng. **4**(3)
21. Liu, J., Wang, X.: Tomato diseases and pests detection based on improved Yolo V3 convolutional neural network. Front. Plant Sci. **11**(898), 1–12 (2020)
22. Ferentinos, K.P.: Deep learning models for plant disease detection and diagnosis. Comput. Electron. Agric **145**, 311–318 (2018)

Optimization of Random Forest Hyperparameter Using Improved PSO for Handwritten Digits Classification

Atul Vikas Lakra[1](✉) and Sudarson Jena[2]

[1] VSSUT, Burla 768018, Odisha, India
[2] SUIIT, Sambalpur University, Burla 768018, Odisha, India

Abstract. In machine learning, classification is one of the important methods used to train a model for the identification of each class on a labelled dataset. The performance of the algorithm can be enhanced using ensemble techniques such as bagging and random subsampling. Random forest (RF) is an ensemble machine learning algorithm to address multiclass classification problems. Several RF algorithms have been proposed to obtain various levels of accuracy on different datasets during classification. But it has been observed that the manual configuration of RF hyperparameter and its accuracy varies significantly depending upon different datasets. Manual configuration of hyperparameter is a time consuming job. Thus, the hyperparameter optimization process is used to generate optimal hyperparameter efficiently. Hyperparameter optimization also enhances the performance of machine learning algorithms. This paper proposes improved particle swarm optimization (PSO) method as hyperparameter optimizer to identify the optimal hyperparameter of the random forest algorithm. We compare the performance of RF model using improved PSO optimizer and existing RF model with default hyperparameter. The improved PSO outperforms the improvement of accuracy during the classification of each digit of the handwritten dataset.

Keywords: Random forest · PSO · Hyperparameter · Optimization

1 Introduction

In today's trending scenarios machine learning algorithms are widely adopted in many research and application areas such as classification, natural language processing, object detection, and identification, computer vision, and recommendation systems. A single machine learning algorithm can't be used to solve all types of problems; for this reason, depending upon the problem requirement, various ML algorithms are used. To build an efficient machine learning model requires a deep understanding of an algorithm and a huge amount of time to identify the optimal parameter for an algorithm. Most machine learning algorithms have two types of parameters. The first type of parameters was generally initialized prior to the execution of the algorithm and with each iteration, these parameters are updated during the learning process of an algorithm. The second type of parameter which is used to define the model and its value cannot be obtained

S. K. Panda et al. (Eds.): CoCoLe 2022, CCIS 1729, pp. 266–276, 2022.
https://doi.org/10.1007/978-3-031-21750-0_23

through a learning process. These parameters are also initialized before the execution of an algorithm and cannot be modified during the learning process. These second types of parameters are known as hyperparameters. Hyperparameters of an algorithm or model have a greater impact on its architecture and performance. The process of building an optimal machine learning algorithm or model requires the exploration of a wide range of possible hyperparameter values. The process of identifying optimal hyperparameters to design an optimal model is called hyperparameter tuning. Hyperparameter tuning is a critical phase of designing an optimal algorithm or model, especially in the case of machine learning models such as random forest and deep neural networks. These two models have many numbers of hyperparameters to be tuned to obtain optimal hyperparameters. The process of tuning a hyperparameter is different from one machine learning model to another machine learning model, as the value of the hyperparameter can be continuous, discrete, or categorical. Manual tuning of all the hyperparameters of a machine learning algorithm or model is a very time taking job and it requires a complete understanding of the machine learning algorithm or model and its hyperparameter value. With the increase in the available dataset, numbers of hyperparameters, and complexity in the ML model manual tuning is not suitable to address the problem efficiently. The problem in the manual tuning of hyperparameters motivated research in techniques for automatic optimization of hyperparameters known as hyperparameter optimization.

The paper is organized as follows. In Sect. 2, related work on the hyperparameter optimization model proposed by various authors has been discussed. In Sect. 3, explanation of the hyperparameter optimization proposed methodology. In Sect. 4, experimental results and analysis to evaluate the performance of the proposed model compared to other models are presented. Finally, the paper concludes in Sect. 5.

2 Related Work

In previous studies, the problem of hyperparameter tuning has been researched and solved by many methods. Widely researched machine learning methods and their hyperparameter optimization are random forest [1–3, 5, 20], support vector machine [13, 16], artificial neural network (ANN) [10], convolution neural network (CNN) [7, 9, 12], and deep neural network (DNN) [4, 6, 8, 11]. These machine learning methods have been optimized using various optimization methods such as genetic algorithm, particle swarm optimization and other natural inspire methods of optimization. Many authors proposed various forms of particle swarm optimization for tuning hyperparameters of a Machine learning algorithm as it can achieve a high level of parallelism and exploration of the search domain.

A classification of the handwritten digit is mostly researched to enhance classification accuracy. In paper [2] random forest algorithm is used for the classification of handwritten digits. In paper [6, 8] deep neural network is used using a parallel PSO optimizer. CNN based on distributed PSO and multilevel PSO hyperparameter optimization in paper [9, 12, 13] used for classification. Classification based on RF using the Bayes algorithm [3] provides the highest accuracy of classification but it is inefficient in parallelism. Apart from handwritten digits; Swedish historical digits [13] and Japanese script are also classified using optimized RF. Authors in [3, 5] propose hyperparameter optimization of random forest algorithm over various problem domains. Research related to hyperparameter optimization has also been studied on different image datasets [19]. The deep learning approach is generally used for image identification and detection. In Parallel version of the PSO algorithm [4, 11], the population of particles are executed in parallel, for the searching of the hyper-parameters which determine the best possible classification performance of the DNN model. This parallel version of PSO has been used over various problem domains and datasets. Authors in [7] proposed hyperparameter optimization of the CNN model using level-based PSO. A large number of GPUs for large swarm sizes is required for CNN and DNN.

The proposed paper contributes to building a model using an improved PSO hyperparameter optimizer implemented on the random forest algorithm for classifying handwritten digits. There has been previous research comparing the performance of the random forest algorithm for handwritten digits classification [2, 14, 15, 17]. However, that study focused more on the hyperparameter optimizer for the random forest classification method. The proposed model has experimented with the handwritten digit dataset and performance in terms of accuracy is compared with the existing RF model to find out efficiency in classification problems.

3 Hyperparameter Optimization

Hyperparameters are the parameter of an algorithm which is required to be set prior to the execution of an algorithm. For a large set of hyperparameters in an algorithm manual configuration of each hyperparameter is difficult. Manual configuration of hyperparameter takes a huge amount of time and also required a deep understanding of an algorithm and its hyperparameter. To overcome the problems related to the manual configuration of hyperparameters, hyperparameter optimization is required which will help to find optimal configuration automatically. A random forest algorithm is used in this paper and improved PSO is used as an optimizer for the finding of optimal hyperparameter. In this paper, the random forest algorithm or model is used for the classification of handwritten digits classification after its hyperparameters are optimized using improved PSO. The detailed working of the random forest model improved PSO optimizer and the proposed model is explained in the following section.

3.1 Random Forest

Random forest (RF) is the supervised machine learning methods mainly used to address classification and regression problems. Random forest [20] is a tree-structured ensemble classifier based on bagging. It creates 'n' number decision tree in the forest and 'p' number of features selected for the splitting process prior to its execution. RF constructs a decision tree on different samples and considers the majority voting for classification.

Bagging selects 'n' random sample from the dataset of size m (m > n). Then 'n' number of decision trees have created a model from the samples provided by the original dataset with a replacement called row sampling. The process of row sampling with replacement is known as bootstrap. After this, all the models are trained separately and the final result is obtained from the majority voting out of all the generated model results as shown in Fig. 1. In a random forest algorithm, while creating an individual

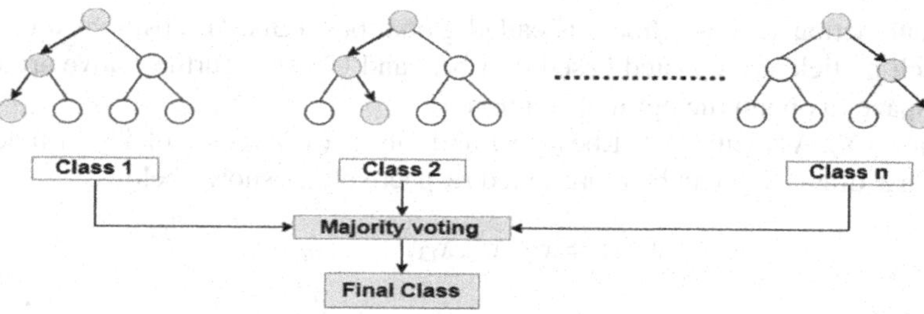

Fig. 1. Random forest

decision tree all the features and data are not considered at the same time which reduces dimensionality problems, able to create multiple decision trees which are different from each other and parallelization can be achieved.

Table 1. Random forest hyperparameter

Hyperparameters	Description
Criterion	Measure for the split quality. Criteria can be "gini" or "entropy"
n_estimators	Number of trees in the forest
min_samples_leaf	Minimum number of samples at leaf node
min_samples_split	Minimum number of samples consider to split an internal node:
max_depth	Maximum depth of the tree
max_features	Number of features taken for the best split:

RF hyperparameters (Table 1) required to be initialize prior to the evaluation of the RF classification model. Apart from this other hyperparameters need to be initialized to increase the performance of the RF classifier model such as n_job to inform the number of processors used during evaluation and randomness of the sample is set using random_state hyperparameter.

3.2 Improved Particle Swarm Optimization (PSO)

Particle swarm optimization [18, 22, 23] uses random initialization of individual swarm particles in the n-dimensional search space problem. These particles move around in the search space with some velocities. Particle Swarm Optimization is an adaptive algorithm based on particle movements, where each particle learns to move in the right direction from its own experience as well as thought interaction with other particles. The importance of a particle in the search domain is defined by its fitness value. Particles with higher fitness values influence their neighbors. Each individual particle in the solution domain is assigned with position and velocity. Each individual particle [1] with its best solution experienced so far is called local best (Lbest) and the best solution achieved through interaction with neighbors is called global best (Gbest). Positions and velocities of each particle are updated based on Lbest and Gbest to further move around the solution space to obtain the optimal solution.

Position (X), Velocity (V), Lbest (Y) and Gbest (Y′) vector of ith particle at t^{th} iteration in d dimension can be represented respectively as shown below:

$$X_i(t) = x_{i1}, x_{i2}, x_{i3}, \ldots\ldots.x_{id}$$

$$Y_i(t) = y_{i1}, y_{i2}, y_{i3}, \ldots\ldots.y_{id}$$

$$V_i(t) = v_{i1}, v_{i2}, v_{i3}, \ldots\ldots.v_{id}$$

$$Y_i^{'}(t) = y_{i1}^{'}, y_{i2}^{'}, y_{i3}^{'}, \ldots\ldots.y_{id}^{'}$$

The position and velocity of particles are updated each time based on the following equations.

$$V_{ij}(t+1) = V_{ij}(t) + C_1 \times R_1 \times \left(Y_{ij}(t) - X_{ij}(t)\right) + C_2 \times R_2 \times \left(Y_{ij}^{'}(t) - X_{ij}(t)\right) \quad (1)$$

$$X_{ij}(t+1) = X_{ij}(t) + V_{ij}(t+1) \quad (2)$$

where, R_1 and R_2 are uniformly distributed random numbers in the range [0, 1]. C_1 and C_2 are the positive constants in the range [0, 2]. C_1 and C_2 are termed acceleration coefficients. C_1 guides the particle's movement towards the particle's Lbest and C_2 guides the particle's movement towards global best (Gbest). In Eq. 1, the expression $C_2 \times R_2 \times (Y_{ij}\ (t) - X_{ij}(t))$ is used to describe how a particle collaborates with its neighbors. The expression $C_1 \times R_1 \times (Y_{ij}(t) - X_{ij}(t))$ describes a particle's ability to recognize its own optimal solution. These two expressions are often referred to as cognitive acceleration and social acceleration because they are both related to particle acceleration (pace of change in velocity). To improve the performance of the existing PSO, inertia weight is multiplied by the velocity in Eq. 1. The velocity formula Eq. 2 is used to change the acceleration of the particle instead of a fixed increase in velocity at each iteration.

$$V_{ij}(t+1) = \omega \times V_{ij}(t) + C_1 \times R_1 \times \left(Y_{ij}(t) - X_{ij}(t)\right) + C_2 \times R_2 \times \left(Y_{ij}^{'}(t) - X_{ij}(t)\right) \quad (3)$$

The inertia weight (ω) is fixed for all iterations. PSO-RANDIW, the concept of random inertia weight, is proposed [21] instead of utilizing the same value for all iterations. The randomness in Inertia Weight is defined as:

$$\omega = 0.5 + \frac{1}{2} \times rand() \quad (4)$$

Knowledge about the Pbest and Gbest helps the particle to move in the direction which leads to convergence of the optimal solution. With the known global best position neighbour particles may move towards the solution which leads to a local optimal solution instead of the optimal solution of the problem. So, there is a possibility that a particle with Lbest may be leading to an optimal solution but with the interaction with the neighbour particle and Gbest position; the particle may take the wrong direction and acceleration. To avoid the movement of particles in the wrong direction another term is added in Eq. 3 called cognitive avoidance [1]. So, the new equation for velocity update is

$$V_{ij}(t+1) = \omega \times V_{ij}(t) + C_1 \times R_1 \times \left(Y_{ij}(t) - X_{ij}(t)\right) + C_2 \times R_2 \times \left(Y'_{ij}(t) - X_{ij}(t)\right) \\ -C_3 \times R_3 \times \left(Z_{ij}(t) - X_{ij}(t)\right) \tag{5}$$

where, Z denotes the vector for the particle's local worst position (Lworst). Lworst of an ith particle is defined as $Z_i(t) = (z_{i1}, z_{i2}, z_{i3}, \ldots\ldots\ldots z_{id})$. Lworst of each particle help to take the right movement by avoiding the influence of its neighbor's best position. Hence every iteration inertia weight, velocity, and position will be updated considering Lbest, Gbest and Lworst using Eqs. 4, 5, 2 respectively.

The steps of Improved PSO are as follows

1. Create a population of Particles and initialize uniform random velocities and positions.
2. Evaluate fitness for each particle's position.
3. If the current position is better than the position of the previous particle, Lbest will be updated. Otherwise, update Lworse.
4. Set best of all Lbest of particle's position as Gbest.
5. Update the particle's velocity and position using Eqs. 4, 5, 2
6. Repeat steps from 2 to 5 till the iteration reaches to N (total number of iteration).

3.3 Proposed Model Using Improved PSO Optimizer

The proposed model is built using an improved PSO optimizer for the random forest algorithm. In this paper, a handwritten digit dataset is considered for classification using the proposed model. The proposed model is going through the process of training, testing, and finding an optimized hyperparameter for the RF model as shown in Fig. 2. In the process of training and testing the model; initially ensure the handwritten dataset consistency using cross-validation. In this model 10-fold cross-validation is used to avoid over-fitting or under-fitting of both hyperparameter and model.

The algorithm steps are as follows:

1. Split the dataset into training and test dataset.
2. Providing the hyperparameters range value of random forest classification model as mentioned in Table 1.
3. The range of hyperparameters of RF classifier are passed to Improved PSO optimizer. Improved PSO creates a solution space using these hyperparameters and initializes uniformly for randomized particles.
4. With the initialized population of particles, evaluate the particle's fitness value based on the accuracy obtained from the RF classifier model.

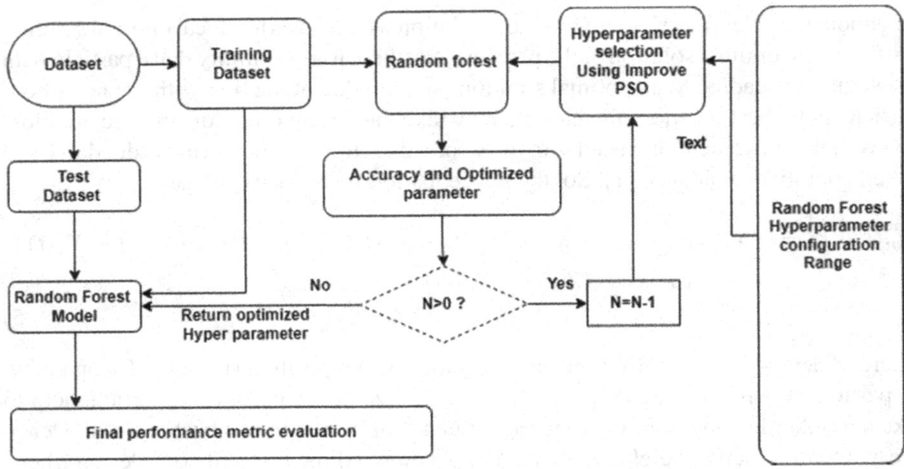

Fig. 2. Process of improved PSO-RF

5. Build the RF classifier model using the values of the hyperparameter given by the current best particle.
6. Train the model and predict the fitness value. Calculate Lbest, Lworst and Gbest.
7. Update the velocity and position using Eqs. 4, 5, 2.
8. If the maximum number of iterations reaches, then return the optimal hyperparameter, else jump to step 5.
9. At the end of iteration build the RF classifier model using the optimal hyperparameter and evaluate the performance metrics.

4 Result and Analysis

Optical recognition of UCI ML handwritten digits dataset having characteristics such as number of Instances is 5620, number of attributes is 64, 8 × 8 images of integer pixels, and no missing attribute values. The dataset contains images of handwritten digits of 10 classes where each class represents an English digit. A sample handwritten digit's images are shown in Fig. 3.

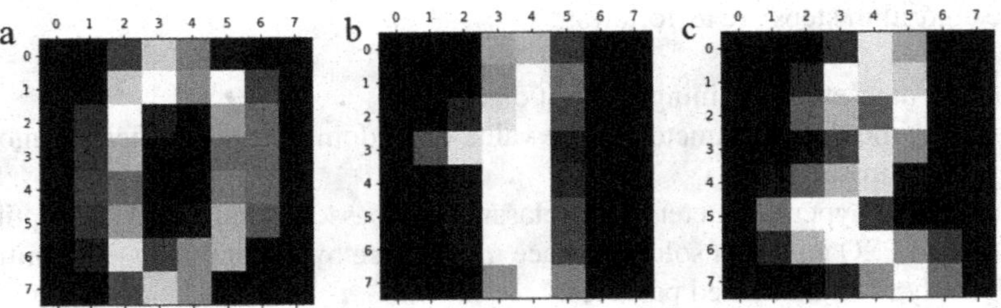

Fig. 3. Sample 8 × 8 images (a) 0, (b) 1, (c) 2 integer value

In this paper, 10-fold cross-validation is used to validate the dataset. Each model's evaluation of performance metrics is implemented using python code and sklearn libraries on the google collab platform. Handwritten digit dataset has been split in 80:20 ratio into training and testing dataset. Hyperparameter configurations for each model used in the experiment before evaluation are shown in Table 2.

Table 2. Hyperparameter initial configuration for RF and improved PSO-RF model

Hyperparameters	n_estimators	criterion	max_depth	min_samples_split	min_samples_leaf	max_features
Random Forest (RF)	10	Gini	None	2	1	Auto
Improved PSO-RF	[10–100]	[0–1]	[5–50]	[2–11]	[1–11]	[1–64]

After the evaluation of the random forest classifier model using default hyperparameter and optimal hyperparameter generated by RF and RF using improved PSO (PSO-RF) optimizer following performance metrics are obtained.

The confusion matrix for the RF model is shown in Fig. 4(a). It is observed from the figure that the RF model is unable to predict 0, 1 and 2 classes in a few samples of test data. The confusion matrix for the RF using an improved PSO optimized (PSO-RF) model is shown in Fig. 4(b). It is clear from the figure that the model is unable to predict 6 and 9 classes in a few samples of test data. Overall RF using an improved PSO optimized model can predict the classes more accurately compared to the existing RF model.

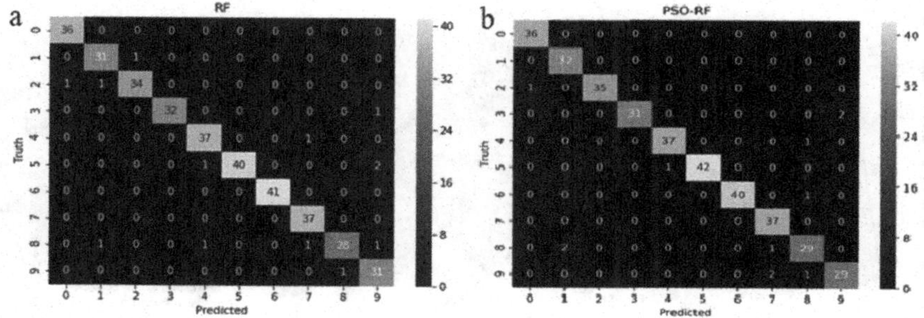

Fig. 4. Confusion matrixes for (a) RF and (b) improved PSO-RF

In handwritten digit classification accuracy is one of the most important performances evaluation metrics and it represents the overall performance of the model. The precision metrics calculate the true positive ratio, out of total actual positive class value how many are positive class values predicted correctly, and the recall metrics are used to find the percentage of total actual predicted results and how many are actually positive. The following equations are used to evaluate the accuracy, precision, recall, and F1-Score for the handwritten digit data set. The true positive (TP), true negative, false positive, false negative.

$$Accuracy \quad \frac{\mathrm{TP}+\mathrm{TN}}{TP+FP+TN+FN} \tag{6}$$

$$Precision \quad \frac{\mathrm{TP}}{TP + FP} \tag{7}$$

$$Recall \quad \frac{\mathrm{TP}}{TP + FN} \tag{8}$$

$$F1Score \quad 2 \times \frac{\mathrm{Precision} * \mathrm{Recall}}{Precision + Recall} \tag{9}$$

The performance metrics are calculated from the confusion matrix and accuracy obtained through the classification of the test dataset. The proposed model shows improvement of accuracy in predicting classes of handwritten digits as tabulated in Table 3.

Table 3. Performance metrics of the models

Model	F1-score	Recall	Precision	Accuracy
Random Forest (RF)	0.947	0.947	0.948	0.947
Improved PSO-RF	0.967	0.966	0.967	0.967

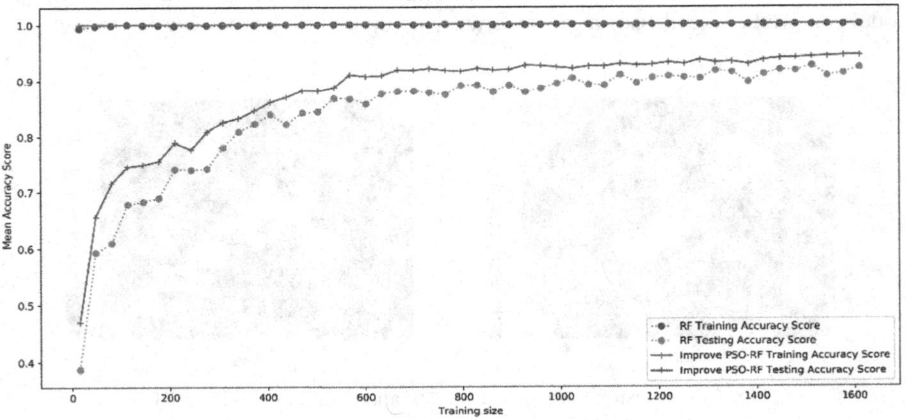

Fig. 5. Learning curve for the models

Finally, a learning curve is drawn to check how a model will perform with respect to the varying training sample size. The accuracy of the model is achieved in terms of how a model is able to classify correctly the training and testing dataset. RF model is able to achieve training mean accuracy of about 99% to 100% with few samples size between 10 to 100 samples shown in Fig. 5. Improved PSO-RF model also able to achieve training mean accuracy about 99% to 100% with few samples size between 10 to 100 samples shown in Fig. 5. It is observed from the learning curve (Fig. 5) that the proposed PSO-RF model is able to achieve a better accuracy score compare to the existing RF.

It is also been observed that from the smallest sample dataset to the maximus sample dataset the proposed model is able to achieve 96% accuracy whereas RF model is able to achieve 94% accuracy. The gap between training and testing mean accuracy gradually decreases, shows low variance in mean accuracy. For the handwritten dataset in both RF and PSO-RF model small dip in the learning curve implies the model suffers from under fitting. RF model and has lager number of dips compares to PSO-RF model this shows proposed model has a good fitting.

5 Conclusion

In this paper random forest (RF) model is used to classify the handwritten dataset. Using ensemble technique RF model combines 'n' number of decision tree to predict multiple classes of dataset. Further to improve the accuracy, improved PSO optimizer is proposed to optimize hyperparameter of RF model. This model restricts the movement of particle towards unsuitable solution. With the inclusion of Lworst for each particle; particle movements restricted towards local optimal solution. Simulation results shows improved PSO optimizer enhances the performance of RF model. In future model can be more optimized using better selection of hyperparameter and attribute selection in dataset.

References

1. Biswas, A., Lakra, A.V., Kumar, S., Singh, A.: An improved random inertia weighted particle swarm optimization. In: 2013 International Symposium on Computational and Business Intelligence, pp. 96–99. IEEE (2013)
2. Bernard, S., Adam, S., Heutte, L.: Using random forests for handwritten digit recognition. In: Ninth International Conference on Document Analysis and Recognition (ICDAR 2007), vol. 2. IEEE (2007)
3. Sun, D., Wen, H., Wang, D., Xu, J.: A random forest model of landslide susceptibility mapping based on hyperparameter optimization using Bayes algorithm. Geomorphology **362**, 107201 (2020)
4. Sandha, S.S., et al.: Mango: a python library for parallel hyperparameter tuning. In: ICASSP 2020–2020 IEEE International Conference on Acoustics, Speech and Signal Processing (ICASSP). IEEE (2020)
5. Daviran, M., Maghsoudi, A., Ghezelbash, R., Pradhan, B.: A new strategy for spatial predictive mapping of mineral prospectivity: automated hyperparameter tuning of random forest approach. Comput. Geosci. **148**, 104688 (2021)
6. Lorenzo, P.R., Nalepa, J., Ramos, L.S., Pastor, J.R.: Hyper-parameter selection in deep neural networks using parallel particle swarm optimization. In: Proceedings of the Genetic and Evolutionary Computation Conference Companion, pp. 1864–1871 (2017)
7. Yang, Q., Chen, W.N., Deng, J.D., et al.: A level-based learning swarm optimizer for large-scale optimization. IEEE Trans. Evol. Comput. **22**(99), 578–594 (2018)
8. Lorenzo, P.R., Nalepa, J., Kawulok, M., Ramos, L.S., Pastor, J.R.: Particle swarm optimization for hyper-parameter selection in deep neural networks. In: Proceedings of the Genetic and Evolutionary Computation Conference, pp. 481–488 (2017)
9. Guo, Y., Li, J.Y., Zhan, Z.H.: Efficient hyperparameter optimization for convolution neural networks in deep learning: a distributed particle swarm optimization approach. Cybern. Syst. **52**(1), 36–57 (2020)

10. Silva, R.C.C., de Menezes Jr, J.M.P., de Araújo Jr., J.M.: Optimization of NARX neural models using particle swarm optimization and genetic algorithms applied to identification of photovoltaic systems. J. Solar Energy Eng. **143**(5) (2021)
11. Mythili, K., Rangaraj, R.: Deep learning with particle swarm based hyper parameter tuning based crop recommendation for better crop yield for precision agriculture. Indian J. Sci. Technol. **14**(17), 1325–1337 (2021)
12. Singh, P., Chaudhury, S., Panigrahi, B.K.: Hybrid MPSO-CNN: multi-level particle swarm optimized hyperparameters of convolutional neural network. Swarm Evol. Comput. **63**, 100863 (2021)
13. Kusetogullari, H., Yavariabdi, A., Cheddad, A., Grahn, H., Hall, J.: ARDIS: a Swedish historical handwritten digit dataset. Neural Comput. Appl. **32**(21), 16505–16518 (2019). https://doi.org/10.1007/s00521-019-04163-3
14. Rasyidi, M.A., Bariyah, T., Riskajaya, Y.I., Septyani, A.D.: Classification of handwritten Javanese script using random forest algorithm. Bull. Electr. Eng. Inf. **10**(3), 1308–1315 (2021)
15. Hand written digits. http://archive.ics.uci.edu
16. Ramasamy, L.K., Kadry, S., Lim, S.: Selection of optimal hyper-parameter values of support vector machine for sentiment analysis tasks using nature-inspired optimization methods. Bull. Electr. Eng. Inf. **10**(1), 290–298 (2021)
17. Keysers, D., Deselaers, T., Rowley, H.A., Wang, L.L., Carbune, V.: Multi-language online handwriting recognition. IEEE Trans. Pattern Anal. Mach. Intell. **39**(6), 1180–1194 (2017)
18. MNIST digit dataset. http://yann.lecun.com/exdb/mnist/
19. Kennedy, J., Eberhart, R.: Particle swarm optimization. In: Procedings of IEEE International Conference on Neural Networks, pp. 1942–1948 (1995)
20. Bhowmick, P., Gajjar, S., Chaudhary, S.: Hyperparameter tuning and comparison of k nearest neighbor and decision tree algorithms for cardiovascular disease prediction. Int. J. Swarm Intell. **6**(2), 118–129 (2021)
21. Breiman, L.: Random forests. Mach. Learn. **45**(1), 5–32 (2001)
22. Eberhart, R.C., Shi, Y.: Tracking and optimizing dynamic systems with particle swarms. In: Proceedings of the 2001 IEEE International Congress on Evolutionary Computation, pp. 94–100 (2001)
23. Qin, C., Zhang, Y., Bao, F., Zhang, C., Liu, P., Liu, P.: XGBoost optimized by adaptive particle swarm optimization for credit scoring. Math. Probl. Eng. **2021**, Article ID 6655510, 18 (2021)

Risk Identification Using Quantum Machine Learning for Fleet Insurance Premium

K. S. Naik[1(✉)] and Archana Bhise[2]

[1] Department of Computer Engineering, SVKM's NMIMS MPSTME, Mumbai, India
kalyani.naik41@nmims.edu.in
[2] Department of Electronics and Telecommunication Engineering, SVKM's NMIMS MPSTME, Mumbai, India

Abstract. It is feasible to hypothesize that quantum computers may perform better on certain deep learning applications than classical computers because quantum systems exhibit distinctive patterns that classical systems are assumed not to produce effectively. We explore one such application in this study leveraging Quantum Machine Learning (QML). This study proposes a different approach that provides a comprehensive analysis of telematics data through the extraction of relevant features, followed by feature transformation into a valid weighted risk score. We apply QML frameworks to improve our classification model for the insurance industry by building an experimental Hybrid Classical and Quantum-based Deep Neural Network, a classical Deep Neural Network and a Recurrent Neural Network. Our technique presents an opportunity for insurers to predict a driver's driving pattern, under different travel conditions, by adding multiple constraints to parameters, for determining personalized premium rates and therefore assign an insurance premium for new drivers or renewal of insurance using predictive modeling. This paper allows insurers to gain a competitive edge by accurate estimation of risk premiums.

Keywords: Quantum computing · Deep learning · Telematics · Insurance premium

1 Introduction

Road safety is an indispensable challenge worldwide with multiple organizations trying to tackle the issue of excessive harsh driving. NHTSA (National Highway Traffic Safety Administration) [20] published an article in 2020 highlighting risky driving behavior such as violation of speed limits, driving under the influence of drugs or alcohol, drowsy driving (due to fatigue, lack of sleep, etc.), among others.

Here is where insurance companies come into the picture. Insurance companies seek to charge a premium at regular intervals, to cover any damage or medical costs incurred on the occurrence of an accident or fire in the future.

S. K. Panda et al. (Eds.): CoCoLe 2022, CCIS 1729, pp. 277–288, 2022.
https://doi.org/10.1007/978-3-031-21750-0_24

Insurance companies charge following a comprehensive assessment of a driver's driving style integrated with the behavior of the milieu and forecasting the risk associated with each driver in conjunction with the behavior of their surrounding environment. For example, if the acceleration patterns of drivers in specific road curvatures can be classified using vehicle dynamics and compared to the speed limit and accident statistics of the road segment under study, confident decisions can eventually lead to increased premiums or reduced liability for reckless driving.

Essentially, driving is a multi-factor cognitive effort discerned relative to its immediate surroundings, including speeding, braking action, road condition, underlying traffic circumstances, and weather conditions. Consequently, the driver's driving pattern is significantly influenced by the activities of other drivers who share the environment. Each driver develops a distinct driving style with time that can impact traffic congestion, safety, and other issues. Traditional insurance firms rely on actuarial methods to design commercial and sustainable policies that, while appealing to customers, are impossible to anticipate claim amounts on an individual basis. Telematics proves to be an effective approach to evaluate driving profiles based on available data and calculating claim amounts.

Evolution and emergence in telematics have instigated effective management of vehicle fleets. An interesting and blooming trend of telematics is associated with the insurance industry wherein insurers collect driving data of vehicles to ameliorate the domain of risk estimation. Particularly, telematics renders insurers the license to vie for a more accurate risk assessment and adjust the insurance pricing accordingly. Moreover, as per Marano, P., & Noussia, K. (2021), telematics enables insurance companies to render feedback to the concerned drivers, through analysis of the driving data, to enhance road safety and mitigate the threat of moral hazard by rewarding drivers, for example with a bonus or premium reduction, to boost secure driving [17].

In this paper, we introduce techniques that enable insurers to examine and render adequate risk assessments and personalized pricing. Modern vehicles are increasingly equipped with advanced sensor technologies that generate vast amounts of data on users' driving location every second. Possessing access to this data in combination with increasingly advanced data analytics has not only made it possible for us to comprehend the functioning and driving style but also, allowed insurers to upgrade their strategies by innovating and expanding their services and products. Presently, the installation of a telematics device in the policyholder's vehicle generates data, through which features such as late night and long-distance driving, speeding and heavy braking can be derived, to determine the conjugated risk.

The objective of this research is to extract key features from driving data of vehicles and calculate their weighted average, to assess the uncertainty involved, followed by the computation of the insurance premium imposed on each driver. The outcome of this project will be useful for the insurance industry to determine the risk posed by drivers with greater accuracy and propose a solution to augment the safety of business fleets. Accordingly, to adopt fairer insurance pricing approaches [2], we adopt Deep Learning techniques to assess the attributes of the trips taken by a certain driver and evaluate its risk rate based on a weighted mean score. The paper concludes with a discussion of the results and their implications for drivers and other stakeholders.

2 Related Work

Our data is derived from each vehicle's coordinates every second, as long as the engine is running. Similarly, [16] generates data through GPS technology that periodically establishes the position of a vehicle. Developing three important categories, namely travel features, event features, and car models, the authors concluded that Random Forests yielded the most accurate results. Internet of Vehicles (IoV) is known to gather data about vehicles and their surroundings, making it a valuable source of driving risk indicators. Highlighting the significance of IoV sensors in telematics analysis, [22] focuses on the exploitation of pay-how-you-drive applications by identifying dangerous drivers via a scoreboard.

The research conducted by [5] demonstrates the use of dimensionality reduction, to reduce the data dimensions and choose critical attributes, to explain the target variables. Techniques implemented by [19] involves the usage of the clustering algorithm under unsupervised learning to categorize the data on basis of driving patterns and determine a rewarding or penalizing factor for each group.

Introducing two different set-ups, [8][7] combines the Poisson generalized linear model (GLM) and Poisson neural network regression model based on actuarial risk factors and telematics data respectively to develop a more powerful predictive model. Similar to the approach implemented in this paper, [9] utilizes a deep convolution neural network to recognize patterns and classify individual trips of manually selected drivers. Neural networks with three hidden layers are proposed in [6] to overcome the shortcomings of GLM and to return the most accurate model with fast convergence. [3] collected GPS data in sunny weather to ensure consistency and used three deep learning algorithms for label classification, with CNN delivering the best performance. While dealing with a multi-label classification problem, [4] evaluated three types of RNN: LSTM, GRU, and SimpleRNN, where GRU proved to be the most accurate. In the thesis authored by [2], each driver's score was calculated based on conditional probability, recording the numbers of recorded crashes and near-crash events. Using these values to identify the risk profile, the author formulated this problem into a classification and regression problem based on the reckoned risk probability.

3 Data Description and Generation

Firstly, we will introduce the telematics dataset and all of its features that are critical in the assessment of driver behavioral analysis. Intending to label individual driving trips as risky, we collect GPS location data of 800 drivers, each having 200 trips per day. The trips were rotated at random, commencing from origin, to safeguard the drivers' locations.

3.1 Feature Extraction Process

Features that best describe the driving behavior of the driver and also the road conditions need to be extracted. Research on driving behavior started in 1978 when Karstens and Kuhler [13] introduced 10 behavioral parameters that account for an aggregate driving profile: "mean speed with and without the stops, average acceleration, mean deceleration, average trip length, the mean number of acceleration/deceleration changes within a trip, standstill time proportion, acceleration time proportion, deceleration time proportion, and constant speed time proportion". Before beginning the calculations, we assume that all vehicles are of the same age and model.

With the help of these coordinate values captured every second, we intend to develop a dataset to address the following questions:

1. At what speed is the vehicle driven?
2. Is the driver on a highway or in an urban area?
3. Is jerkiness observed?
4. How many times does the driver cross the speeding limit?

To find solutions to these queries, using the coordinates provided in the telematics dataset, we created a new dataset that features important characteristics such as speed, turning angle, acceleration, jerks, and stops.

The initial position of all vehicles is at the origin (0, 0). Let $(\mathrm{x}_{(s)}, \mathrm{y}_{(s)})$ denote the location of a vehicle at any given instances. The total distance covered per second (s) can be measured using the formula

$$d_{(t)} = \sum_{s=0}^{t} \sqrt{(y_{(s)} - y_{(s-1)})^2 + (x_{(s)} - x_{(s-1)})^2} \tag{1}$$

where t denotes the total time per trip in seconds. We convert the total time (t) into hours.

Since the GPS records location every second, the average speed $(\mathrm{v}_{(t)})$ is equal to the total distance measured per total time of the trip (in hours), denoted by t. We also convert the total distance (in meters) to miles. By analyzing vehicle-associated signals such as acceleration, an accurate assessment of the driver can be derived, as aggressive acceleration is an indicator of risky drivers. We define the average acceleration per trip and jerk $(\mathrm{j}_{(t)})$ by the change in acceleration with respect to for total time t by

$$a_{(t)} = \frac{v_{(t)}}{t} \tag{2}$$

$$j_{(t)} = \frac{a_{(t)}}{t} \tag{3}$$

To find out how many times a vehicle halts or slows down, we extract the values when there is a decline in speed. To get a better idea of the driver's behavior, we check the speed by which the driver slowed down. If a sharp decline in speed, or hard braking, is commonly observed in a driver's driving history, it is indicative of high-risk driving with a greater probability of a crash.

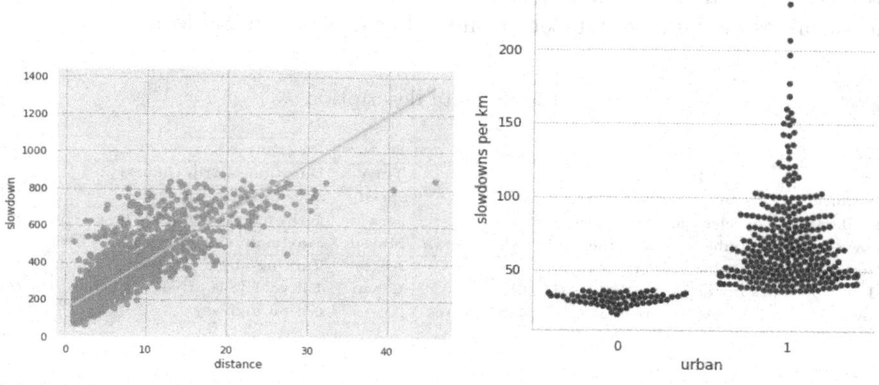

(a) Slowdown vs distance plot for 1500 trips (b) Distribution of urban & highway trips (1 - urban, 0 - highway)

Fig. 1. Distribution of trips.

A critical feature is to compute the risk rate of a trip and determine whether the driver is speeding. A trip that we may presume to be risky based on higher speed, could be the vehicle being driven on a highway. To avoid this situation, we investigate the ratio of slowdown to distances. In Fig. 1, we randomly select 1500 trips from our data and plot slowdowns and distance. The upper portion of the graph, as separated by the slope, highlights the trips where for the same amount of distance covered, the number of slowdowns is greater.

To understand if the trip is on urban roads or highways, we decide on the basis of the count of slowdowns per mile, by setting a threshold value for urban ($\mathrm{u_{th}}$) and highway driving ($\mathrm{h_{th}}$).

$$urban_i = \begin{cases} 1 & \text{if } sd_i > \mathrm{u_{th}} \\ 0 & \text{if } sd_i > \mathrm{h_{th}} \end{cases} \tag{4}$$

We also formulate the weighted mean for each trip k by assigning weights to N features according to their significance, based on our understanding, to express the risk profile of a specific driver. It is estimated through:

$$wavg_{(k)} = \sum_{j=0}^{N-1} [w_{(j_k)} \times feature_{(j_k)}] \tag{5}$$

where,

$$\sum_{j=0}^{N-1} w_{(j)} = 0 \tag{6}$$

and feature contains a list of all features in our data with their allotted weightage. The variables of the new dataset are introduced below in Table 1.

Table 1. Data description

Feature	Description	Feature	Description
Drid	Driver ID	Time	Duration of trip (hours)
Distance	Distance covered in trip (mi)	speed	Speed of trip (mi/hr)
Acceleration	Acceleration of trip (mi/hr^2)	Jerk	Jerks per trip (mi/hr^3)
Slowdown	Number of times the vehicle slows down	Maxsd	Maximum slow down speed (mi/hr)
Ang_vel	Angular velocity of vehicle	Angle	Turning angle of vehicle
sd	Number of slowdowns per mile	Urban	1 if vehicle is driven on urban streets
wavg	Weighted average of important features		0 if on highway

3.2 Dependent Variable Selection

To deduce if a trip is risky, we inspect if the vehicle crosses the speed restrictions imposed by the Government, in addition to the surrounding location of the vehicle. To tackle this risk prediction problem, we formulate it as a binary classification problem using the following expression:

$$risky_i = \begin{cases} 1 & \text{if } v_i > \mathrm{v_{urban}} \& urban_i = 1 \& wavg_i > \mathrm{wm_{urban}} \\ 1 & \text{if } v_i > \mathrm{v_{highway}} \& urban_i = 0 \& wavg_i > \mathrm{wm_{highway}} \\ 0 & \text{otherwise} \end{cases} \quad (7)$$

where v_{urban} and $\mathrm{v}_{highway}$ reflect the speed limits on urban streets and highways respectively, and v_i represents the average speed for trip i. Another condition factored in for the trip to be classified as risky was the requirement of each trip's weighted mean (wavg_i) to surpass the threshold value assigned for urban ($\mathrm{wm_{urban}}$) and highway ($\mathrm{wm_{highway}}$) trips.

Taking the risky trip outcome values as our dependent variable, we come across a class imbalance with the minority class having a weightage of 6%. We chose to perform oversampling on our data by generating synthetic samples via Borderline SMOTE [10], after splitting the dataset for training (60%) testing (20%), and validation (20%) purposes. To avoid overfitting later, we perform oversampling on the training set only.

4 Driving Risk Classification

4.1 Deep Neural Network Evaluation

As per Haykin's [11] understanding, an Artificial Neural Network (ANN) is comparable to a human brain, in terms of its functioning abilities. A human brain constitutes multiple interconnected neurons, working together to perform tasks by transferring and receiving signals. A deep Neural Network (DNN) is equivalent to a Feed-forward ANN that has at least two layers of hidden units between its inputs and outputs layers [4].

On obtaining input characteristics, the input layer passes them to hidden layers, that are responsible for the transformation of input features through an activation function. Rectified Linear Unit (ReLU), an activation function, is utilized at each layer by DNN to diminish the occurrence of gradient vanishing in neural networks. DNNs learn data representation through several levels of abstraction using numerous consecutive computational layers, as seen in Fig. 2. To achieve an effective outcome at the output layer, each hidden layer develops increasingly complicated features based on interactions of features from previous layers, based on the initial features from the input layer. The error is relayed backward and the parameters are changed to produce more accurate results by comparing the algorithm's output with the actual data. DNNs do not require feature engineering because higher-level abstraction features are derived spontaneously during backpropagation.

The DNN-based classification model is a good fit for this study's research goal. The attributes of the driving behavior are mapped in the hidden layers for transformation. The ability to gather data from several sources and create new characteristics to access driving danger is made feasible by multi-layer neural network learning, which outperforms classic machine learning algorithms in picking behavioral variables. The hyper-parameters where we adopted the number of epochs as the stopping criteria, shown in Table 2, returned the best performance.

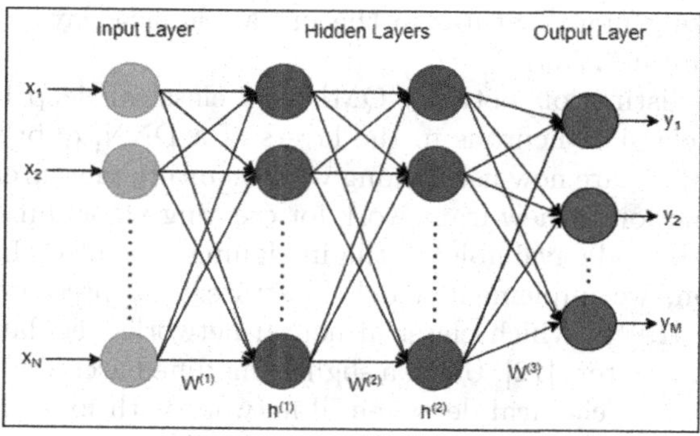

Fig. 2. Feed forward DNN

4.2 Recurrent Neural Network Evaluation

Recurrent Neural Networks (RNN) are a type of Feed-forward Neural Network with recurrent hidden states that can handle variable length sequences. Through

Table 2. RNN adopted hyper-parameters

DNN parameter	Adopted value	LSTM-RNN parameter	Adopted value
L1 & L2 penalty	0.0001	Dropout penalty	0.2
Number of hidden units per layer	7, 8, 5, 15	Number of LSTM units per layer	5, 5, 5
Optimization algorithm	ADAM	Optimization algorithm	RMSPROP
Activation function	RELU		

the recurrent states, the internal memory rendered by RNNs enables them to store past information and exhibit dynamic temporal behavior that allows them to update their hidden state using non-trivial ways.

Long Short-Term Memory (LSTM) networks are more efficient than traditional RNNs, especially when they have multiple layers for each time step [14]. LSTM tackles the vanishing gradient issue by employing three gates, namely input, output, and forget, to determine which information to keep [3]. To enhance the performance of our model and regularization, we added two dropout layers before the compilation of the model.

4.3 Hybrid Classical-Quantum Neural Network

The paradigm of Quantum Computation incorporates phenomena like superposition, interference, and entanglement, which could give it an edge over traditional computing models. These elements work together to make quantum computers an appealing platform for researching novel neural network architectures, especially hybrid classical-quantum methods. Hybrid neural networks are built by concatenating classical and quantum neural networks and have the significant advantage of having more features in the initial classical layers than there are qubits in the quantum layer.

The primary distinction between QML and classical deep learning is that instead of using classical neurons in the layers of a DNN, qubits and quantum gates acting on qubits are now used, along with quantum measurements acting as the activation function. A new framework for creating algorithms with quantum speedups has been made available by the intriguing field of QML [21].

In this section, we implement a hybrid strategy as presented by Killoran, Nathan, et al. (2019) in which classical neural networks regulate the quantum network's gate parameters [12]. Using a slightly modified architecture of our DNN model, we construct a classical deep neural network with four hidden layers, all of varying sizes. Defining the classical layers, we perform an encoding operation where classical data is encoded into quantum states using linear as well as non-linear gates of photonic quantum computing. Two nodes initially in the vacuum make up the quantum neural network, which is controlled by the output neurons of our classical model. The output layer, which takes the form of measurement of the photon number, is then sent from the input layer through four hidden levels with fully controllable parameters.

Pennylane is an open-source software platform for differentiable programming of quantum computers [1]. This framework provides the foundation for our hybrid model. In Pennylane, a quantum node in the hybrid computational graph is represented as an object QNode. In this case, a quantum function is used to build a quantum node, or QNode object, which contains both the quantum function and the tool used to execute it.

With over 150,000 trips, we train the hybrid network on smaller datasets using the MSE loss function and ADAM as optimizers. We determine the probability of a single photon being observed in the mode corresponding to the right label after training and classify single photon events using the post-selected probability after training.

5 Results

To ensure that our model is not overfitting, we studied the differences between training, testing, and validation accuracies. The goal of the validation set is to evaluate the effectiveness of the suggested model for categorizing risk levels based on the behavior exhibited by a particular driver. We assess how well trip-based driving behavior analysis works and put our deep learning-based classification model and hybrid model for driving behavior to the test.

A training accuracy of 0.9917 was observed for our hybrid classical-quantum model. Its testing accuracy crossed 0.98 after the third epoch. For DNN, we noticed that the training accuracy (0.9347) and testing accuracy (0.9329) surpassed the F-1 score of 0.9184. Similarly, for LSTM-RNN, the training and testing accuracies were 0.8928 and 0.8841 respectively. The behavior loss is depicted below in Fig. 3.

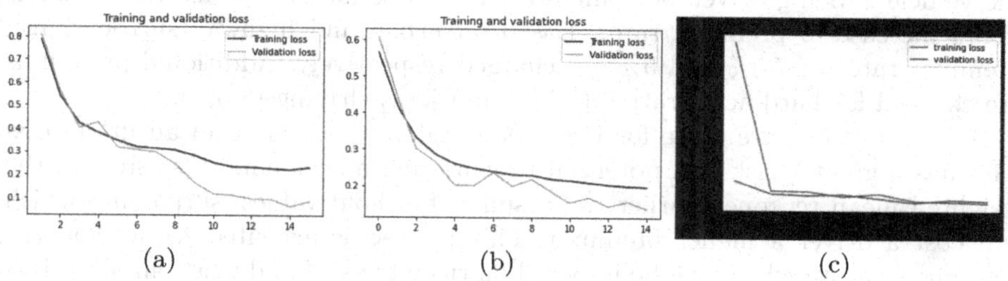

(a) (b) (c)

Fig. 3. Loss prediction for DNN, LSTM-RNN and hybrid model respectively

As a result, we found that the Hybrid Classical-Quantum Network reflects highest accuracy of 0.985. Our experimental results indicate that the proposed behavior-centric model is an appropriate method for driving risk level classification. LSTM-RNN presented the lowest results because of the nature of the LSTM layers that are more suitable for sequential data.

We examined the loss function of the DNN and LSTM-RNN model across 20 simulations and used the Shapiro-Wilk test on the data to further draw definitive conclusions from the classical models. The p-values of the LSTM-RNN model

(0.142) and the DNN model (0.0723) both exceeded the alpha level of 0.05, indicating that the results are normally distributed.

6 Insurance Premium

To make this model deployable for real-life insurance cases, we utilize indicative rates, to work out the on-ground risk premiums, and to give a sense of how this model would work in realistic scenarios. After classifying the trips, we suggest an approach to determine a driver's insurance premium. As observed, a high-mileage driver is more likely to cause an accident than a low-mileage driver. Lee, Kristine (2021) and Martin, Ross (2021) accent the significance of annual mileage and its impact on car premium in their respective articles by highlighting the average six-month premium charged based on different value ranges of annual mileage [15,18].

The premium costs shown in Table 3 are charged semi-annually. Since the trip duration in our data is much lesser, we reduce the cost in accordance with the total trip duration taken by a certain driver and employ those costs as an addition to the base annual insurance cost applicable to every vehicle.

The next factor taken into consideration is the location of the vehicle. As an example, using speed limits imposed by federal law in the United States of America, we can realize if a vehicle is on a highway or a busy urban street. If a vehicle crosses the speed limits of an urban area and tends to stop more frequently at shorter distances, it can be inferred that the vehicle is located in an urban locality at that particular moment. In contrast, if a vehicle crosses both speed limits and travels longer distances without halting often, it is deduced that the vehicle is being driven on a highway. For these factors, we assume a conditional increase in premium rates. Based on urban and highway surroundings, premium rates of 7.5% and 5% are charged respectively. Additional premiums are charged for hard acceleration (4.5%) and jerky driving (8.5%).

Premium rates are more for the urban region as speeding in an urban district has a greater risk and potential to cause more accidents. Focusing on the weighted mean reckoned earlier, we assume threshold values, surpassing which will cost a driver a higher premium. This process is executed to develop the insurance feature which will be imposed on risky trips. If and when an old driver wishes to renew their insurance or a new driver wishes to purchase insurance, these parameters will be factored into insurance calculations.

Table 3. Car insurance for low and high-mileage drivers (The Zebra, 2021)

Low-mileage	Average six-month premium	High-mileage	Average six-month premium
0–7,500 mi	$1,409	15,000–20,000 mi	$972
7,500–10,000 mi	$1,470	20,000–25,000 mi	$974
10,000–15,000 mi	$965	25,000–30,000 mi	$976

7 Conclusion and Discussions

In this paper, we demonstrated the significance of telematics data in the insurance industry with a comprehensive view of various driving indicators. Studying a total of about 150,000 trips driven by roughly 800 drivers, we built a new dataset and derived vital characteristics of each. Using these characteristics, we demonstrated techniques utilized to determine a trip's exposure to risk and therefore, compute the premium cost levied on each driver. With a view to bringing in an evolution in the manner in which risk is computed, we introduced QML, by implementing a hybrid classical-quantum model. Furthermore, we implemented Deep Neural Networks as well as LSTM-RNN and discussed which hyper-parameters of this trip could provide us with an accurate outcome.

The findings of this study are expected to benefit insurance companies and their clients. We recommended a base insurance amount charged to all drivers succeeded by the application of a premium rate on the basis of each trip's weighted average as well as other essential features such as hard braking, and speeding on urban roads or highways. Albeit the weights considered for each attribute in our data, used to measure the weighted mean were assumed, they gave us a fair idea of the influence each attribute holds in a risky trip. Insurance companies can modify the weights as per their requirements and perform the computations accordingly. Likewise, the premium rates for various driving conditions were an assumption, but the insurers may choose to modify the premium rates as per their suitability. This strategy may eventually lead to the development of a new, more distinctive, and individualized insurance pricing structure.

Future work relates to a more in-depth analysis of the problem and new approaches to address certain mechanisms. An interesting addition to our study which could have been a major improvement is the vehicle's model and age. Learning about a car's model and age, we could have tried to distinguish two vehicles based on their speed and a similar number of slowdowns and thereby impose a more accurate premium cost. Further exploration includes understanding the mechanism behind quantum speedups for advanced Quantum Neural Networks. Potential algorithms that can be explored further to shed a better understanding of the data include Generative Adversarial Networks (GANs), Generalized Linear Models (GLMs).

References

1. What is Quantum Machine Learning? PennyLane (2020). https://pennylane.ai/qml/whatisqml.html
2. Abdelrahman, A.: Driver behavior modelling and risk profiling using large-scale naturalistic driving data. Ph.D. thesis, Queen's University (Canada) (2019)
3. Al-Hussein, W.A., Por, L.Y., Kiah, M.L.M., Zaidan, B.B.: Driver behavior profiling and recognition using deep-learning methods: in accordance with traffic regulations and experts guidelines. Int. J. Environ. Res. Public Health **19**(3), 1470 (2022)

4. Bian, Y., Lee, C.H., Zhao, J.L., Wan, Y.: A deep learning based model for driving risk assessment. In: Proceedings of the 52nd Hawaii International Conference on System Sciences (2019)
5. Boodhun, N., Jayabalan, M.: Risk prediction in life insurance industry using supervised learning algorithms. Complex Intell. Syst. **4**(2), 145–154 (2018). https://doi.org/10.1007/s40747-018-0072-1
6. Ferrario, A., Noll, A., Wuthrich, M.V.: Insights from inside neural networks. Available at SSRN 3226852 (2020)
7. Gao, G., Meng, S., Wüthrich, M.V.: What can we learn from telematics car driving data: a survey. Insur. Math. Econ. **104**, 185–199 (2022)
8. Gao, G., Wang, H., Wüthrich, M.V.: Boosting poisson regression models with telematics car driving data. Mach. Learn. **111**(1), 243–272 (2022)
9. Gao, G., Wüthrich, M.V.: Convolutional neural network classification of telematics car driving data. Risks **7**(1), 6 (2019)
10. Han, H., Wang, W.-Y., Mao, B.-H.: Borderline-SMOTE: a new over-sampling method in imbalanced data sets learning. In: Huang, D.-S., Zhang, X.-P., Huang, G.-B. (eds.) ICIC 2005. LNCS, vol. 3644, pp. 878–887. Springer, Heidelberg (2005). https://doi.org/10.1007/11538059_91
11. Haykin, S.: Neural networks and learning machines, 3/E. Pearson Education India (2009)
12. Killoran, N., Bromley, T.R., Arrazola, J.M., Schuld, M., Quesada, N., Lloyd, S.: Continuous-variable quantum neural networks. Phys. Rev. Res. **1**(3), 033063 (2019)
13. Kuhler, M., et al.: Improved driving cycle for testing automotive exhaust emissions (1978)
14. LeCun, Y., Bengio, Y., Hinton, G.: Deep learning. Nature **521**(7553), 436–444 (2015)
15. Lee, K.: Car insurance for high-mileage drivers. The Zebra. https://www.thezebra.com/auto-insurance/driver/other-factors/car-insurance-high-mileage-drivers/
16. Longhi, L., Nanni, M.: Car telematics big data analytics for insurance and innovative mobility services. J. Ambient Intell. Humanized Comput. **11**(10), 3989–3999 (2020)
17. Marano, P., Noussia, K.: Insurance Distribution Directive: A Legal Analysis. Springer, Cham (2021)
18. Martin, R.: Car insurance for low-mileage drivers. The Zebra. https://www.thezebra.com/auto-insurance/driver/other-factors/car-insurance-low-mileage-drivers/
19. Narwani, B., Muchhala, Y., Nawani, J., Pawar, R.: Categorizing driving patterns based on telematics data using supervised and unsupervised learning. In: 2020 4th International Conference on Intelligent Computing and Control Systems (ICICCS), pp. 302–306. IEEE (2020)
20. NHTSA: risky driving (2020). https://www.nhtsa.gov/risky-driving/speeding
21. Schetakis, N., Aghamalyan, D., Boguslavsky, M., Griffin, P.: Binary classifiers for noisy datasets: a comparative study of existing quantum machine learning frameworks and some new approaches. arXiv preprint arXiv:2111.03372 (2021)
22. Sun, S., Bi, J., Guillen, M., Pérez-Marín, A.M.: Assessing driving risk using internet of vehicles data: an analysis based on generalized linear models. Sensors **20**(9), 2712 (2020)

An Improved Machine Learning Framework for Cardiovascular Disease Prediction

Arati Behera(✉), Tapas Kumar Mishra, Kshira Sagar Sahoo, and B. Sarathchandra

SRM University, Amaravati, AP, India
{arati_behera,sarathchandra_banala}@srmap.edu.in

Abstract. Cardiovascular diseases have the highest fatality rate among the world's most deadly syndromes. They have become stress, age, gender, cholesterol, Body Mass Index, physical inactivity, and an unhealthy diet are all key risk factors for cardiovascular disease. Based on these parameters, researchers have suggested various early diagnosis methods. However, the correctness of the supplied treatments and approaches needs considerable fine-tuning due to the cardiovascular illnesses' intrinsic criticality and life-threatening hazards. This paper proposes a framework for accurate cardiovascular disorder prediction based on machine learning techniques. To attain the purpose, the method employs an approach called synthetic minority over-sampling (SMOTE). The benchmark datasets are used to validate the framework for achieving better accuracy, such as Recall and Accuracy. Finally, a comparison has been presented with existing state-of-the-art approaches that shows 99.16% accuracy by a collaborative model by logistic regression and KNN.

Keywords: Machine learning · Ensemble · SMOTE · Cardiovascular prediction · Feature selection

1 Introduction

Unhealthy living styles of humans have resulted in ill health of humans. Rising cases of Cardio Vascular Diseases have put humans in a dilemma as to the exact reason for getting hooked up with this. The non but yet unknown conditions have been considered as the habit of excessive exercise, smoking, drinking, and drug usage. All of these factors play a role in the development of a variety of severe diseases, such as Cardio-Vascular Disease (CVD) and cancer. Early detection of these disorders is critical so that preventative steps can be implemented before something terrible occurs. A disorder that damages the heart and the blood vessels is referred to as cardiovascular disease Coronary heart disease, stroke/Transient Ischemic Attack (TIA/ Mini-stroke), peripheral arterial disease, and aortic disease are the four main kinds of CVD [5,11]. CVD is associated with hypertension, smoke, diabetic, body mass (Bms), fat, age, and

S. K. Panda et al. (Eds.): CoCoLe 2022, CCIS 1729, pp. 289–299, 2022.
https://doi.org/10.1007/978-3-031-21750-0_25

family history. For several people, these factors are different. The different factors of CVD are brought on by a number of factors, like youth, genetics, strain, as well as an addictive personality. The main problem is to accurately forecast these diseases in a timely manner so that mortality can be decreased through appropriate medicine and other countermeasures. Using various datasets and approaches, researchers have suggested multiple algorithms in order to anticipate cardiovascular diseases. Heart disease [4], Cleveland [2], Framingham [3], and cardiovascular disease [1] are some of the most commonly used datasets for CVD prediction. These datasets are made up of several attributes that are used to predict CVD. The factors that lead to cardiovascular disease include both changeable and non-changeable risks. The Framingham dataset [3], which is gathered against these parameters, is one of the most well-known datasets. Several researchers have utilized this data collection to validate their prediction models. In the given study context, various ML and DL based algorithms for the diagnosis of cardiovascular disease were developed. On the other hand, the problem of class imbalance is not being addressed by researchers as they instead concentrate on feature selection methods and classification algorithms. The problem of class imbalance substantially impacts the classification algorithm's accuracy. When the data is uneven, a large number of qualities are further required for prediction. This significantly raises the solution's computational complexity, making it unusable in real-world situations. Furthermore, to decrease computing while maintaining a reasonable level of accuracy, it is necessary to update the current feature selection techniques. Similar to this, improved classifier results are required to generate trustworthy results.

In conclusion, a framework for cardiovascular machine learning that incorporates unified machine learning diseases is urgently needed. Data balance, feature selection, and classification augmentation are all carried out methodically. Figure 1 shows a high-level representation of the framework. In contrast to previous research, which has mostly absorbed on feature selection and standard classification approaches, by addressing missing values and data, the framework tries to boost overall correctness that is imbalanced. By addressing missing values and data, the framework seeks to improve unbalanced overall correctness, in contrast to prior research, which has mainly focused on feature selection and conventional classification methodologies. The average of all values for a relevant attribute was used to fill in the gaps left by missing values. The framework proposes Synthetic Minority Over-sampling Technique (SMOTE) to deal with data imbalance.

1.1 Key Contributions

The key contributions are highlighted as follows.

- Feature importance technique is used to select the best set of features.
- Synthetic Minority Over-sampling Technique (SMOTE) is used to deal with data imbalance.
- An ensemble of Logistic Regression and K-Nearest Neighbor (KNN) models is presented for enhanced prediction.

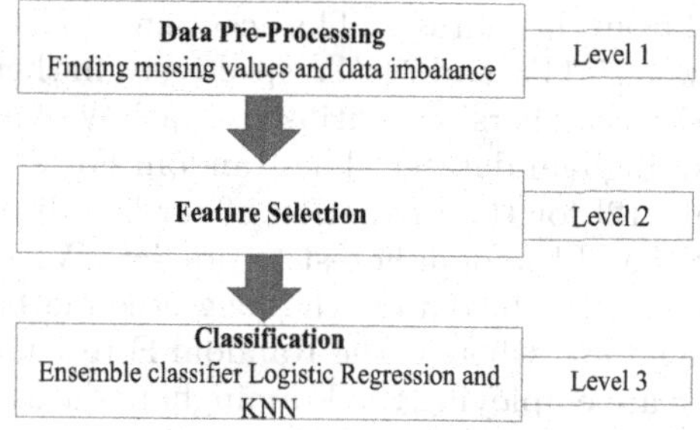

Fig. 1. Framework for cardiovascular diagnosis based on ML.

The remaining of the paper is structured as follows. A few important pieces of literature are mentioned in Sect. 2. Our suggested model is described in Sect. 3. Finally, Sect. 4 presents the effectiveness of the suggested model, and Sect. 5 draws conclusions and future works.

2 Literature Review

The heart and blood arteries are affected by cardiovascular diseases. Cardiovascular diseases come in a variety of forms and can have a wide range of effects on the human body. High blood pressure, smoking, diabetes, body mass index (BMI), cholesterol, age, family history, and other risk factors have been identified as potential causes of CVD [13]. CVDs are caused by a variety of variables, including age, gender, stress, and an unhealthy lifestyle [9]. Similarly, the researchers have employed a variety of datasets to validate their proposed methodologies. Cleveland [2], Framingham [3], and the heart disease dataset [4] have all received a lot of attention. The properties of these datasets are mostly the same. The experimental setup, or how the dataset is acquired, is the major variation in these datasets. The research on CVD prediction that was done by deserving academics, as well as the necessary datasets, are presented in the following paragraphs. The Cleveland [2] dataset was utilised by Tanvi et al. [13] to predict heart disorders. The model was trained using 14 characteristics as part of the prediction process. From all these models, Decision Tree (DT) has had the best accuracy. However, the sequence of features used on DT plays a major role in prediction. The authors in [14] suggested some feature selection techniques. On the cardiac disease dataset [4] accessible in the UCI repository, Singh et al. [10] used various categorization techniques. The use of Logistic Regression, which was the most accurate of all the other models, yielded 87.1% accuracy. Amanda et al. [8] used ten distinct features from a South African dataset on cardiac disease. The dataset is subjected to three distinct models: Decision Tree, Nave Bayes, and support vector machine (SVM), which are then evaluated using the Confusion Matrix. Naive Bayes generated the best outcomes of the three models. The dataset utilised by Ketut et al. [7] was obtained from Harapan Kita Hospital. For the prediction of cardiac disorders, 18 factors were extracted from this dataset. The accuracy of KNN with and without parameter weighting was 75.11% and 74%, respectively, in their investigation. For the forecast of disease, researchers have utilised a variety of approaches and procedures using the Framingham dataset. The Random Forest algorithm was proposed by Rubini et al. [12] for the prediction of cardiac disease. Hoda et al. [6] proposed utilising KNN and Random Forest to predict CVD. KNN and Random Forest were utilised to classify the data in the suggested method. The accuracy of KNN was found to be 66.7%, whereas the Random Forest method was found to be 63.4% accurate. We are employing the Framingham dataset in our study with necessary variables to aid in the prediction of these diseases. There are 16 features in the dataset that can be used to make a prediction. The Framingham dataset contains information from three generations of people, including those who took part in the original study.

3 Proposed Solution

For the prediction of cardiovascular disorders, a customized ML based Cardiovascular Disease Diagnosis Framework is presented. The purpose of this research is to develop a ML model that can correctly identify cardiovascular illnesses from patient clinical data. The steps in the proposed strategy are as follows: 1) Outlier elimination, missing value replacement, and data imbalance class handling are all part of data preparation using SMOTE, 2) feature importance technique is used for feature selection, 3) combination of logistic regression and KNN is used for ensemble classification. The trained model is then used to make predictions.

Most outliers are considered noise, which does not affect the data's significance and hurts the model's performance. If the data contains missing values, the model cannot be trained on such data because to the restricted amount of training samples. This has an impact on the model's accuracy. Thus, in this proposed framework, missing values are replaced by the average of all values of the associated property. It lowers the possibility of over-fitting by allowing the retention of training data without adding new data to the dataset. The next stage of pre-processing in our suggested architecture involves handling the issue of an imbalanced class using the SMOTE approach and K- Means clustering algorithms after handling the issues of outliers and missing values using the mean replacement technique.

By locating the minority class's k nearest neighbour, SMOTE improves the sample size of the minority class. Then, at random, one of the k closest neighbours is chosen to boost the smaller class samples. This approach can generate as many smaller class samples as needed.

This method generates samples that are very identical to the original, enhancing reliability and lowering randomness. Finally, the framework recommends an ensemble for classification utilising the boosting technique.

3.1 Dataset

We have used the Framingham [2] data set to demonstrate the framework's applicability. Data collection was done in three phases. This round, that took

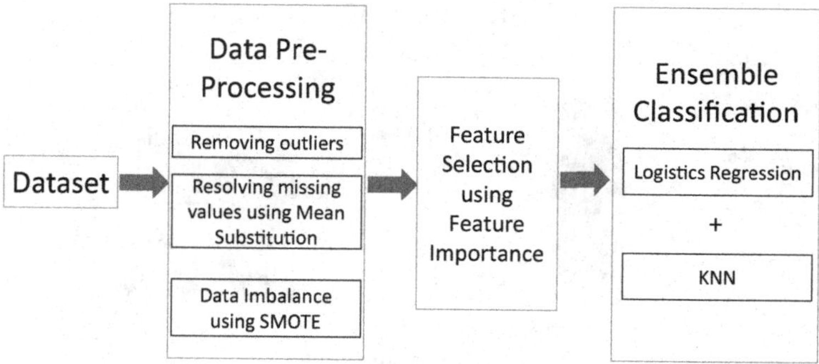

Fig. 2. Flowchart of the cardiovascular diagnosis perdition framework based on ML.

place in 1948, gathered information from 5209 participants aged 30 to 62. In 1971, 5124 people took place in the second stage, and they're all given the same examination. Those are the children of the first-round draftees. Finally, data from the first cohort's 3rd generation was obtained.

Table 1. Attributes and its type of Dataset

Attribute	Type	Attribute	Type
Sex	Nominal	Diabetes	Nominal
Age	Continuous	Total Cholo	Continuous
Education	Continuous	Sys BP	Continuous
Current Smoker	Nominal	Dia BP	Continuous
Cigarettes per day	Continuous	BMI	Continuous
BP Meds	Nominal	Heart Rate	Continuous
Prevalent Stroke	Nominal	Glusoce	Continuous
Prevalent Hyp	Nominal	Ten-year CHD	Nominal

The Framingham dataset contains information from three generations of people, where class 1 sample represents patients and class 2 represents persons without cardiovascular disease. Table 1 shows 16 attributes in this data collection.

3.2 Data Imbalance

The Framingham dataset is an imbalanced dataset with a total of 644 examples of class 1 and 3596 samples of class 2. A quantitative value of different classes are shown in Fig. 3.

One of the most popular oversampling techniques to address imbalance issues is the synthetic minority oversampling method (SMOTE), which creates synthetic training samples for the minority class using linear interpolation. These

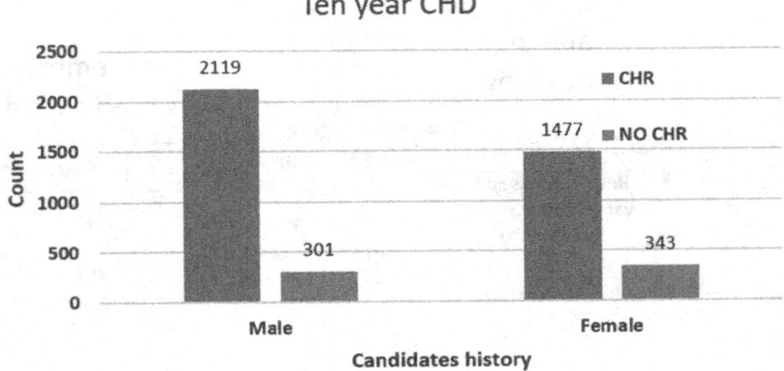

Fig. 3. Data imbalance

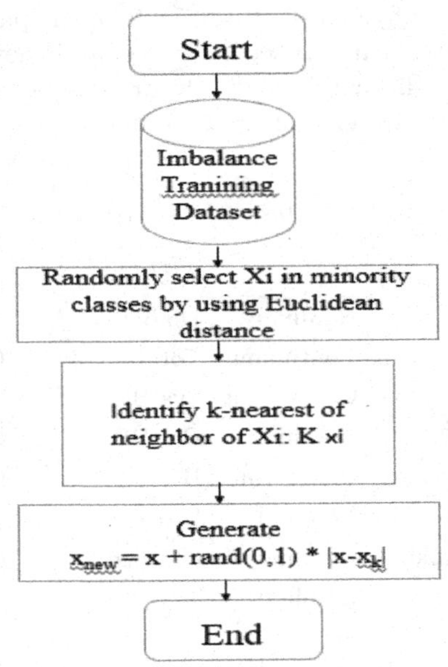

Fig. 4. Flowchart of the SMOTE

synthetic training cases are constructed by randomly selecting a subset of the k-nearest neighbours for each instance in the minority class. The SMOTE flowchart is shown in Fig 4.

The data is rebuilt just after oversampling process, and the modified data can be classified using a variety of methodologies. The following is the basic idea:

Step 1. Measuring the Euclidean distance among x and any minority classes A yields the k-nearest neighbours of x for each $x \in A$.

Step 2. The uneven proportion determines the sampling rate N. For each x $\in$ A , N examples x_1 , x_2 ,x_3,..... x_N (N$\leq$K) are chosen at random from its k-nearest neighbours and used to create the class A_1.

Step 3. For each example x $\in$ A_1 (k=1,2....N) , To create a new example using Eq. 1.

$$x_{new} = x + rand(0,1) * |X - x_k| \tag{1}$$

where rand (0,1) denotes a randomized values 0 or 1.

Our Framework works used SMOTE to resolve data imbalance while choosing the classes of dataset.

3.3 Feature Importance

Each data feature is given a score by *feature importance*, the higher of the score, the more important or pertinent the feature is for predicting. Tree-Based Classifiers provide a built-in class for feature significance; our proposed method uses the SelectKBest class to extract the most crucial features.

The weighted average of the node impurity multiplied by the chance of accessing that node determines the relevance of a characteristic.

Table 2. Specs Score

Attribute Name	Score	Attribute Name	Score
sysBP	727.935535	BPMeds	30.759595
age	319.266019	male	18.899930
totChol	235.502392	prevalentStroke	16.109887
cigsPerDay	209.897040	BMI	15.227367
diaBP	152.748563	education	6.318253
prevalentHyp	92.048736	heartRate	4.232372
diabetes	39.144944	currentSmoker	0.811334

The importance of a character is determined by the weighted average of the node impurity times the probability of accessing that node. In this regard, the *feature importance* technique has been used in our suggested framework. Table 2 displays our dataset specifications score. The results of this method are shown in Fig. 5. The overfitting is reduced by feature significance by deleting the duplicate feature, and misleading features from the data. This will give better accuracy in results.

Features with high score are selected for find probability. In this, selected features for applying models to predict more accuracy are SysBP, Age, totChol, cigsperday, and diaBP.

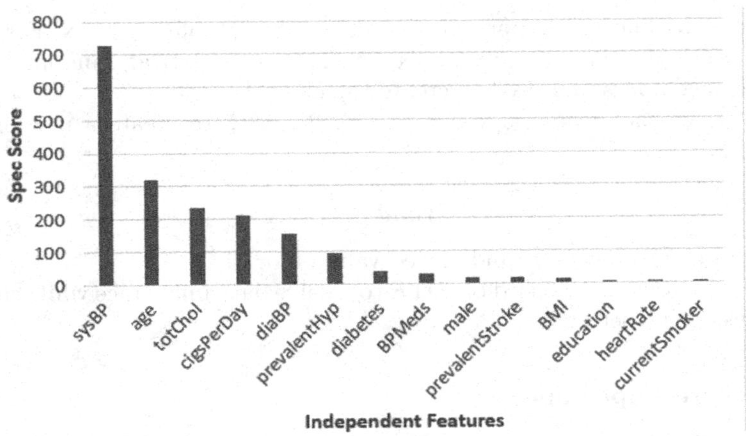

Fig. 5. Feature importance

4 Evaluation of Proposed Solution

4.1 Applying LR

Logistic regression is the best regression technique to utilize when the variable is categorical (binary data). Like all other regression techniques, logistic regression is essentially a predictive analysis. A statistical method known as logistic regression is used to describe and explain correlations between one category dependent variable and independent variables that can be numerical, continuous, interval, or proportional.

Consider a categorical dependent variable Y and really want to model the probability p(Y = 1/X = x) as just a function of x; any latent variables in the function must be estimated. The outcome of linear regression is squeezed between 0 and 1 using logistic regression.

Here, we are using the P function since to predict probability rather than the log of odds. This approach achieves an accuracy of 94.19%.

4.2 Applying KNN

One of the most fundamental adaptive algorithms being used supervised learning is the K-Nearest Neighbour(KNN) approach. In supervised learning, the training data is being labelled and found unknown sample, the model forecasts it using a trained model. KNN performs effectively on datasets with just a large number of samples. It works well with numeric properties as well.

The average output variable in regression, or the modal category value in classification, could be used. A distance metric is used to identify which of the K examples inside the training data are closest to the new input.

Euclidean distance is the widely used distance measure for input variables with real values. Euclidean distance is measured using Eq. 2, for all 11 input variables of k with the square root of the sum of squared differences between every new distance point(a) and existing distance point(b).

Formulae for Euclidean distance (ED),

$$ED(a,b) = \sqrt{\sum(a-b)^2} \tag{2}$$

The k value is picked, and the distance between the k closest neighbours is determined using that value. Euclidean geometry is widely used. The distance between neighbours is measured. In our simulation, k is taken as 5. This approach achieves an accuracy of 84.19%.

4.3 Applying Decision Tree

The selection of attribute for root node within every level is the most difficult task in Decision Tree. Attribute selection is the term for this process. There are two popular methods for selecting attributes.

In machine learning, the Decision Tree algorithm works on attribute-based parameter technique. If there is a single attribute that really can simply segregate data and improve decision-making, it works well. Range of the root node poses a hurdle in this approach. When the root node is chosen carefully, the algorithm's computational complexity is reduced, and it becomes extremely effective. This model has a 74.3% rating.

4.4 Applying Ensemble Classifier

Ensemble is a strategy for improving the accuracy of outcomes by combining different ML algorithms. Ensemble has substantially contributed in the improvement of accuracy. In our proposed Framework classification, we use an ensemble of LR and KNN. Prediction accuracy of 99.16% is attained with this ensemble.

4.5 Result Analysis

Our proposed machine learning based Cardiovascular Disease Diagnosis framework has analysed the accuracy of the ML models without SMOTE and with SMOTE technique. Accuracy of the models without SMOTE is good but the recall of the minority class is very less, i.e. the model is more depends on majority class.

In order to improve recall from both the minority and majority of classes, we need to consider data imbalance problem of minority class using SMOTE. SMOTE generates the virtual training records by linear interpolation for the minority class. Above ML models gives accuracy after applying SMOTE technique. The detailed analysis is listed below in Table 3.

Table 3. Accuracy and Recall Value Analysis

ML Model	With SMOTE			Without SMOTE		
	Recall		Accuracy	Recall		Accuracy
	Male	Female		Male	Female	
LR	0.88	0.84	0.94	0.97	0.72	0.99
KNN	0.94	0.95	0.84	0.96	0.75	0.865
DT	0.97	0.92	0.74	0.97	0.72	0.84
Ensemble	0.99	0.47	0.99	0.97	0.72	0.99

5 Conclusion and Future Work

The framework is divided into four primary phases, the first of which deals with the mean replacement technique for addressing missing values. In the second phase, the Synthetic Minority Over-sampling Technique is used to correct the data imbalance problem. Feature selection is done in the third phase utilising the feature significance technique to reduce the computational complexity of the model. Finally, an improved prediction framework is modeled using combination of Logistic Regression and KNN. The framework is validated using Framingham dataset that shows accuracy of 99.16%. Thus, the proposed framework combines pre-processing using SMOTE, feature selection using SelectKBest technique, and an improved ensemble technique for prediction. In future, the model will be tested on different benchmark data-sets for its validation and performance measurement.

References

1. Cardiovascular disease by kaggle. Accessed 17 Jan 2022. https://www.kaggle.com/sulianova/cardiovascular-diseasedataset
2. Cleveland dataset by keel. Accessed 15 Jan 2022. https://sci2s.ugr.es/keel/dataset.php?cod=57
3. Framingham dataset by kaggle. Accessed 17 Jan 2022. https://www.kaggle.com/amanajmera1/framingham-heartstudy-Dataset
4. Heart disease dataset by UCI. Accessed 15 Jan 2022. https://archive.ics.uci.edu/ml/datasets/Heart+Disease
5. El-Hasnony, I.M., Elzeki, O.M., Alshehri, A., Salem, H.: Multi-label active learning-based machine learning model for heart disease prediction. Sensors **22**(3), 1184 (2022)
6. Elsayed, H.A.G., Syed, L.: An automatic early risk classification of hard coronary heart diseases using framingham scoring model. In: Proceedings of the Second International Conference on Internet of Things, Data and Cloud Computing, pp. 1–8 (2017)
7. Enriko, I.K.A., Suryanegara, M., Gunawan, D.: Heart disease diagnosis system with k-nearest neighbors method using real clinical medical records. In: Proceedings of the 4th International Conference on Frontiers of Educational Technologies, pp. 127–131 (2018)

8. Gonsalves, A.H., Thabtah, F., Mohammad, R.M.A., Singh, G.: Prediction of coronary heart disease using machine learning: an experimental analysis. In: Proceedings of the 2019 3rd International Conference on Deep Learning Technologies, pp. 51–56 (2019)
9. Hajar, R.: Risk factors for coronary artery disease: historical perspectives. Heart Views Official J. Gulf Heart Assoc. **18**(3), 109 (2017)
10. Kohli, P.S., Arora, S.: Application of machine learning in disease prediction. In: 2018 4th International Conference on Computing Communication and Automation (ICCCA), pp. 1–4. IEEE (2018)
11. Mousa, D., Zayed, N., Yassine, I.A.: Automatic cardiac MRI localization method. In: 2014 Cairo International Biomedical Engineering Conference (CIBEC), pp. 153–157. IEEE (2014)
12. Rubini, P., Subasini, C., Katharine, A.V., Kumaresan, V., Kumar, S.G., Nithya, T.: A cardiovascular disease prediction using machine learning algorithms. Ann. Rom. Soc. Cell Biol. **25**, 904–912 (2021)
13. Sharma, T., Verma, S.K., et al.: Prediction of heart disease using cleveland dataset: a machine learning approach. Int. J. Rec. Res. Asp **4**, 17–21 (2017)
14. Tripathy, J., Dash, R., Pattanayak, B.K., Mishra, S.K., Mishra, T.K., Puthal, D.: Combination of reduction detection using TOPSIS for gene expression data analysis. Big Data Cogn. Comput. **6**(1), 24 (2022)

Telecommunication Stocks Prediction Using Long Short-Term Memory Model Neural Network

Nandini Jhanwar(✉), Pratham Goel, and Hemraj Lamkuche

Symbiosis University of Applied Sciences, Indore, India
nandinijhanwar67@gmail.com

Abstract. This study looks at how LSTM networks can be used to predict destiny stock fee patterns primarily based on fee history and technical evaluation. To achieve this, a methodology was developed, several tests were conducted, and the results were evaluated against a number of measures to see if this kind of algorithm outperforms other machine learning techniques. A major current trend in scientific study is machine learning, which involves teaching computers to perform tasks that would require human intelligence. This study uses Long-Short Term Memory Model, to develop a model that predicts future stock market values. The main goal of this paper is to evaluate the predictive accuracy of the machine learning algorithm and the extent to which epochs can improve our model.

Keywords: Long short-term memory · Recurrent neural network · Stock market · Data analytics · Artificial neural network

1 Introduction

Basically, large-capitalized quantitative traders acquire stocks, futures, and equities at low prices and then sell them at higher prices. Even though the tendency in stock market forecasting is nothing new, numerous organizations continue to discuss it. Before purchasing a stock, investors do two different types of stock analyses. The first type is called fundamental analysis; during this research, investors consider the intrinsic worth of the stock as well as the performance of the market, the economy, and the political environment. On the other side, technical analysis tracks the development of stocks by examining data produced by market activity, such as historical prices and volume[1–7].

Machine learning has gained more and more traction in a variety of industries recently, which has inspired many traders to apply these techniques to their trades. Some of these applications have shown some very encouraging outcomes. The random walk model that governs the stock market suggests that the best indicator of tomorrow's value is today's value. It is undeniably tough to forecast stock indices due to market volatility, which necessitates an accurate forecast model. The stock market indices fluctuate a lot, which affects investor confidence. Due in part to the combination of known elements (such as the previous closing price, the P/E ratio, etc.) and unknown factors,

S. K. Panda et al. (Eds.): CoCoLe 2022, CCIS 1729, pp. 300–310, 2022.
https://doi.org/10.1007/978-3-031-21750-0_26

stock prices are thought to be highly dynamic and subject to sudden adjustments (like news on elections, rumours, etc.). There have been various initiatives to use machine learning to predict stock price. Each study project's focus differentiates in three ways:

1. The goal price change can be short-term (few days), long-term (weeks later), or near-term (less than an hour).
2. The set of stocks can be restricted to fewer than ten specific stocks, stocks in a specific industry, or generally all stocks.
3. The predictors utilized might be anything from a general trend in the news and economy to specific firm features to purely time series data on the stock price.

This essay will concentrate on making future stock price predictions for various Indian telecommunications companies. We have selected a particular group of Indian telecommunications companies to use in the development of a financial data predictor programme. The programme will use the dataset of previous stock prices as training data. The fundamental goal of the prediction is to lessen the uncertainty involved in choosing an investing strategy.

1.1 Data Analysis

Here is a quick visual that shows which Indian telecommunications firms we choose to include in our dataset.

One equity share among the many sellable shares of a firm is valued at one share price. Revenue is the entire amount received from the sale of goods or services related to a company's main operations. The final result, or net profit, is the net income. It depicts a company's financial situation after all of its costs have been reduced from its overall revenue [8–12].

The graphs in Figs. 1, 2, 3, and 4 show the stock price, revenue, and net profit of some of the companies over the previous five years with respect to dates.

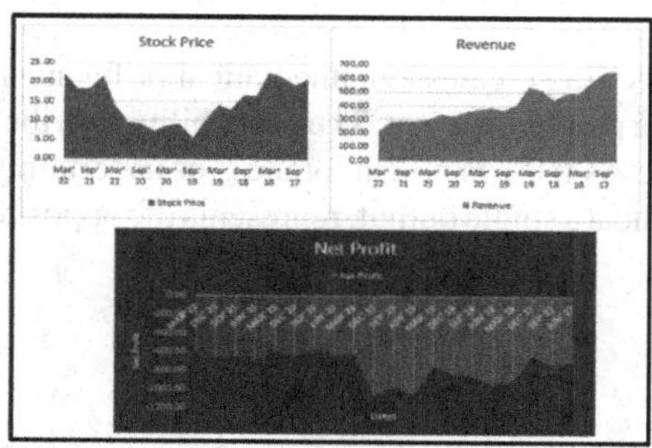

Fig. 1. Mahanagar Telephone Nigam Limited

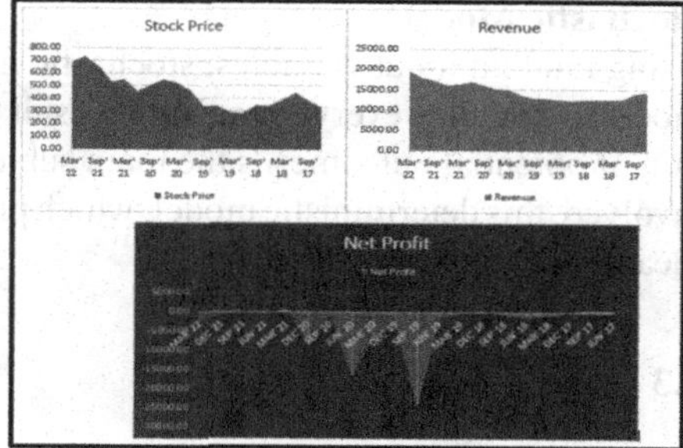

Fig. 2. Bharti Airtel

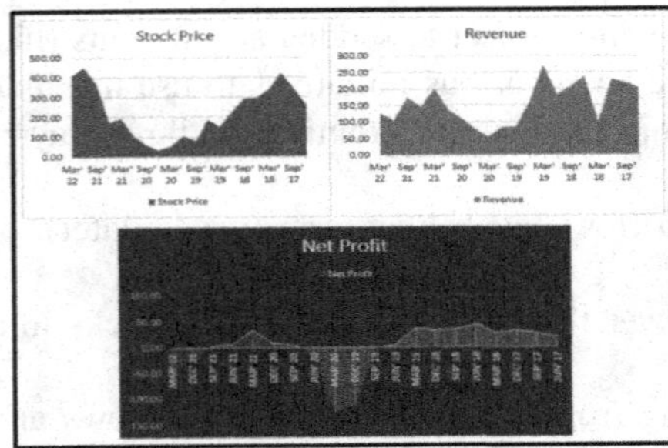

Fig. 3. Tata Teleservices (Maharashtra) Limited

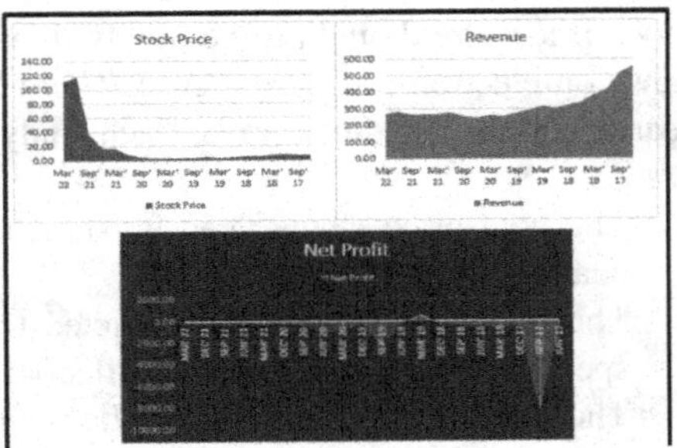

Fig. 4. Tejas Network

1.2 Neural Network Classifications

There are many authors uses various techniques: ARIMA, ANN, and Stochastic Models to predict stock prices [13–17].

Autoregressive Integrated Moving Average Process (ARIMA)
ARIMA, is a statistical analysis technique that employs time collection records to forecast destiny developments or to better recognize the modern-day information collection. If a statistical model forecasts destiny values the usage of facts from the past, its miles stated to be autoregressive.

Artificial Neural Network (ANN)
Similar to the human brain systems are greatly simplified in ANN models. Artificial neurons are computational units that are similar to the neurons found in the nervous system. Multiple layers(input, output, and hidden) make up the major part of the ANN model.

Stochastic Model
Using random input variables, stochastic modelling creates a mathematical or financial model to calculate every conceivable result of a particular event. The probability distribution of potential outcomes is the main subject. As there is no randomness or uncertainty involved, this deterministic model, which predicts a single output, represents the opposite idea of the stochastic model.

1.3 Aim

The purpose of this study is to keenly understand the performance of a long short-term memory model neural network as a training model for predicting stock prices of Indian telecommunication companies. One of the most frequently utilized recurrent structures in sequence modelling is the LSTM. Information flow in the recurrent computations is controlled by gates.

Long-term memory retention is a strong suit of LSTM networks. Depending on the data, the network may or may not keep the memory. The network's Gating mechanisms maintain the network's long-term interdependence. Using random input variables, stochastic modelling creates a mathematical or financial model to calculate every conceivable result of a particular event. The main subject is the probability distribution outcomes. As there is no randomness or uncertainty involved, this deterministic model, which predicts a single output, represents the opposite idea of the stochastic model [18–23].

By incorporating new gates, such as input and forget gates, which improve the preservation of "long term dependencies," LSTM addresses the vanishing expanding gradient problem. Because it is frequently employed to analyze and generate predictions given data sequences, it is superior to other models.

2 Related Work

2.1 Neural Network

Neural networks, or artificial neural networks (ANNs) or simulated neural networks (SNNs), is a subset of system studying and are the main part of deep gaining knowledge of algorithms. Their call and structure are stimulated with the aid of the human mind and mimic the procedure organic neurons signal to each different.

ANNs consist of a layer that contains nodes in form of an input layer, more than zero hidden layers, and a single output layer [23–26].

2.2 Recurrent Neural Network

Recurrent neural networks come under artificial neural network in which the strings between nodes can form a cyclic structure, allowing output from some nodes to influence future input to other nodes in the same network. Thanks to this, it can behave dynamically in time.

2.3 Long Short-Term Memory

The term "LSTM" refers to a type of artificial neural network used in deep learning and artificial intelligence. The LSTM has feedback connections as opposed to typical feedforward neural networks. Such a recurrent neural network can process complete data sequences in addition to single data points (like photos) (such as speech or video). Figure 5 shows the Long Short-Term Memory Network.

3 Methodology and Datasets

3.1 Methodology

The Methodology section contains basically contains four subsections. The first subsection describes the data that is used to make the model. Then preprocessing has been

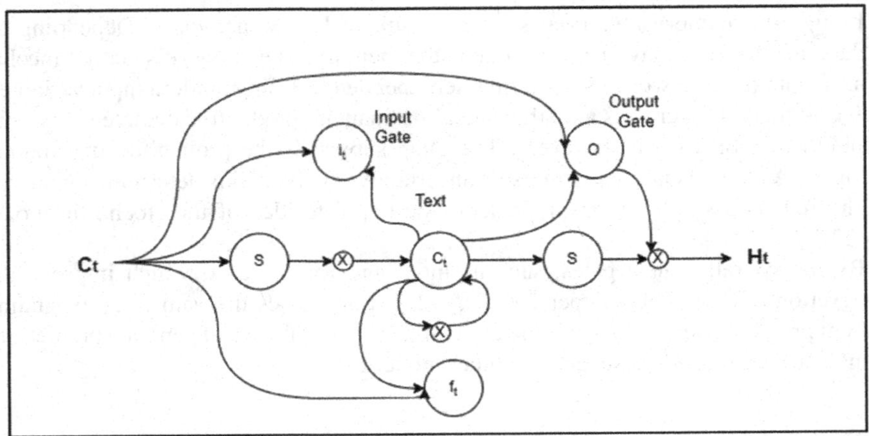

Fig. 5. LSTM Network

done on the data set to transform the raw data into useful and efficient format. Further the dataset has been normalized by converting the dataset's numerical columns' values to a common scale is a helpful change in better performance of our model. To scale the training dataset, we have used scikitLearn's MinMaxScaler for the same. Further, the next subsection contains the LSTM model that is fitted into the particular dataset and the model is been trained. The overall performance of the model is crosschecked by the analysis of the residuals and the root error measure mean square error (RMSE). The formula to calculate root mean square error is:

$$RMSE_{fo} = \left[\sum_{i=1}^{N} (Z_{fi} - Z_{oi})^2 / N\right]^{1/2} \tag{1}$$

where,

Σ = summation

$(Z_{fi} - Z_{oi})^2$ = squared differences

N = sample.

So, this provides the prediction on stocks for the experimental analysis. The whole methodology is been done for seven Indian telecommunications companies (Fig. 6).

3.2 Algorithmic Steps

Algorithmic steps for telecommunication stocks prediction:

1. Import the required libraries and the dataset.
2. Create a temporary database using the columns "Close" and "Date" as the index.
3. Apply the MinMax scaler because LSTM is sensitive to data scale.
4. Split the dataset into train and test sets.
5. Convert the array into a dataset matrix.

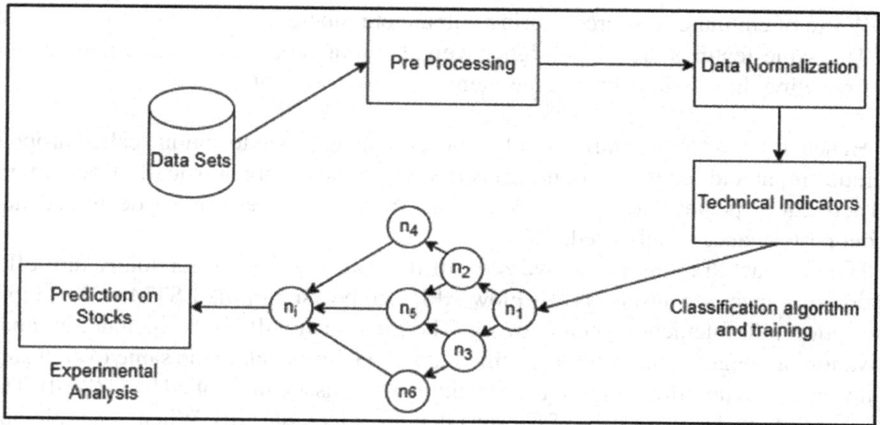

Fig. 6. Methodology for stock price prediction

6. Reshape the equation in x = t, t + 1, t + 2, t + 3, and Y = t + 4, where t is the timeStep.
7. Create a stacked LSTM model with the optimizer Adam and loss as "mean squared error."
8. Fit the train and test sets with an epoch value of 100 into the model.
9. Make test and train predictions and transform them back to original form.
10. Determine the performance indicators for test and train data using the RMSE.
11. Make graphs for train and test predictions and demonstrate predictions for next 29 days.

3.3 Datasets

The dataset includes the daily stock price for each firm for the five years from 1 January 2017 to 30 June 2022. We used Google Collab for the coding and got the data from Business Standard. Date, Open, High, Low, Close, Number of Shares, and Number of Trades are the first seven columns in the dataset. The ratio used to divide the train and test datasets was 7:3. Then, a stacked LSTM model for each of the test and train data was fitted. How many times the learning algorithm will go over the entire training dataset before changing the internal model parameters is indicated by the Epochs parameter, which can have values of 20, 30, 50, or 100. Additionally, predictions are formed, performance metrics are computed on the training dataset using RMSE (Root Mean Squared Error), tested on the testing dataset, and shown for the next 29 days. The entire article has been illustrated with graphic examples.

LSTMs have the drawback of easily overfitting training data, which lowers the accuracy of their predictions. Co-adaptation is more likely to occur when a layer is fully linked and has a significant number of neurons. When the connection weights of two separate neurons are remarkably similar, co-adaptation occurs, in which many neurons in a layer get the same or extremely comparable hidden properties via input layer. Therefore, it presents our model with two distinct issues:

1. Waste of computer resources during output computation.
2. The same features are given higher weight in our model if multiple neurons are extracting them, which causes the training set to be overfit.

Hence, we need to minimize co-adaption. A regularization technique called dropout excludes input and recurrent connections to LSTM units probabilistically from weight and activation updates during network training. As a result, overfitting is decreased, and model performance is enhanced.

Here, at each training phase, we zero off the neuron values to randomly turn off a portion of a layer's neurons. TensorFlow APIs can be used in the LSTM nodes' input connection to implement it on a network. The input data will not be included in node activation or weight updates for a specific likelihood. To maintain the same overall sum of the neuron values, the values of the remaining neurons are multiplied by (1/1- rd). The Dropout Rate is the proportion of neurons that are wiped out (rd). When generating an LSTM layer in Keras, this is provided with a dropout argument. The dropout percentage varies from 0 (no dropout) to 1. (no connection). Here is a diagrammatic representation for dropout algorithm (Fig. 7).

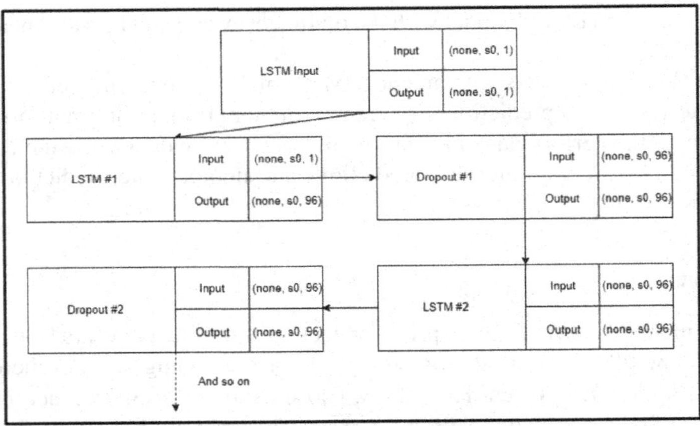

Fig. 7. LSTM model structure with dropouts

4 Result and Discussion

Figures 8, 10, and 12 shows the test predictions and the prediction from the model for different companies. The blue line resembles the actual prices with respect to previous days. The LSTM model has been applied on the train and test sets where the orange color represents the outcome of the model on training data set, and the green for the test. The graphs clearly represent that the test prediction is really close to the actual values.

Figures 9, 11, and 13 shows the future prediction for next 29 days via orange color on the basis on the previous 100 days.

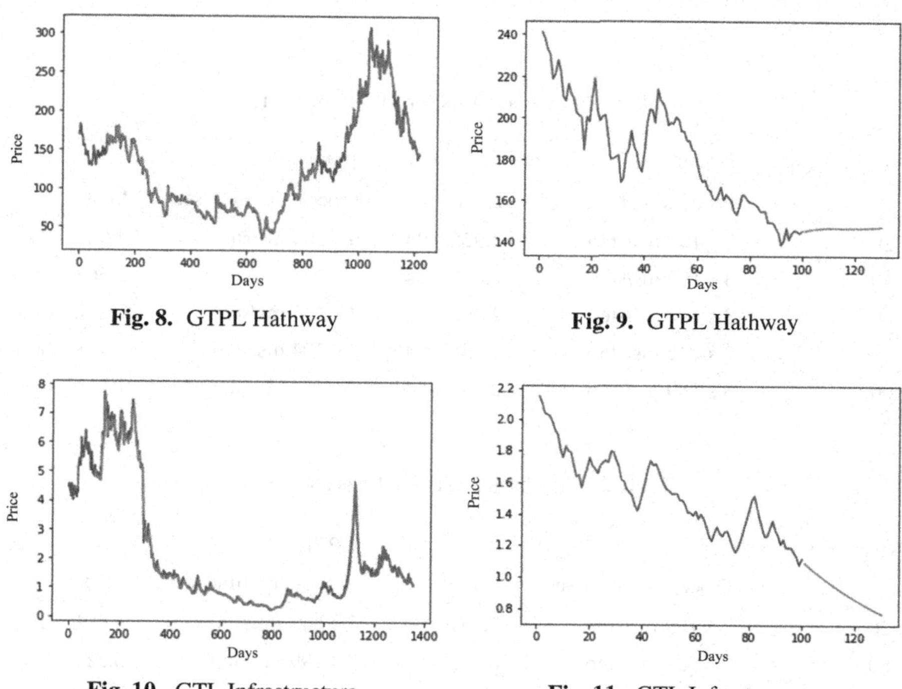

Fig. 8. GTPL Hathway

Fig. 9. GTPL Hathway

Fig. 10. GTL Infrastructure

Fig. 11. GTL Infrastructure

Tables 1, 2, and 3 show that increasing the number of training epochs for our model, which is limited to a maximum of 100, increases the precision of prediction.

4.1 Application of LSTM

Long Short-Term Memory is the 20th century's most used neural network model. Telecommunications are crucial to the development of developing countries like India. Investors may use this methodology to more carefully select their telecommunications stock purchases because India only has a small number of these businesses.

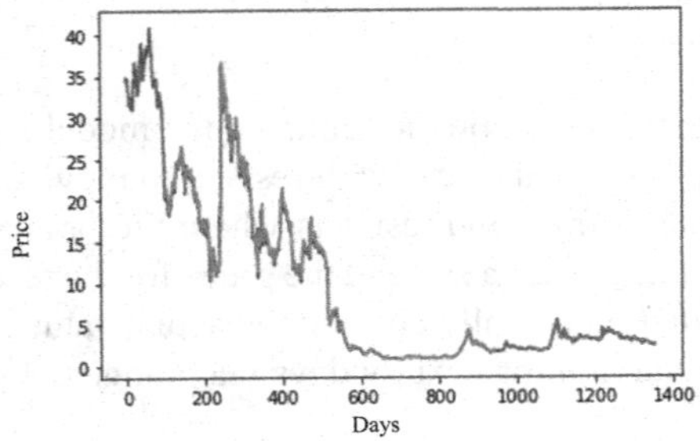

Fig. 12. Reliance Communication

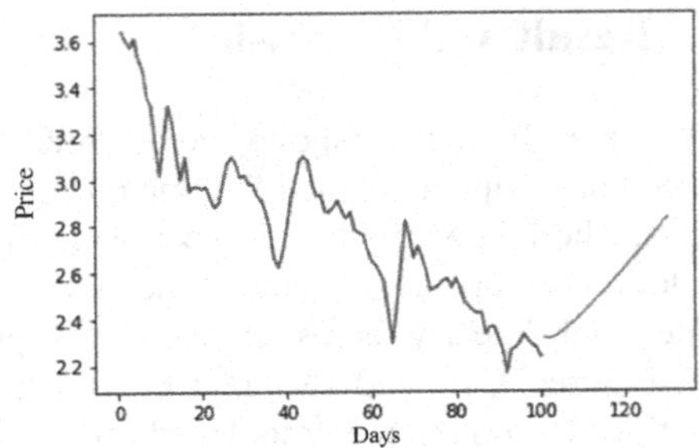

Fig. 13. Reliance Communication

Table 1. Epochs analysis for MTNL and TTMS

No of epochs	MTNL		TTMS	
	Processing time/sec	Loss	Processing time/sec	Loss
20	3 s 193 ms/step	2.92E−04	3 s 204 ms/step	4.06E−06
40	3 s 196 ms/step	2.41E−04	3 s 204 ms/step	2.56E−06
60	3 s 197 ms/step	2.36E−04	3 s 206 ms/step	2.30E−06
80	3 s 192 ms/step	2.35E−04	3 s 204 ms/step	1.79E−06
100	3 s 189 ms/step	2.28E−04	6 s 424 ms/step	1.23E−06

Table 2. Epochs analysis for Tejas and GPTL

No of epochs	Tejas		GPTL	
	Processing time/sec	Loss	Processing time/sec	Loss
20	2 s 199 ms/step	7.98E−04	3 s 248 ms/step	8.60E−04
40	2 s 196 ms/step	6.20E−04	2 s 199 ms/step	5.31E−04
60	2 s 206 ms/step	4.90E−04	2 s 199 ms/step	4.30E−04
80	2 s 196 ms/step	4.61E−04	2 s 198 ms/step	3.16E−04
100	2 s 197 ms/step	3.14E−04	2 s 200 ms/step	2.92E−04

Table 3. Epochs analysis for GTL and Reliance

No of epochs	GTL		Reliance	
	Processing time/sec	Loss	Processing time/sec	Loss
20	3 s 209 ms/step	0.0013	3 s 231 ms/step	0.0014
40	3 s 210 ms/step	0.001	3 s 197 ms/step	8.06E−04
60	3 s 209 ms/step	7.33E−04	3 s 193 ms/step	5.39E−04
80	3 s 206 ms/step	6.11E−04	3 s 193 ms/step	3.87E−04
100	3 s 207 ms/step	5.27E−04	3 s 202 ms/step	3.73E−04

5 Conclusion

This research paper suggests using RNN based on LSTM to predict future values for telecommunication stocks from assets listed on the National Stock Exchange. The results of our model have been encouraging. The results of the testing support the claim that our model can track the development of opening prices for both assets. The suggested approach accurately forecasts future stock prices so that investors can make better investment decisions in telecommunications stocks. The future scope if this paper can be used to identify distinctions between various algorithms such as the Random Forest Classifier and Multiple Regression, with other trend analysis algorithms, such as EMA(Exponential Moving Averages), MACD(Moving Average Convergence Divergence), and WMA(Weighted Moving Average) and determine which algorithm is most effective for various markets. In order to determine whether there is no pattern or whether there are specific patterns exclusive to certain markets and companies, we will also examine datasets from other stock markets and datasets from various sorts of companies.

References

1. Fama, E.F., Malkiel, B.G.: Efficient capital markets: a review of theory and empirical work. Journal of Finance **25**(2), 383–417 (1970). https://doi.org/10.1111/j.1540-6261.1970.tb00518.x
2. Malkiel, B.G.: A Random Walk Down Wall Street. Norton, New York (1973)
3. Biondo, A.E., Pluchino, A., Rapisarda, A., Helbing, D.: Are random trading strategies more successful than technical ones? PLoS ONE **8**, e68344 (2013)
4. Lo, A., MacKinlay, A.: A Non-random Walk Down Wall Street. Princeton Univ. Press, Princeton, NJ (1999). http://gso.gbv.de/DB=2.1/CMD?ACT=SRCHA&SRT=YOP&IKT=1016&TRM=ppn+249613484&sourceid=fbwbibsonomy
5. Glantz, M., Kissell, R.: Multi-asset Risk Modeling, 1st ed. Academic Press (2013)
6. Kirkpatrick, C., Dahlquist, J.: Technical Analysis: The Complete Resource for Financial Market Technicians, 1st ed. FT Press (2006)
7. Allen, F., Karjalainen, R.: Using genetic algorithms to find technical trading rules. J. Finan. Econ. **51**(2), 245–271 (1999). http://www.sciencedirect.com/science/article/pii/S0304405X9800052X

8. Kim, K.: Financial time series forecasting using support vector machines. Neurocomputing **55**(1–2), 307–319 (2003). http://www.sciencedirect.com/science/article/pii/S0925231203003722
9. Melo, B.: Considerac¸ ˜oes cognitivas nas t´ecnicas de previs˜ao no mercado financeiro. Universidade Estadual de Campinas (2012)
10. Batres-Estrada, B.: Deep learning for multivariate financial time series (2015)
11. Sharang, A., Rao, C.: Using machine learning for medium frequency derivative portfolio trading. CoRR, vol. abs/1512.06228 (2015). http://arxiv.org/abs/1512.06228
12. Heaton, J.B., Polson, N.G., Witte, J.H.: Deep learning in finance. CoRR, vol. abs/1602.06561 (2016). http://arxiv.org/abs/1602.06561
13. Greff, K., Srivastava, R.K., Koutník, J., Steunebrink, B.R., Schmidhuber, J.: LSTM: A search space odyssey (2015). arXiv:1503.04069
14. Hochreiter, S., Schmidhuber, J.: Long short-term memory. Neural Comput. **9**(8), 1735–1780 (1997). https://doi.org/10.1162/neco.1997.9.8.1735
15. Graves, A.: In: Supervised Sequence Labelling with Recurrent Neural Networks. Studies in Computational Intelligence, vol. 385. Springer (2012). https://doi.org/10.1007/978-3-642-24797-2
16. Graves, A., Liwicki, M., Fernández, S., Bertolami, R., Bunke, H., Schmidhuber, J.: A novel connectionist system for unconstrained handwriting recognition. IEEE Trans. Pattern Anal. Mach. Intell. **31**(5), 855–868 (2009)
17. Chen, K., Zhou, Y., Dai, F.: A LSTM-based method for stock returns prediction: a case study of china stock market. In: 2015 IEEE International Conference on Big Data (Big Data), pp. 2823–2824 (2015)
18. Di Persio, L., Honchar, O.: Artificial neural networks approach to the forecast of stock market price movements. Int. J. Econ. Manage. Syst. **1**, 158–162 (2016)
19. Khaidem, L., Saha, S., Dey, S.R.: Predicting the direction of stock market prices using random forest. CoRR, vol. abs/1605.00003 (2016). http://arxiv.org/abs/1605.00003
20. Pramod, D., Lamkuche, H.S.: CSL: FPGA implementation of lightweight block cipher for power-constrained devices. Int. J. Inf. Comput. Secur. **12**(2–3), 349–377 (2020). https://doi.org/10.1504/IJICS.2020.105185
21. Lamkuche, H.S., Kondaveety, V.B., Sapparam, V.L., Singh, S., Rajpurkar, R.D.: Enhancing the security and performance of cloud for e-governance infrastructure: secure E-MODI. Int. J. Cloud Appl. Comput. **12**(1), 1–23 (2022). https://doi.org/10.4018/IJCAC.2022010108
22. Gaikwad, D., Lamkuche, H.: Segmentation of services provided by E-commerce platforms using PAM clustering. J. Phys. Conf. Ser. **1964**(4), 042036 (2021). https://doi.org/10.1088/1742-6596/1964/4/042036
23. Sarma, K.N.S., Lamkuche, H.S., Umamaheswari, S.: A review of secret sharing schemes. Res. J. Inf. Technol. **5**(2), 67–72 (2013). https://doi.org/10.3923/rjit.2013.67.72
24. Kumar, S., Kumar, D., Lamkuche, H.S.: TPA auditing to enhance the privacy and security in cloud systems. J. Cyber Secur. Mobil. **10**(3), 537–568 (2021). https://doi.org/10.13052/jcsm2245-1439.1033
25. Ramesh, A., Pradhan, V., Lamkuche, H.: Understanding and analysing resource utilization, costing strategies and pricing models in cloud computing. J. Phys. Conf. Ser. **1964**(4), 042049 (2021). https://doi.org/10.1088/1742-6596/1964/4/042049
26. Lamkuche, H.S., Pramod, D., Onker, V., Katiya, S.A., Lamkuche, G.S., Hiremath, G.R.: SAL – a lightweight symmetric cipher for Internet-of-Things. Int. J. Innov. Technol. Explor. Eng. **8**(11), 521–528 (2019). https://doi.org/10.35940/ijitee.K1088.09811S19

Author Index

Printed in the United States
by Baker & Taylor Publisher Services